THE AFRICAN EMPEROR

SEPTIMIUS SEVERUS

THE AFRICAN EMPEROR

Septimius Severus

Anthony R. Birley

B.T. BATSFORD LTD · LONDON

Typeset by Latimer Trend and Company Ltd, Plymouth
and printed in Great Britain by
Adlard & Son Ltd, Letchworth
for the Publishers, B.T. Batsford Ltd
4 Fitzhardinge St, London W1H 0AH

ISBN 0 7134 5694 9

Contents

CONTENTS

List of Illustrations

vii

Preface

ONCE THE ROMAN IMPERIAL SYSTEM became well established, it did not matter much – so it can be argued – who was emperor. 'As for the Emperor and the Emperor's friends', Synesius wrote in a letter, 'and fortune's dance . . . certain names shooting up like flames to a great height of glory and being extinguished – there is complete silence on these things here, our ears are spared from news of that sort. Maybe people know well enough that there always is some Emperor who is alive, because we are reminded of this every year by the tax-collectors. But *who* the Emperor is, that is not so clear, in fact there are some among us who think Agamemnon is still on the throne.' Synesius could make a joke out of the remoteness of Arcadius and the sheltered ignorance of Cyrenaica. But he strongly disapproved, as he told Arcadius in his address *On Kingship*: the emperor should lead his armies in person, and tour the provinces to see and be seen. Septimius Severus is not known to have visited Cyrenaica; but this is one of the very few parts of the empire that he did not see. For one thing, he was the first emperor born and raised away from Rome and Italy, in his ancestral Tripolitania. His career as a senator took him to Sardinia, Spain, Syria, Gaul, Sicily and Pannonia, with a stay at Athens while out of office. Once he had seized power he spent all but four of his eighteen years as emperor on the move, notably in the east, where he extended Rome's borders to the Tigris; in Egypt; the Balkans and Rhineland; Africa; finally remote Britain, where he stayed longer than any other ruler. Such a man deserves close scrutiny, even if it is difficult, impossible no doubt, to get beneath his skin.

His African origin is not the least remarkable aspect of Septimius. As the work of numerous scholars, archaeologists and epigraphists in the main, now makes clear, Tripolitania stood apart from the rest of Roman Africa, deeply conservative after centuries of virtual independence, with its Punic or Libyphoenician identity still strongly apparent when it finally entered Rome's orbit under Augustus. No influx of colonial migration disturbed the dominance of the Punic élite; yet they responded with alacrity to Rome's presence – as a free city Lepcis had won allied status long before. Septimius' ancestors became Romans, his grandfather emerges as a knight owning land near Rome and a minor figure in

ix

fashionable literary circles of late Flavian Italy – but he returned to Lepcis to preside over the culmination of its transformation, into an honorary *colonia*. Septimius' father spent his entire life in Tripolitania, Septimius himself grew up there.

My interest in Septimius goes back a long way. He is a key figure for the student of Roman Britain, and it was a matter of great excitement when Robin Birley's excavations at Carpow on the Tay in 1961–2 revealed that the site was Severan, with stone *principia* and *praetorium*. This made it clear that Septimius really had sought to conquer the whole of Britain (as Dio said), not just to crush Caledonia before returning to the Wall. A few years later I was lucky enough to visit Lepcis Magna, and by an unusual route, coming up across the desert from the Garamantian country, past the Black Mountain and the outpost fort at Bu-Ngem which Septimius built, grateful to reach the coast after the searing heat of the *ghibli*. Meanwhile I had been plunging 'into the ocean of the Augustan History', but not 'insensibly' (as Gibbon recalled he had done). I was fortunate to have been guided by Sir Ronald Syme in my first steps through what he has called a 'Serbonian bog'. The *Historia Augusta* – which I abbreviate *HA* throughout this book – is a problem that must be confronted by any student of the second and third centuries AD. Participation in several of the *Colloquia* organised by Professor Johannes Straub proved very beneficial. At the first one that I attended the late H.-G. Pflaum urged me to undertake a biography of Septimius. The result, mostly written at Duke University, was published in 1971. It has long been out of print and I have often enough been asked for spare copies by would-be readers. In the meantime a considerable body of new evidence and a mass of new literature have appeared. The invitation to produce a completely new version was thus both welcome and daunting. I have had to be selective, some might call it eclectic, in what I have cited, to avoid excessively ponderous documentation. I have subdivided the bibliography, in some cases by a group of chapters, often chapter by chapter. To a limited extent the bibliographies give a conspectus of the literature, but I have refrained from listing a fair number of standard works if they have not been expressly cited in the notes.

Work of this kind is only made possible by the work of a host of scholars. It is proper to register the benefit I derived from the studies by De Ceuleneer, Platnauer and Hasebroek, the last of whom remains of great value on the *HA vita Severi*. When I began my own research I gained particular inspiration from a series of articles by Julien Guey and great benefit from the work of the late Guido Barbieri. My debt to Eric Birley is incalculable, but I can express it best by stating the conviction I have derived from him that Roman history, epigraphy and provincial archaeology are essential to one another. Those to whom I owe thanks – for discussion of detail, for sending me copies of their work, for fruitful debate – are very numerous: some fifty names deserve listing, but I must refrain lest I appear to shelter behind their authority. I must nonetheless explicitly thank Géza Alföldy, who not for the first time let me see some of his new work before publication; Charles Daniels, who made possible my visit to Tripolitania and has provided illustrations for this book; Barri Jones, for generous help while I was preparing my text and other kindnesses over many years; David Kennedy, for advice on eastern frontiers; and David Mattingly, for guidance on the most recent work in Tripolitania. The interpretations offered here – and responsibility for error – remain my own, something which I need to stress since I am aware that some of my views may be controversial. Imperial biographies are frowned on in some quarters as a genre and, to return to the subject of this one, my emphasis on his African nature may be unwelcome. There are difficult and delicate questions here, not to mention the ethnic identity of his wife, Julia Domna: her city, Emesa, was founded by Arabs. Not all consent to call her one. Further, I lay weight not merely on the 'otherness' of Tripolitania and her most famous son, but on the strong involvement of Roman Africans, including Septimius and his brother, in the conspiracy which toppled Commodus. Anglo-Saxons, mostly monoglot, may not always grasp the complexity of a society in which there were two languages of culture, Latin and Greek, and a variety of other tongues in common use. Septimius Severus is an instructive phenomenon. My belief that his origin mattered has led me to call this story of his life *The African Emperor*.

ANTHONY BIRLEY
Manchester
27 February 1988

THE EMPORIA

SEPTIMIUS SEVERUS WAS BORN ON 11 April 145, at Lepcis Magna in Tripolitania, son of P. Septimius Geta and Fulvia Pia. Lepcis had had the status of a Roman colony for a generation and was one of the great cities of Roman Africa. Tripolitania, land of three cities, took its name from Lepcis and her two western neighbours, Oea (Tripoli) and Sabratha. The Roman empire was then at the height of its prosperity. Antoninus Pius, the emperor, give his name to an era synonymous with peace and affluence. In 145 he himself was consul with his adopted son as colleague. The year of Septimius' birth was thus the year of 'the emperor Antoninus for the fourth time and Aurelius Caesar for the second time'.[1]

The son born to Geta and Fulvia was given the names of his paternal grandfather: 'Lucius Septimius Severus'. Fifty years later Septimius was to denote himself 'son of the deified Marcus' in place of 'son of Publius'. Soon after this retrospective adoption into the Antonine dynasty a cynical senator congratulated Septimius on 'finding a father', implying that the real parent was a nobody. Geta was an obscure provincial, it is true (and long dead by 195). But men of his family in the same generation as himself were already senators when his son was born: P. Septimius Aper and C. Septimius Severus, both on the road to high office in 145. These men, probably Geta's first cousins, were no doubt older than him. But Geta never held public office. Ill health may have been a bar, or lack of ambition, but hardly poverty. His sister Polla, who apparently died unmarried, was a very wealthy woman, and the family had property in Italy as well as estates at Lepcis. For whatever reason, Geta seems to have stayed in Africa with his wife and three children. There was another son, named after himself, hence probably the elder, and a daughter, Octavilla. However obscure his life, the biographer Marius Maximus discoursed 'quite copiously' about him and his character in his life of Septimius, according to the *HA* (which fails to reproduce any details).[2]

Even within so variegated an empire, Septimius' home town, where he spent the first seventeen years of his life, was a very exceptional place, and the 'three cities' markedly different from the rest of what the Romans called 'Africa'. A look at Lepcis' origins is required to understand better who Septimius Severus was. 'Civilisation' came to North Africa with Canaanite traders from Tyre and Sidon, their language—Phoenician, later called Punic in the western Mediterranean—closely related to Hebrew. They began exploring the coasts of the west in the late second millennium BC. Phoenicia had acquired expertise in seamanship and trade over the preceding centuries, when Ugarit on the Syrian coast played no small part in the economy of Egypt. The great disturbances caused by the 'Sea Peoples' in about 1200 BC forced her to look further afield. North Africa's few natural harbours became Phoenician staging-posts on the route to southern Spain. Not quite the earliest, but soon the most important, was Carthage, *Qart-Hadasht*, 'new city'. During the first half of the first millennium BC these trading-stations began to take on the character of towns. The process was accelerated and stimulated by the march of events in Asia. Assyria crushed the mother-cities Tyre and Sidon in the eighth century. Further colonists, this time refugees, arrived. Carthage and her fellow Punic cities prospered. They faced rivalry, before long, from the Greeks, active in southern Italy and Sicily from the eighth century, and from the mid-seventh interested in Africa, 'Libya'. Dorian Greeks from the island of Thera established themselves in eastern Libya, the 'Green Mountain', founding Cyrene in 531 BC. From there daughter-cities were sent out, extending Greek settlement from the borders of Egypt to the Syrtica. Carthage responded, it is clear, by planting a settlement at a site called *Lpqy* in Tripolitania, at first perhaps on a little island opposite the mouth of the wadi, but soon on the mainland. Later two more colonies followed, to the west, *Wy't* and *Sbrt'n*. All three names are Libyan, not Punic. They were trading stations, and the Greeks subsequently still called them the *emporia*—and Lepcis was often known as *Neapolis*. Tripolitania lies hundreds of kilometres closer to black Africa than Carthage herself. It was clearly to control the shortest paths to the interior by the transsaharan routes that Carthage planted the *emporia*. But the hills to the south-west of Lepcis, the Gebel Msellata, Herodotus' 'Hill of the Graces', cried out for exploitation, likewise the rich valley of the River Cinyps (Wadi el-Caam), which rises in the Gebel and flows into the sea twelve and a half miles (20 km) east of Lepcis. 'It is equal to any country in the world for cereal crops and is nothing like the rest of Libya. The soil here is black and springs of water abound so that there is no fear of drought and heavy rains—for it rains in that part of Libya—do no harm when they soak the ground. The returns of the harvest come up to the Babylonian measures ... the Cinyps region yields three hundred-fold', Herodotus wrote. Further, 'the Hill of the Graces is thickly wooded and is thus very unlike the rest of Libya, which is bare'.[3]

In about 514 BC a Spartan adventurer, Dorieus, guided by men of

Thera, 'came to Cinyps, where he colonised a place which has not its equal in all Libya, on the banks of a river', Herodotus records. But 'he was driven out in the third year by the Macae, the Libyans and the Carthaginians'. Greeks from Asia Minor had managed to found Massilia in about 600 BC and exploited much of southern Gaul. But Carthage was by then strong enough virtually to exclude them from Spain, expelled them from Corsica and dominated Sardinia and western Sicily. Northern and central Italy were controlled by the Etruscans, with whom Carthage allied herself, as she did with the infant Roman republic. Only in southern Italy, eastern Sicily and Cyrenaica could the Greeks secure a firm foothold. The western Mediterranean was virtually a Punic preserve until the third century BC.[4]

Tripolitania, the land between the two Syrtic Gulfs, is lost to history between the expulsion of Dorieus and the end of the third century. During these three hundred years the *emporia* clearly flourished, in spite of the obstacles. In its physical relief and climate Tripolitania stands apart from the rest of North Africa, a hybrid between Mediterranean and Sahara, with a fertile margin along and near the coast and a vast desert hinterland. A wide coastal plain, the Gefara, stretches from just west of Lepcis to the mainland opposite Meninx (Djerba), the 'Isle of the Lotus-eaters', bounded on the south by the great rocky escarpment of the Gebel. This band of hills, some twelve and a half miles (20 km) wide for the most part, merges with the Saharan plateau, the Dahar, which in turn slopes away to the southwest into the Great Eastern Erg or sand sea, an almost impassable barrier, further to the east into the 'red rock', Hamada el-Hamra, which divides Tripolitania from the Fezzan. Much of the Gefara plain itself is arid scrub, apart from a band of oases along the coast. Rainfall in Tripolitania is far lower than in the Maghreb proper and the scorching wind from the Sahara, the *ghibli*, is an added hazard. Another might have been the presence of hostile Libyan tribes. Yet Herodotus knew that Carthage had combined with the largest of these, the Macae, to expel Dorieus. The Libyans were the ancestors of the modern Berbers, who have seemingly preserved their identity through three thousand years of domination by Phoenicians, Greeks, Romans, Vandals, Arabs, French and Italians. Neither they nor the Phoenicians practised cultural or social apartheid. There was considerable intermarriage, and the population of Carthage's Tripolitanian colonies were to become known as 'Libyphoenicians'. Further east, the Nasamones of the Syrtica were semi-nomadic, moving from the oasis of Augila to the coast, where they were feared by passing traders. To the south, in the oases of the Fezzan, lay the Garamantes, around whom legend accumulated. They were clearly important middlemen in the transsaharan trade, but from time to time were liable to raid their northern neighbours. Other indigenous peoples of the interior, between the coast and the Garamantes, are labelled 'Gaetuli', doubtless linked to the semi-nomads of Numidia and with the Numidae themselves, the most powerful people of the Maghreb. The Moors, Mauri, of the far west, were too distant to affect Lepcis.[5]

Until the third century only the Greeks had challenged Punic dominance. But the steady advance of Rome was to lead to Carthage's downfall. Her mercenary armies lost the first long war (264–241 BC) to Rome's citizen legions. She surrendered Sicily, and soon after Sardinia and Corsica. Hannibal came within an ace of destroying Rome during the second war (218–202 BC) and Carthaginian armies roamed Italy for thirteen years. But Carthage lost again, when Rome took the war first to Spain and then to Africa. She had invaded, to be sure, during the first war (the expedition of Regulus in 256 BC) but that venture had ended in disaster. This time there was no mistake.

Near the end of the Hannibalic war a Numidian chief who had served with Carthage, Massinissa, son of Gaia, defeated by a rival, took refuge in the region 'between the Emporia and the Garamantes'. He did not forget what he saw there. Lepcis was still small, no doubt, clustered on the headland on the left bank of the Wadi Lebdah, but its control of the Gebel and the Cinyps valley made it rich from the cultivation of cereals and olives. It was paying Carthage tribute of one talent a day. The peace settlement between Rome and Carthage in 201 BC made Massinissa, who had switched sides opportunely, king of a united Numidia. For over half a century this remarkable man greatly enlarged his dominions, at the expense of Carthage. He repeatedly attempted to take over the *emporia*. In the 190s Roman commissioners came to Lepcis, three eminent men, Cornelius Cethegus, Minucius Rufus and the great Scipio himself, Hannibal's conqueror. No clear decision seems to have been made, but by the 160s Carthage's rights were finally lost. However, Lepcis and her neighbours were left in relative independence from the distant Numidian king. Links with the eastern Mediterranean were developed, not least with Alexandria.[6]

In 149 BC Roman fear and greed brought about her third and final war with Carthage. After three years the old enemy was destroyed by the younger Scipio, who formally cursed the levelled ruins. Her former territory in north-eastern Tunisia now became the Roman province Africa, with Utica as the governor's residence. Little is heard of it until 122 when C. Gracchus attempted a refoundation. His embryonic *colonia* was abandoned on his death the next year although numbers of the settlers retained their land-allotments. Soon afterwards the Numidian kingdom entered a crisis. In 112 the most powerful claimant to the contested throne,

4

Jugurtha, was at war with Rome. 'As soon as war broke out the Lepcitani sent envoys to the consul Bestia, then to Rome, requesting friendship and alliance', Sallust wrote. It was granted: Lepcis became a 'treaty state', *civitas foederata*, a friend and ally of the Roman people, and steadily provided assistance to successive consuls, Bestia, Albinus and Metellus. In 109 an internal conflict broke out: a noble called Hamilcar was plotting a coup, perhaps in Jugurtha's interests. Metellus sent four Ligurian cohorts to Lepcis in response to an appeal. After numerous blunders the 'new man' C. Marius ended the war in 105 BC. The boundaries of the Roman province, defined by the 'royal ditch' (*fossa regia*) traced from the north-west to south-east by Scipio in 146, remained unchanged; but Marius settled some veterans in northern Numidia.[7]

After the war Lepcis and the other *emporia* remained free states, allies of Rome. In due course they issued their own coinage, that of Lepcis depicting the city's two guardian deities, *Mlkqrt*, the 'king of the city', the main god of Phoenician Tyre, worshipped at Lepcis under the name *Mlk'shtrt* or Milk'ashtart, underlining an association with Astarte, or 'Ashtaroth the abomination of the Sidonians', and *Shdrp'*, or Shadrapa. 'Only the language of the city has been affected by intermarriage with the Numidians', Sallust wrote in the late first century BC. 'The laws and customs are Sidonian [i.e. Punic]: they were able to retain them because of their great distance from the king's authority. There are considerable tracts of desert between them and the settled part of Numidia.' As it happens, an inscription from the late second or early first century BC shows that the Punic language was not affected either. Only the script was debased, the so-called 'Neo-Punic' or cursive script being used rather than the lapidary forms found in Punic areas before the fall of Carthage. The stone honours 'the Lord *Shdrp'* and *Mlks'htrt*, patrons of Lepcis', to whom a statue was set up by *'drb'l* (Adherbal), during the terms of office as *šptm*—*sufetes*—of *'rš* (Arish) and *Bdmlqrt* (Bodmelqart or Bomilcar), in accordance with a decision of 'the great of Lepcis and all the people of Lepcis' (*'dr 'Lpqy wkl 'm 'Lpqy*, in other words the council and assembly). The *sufetes*, as the title of these magistrates was written in Latin, were the twin annually elected magistrates at Carthage and all over the Punic world, equivalent to the 'Judges' of their Israelite cousins. Melqart, identified with the Greek Heracles and Roman Hercules, and Shadrapa, equated with Dionysus or Bacchus, and with the Roman Liber Pater, were to remain the guardian deities of Lepcis down to Septimius' day. The Carthaginian Ba'al Hammon, whom the Romans called Saturn, and Tanit, the Roman Juno Caelestis, seem to have had a more restricted following than in the more westerly Punic cities.[8]

After the Jugurthine war Lepcis is lost to history for half a century, avoiding entanglement in the civil wars that wracked Rome in the 80s. But the tide of events was soon to sweep her firmly into the Roman orbit. The silence is broken only by Cicero's mention, in 70 BC, of a Roman banker, T. Herennius, in business at Lepcis, and a victim of the notorious governor of Sicily, Verres. Neighbouring Cyrenaica, bequeathed to Rome by her last Ptolemaic king early in the century, was finally annexed in the 70s. An inscription from one of the Greek cities, Arsinoe, mentions the possibility of importing corn from Lepcis during a food shortage. Lepcis continued to prosper, although it was olive oil, for which the Gebel and even the pre-desert beyond could be exploited, which was her main source of wealth. It was probably before the end of the second century that a new city centre was laid out, with twin temples of the ancestral gods as its main focus.[9]

The last of the Numidian kings (as it turned out), Juba, resumed the practices of Massinissa at this time, seizing 'property' and perhaps land from Lepcis. The city complained to the Roman senate, which appointed arbitrators: her losses were restored. But in 49 BC, when Rome's greatest civil war began, Juba was again in conflict with Lepcis, and was only recalled from Tripolitania by news that Caesar's supporter Curio had landed with an army in Africa. Juba backed the Pompeians and Curio was crushed near Utica. After Pompey's death in Egypt in 48, the Republican forces regrouped in Africa. The redoubtable Cato led a force right across the scorching Syrtica to join them, and wintered at Lepcis. Two years later retribution followed. Caesar arrived at the beginning of 46: the Pompeians were defeated, their vicious ally Juba committed suicide and the bulk of his kingdom was annexed as the province 'Africa Nova', 'New Africa'. Lepcis paid dearly for its assistance to Caesar's enemies. The dictator imposed a fine of three million pounds weight of olive oil, presumably as an annual payment. To be able to produce such a quantity as a surcharge—over one million litres—the Lepcitani must have possessed in the region of a million trees.[10]

Caesar took other, vital steps in Africa. Carthage was once again refounded as a Roman colony. This time it worked, and the new city was to become great again, second only to Rome in the western Mediterranean. Caesar sent veteran settlers to a number of other places in Africa. Augustus' victory in the renewed civil wars that followed Caesar's murder meant further changes. The two provinces were amalgamated and administered by a proconsul with a standing army, of which the main force was the legion III Augusta. The western part of North Africa became the kingdom of Mauretania, and was given to the younger Juba, who had married a daughter of Antony and Cleopatra. Both in Mauretania and in the enlarged province Augustus founded further colonies, mainly for veteran soldiers. A particular region around the old Numidian royal city of Cirta (Constantine) had been briefly seized, during the confused years when the Republic was collapsing, by the Campanian *condottiere* Publius Sittius, with a host of mercenary followers. He and his men at first retained Cirta as a private empire in northern Numidia, but Sittius was dead before Caesar Augustus gained sole power, and this area too, with its now strong Italian element, formed part of the province. Lepcis and the other *emporia* were probably left out; but not for long.[11]

LEPCIS MAGNA: FROM FREE STATE TO COLONIA

CAESAR'S MASSIVE FINE DOUBTLESS ACTED as a stimulus to Lepcis to develop its olive cultivation further in the Gebel and indeed in the valleys south and east. How long she had to go on paying is unknown, but the *emporia* clearly regained their status as free cities during the Triumviral period. Lepcis' independent coinage continues, and before long the image of Caesar Augustus appears on it, as an additional and potent presiding deity. During the period from the mid-forties to the mid-twenties large numbers of Italians settled in Africa, not merely government-sponsored colonists but people dispossessed from their own land. '*At nos sitientes ibimus Afros*', says an Italian farmer whose land was confiscated, in Virgil's first *Eclogue*, 'but we will go off to the thirsty Africans'. Not, however, to Tripolitania—more likely than not to Sittius' 'New Campania' (with *sitientes* a punning allusion to the founder), in the Cirta region. Nor did Tripolitania receive any official settlers. A few Italians may be detected at Lepcis, probably traders or bankers (like Cicero's Herennius). There is a man called Perperna, an Etruscan by his name; and a family of Fulvii: these were Septimius' maternal ancestors. Lepcis, Oea and Sabratha were in a different position to the rest of Punic Africa. They had enjoyed virtual independence for a century and a half, had never been conquered and had not had to surrender land to settlers from Rome. The Punic heritage was thus unusually strong, although the *emporia* had clearly developed strong links with Alexandria, continuing the tradition of trade and contact with Egypt that went back long before the great Greek metropolis was founded. Lepcis was going to become a Roman city, in the end; but on her own terms. She is generally referred to as 'Lepcis Magna', 'Great Lepcis', to distinguish her from Lepti in Byzacena. The label was apt.[1]

Africa occupied an anomalous position in the new order of Caesar

Augustus. Alone among the proconsular provinces it was to retain a legion, the III Augusta. The proconsuls had fighting to do. There had already been three triumphs 'from Africa' before the settlement of 27 BC which divided the provinces between *princeps* and senate. In 21 there was another, then, in 19, the last to be celebrated by any Roman other than an emperor. The proconsul L. Cornelius Balbus, himself of Punic origin, from Gades, had achieved a remarkable feat in the south. As well as campaigning against the Gaetuli, he took an army across the Black Mountain (*mons Ater*) and deep into the oases of the Fezzan, as far as Garama, 'the most famous capital of the Garamantes', whose name was synonymous with the ends of the earth. His expedition had important results on the Garamantes themselves. Within a few decades this people across the Sahara was constructing stone houses and tombs of Roman type, and using imported Roman pottery. Balbus must have imposed a treaty on them, by which peaceful trade would be guaranteed. Ivory, gold dust, gems, ostrich feathers—and slaves—were among the items traded, also exotic wild beasts. Lepcis and the other *emporia* must have benefited.[2]

Just over ten years later (8 BC) the first dated inscription in Latin is found. As with most public inscriptions at Lepcis for the next century it was bilingual, in Punic and Latin. The text is carved on thirty-one sandstone blocks, each half a metre square on the face, placed round the precinct wall of the market (*macellum*). It honours Augustus, with all his titles, and the proconsul Crassus Frugi. In the Punic text *imperator* is rendered *mynkd*, perhaps a Libyan word related to the Tuareg *amanukal*, 'paramount chief'. Muttun son of Anno was *sufes* (his colleague's name is missing), Iddibal son of Arish and Bodmelqart son of Annobal were priests, *flamines*, of Caesar Augustus. The work was paid for by Annobal Tapapius Rufus, son of Himilcho, *flamen*, former *sufes*, and 'prefect of sacred affairs'. The names are typically Punic, with the termination *-bal* referring to the god Ba'al. 'Annobal' is the name more familiar to Romans as 'Hannibal' (likewise 'Anno' as 'Hanno', and 'Bodmelqart' as 'Bomilcar', which means 'in the hands of Melqart'). Annobal had taken steps to adapt his names. His family name, the Punic 'Tabahpi', was given a Latin-style termination and he had taken the additional name Rufus. The *flamines* of Caesar Augustus, from their position in the dedication, were persons of major importance in the town. The worship of the emperor was now firmly implanted in the heart of Lepcis. What had presumably been built as the temple of Milk'ashtart or Melqart was now rebuilt as a shrine for 'Roma et Augustus'.[3]

Annobal Rufus appears on three other monumental inscriptions, lintels in grey limestone, from a new quarry, better adapted for elaborate moulding and fine lettering. Eight or nine years later Annobal paid for

① GERMANIA INFERIOR
② GERMANIA SUPERIOR
③ PANNONIA SUPERIOR
④ PANNONIA INFERIOR
⑤ MOESIA INFERIOR
⑥ LYCIA et PAMPHYLIA
⑦ OSRHOENE
⑧ MESOPOTAMIA
⑨ SYRIA COELE
⑩ SYRIA PALAESTINA

— Frontier
---- Provincial boundary

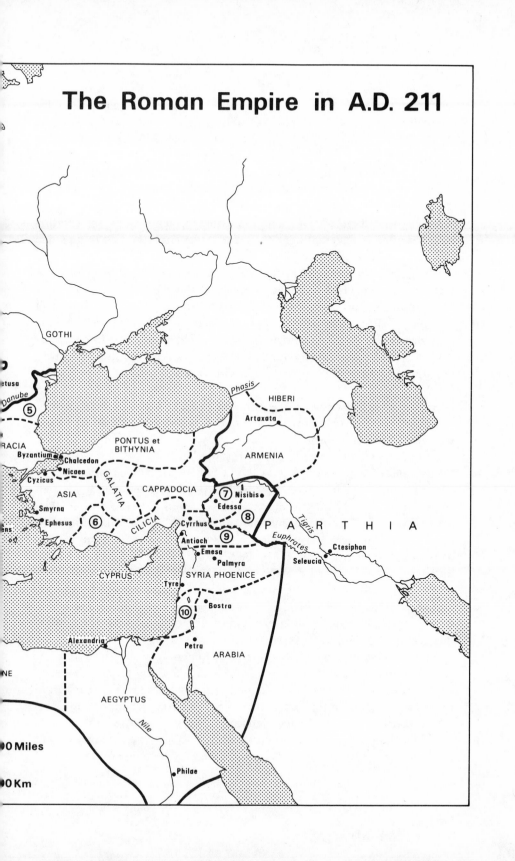

The Roman Empire in A.D. 211

GOTHI

⑤

RACIA

Byzantium• ⑤Chalcedon

•Nicaea

Cyzicus•

ASIA

•Smyrna

•Ephesus ⑥

ns•

Danube

Phasis

HIBERI

Artaxata•

PONTUS et
BITHYNIA

GALATIA

ARMENIA

CAPPADOCIA

⑦ Nisibis•

•Edessa

⑧

CILICIA   •Cyrrhus

•Antioch   ⑨

CYPRUS

•Emesa
•Palmyra

SYRIA PHOENICE

Tyre•

⑩

•Bostra

Alexandria•

•Petra

ARABIA

AEGYPTUS

P A R T H I A

Tigris

Euphrates   •Ctesiphon

•Seleucia

etusa•

NE

0 Miles

0 Km

Nile

•Philae

additions to the theatre. He bears additional titles, traditional in Punic cities, 'adorner of his country' and 'lover of concord'. The theatre already had a statue of Augustus, set up in 3 BC to 'their protector' (*conservatori*) by the 'Fulvii Lepcitani' along with one of his adopted sons, Gaius Caesar. At about this time the remodelling of the Forum was being completed. The proconsul Piso's name, in massive bronze lettering in the pavement, presumably marked the dedication of a new small temple alongside those of Liber Pater (Shadrapa) and of Rome and Augustus; it was perhaps a new home for Melqart.[4]

Lepcis needed protection. The semi-nomadic peoples of the interior were reacting with resentment to Rome's ever more pervasive presence and the transformation of North Africa's economy. Several proconsuls campaigned in the area. Sulpicius Quirinius was successful, but Cornelius Lentulus was killed by the Nasamones. Another Lentulus, Cossus, won victories against a series of Gaetulian peoples, including the Musulamii and the Cinithii. The *civitas Lepcitana* marked 'the liberation of the province Africa in the Gaetulian war under the auspices of Imp. Caesar Augustus, *pontifex maximus*, *pater patriae*, and the generalship of Cossus Lentulus, consul, *XVvir*, proconsul', with a dedication to 'Mars Augustus'.[5]

At Rome itself the cult of Augustus reached a new stage when Tiberius dedicated an altar to his *numen* in AD 10. Lepcis became the first 'free state' within the Roman world to follow suit when another imposing new building, the Chalcidicum, next to the market, was consecrated to the '*Numen imp. Caesaris divi f. Aug.*' by a college of 'fifteen priests'. The Chalcidicum, together with its double porticoes, gate and adjacent structures, was paid for by Iddibal Caphada Aemilius, son of Himilis. The experiences of Cossus and his predecessors no doubt made it seem imperative to improve communications between Tripolitania and the rest of Africa. Late in Augustus' reign the proconsul Caecina Severus set up a milestone on the coast road between Sabratha and Oea, presumably only one stage in what was to become the imperial Carthage to Alexandria highway. In AD 14 the proconsul Asprenas built a road joining Tacape on the coast, just beyond the western end of Tripolitania, with the winter-quarters of III Augusta far to the north-west.[6]

Soon another proconsul was to render Lepcis very special favour. As recorded on a stone at a major crossroad in the city, 'by order of Tiberius Caesar Augustus, Lucius Aelius Lamia, proconsul, directed (a road) from the town to the south for forty-four miles'. The road ran along the·Gebel to the furthest limit of Lepcis' territory. Lamia is also recorded in the Gebel itself, on a Neo-Punic inscription close to Mesphe (Medina Doga), about five miles from the terminus of his road, where one of 'the sons of

Masinkaw', a native Libyan, paid for 'a beautiful statue of the Lord Ammon ... and the sanctuary of his temples and the porticoes, which were built and dedicated in the year of "the general in place of the general of the army" (t'ht rb mhnt) [proconsul] "over the land of the Libyans" (shd Lwbym) [of Africa], Lwqy 'Yly L'my'.[7]

Shortly after Lamia's departure a guerrilla war began that overshadowed anything that Lepcis had seen before, an uprising of the semi-nomadic peoples of the 'south that spread right across from the *emporia* to the Atlas mountains. Their leader Tacfarinas, a Numidian from the Musulamii, won allies among the Moors, the Cinithii and the Garamantes. The first proconsul to face the rebels, a man with the resplendent name of Furius Camillus, inflicted an initial defeat on Tacfarinas in AD 17, but the war spread and was to last for seven years, even though a succession of proconsuls won victory honours. At one stage an extra legion, IX Hispana, was despatched from the Danube. For a time it was stationed, under the command of a Scipio, 'where there was a possibility of ravaging the territory of the Lepcitani and where there were escape-routes to the Garamantes', Tacitus wrote. The king of the Garamantes had supported Tacfarinas 'not to the extent of invading with an army but by sending light troops, whose strength was exaggerated in view of the distance, and acting as a repository for booty and ally in plunder'. The proconsul Dolabella, though deprived of the Ninth legion, eventually trapped and killed Tacfarinas far away in the north-west. Inscriptions at Oea and Lepcis commemorated his achievement. The Garamantes actually sent envoys to Rome to plead for mercy, 'a rare sight', Tacitus commented.[8]

During the troubles Lepcis confirmed its loyalty by further embellishment to the temple of Rome and Augustus, which became in effect a shrine to the entire Julio-Claudian family. Statues were erected in the covered courtyard, not only of Augustus and Roma, but of Tiberius and Livia, and of Germanicus and Drusus Caesar and their wives and mothers. The inscription in Punic listed their names and recorded that the work was done during the sufeteship of Balyaton ben Hanno G[..] Saturninus and Bodmelqart ben Bodmelqart Tabahpi. When the war ended, the proconsuls took some time to deal with its effects. In the late 20s Vibius Marsus was busy defining tribal boundaries at the western limits of Tripolitania; but found time to dedicate an arch of Augusta Salutaris at Lepcis. It was as late as 35–6 before Rubellius Blandus, husband of Tiberius' grand-daughter, could instruct his legate Etrilius Lupercus to arrange 'the paving of all the streets of Lepcis', to be paid for 'from the revenues on the lands restored to the Lepcitani'—presumably parts of the Gebel and the valleys taken over first by rebels, then perhaps by the army. Two arches were erected spanning major streets, bearing an inscription that commemorated this action.[9]

Whatever the exact status of the *emporia*, they were clearly now treated as effectively part of Roman Africa. Tiberius' death and the accession of Caligula marked a major change in the province. Control of the legion was removed from the proconsul and the legate of III Augusta was now a separate source of authority, commander of the 'army of Africa'. For the *emporia*, it meant that whereas the proconsul was still supreme within their territory, the legate policed and guarded the pre-desert hinterland from his base in Numidia. Caligula also deposed and killed the Mauretanian king Ptolemy, son of Juba. At the beginning of Claudius' reign his territory was pacified and converted into two provinces. The Roman writ now ran uninterrupted from the straits of Gibraltar to Egypt.[10]

Claudius was notoriously generous with grants of Roman citizenship. Some beneficiaries took his name, at Lepcis as elsewhere, becoming 'Ti. Claudius'; but others chose the name of the proconsul or legate through whose good offices the boon was obtained. In 43 one of the Tapapii, Iddibal son of Mago, dedicated a shrine to the 'Di Augusti', the 'August deities', probably the deified Augustus and his widow Livia, herself deified by her grandson Claudius. The little shrine was dedicated by the proconsul Q. Marcius Barea. It can be no coincidence that the name of this early Claudian proconsul is well represented at Lepcis: the Marcii of this place descend from persons enfranchised through him. Iddibal son of Mago may have been one. Other Lepcitani became Romans at this time, the best known being a Stoic philosopher, L. Annaeus Cornutus, friend and teacher of the poets Persius and Lucan. Cornutus' first two names point to the patronage of his fellow-Stoic and Lucan's uncle—Seneca. Cornutus could have met him much earlier, perhaps at Alexandria.[11]

The proconsul Barea, like others active at Lepcis, is described as the city's patron. Predecessors include the first proconsul recorded there, the aristocratic Crassus Frugi, Caninius Gallus, Blandus and his legate Lupercus. Others for whom the evidence is not explicit may be postulated, such as Aelius Lamia; and often a son would continue the role, prepared to offer support at Rome if Lepcis asked for it. The uniform high rank of Lepcis' patrons is yet another indication of the exceptional influence of the city.[12]

At the very end of Claudius' reign Pompeius Silvanus, proconsul and patron, dedicated to the emperor another piece of largesse. The Forum was paved and provided with a colonnaded portico, paid for by G'y ben Hanno in honour of his grandson G'y. The grandson's adoptive brother Ba'alyaton Qmd' ben M'qr supervised the completion of the work, as the Neo-Punic version of the bilingual dedication expressed it. The council, called *senatus*, and people of Lepcis set up a statue of the grandson, here called Gaius Phelyssam, son of Macer, grandson of Gaius Anno; and the adoptive brother is called Balitho Commodus, son of Macer. The family display a variety of Latin names, 'Gaius', 'Macer' and 'Commodus'; but are not yet citizens. Still, the family was clearly eminent; Gaius Anno was perhaps brother of the *sufes* in whose year of office the statues had been dedicated in the main forum temple.[13]

Early in Nero's reign, when Silvanus—who served three years—was still proconsul, Lepcis achieved an amphitheatre of its own, located beyond the eastern limit of the city, between the Alexandria road and the sea. In AD 62 the proconsul Orfitus was at Lepcis, with his legate Silius Celer, dedicating to Nero another grandiose new building, a portico by the harbour. The work was supervised by a Tapapius, Ithymbal Sabinus, son of Arish, *flamen* of Augustus and 'curator of public money'. Ithymbal is elsewhere on record, in Punic, honouring his aunt Arishut bat Yatonbaal, 'the builder'. Ithymbal's grandfather, to judge from this title, had also played a part in the growth of Lepcis. The building by the harbour no doubt represented merely the top dressing for a programme of improvement to the port. For a long time Lepcis had relied on a roadstead a few kilometres west at Cape Hermes (Homs), where the headland offered protection from the north-east wind. Now the olive oil exports could be shipped more conveniently.[14]

A Punic inscription from the 60s records the *sufetes* Abdmelqart Tabahpi and Arish, and lower officials, *mahazim*, equivalent to the Roman aediles, two pairs of them: one called Candidus and Donatus, the other Idnibal ben Hannobal and Hanno ben Arish. It would not be long before the Roman names took over, among the élite. Lepcis no doubt watched nervously the upheavals which began in 68, with Nero's fall. Africa, not the centre of the struggles, was nonetheless affected. The legate of III Augusta, Clodius Macer, apparently bidding for power, raised a new legion and minted his own coins before he was suppressed. His successor Valerius Festus studied developments anxiously, as a kinsman of Vitellius but seeing Vespasian's forces on the way to victory. Lepcis will have known both men, recent proconsuls—and Vespasian's wife, now dead, had once been the mistress of a Roman knight from Sabratha, T. Statilius Capella. Soon there were more immediate concerns. Confident that Lepcis' powerful patrons could not intervene and that the legion would remain elsewhere, Lepcis' neighbour Oea seized the chance to settle a dispute. 'It had a trivial origin', Tacitus relates, 'in thefts of fruit and cattle by peasants, but now they were trying to settle them in open warfare.' (Did the 'free states' have their own militia?) 'Oea, being inferior in numbers, had called in the aid of the Garamantes, an invincible tribe, who were always a fertile source of damage to their neighbours. Thus the people of Lepcis were in great straits. Their fields had been wasted far and wide, and they had fled in terror behind their walls'—temporary earthworks, it would seem. Festus, who had just acquired a reputation for ruthlessness by eliminating the proconsul, probably welcomed the excuse for a campaign. He followed up his suppression of the disturbance with a lightning raid to the far south which recalled Balbus' expedition ninety years before. The Garamantes were battered into submission, and gave no more trouble for over a century.[15]

Lepcis had thus come to the attention of the new emperor at the very outset of his reign; and Vespasian was interested in Africa. He needed revenue, Africa was rich as he must have known well. Nero had confiscated large estates in the 'old province', which needed organisation; and the taxation yield could be increased. Among other measures he sent in a special commissioner in 73, Rutilius Gallicus, as imperial governor (instead of a proconsul). Gallicus is attested, with an assistant of high rank, adjusting boundaries, including the old 'royal ditch' marked out in 146 BC. He also confirmed the dividing line between Oea and Lepcis, as two stones from the Gebel show: to the benefit of Lepcis, it is clear. The people of the city honoured the governor's wife, Minicia Paetina, with a statue in their home town, Turin (and, no doubt, Gallicus himself, though no inscription has survived). It would not be surprising if Lepcis struck home her advantage, whether through the good offices of Rutilius Gallicus or of another patron, perhaps the son of the Tiberian proconsul Lamia, Plautius Silvanus Aelianus, a figure of great eminence under Vespasian, City Prefect at Rome and a consul a second time in 74. (The name Plautius was perpetuated at Lepcis.) At all events, at the latest by the year 78 Lepcis had become a *municipium*, a chartered town with the *ius Latii*, the 'Latin right'. In 77 or 78 the proconsul Paccius Africanus dedicated an arch in honour of Vespasian. He and his legate could now be called *patronus municipii*. The grant was fully in accord with Vespasian's overall policy—he gave the same privilege to the whole of Spain. What it meant was that the Roman authorities recognised the Latin nature of a formerly alien community, *civitas peregrina*. In particular, the new status automatically conferred full Roman citizenship on those annually elected as magistrates. It was normal in such cases for the city to give the traditional Latin style of *quattuorviri* to their chief officers, two senior, and two aediles. At Lepcis, although the *mahazim* became *IIIIviri aedilicia potestate*, the two senior magistrates retained the ancient Punic style of *sufetes*. It is an anomaly, but a sign of Lepcis' self-confidence and pride: she could have the best of both worlds.[16]

The change of status did mean that the élite of Lepcis changed their names. Iddibal, son of Balsillec, grandson of Annobal, great-grandson of

Asmun, who paid for the temple of the 'Great Mother', Magna Mater, in the Forum in 72, was probably to be the last Punic notable to go on record with his Punic names. Within a few years the Annobals, Balsillechs, Balithos, the Bodmelqarts, Magos and Ithymbals, disappear from public records, to be replaced by Claudii and Flavii, Marcii, Paccii, Cornelii and Plautii. Back in 8 BC Annobal Rufus had pointed the way, adding a Latin *cognomen* to his native style, followed by the family of Anno who chose both 'Macer' and a *praenomen*, 'Gaius'. By 92, when Ti. Claudius Sestius, son of Ti. Claudius Sestius, in the Quirina tribe (to which new citizens were attached between the years 41–96) erected a massive podium and altar in the orchestra of the theatre, the transition might seem complete— except that Sestius bears the peculiarly Punic titles 'adorner of his country', 'lover of concord', and the text is given in both Latin and Punic. Still, that is the latest recorded public inscription in the old language. Punic continues, written sometimes in the Latin alphabet, for which it was ill-suited, as well as in the Neo-Punic script, but in the city it recedes into the background. The language was still spoken and used by the Lepcitani, above all in the countryside.[17]

If Festus' expedition had removed the Garamantian peril from Lepcis, it probably revived Roman interest in the Sahara too. The elder Pliny, writing a few years later, lists the places Balbus had conquered long before, and adds that Festus had discovered a new and shorter route 'by the Head of the Rock', *praeter caput saxi*, and that the Garamantes were no longer preventing passage by filling up the wells en route with sand. They had indeed been brought to a cooperative attitude: a mosaic from Zliten, east of Lepcis, seems to show Garamantian prisoners being punished in the Lepcis amphitheatre. Not long after Festus another Roman officer, Septimius Flaccus, took a force from Lepcis to the Garamantian oases and went on further south 'for three months' journey, towards the Ethiopians'—in other words into black Africa. The second century Alexandrian geographer Ptolemy derived his information from Marinus of Tyre, with which Lepcis still had links. Marinus may be supposed to have taken special interest in this mission, in which men of Lepcis probably played a part, and also to have supplied Ptolemy with evidence for a second transsaharan venture. This one, evidently not military, was led by 'Julius Maternus from Lepcis', who went from Garama, accompanied by the Garamantian king, for 'four months' journey to the south', reaching 'Agisymba, where the rhinoceroses congregate'. Ptolemy was sceptical; but the emperor Domitian was to display a rhinoceros at Rome for the first time in the early 90s. Well before that the Colosseum, or Flavian amphitheatre, had been opened by Titus, in June 80: nine thousand wild beasts were slaughtered for the delectation of the Roman people. Flaccus' expedition may have been prompted by orders to obtain choice specimens.[18]

Septimius Flaccus has been identified by some with Suellius Flaccus, legate of III Augusta, on record as fighting the Nasamones of the Syrtica who had rebelled against Roman tax-collectors. He also adjudicated a boundary between two tribes on the coast in 87. Nonetheless, it seems plausible that a Roman senator called Septimius was active in Tripolitania in the early Flavian period, when a boy called Septimius Severus was taken from Lepcis by his wealthy father and brought up near Rome. The father must have been one of the notables of Lepcis who had acquired Roman citizenship and had taken a Roman *gentilicium*, 'Septimius'. The *HA*, in the slightly garbled opening to the life of Septimius, assigns him an ancestor called 'Macer', and one of his grandfather's brothers was called 'Gaius Septimius'. It is reasonable to detect the emperor's pre-Roman paternal ancestors in the family of Gaius Anno, son of Anno, father of Anno Macer and grandfather of Gaius Phelyssam and Balitho Commodus. The first to be enfranchised may have taken the names 'Gaius Septimius Macer'. It is conceivable that he had become wealthy in part through the transsaharan trade; but the Septimii certainly possessed olive plantations as well.[19]

The Italian estates of the Septimii were near Veii, north of Rome, some seventeen Roman miles along the Via Cassia at a place perhaps called Baccanae; at Cures Sabini further north-east, close to the Via Salaria; and in Hernican country south-east of Rome, perhaps at Anagnia on the Via Latina. The young Septimius Severus was evidently a child when he first came to southern Etruria and to Rome to be educated with the sons of the great, in the 80s. He lost any trace of an African or Punic accent, was imbued, no doubt, with Greek and Latin literature, and completed his education by studying with the great Quintilian, first holder of an imperially endowed chair of rhetoric. His fellow-pupils included senators, such as Vitorius Marcellus, a 'new man' from Teate Marrucinorum on the east side of Italy, but married into the by now aristocratic house of the Hosidii. Quintilian was to dedicate his treatise on oratory to Marcellus. Another pupil of his was the younger Pliny. Severus could have acquired senatorial rank, but was content with the 'narrow stripe' of a Roman knight. He began to practise as a barrister, wrote verses and had literary friends, among them the poet Statius, author of the *Thebaid*. Statius wrote a poem in 91 or 92 to celebrate the recovery from illness of an eminent man, Rutilius Gallicus, by then City Prefect. By the time it was published, in the first instalment of Statius' occasional pieces, the *Silvae*, Gallicus had died. The Septimii may have found Gallicus a helpful patron after their migration to Italy. Gallicus had probably met Severus' father when he was at Lepcis in the 70s. Statius' poem recalled, among the other highlights of Gallicus' career, 'the tribute and wondrous obedience of Libya ... and such wealth as not even he who gave the order dared to expect'. Africa's wealth, of which the Septimii possessed a share, gave them the entrée to Rome's high society.[20]

The overthrow of Nero had begun in the west and the new dynasty was first proclaimed in the east. Civil war accelerated the opening up of the highest positions to provincial Romans, already well advanced: the government of Nero had been handled for some years by Seneca, from Spain, and Burrus, from southern Gaul. 'Colonials' from the west had achieved the consulship long before. Now they were joined by men from the east and from Africa, at first descendants of Italian settlers, such as Junius Montanus of Alexandria Troas and Pactumeius Fronto of Cirta in the Numidian 'New Campania'. Before the Flavian dynasty finished Greek senators with Roman names would be consuls; and by the year 98 a western colonial would be emperor. In this society a family from Lepcis could have felt at ease. Still, the Punic background was a potential embarrassment. The very label could be held pejorative. Rome still remembered Hannibal. Anyone with literary interests who preferred to forget him might have had difficulty in evading recitals of Silius Italicus' *Punica*. The distinguished senator was producing the longest epic in the Latin language, devoted to the Hannibalic war. Statius himself, in a poem to celebrate a road built by Domitian in 95, starts by expressing relief that 'no Libyan hordes' were marching on it, that no 'foreign general' was 'scouring the Campanian fields in treacherous warfare', alluding to the proverbial *Punica fides*, 'bad faith', of the old enemy. Another poem in the same book of the *Silvae*, on a statuette of Hercules, imagines its former owners, including Hannibal, variously labelled the 'Nasamonian king' and the 'Sidonian general'—and as 'ruthless, treacherous and arrogant', hated by the god as being 'drenched in Italian blood'. Not surprisingly, when—in the same book—he dedicated an Ode to his friend Septimius Severus, in fifteen four-line stanzas, he was careful to make it clear that his friend was different.[21]

No one would imagine that he had been born at Leptis (outside Tripolitania the name was almost invariably misspelled):

> *tene in remotis Syrtibus avia*
> *Leptis creavit?*

> Did far away Leptis really bear you,
> in the remote Syrtes?

No, says Statius, 'who would not assume sweet Septimius had crawled in infancy on all Romulus' hills? But, after all, he had been brought to Italy as a boy and swam in Tuscan pools: the language echoes Aeneas' arrival— from Carthage— with his son Iulus. The young Severus 'grew up among the sons of the senate, but content with the glory of the narrow purple'. Then come the striking lines:

> non sermo Poenus, non habitus tibi,
> externa non mens: Italus, Italus.

> Your speech is not Punic, nor your dress,
> Your mind not foreign: you are Italian, Italian!

Had his 'speech been Punic', which may mean 'a Punic accent', Statius' friend might have pronounced his own name as 'Sheptimiush Sheverush', it might be guessed. The young man had become completely assimilated, 'Romanised' (to use a modern term). Statius' poem shows the facility with which the process could take place. His fellow poet and contemporary Martial (himself from Spain) praised a young British woman, Claudia Rufina, in rather similar terms:

> Claudia caeruleis cum sit Rufina Britannis
> edita, quam Latiae pectora gentis habet!
> quale decus formae! Romanam credere matres
> Italides possunt, Atthides esse suam.

> Though brought up among the sky-blue Britons,
> Claudia Rufina has the spirit of the Latin race.
> What graceful beauty—the Italian ladies can
> believe she is Roman, the ladies of Athens that she is theirs.

Martial too may have been a friend of Septimius Severus—he had a poet friend called Severus, but that name was very common. Statius had been supported by his friend during Domitian's literary competition at Alba; and he encouraged Severus to write more poetry in his country retreat, after his exertions in the courts.[22]

In September 96 Domitian was assassinated. The new emperor Nerva and his heir Trajan, adopted in 97 and emperor from January 98, were generally welcomed, especially by senators. But poets like Martial and Statius, who had flattered Domitian with sickening adulation, may have found the change less advantageous. Martial returned to Spain. Old Silius Italicus committed suicide. Statius is not heard of again. The young Severus may have abandoned thoughts of a career at the bar or of an official post. He did obtain a minor distinction at some stage, being appointed a 'select judge' or juryman, iudex selectus, and would have served in one of the first three of the five panels, or decuriae, that heard cases at Rome. Whether or not he decided to return to 'far off Lepcis' straightaway, events there may have made his return mandatory. The change of ruler had had unwelcome effects in some provinces. With the removal of Domitian's iron control some governors practised graft on a colossal scale. The proconsul of Africa, Marius Priscus, perhaps in office in 96–7, oppressed his province greedily, not least Lepcis Magna. A member of the town council, Flavius Marcianus, bribed him with the enormous sum of 700,000 sesterces to eliminate an enemy, who was a Roman knight. The man had been flogged, sentenced to the mines, and finally executed by strangulation. In another case which may also have taken place at Lepcis a certain Vitellius Honoratus had paid 300,000 for a knight to be exiled and seven of the man's friends to be killed.[23]

Priscus had acted at Lepcis through the agency of his legate Hostilius Firminus. He too received money from Marcianus, though less than he had hoped for: 'it was proved from Marcianus' accounts and a speech he had made in the Lepcis council that Firminus had helped Priscus with a particularly shameful service, and had bargained with Marcianus to get 200,000 sesterces. He had in fact been given 10,000, entered in the accounts under the heading of "cosmetics".' When Priscus' proconsulship ended action against him commenced. 'Many private individuals and one particular city'—surely Lepcis—preferred charges. The case came to the senate, and was prolonged. Priscus was at first accused of minor extortion, and pleaded guilty, asking for damages to be assessed by a senate committee. Pliny and Tacitus were appointed to represent the Africans. It is from the former's correspondence that the account of the trial derives; Tacitus may have learned details of Lepcis' history at this time, later to be incorporated in his *Histories* and *Annals*. The two eminent and eloquent prosecuting counsel revealed that Priscus was trying to evade trial on more serious charges by a plea of guilty to minor ones. A commission of enquiry, *inquisitio*, was set up to summon witnesses from the province. Priscus was in the meantime convicted on the minor charges and deprived of his rank. At least twelve months after the case began the main hearing was opened. At the second session, in January 100, Trajan himself presided, as consul. It was one of the new emperor's first appearances at Rome since his accession.[24]

Pliny opened with a speech lasting nearly five hours. Salvius Liberalis, defence counsel, replied the next day, followed by Tacitus for the prosecution, 'eloquent, with all the solemnity that typifies his style of public speaking'. After this the defence could only appeal for leniency. On the third day Priscus was found guilty, but his punishment was merely banishment from Rome and Italy and repayment of the bribes; his legate Firminus lost some privileges, but not his senatorial rank. The poet

Juvenal recalled the case some years later: the guilty proconsul begins 'drinking from the eighth hour, while you, victorious province, lament'. All the same, Lepcis had once again managed to capture the attention of a new dynasty. Shortly after this at least one Lepcitane, a man called Fronto, entered the Roman senate. The city's powerful patrons had redressed her grievances and her position was enhanced. A few years later this was recognised formally. Lepcis was granted the rank of *colonia*, taking the titles *Ulpia Traiana fidelis*. All its inhabitants became Roman citizens and its chief magistrates now, at last, shed the Punic name *sufetes* and were entitled *duoviri*. Lucius Septimius Severus, who had already been *sufes* of the *municipium*, was given a special post as prefect at the time when the grant of *civitas*, Roman citizenship, was made, and became one of the first two *duoviri* of the new *colonia*. Lepcis was now in the fullest sense Roman, so it might seem. Another feature of the town's constitution might appear to confirm this: the division of part of the population into *curiae*, 'wards', evoking the primeval organisation of the Roman people. In fact the *curiae*, each given a name associated with the imperial family, Ulpia, Traiana, Nervia, Plotina, and so on, mask an ancient Punic institution. Punic culture did not disappear and the Punic language was still used. Besides, the Roman *colonia*, with its impressive and gleaming array of public buildings, actually looked more like a Greek city than a Roman one. At all events, Lepcis in the year 110 erected another arch, in grateful thanks to Trajan.[25]

· 3 ·

LIFE IN ROMAN
TRIPOLITANIA

WHEN LEPCIS BECAME A *colonia*, Lucius Septimus Severus, its leading
man, was doubtless already married. His wife's name and origin are
unknown—and he could have married more than once. He might have
found a wife in Italy; a local heiress is perhaps more probable. Nothing is
known of his daughter Polla's date of birth; the son, Geta, old enough to
father children himself by the year 144 at latest, can hardly have seen the
light of day much after Hadrian's accession. Some comment is required on
the choice of names for his children by the *sufes* and *duumvir*. 'Geta' is very
rare (and originally a slave's name), but it was borne by the son of Vitorius
Marcellus. The *sufes* was surely recalling his days in Italy and honouring
his old fellow-student. 'Polla' is commoner; but the charming Argentaria
Polla, Lucan's widow and wife of Pollius Felix, is celebrated—more
frequently than Severus himself or Marcellus—in the *Silvae* of Statius.[1]

While Geta grew to manhood Lepcis continued to expand and develop.
Magnificent public baths were built in the south-east part of the town.
The aqueduct, dating to 120, was paid for by Q. Servilius Candidus,
whose generosity is commemorated, with due honour to the emperor
Hadrian, on three Latin inscriptions. He had brought in water from the
River Cinyps and an extension supplied a fountain in the theatre. A
stamped tile from the baths shows that the Punic element, now less openly
displayed, was still present. In the old language, but in the Latin alphabet,
it records that it was 'made in the workshops of Rogate (Rogatus)
the master' (*felioth iadem sy-Rogate ymmanai*). Candidus himself, on
another public inscription, from the temple of Liber Pater, is accorded
traditional Punic titles in Latin translation: *amator patriae, amator civium,
amator concordiae*. He was probably a descendant of the Punic magnate
'Candidus son of Candidus, grandson of Hanno, great-grandson of
Abdmelqart'. Private and official dedications alike, honouring Hadrian
and his successor Antoninus Pius, display the zealous loyalty of the
Lepcitane notables. A Septimius is among them, donating a statue of
Cupid to the Chalcidicum, 'for the welfare of the emperor Antoninus

Augustus Pius and his children'. This man, by his full names Gaius Claudius Septimius Aper, may be presumed the father of Septimius' senatorial kinsmen, Aper and Severus, whom the *HA* calls his 'uncles', *patrui*. The two are known from other evidence, P. Septimius Aper as consul suffect in 153, C. Septimius Severus consul a few years later. The latter turns out to be 'son of Gaius' (*C.f.*), hence not son of Lucius the *sufes*. Perhaps C. Cl. Septimius Aper was a brother of Lucius; his sons would then be cousins, *fratres patrueles*, of Septimius' father Geta, not uncles of Septimius in the strict sense.[2]

P. Septimius Aper, born at latest c. 110, presumably entered the Roman senate under Hadrian. Nothing else is known of him except his consulship: but he is the earliest known man of Lepcis to hold the *fasces*. The career of the other 'uncle' is known in detail. After a compulsory pre-senatorial post, but no military tribunate, he moved through the three 'qualifying' republican magistracies: quaestor, tribune of the plebs, praetor. There followed the curatorship of an Italian road and the command of a legion in Syria, XVI Flavia at Samosata, and, a sign of high favour, two senatorial priesthoods, before he returned to the east as governor of Lycia-Pamphylia in the 150s, with the consulship to follow, probably in 160.[3]

In the Antonine era the Roman Africans were beginning to storm the heights, whether descended from Italian settlers or enfranchised notables, from Numidia and from the 'old province' above all. But the Tripolitanians, who had plenty of links with the rest of Africa, economic as well as of sentiment and common education (at Carthage in many cases), will have benefited too. An early harbinger of the Africans' rise is the literary man and Roman knight, Suetonius Tranquillus, biographer of the Caesars, from Hippo Regius, who popped up as Chief Secretary, *ab epistulis*, of the emperor early in Hadrian's reign. He did not last the course (he was sacked in Britain in the year 122). But one of the two Guard Prefects that Hadrian bequeathed to Antoninus Pius was, it seems, another Numidian, M. Petronius Mamertinus. This man's son or nephew, consul in 150, evidently married a Septimia, quite possibly from the Lepcis family. (C. Septimius Severus later had links with Numidian Thubursicu.)[4]

A kinsman of the Guard Prefect Mamertinus, M. Cornelius Fronto of Cirta, was now at the height of his fame, not merely as the leading orator at Rome: he was the tutor and friend of Antoninus' heir, Marcus Aurelius Caesar. Another of the Caesar's tutors, the *grammaticus* Tuticius Proculus, was from African Sicca, and the doyen of that profession, Fronto's friend Sulpicius Apollinaris, was from Carthage. Fronto's links with his fellow-countrymen, and the wider fellowship of his admirers, pupils and acquaintances from Italy, and the eastern and western provinces, formed a powerful nexus. More influential still, it may be argued, was another man from Cirta, Q. Lollius Urbicus. This younger son of a local magnate at Tiddis, a dependency of Cirta, had a distinguished military record, culminating in a victory over rebellious north Britons in 142 and the re-occupation of southern Scotland. Soon after, probably in 146, Urbicus was elevated to the Prefecture of Rome itself, the pinnacle of the senatorial career. He was to occupy the post for the rest of his life, until 160. Eminence in literature and in war was matched by legal distinction. The greatest jurist of the Antonine era, P. Salvius Julianus, was another African senator, his home town being Hadrumetum in Byzacena. Hadrian had recognised his outstanding talent in the 130s, commissioning him to reformulate the 'praetor's edict'. In the year 148, which marked the 900th anniversary of Rome's foundation, Julianus held office as *consul ordinarius*, a rare honour for a new man.[5]

The 'old province' and Numidia were certainly to the fore. But the leading families of Lepcis, Oea and Sabratha, with some of their own men already senators, some of their women, no doubt, married to other senators, were well placed to push forward. And there were still regular opportunities to canvas proconsuls for assistance, when they visited Tripolitania on assize. The possibilities are illustrated in the writings of another African, Apuleius, the most celebrated Latin author of the age, best known for his novel, the *Golden Ass* or *Metamorphoses*. In the early 160s, Apuleius settled at Carthage, where he commanded vast audiences for public lectures, many on subjects which he preferred to call 'philo-sophy'. Some surviving extracts are elaborate panegyrics of proconsuls and their kin. One of the shorter pieces, to an unknown dignitary, captures the tone well: 'Out of countless men there are but few senators, and of senators few are of noble birth; and of the consulars few are good men, and of those good men few are learned.'[6]

Apuleius was probably born at the beginning of Hadrian's reign, at Madauros, once a Numidian town in the kingdom of Syphax, later part of Massinissa's realm, but given a charter as a *colonia* under Vespasian, who settled veteran legionaries there. Apuleius could call himself, deprecat-ingly, a 'semi-Gaetulian, semi-Numidian', but was doubtless of settler or mixed stock. His father had been a member of the élite, a *duumvir*, and had left Apuleius and his brother an estate worth 2,000,000 sesterces, enough to make them each comfortably qualified for equestrian rank. At an early age Apuleius went to Carthage, some 150 miles (240 km) from his home, to further his education. His affection for Carthage remained immense: 'Carthage is the revered teacher of our province,' he said years afterwards, 'Carthage is the divine muse of Africa, Carthage is the foundation of inspiration for the Roman World.' From Carthage he went to Athens, the greatest university in the ancient world, and travelled further afield: he happens to mention visiting Samos and Phrygian Hierapolis. At Athens he drank in 'the imaginative draught of poetry, the clear draught of geometry, the sweet draught of music, the austerer draught of dialectic, and the nectar of all philosophy'. There he met a student several years younger than himself, Sicinius Pontianus of Oea.[7]

From Athens Apuleius went to Rome, where he gained the entrée to the literary circles of the upper classes, including friends of the patrician senator Scipio Orfitus, as he later recalled. If, as is generally reckoned, the end of his *Metamorphoses* contains some autobiographical material, he went to Rome shortly after his initiation into the mysteries of Isis, became a fervent worshipper at the temple on the Campus Martius, and was initiated further. His funds were by now becoming depleted and to support himself he began to practise as a rhetorician. He had thus found his vocation. When he returned to Africa his talents were greatly in demand.[8]

Apuleius still had an urge to travel, and in winter 156 began a journey by land to Alexandria. On his way he stayed at Oea, with his friend Appius Quintianus. He fell ill, and was visited by his old fellow-student Sicinius Pontianus, who begged him to prolong his visit, adding that he himself would like to accompany Apuleius when he did resume his travels. He urged that Apuleius, because of his illness, should postpone the journey until the following winter (travel in summer along the baking hot Syrtic coast was out of the question). Further, he should move from the house of Appii to Pontianus' own, overlooking the sea.[9]

Pontianus' household consisted of his widowed mother Aemilia Pudentilla, and a younger brother, Pudens—a surly youth, who unlike Pontianus had had no higher education. He was later alleged to speak virtually no Latin: his normal language was Punic, and he had been taught a little Greek by his mother. Even if this description is overdrawn, it must indicate a state of affairs that was possible, even in a family of equestrian rank, with great estates. Pudens was only a few years older than Septimius from neighbouring Lepcis, who was said to have spoken fluent Punic. Apuleius quickly made himself at home. As his health gradually improved, his friends persuaded him to give a public lecture. It took place in the town hall, *basilica*, of Oea, which was packed out. The lecture was a rousing success—the audience shouted their approval (calls of *insigniter!*) and there were cries that Apuleius should stay and become a citizen of Oea. Afterwards, Pontianus put a proposition to Apuleius. 'This universal enthusiasm is a sign from heaven', he said; and then revealed that he wanted Apuleius to marry his mother Pudentilla. 'You are the only friend I can rely on with complete trust and confidence.' His mother had many suitors, although just a plain widow with children. If Apuleius refused, and wanted to reserve himself for a more attractive and wealthier match, he, Pontianus, would regard it as unworthy of a philosopher and a friend. Pudentilla may not have been 'wealthy', but as Pontianus himself had pointed out, there were several men eager to marry her—and she had an estate worth 4,000,000 sesterces.[10]

After the death of her husband Sicinius Amicus some fourteen years before, her father-in-law, who became the guardian of Pontianus and Pudens, was eager that she should marry another of his sons, Sicinius Clarus. Pudentilla was unwilling, but the old man threatened that if she married anyone else he would exclude his grandsons from their father's share of his property. Pudentilla, more or less forced to comply, was betrothed to Clarus, but managed to defer the marriage. It had still not taken place when the old man died, leaving Pontianus and Pudens as his heirs. Pudentilla was ill for some time, and was strongly urged to marry again for her health's sake before her elder son left home for good. He was by this time studying abroad. She refused to marry Clarus despite pressure from her late husband's other brother Aemilianus. But she was determined on a marriage of some kind, to protect herself, and so informed Pontianus, who by now had gone from Athens to Rome. He returned post-haste, determined to make sure that whoever became his stepfather, his own and his brother's inheritance would not be placed in jeopardy. It was at this juncture that Apuleius appeared.[11]

Apuleius had already spent a year or so with the Sicinii by the time that he became personally involved in the question of Pudentilla's remarriage. He had got to know her well, but was reluctant to tie himself down. Still, he soon found—as he himself put it—that he was beginning to love Pudentilla, and agreed. Pontianus had no difficulty in getting his mother's consent, and was all for arranging the ceremony at once. Apuleius and Pudentilla persuaded him that they should wait until Pontianus himself took a wife and Pudens assumed the toga of manhood. Meanwhile Pontianus was beginning to study oratory with Apuleius, who continued to give public lectures. One was attended by the proconsul Lollianus Avitus, who was on a tour of duty in Tripolitania (during which he supervised repairs to the fountain Candidus had given to the theatre at Lepcis). Apuleius, who had probably met Avitus at Rome, recommended his future stepson to the proconsul. Avitus is known from another source as an influential patron. A year or two later he did his best to secure a commission as centurion for a disillusioned *grammaticus*, Helvius Pertinax.[12]

Then came Pontianus' marriage and Pudens' entry into manly status, public occasions because of the high position of the Sicinii at Oea— requiring distribution of largesse to the tune of 50,000 sesterces. Pontianus married the daughter of one Herennius Rufinus, whose character Apuleius later presented in the blackest terms. Pontianus' attitude and behaviour towards Apuleius suddenly changed. He now tried to prevent his mother from remarrying, evidently influenced by Rufinus. Pontianus told his mother that Apuleius practised the black arts and had bewitched her into falling in love with him. Pudentilla wrote to him—in Greek—attempting to calm him down:

> Since I determined to marry, for reasons that I explained to you, you yourself persuaded me to choose Apuleius as a husband in preference to all others, because you admired him and were eager that he should become a member of our family. But now that certain ill-disposed persons have accused us, and are persuading you against us, suddenly 'Apuleius is a magician', and I have been 'bewitched by him and love him'. Come to me then, while I am 'still in my senses'.

Pontianus and his wife, and Pudens, then returned to their mother's house, and stayed there for about two months.[13]

The marriage of Apuleius and Pudentilla took place, quietly, at one of her villas outside Oea, to escape the distribution of presents to the townspeople that had already been necessary when Pontianus married. But the ill-feeling was revived. It was felt by the family that Pontianus and Pudens would now lose their inheritance to the usurping stepfather. Apuleius persuaded Pudentilla to make over a substantial part of her late husband's property to her sons, in the shape of farms—to be valued at a low assessment—and, from her personal property, lands, a large, well-appointed house, a great quantity of wheat, barley, wine and oil, a large number of cattle and 400 slaves. This graphically illustrates the substantial nature of the family's possessions. Pudentilla retained a substantial number of slaves over and above the 400 she gave her sons. She also had fifteen in her fine town house overlooking the sea. It emerges, too, that the estate included property almost 100 Roman miles from Oea. This must have been in the Gebel, south of Thenadassa. Apuleius received from his bride another, modest property worth 50,000 sesterces (the same sum that had been lavished on the people of Oea not long before). The wealth of the Sicinii and Aemilii of Oea was certainly matched, indeed exceeded, by the Septimii and their kin of Lepcis. Lepcis unquestionably possessed the greater share of the best olive growing lands in the Gebel, those of the Tarhuna and Msellata sectors. The élite of Lepcis had most of that relatively small portion of the Gebel plateau where the average annual rainfall reaches twelve inches (300 mm). Further to the south-west, past the terminal point of the forty-four mile road from Lepcis constructed long before by the proconsul Lamia, the levels decline markedly. The area where the landowners of Oea and Sabratha had their olive groves will have had a lower yield and smaller profits than were enjoyed by their neighbours at Lepcis. Tripolitania was an unusual region, set apart from the rest of the province of Africa, not only geographically and in climate, but in its history. Nearly two centuries of virtual independence after the second Punic war had allowed them to consolidate their hold on very large territories. That of Lepcis must have comprised at least 2000 square miles (well over 5000 square km). In the old province and its extension to the west, only Carthage and Cirta exceeded this. Lepcis, city and territory, not only outdid Oea and Sabratha. She was much richer than most other cities in Africa.[14]

Pudentilla's generous provision for her sons won round public opinion at Oea. Pontianus' father-in-law Rufinus was now criticised for setting son against mother. Pontianus and Pudens came to ask for forgiveness. Pontianus asked Apuleius to explain to Lollianus Avitus, to whom he had just written with an account of Pontianus' behaviour, asking him to ignore the earlier recommendation. Apuleius gave Pontianus another letter, to take to Carthage in person. Avitus was awaiting the arrival of his successor, Claudius Maximus. The reconcilation probably took place in early spring of 158. Pontianus set off at once, was favourably received, and given a reply to take back to Apuleius.[15]

But on his homeward journey Pontianus, who had been sending ahead letters written in the warmest tones, fell ill, and died soon after his arrival at Oea. In his will he left everything to his mother and brother. The young widow, Rufinus' daughter, got nothing except some linen worth 800 sesterces. Rufinus would clearly be incensed. His aim had presumably been to lay his hands on the estate of the Sicinii through the marriage connection. He now took steps to entice Pudens away from Apuleius, not a difficult task. Rufinus' daughter exerted her charms again, and Pudens once more left his mother's house, moving to that of his uncle Sicinius Aemilianus. Aemilianus must have been watching the turn of events with impotent rage. He was not the man to give in without a fight—he had previously contested the will of his own uncle, and the case had reached the court of the Prefect of Rome, Lollius Urbicus, who decided against him. He had given an unfortunate exhibition of himself—his violent insistence, in spite of the Prefect's verdict, that the will was a forgery, put him in danger of punishment for *calumnia*. Pudens, away from his mother's guidance, gave up school, spending his time drinking and going to the gladiatorial training establishment. Pudentilla fell ill again under the strain, and wanted to disinherit Pudens. But Apuleius dissuaded her.[16]

The change of proconsul in the spring of 158 perhaps made Apuleius' enemies think that they had a better chance than with Avitus, to whom Apuleius was known. Claudius Maximus, like his predecessor, came to

Tripolitania. He held assizes at Sabratha, probably in the autumn of 158. Apuleius attended, to appear on behalf of his wife in a case brought against her by the Granii brothers. Sicinius Aemilianus, appearing as a witness for the Granii, made a staggering assertion against Apuleius, accusing him of practising black magic to gain the hand of Pudentilla—and of murdering Pontianus. His enemies saw that the proconsul viewed the charge with some scepticism, and decided to modify it. Four or five days later Apuleius was formally indicted on lesser charges: the principal one was that he practised the black arts (which could be treated as a capital offence); further, that he was a dandy and a debauchee who had married an elderly woman for her money. The charges were filed in the name of Sicinius Pudens, with his uncle Aemilianus merely listed as his 'representative'. An advocate, Tannonius Pudens, was engaged to present their case. Apuleius made his own defence, and the speech that he gave, no doubt considerably rewritten, survives as the *Apologia*—the source of virtually all our information about the affair.[17]

Clearly Apuleius goes out of his way to blacken his opponents. But the speech is an authentic record from a trial that actually took place. Apuleius may have been a novelist, among his other accomplishments, but he did not invent the characters in the trial at Sabratha. The names of most of the persons involved can be matched on contemporary inscriptions from Tripolitania. For an account of provincial life 'with the lid off', the only rival to the *Apologia* is Cicero's *pro Cluentio*, even if Apuleius' enemies appear relatively harmless compared with Cluentius' murderous persecutor Oppianicus. The speech casts vivid light on life in Antonine Tripolitania. Its value as a commentary on the agrarian economy has already been indicated. It would be a waste not to quote a little more. There can be no doubt that the Septimii of Lepcis would hear about Apuleius. Some of them perhaps attended his lectures at Oea, and conceivably even attended the trial. It would have been desirable to visit Sabratha when the proconsul was in residence. Apuleius refers to 'the vast multitude, which has flocked together from every quarter to hear this case'. Even the young Septimius himself, as a thirteen-year-old, may have been there.[18]

Among the evidence produced by the prosecution, who had seized on every scrap or detail that could discredit Apuleius, were poems, some alleged to be obscene. Another was to a certain Calpurnianus describing a special toothpowder Apuleius had prepared at the latter's request. The prosecution tried to put on this the connotation of mixing magic potions. Later, they produced the letter from Pudentilla to Pontianus, but quoted only the end of it, out of context: 'Apuleius is a magician and I have been bewitched by him and love him. Come to me then while I am still in my senses.' The accusation of black magic took various forms. Apuleius

30

mocked his accusers—if he were really a magician, it was reckless to attack him, for they would be in danger of supernatural reprisals. He was said to have used a rare fish for magical purposes, to have hypnotised a young slave to make him prophesy, to have kept 'something mysterious' wrapped up in linen among the household goods at Pontianus' house, to have performed a nocturnal ceremony at someone else's house, and to have had a magic image made. Apuleius answered the charges one by one, with evident relish. The fish was dissected for the purpose of scientific research. The slave was a sufferer from epilepsy. The objects covered with a cloth were connected with the Greek mystery-cult into which he had been initiated, and he appealed to fellow-initiates in court for conformation of the necessity to remain silent about their nature. As for the 'nocturnal ceremonies', that was a pure invention, and the 'image', allegedly of a skeleton, was a statuette of Mercury, made for him quite openly by 'the craftsman Cornelius Saturninus, a man whose skill is famous among the townspeople and whose character is above reproach'.[19]

On the two latter charges Apuleius may well have been disingenuous. The 'nocturnal rites' were supposedly performed with his friend Appius Quintianus at the house of Junius Crassus, which Quintianus was renting during Crassus' absence at Alexandria. Crassus did not appear and the prosecution produced written testimony. Apuleius simply denies the charge and discredits Crassus as a glutton and drunkard who had been bribed to invent the whole story. 'Why is Crassus not in court? I myself saw him here at Sabratha yesterday, Aemilianus, belching in your face . . . I tell you that Crassus has long since been snoring in a drunken stupor, and has taken a second bath—or is now sweating out his drunkenness at the baths to be ready for a second binge after supper.' Or perhaps, he suggested, Aemilianus simply thought that the appearance of his witness, 'a young man with his face stripped of the beard and hair that ought to adorn it, his eyes heavy with wine, his eyelids swollen, his vacant grin, his slobbering lips, harsh voice, trembling hands, his breath reeking of the cookshop', would weaken the credibility of his sworn evidence. As for the 'image', Apuleius sidesteps the charge, giving details of a statuette of Mercury, making it obvious that it in no way resembles a skeleton and giving a detailed account of when and how it was made for him—but does not state unambiguously that the Mercury was the 'image' described by his accusers.[20]

After dealing with the accusations of magic he turns at last to the real issue, his marriage with Pudentilla. On specific questions he shows that the prosecution have concocted the evidence, as with Pudentilla's letter. Again, they had tried to prove that she was nearly sixty, whereas Apuleius demonstrated that she was twenty years younger than that. Having attacked Aemilianus and Crassus, he turned the full force of his invective on Rufinus, accusing him of being the prime mover in the conspiracy against him. 'In his boyhood before he became so hideously bald, he readily submitted to pederasts in every unspeakable way; as a young man he was a stage dancer ... except for his immorality he is said to have possessed none of the qualities of an actor.' Now that he is older, 'his house is a home for pimps and the whole household is contaminated: his own character is disgusting, his wife is a prostitute, his sons are like their parents. .... His wife was getting old and worn out and refused to go on supporting the whole family by her own actions'—so the daughter was then set to work, and seduced the affections of young Pontianus. Rufinus was also charged with 'consulting Chaldaean astrologers'—something that Septimius is said to have done not many years later.[21]

Apuleius' portrayal of Sicinius Aemilianus was couched in rather different terms. He mocks his poverty—he had not long before owned no more than a tiny plot of land at Zaratha (far to the west, along the Tripolitanian coast), which he cultivated without any slave labour. He derides the man's show of austerity and his boorish disapproval of erotic verse. In a long passage he points out that Aemilianus has ample scope for criticising him: 'You have the advantage of one who, himself shrouded in darkness, surveys another who chances to have taken his stand in the full light of the day.' Defending himself on the charge of 'the objects wrapped in linen', Apuleius contrasts his own piety with the total lack of interest in religion displayed by Aemilianus, who thinks it:

> a good joke to mock at things divine. For I learn from certain men of Oea who know him, that to this day he has never prayed to any god or frequented any temple. And if he happens to pass any shrine, he regards it as a crime to raise his hand to his lips in token of reverence. He has never given first fruits of crops or vines or flocks to any of the gods of the farmer, who feed him and clothe him; his farm holds no shrine, no holy place, nor grove. But why do I speak of groves or shrines? Those who have been on his property say they have never seen one stone where an offering of oil has been made, one bough where wreaths have been hung.

The combination of an austere character with unmistakable lack of traditional pagan piety hint that Aemilianus was being subtly labelled a Christian. Apuleius actually uses the word 'lucifugus', 'shunning the light of day' to characterise Aemilianus. The term reappears in Minucius Felix's *Octavius* a few generations later describing the Christians. Apuleius also compares his opponent to Thyestes. This was a current insult applied to Christians: the great Cornelius Fronto, whose speeches Apuleius must have known, is quoted by Minucius, accusing Christians of holding 'Thyestean banquets'. It is unnecessary to believe that Aemilianus was really a Christian. Apuleius' hints, which the proconsul and others in the Sabratha court-house would readily follow, would be enough. It was part of Apuleius' attempts to establish the respectability of his own religious practice by discrediting the opposition.[22]

Throughout his defence Apuleius played on his philosophical and literary prowess, to win the respect of the proconsul. Claudius Maximus was a personal friend of Aurelius Caesar, and one of his mentors in philosophy. Apuleius claims him as a fellow-authority on Plato and Aristotle, and praises his patience in listening to the long-winded prosecution, his acuteness in interrogating witnesses. A trump card was the letter to himself from Maximus' predecessor Lollianus Avitus, which he read out in court. 'What witness to my character more worthy of all confidence? What more eloquent advocate? Many eloquent men who bore the Roman name I have known and studied in my life, but never did I admire any as much as him.' The effect of this letter was manifest: 'I see, Maximus, with what pleasure you hear those characteristics described, which you recognise as distinguishing your friend Avitus.' There is no doubt that the defence succeeded. Not long after, Apuleius was at Carthage, highly esteemed by the city and the proconsuls; and he was to be chosen as 'high priest of the province', chairman of the provincial council.

If excuse were needed for introducing the story of Apuleius at Oea into a biography of Septimius Severus, it can only be repeated that for the thirteen-year-old boy the trial must have represented one of the most striking events of his life. Connections between the three cities of Tripolitania were close. It may be that the Granii, whose lawsuit with Pudentilla provided the opportunity for the attack on Apuleius, were from Lepcis Magna. Sicinius Pudens, that unprepossessing youth who was Septimius' near-contemporary, may be the same Pudens who half a century later composed a curious inscription in honour of Septimius as emperor, in gratitude for the advancement of his son, no doubt the senator Q. Sicinius Clarus Pontianus, governor of Thrace in 202. It would be curious—though there is no proof—if the Septimii, from whose ranks the lawyer friend of Statius had come, failed to take note of this *cause célèbre*, worthy indeed of Africa, 'the nurse of pleaders', *nutricula causidicorum*. Septimius certainly would have the chance of hearing Apuleius at Carthage ten years later, and was then to plead his own case in court also, although in an altogether less exciting and brilliant affair.[23]

Few details are recorded of the boyhood of Septimius. It is said that his favourite game was 'judges', and that he himself would make his playmates act the part of lictors, carrying the bundles of rods and axes in front of him, while he took the role of the Roman magistrate. Of course his schooling is referred to—prowess in both Latin and Greek is mentioned in the *HA*. Another late source speaks of his fluency in Punic. One may accept the judgment of his contemporary Cassius Dio, who recalled that Septimius had been eager for more education than he actually got. At seventeen, in 162, he gave a speech, or declamation, in public, no doubt in his home town. This marked the end of his formal schooling. His brother Geta had probably already left Lepcis for the start of an official career. After serving as *decemvir stlitibus iudicandis*, one of the posts in the vigintivirate, he gained a commission as the senatorial tribune of the legion II Augusta in Britain. There was warfare in Britain at this time, and the governor, Sex. Calpurnius Agricola, very probably himself from Africa, may have been persuaded by some mutual acquaintance to give Geta the appointment.[24]

Much of the empire was indeed in a state of ferment. Antoninus Pius had died on 7 March 161, and his two adopted sons succeeded him jointly as M. Aurelius Antoninus and L. Aurelius Verus. The omens were good, but disaster loomed: the long Antonine peace was shattered on the eastern frontiers, the northern barbarians were threatening, there was a war in Britain. But Africa was still prosperous and tranquil, and these troubles may have seemed very remote to a young man with his way in the world to make. Soon after his formal speech at Lepcis, Septimius set out for Rome, 'to study'.[25]

It is far from simple to assess the influence of his Lepcitane background. In many respects he would be a typical representative of the provincial aristocracy, a member of one of the leading families in one of the principal towns of a wealthy province. Lepcis Magna had long had a thoroughly Roman outward appearance, a theatre for more than 150 years, an amphitheatre for more than a century. In the very year that Septimius left for Rome, it acquired its own Circus, a large and imposing structure beyond the eastern end of the city, close to the shore, some fifteen minutes walk away. There may have been some sort of chariot racing stadium there earlier, but the new Circus was a remarkable affair. It was integrated with the amphitheatre, alongside, into a single architectural complex. Its estimated seating capacity, over 20,000, gives a useful indication of Lepcis' total population—more than twice that figure. Lepcis now had all the trappings of a great Roman city. To be sure, the old Punic gods, Melqart and Shadrapa, joint patrons of Lepcis, had long been labelled 'Hercules' and 'Liber'. As Apuleius' speech would suggest, the Lepcitanes, like all Africans, were markedly superstitious, addicted to the science of the stars. The dazzling clarity of the North African night sky might well have inspired faith in astrology. Apuleius indeed accused Herennius Rufinus of consulting 'Chaldaeans'. The streets of Lepcis were liberally adorned with phallic symbols—not a sign of excessive sexual indulgence: it was to ward off the evil eye. There was a wide variety of deities. Septimius, later known as a devotee of Sarapis, the new version of an Egyptian god devised by the Ptolemies, may have first encountered him in the temple by the port at Lepcis.[26]

Septimius' grandfather had become completely Italianised—'non sermo Poenus ... Italus, Italus', Statius had told him; and he was even a Latin poet. But he had been taken to Italy as an infant. Septimius was brought up in Lepcis, surrounded by monuments which still bore the old Punic script; and the language was still spoken and written in his own day, if no longer used on public buildings. He would have needed to speak the old language, certainly when out in the hinterland, on the family estates; no doubt he could write in it too. But he had been educated in Latin and Greek, like Sicinius Pontianus or Apuleius. An anonymous Latin writer, the author of the Epitome de Caesaribus, says that he was 'adequately trained in Latin literature, a polished speaker of Greek, more fluent in Punic eloquence', Latinis litteris sufficienter instructus, Graecis sermonibus eruditus, Punica eloquentia promptior—adding, to explain the last comment, 'because he was born at Leptis in the province Africa'. The source of these remarks was probably Marius Maximus, Septimius' younger contemporary and supporter, later the biographer of the Caesars—and himself, it seems clear, from Africa.[27]

The HA says that his voice was tuneful, but that 'he retained a trace of an African accent into old age'. The statement may be a guess. But it is least plausible: a man from Tripolitania would speak a Latin that was affected by the rhythms and accents of the Punic and Libyan languages still in regular use there. It was possible, no doubt, for an African to achieve perfect 'Roman' diction: Apuleius, in spite of ironic remarks about his 'Numidian-Gaetulian' origins, knew that his sophisticated hearers at Carthage would not forgive him a 'single syllable of barbarous pronunciation'. Occasional mentions in later writers provide some idea of what this African accent was. The Africans dropped their aitches and mispronounced the letter L. They tended to lengthen short syllables at the beginning of words, and made a whistling sound over certain letters. Above all, they had difficulty in adapting sibilants to the restricted sounds of Latin. There is a chance that Septimius pronounced his own names in a manner resembling 'Sheptimiush Sheverush'. His sister Octavilla was later supposed to have been scarcely able to speak Latin. But there is no doubt that Septimius himself, accent or not, was completely fluent. The 'African accent' was a provincial Roman accent, not a foreign accent.[28]

The muddled Antiochene chronicler John Malalas, four centuries later, says that Septimius was dark-skinned. There is not much chance of verifying this statement now (although one colour portrait has survived). Malalas also says that he had a long nose, which is false: portraits show it was short, slightly turned-up. His hair seems to have been naturally curly. Later he would grow a beard, as was still the fashion; not as long as some wore it. He was a small man, but powerful and energetic. The portraits give an idea of this energy: the eyes look keen and searching; but sometimes also he appears brooding and abstracted.[29]

THE BROAD STRIPE

ROME IN THE EARLY 160s must have had an atmosphere of urgency. The long calm ended when the dying emperor breathed the watchword to the officer of the guard: 'Equanimity'. In his last moments Pius 'had spoken only of the foreign kings that angered him'. His adopted sons had scarcely had time to grasp the reins before those kings gave real cause for anger: they provoked a frontier incident on the upper Euphrates. It was blown up into a major war by the rash response of the governor of Cappadocia, Sedatius Severianus. He found himself trapped with inadequate forces. A legion was wiped out, and Severianus committed suicide. The governor of Syria, Attidius Cornelianus, had the clear duty of preserving calm and maintaining Roman defences. But he was defeated by a Parthian force, and put to flight. The Syrian legions were apparently in a poor state. C. Septimius Severus, who had commanded one a few years before, must have had a keen personal interest in the course of events. His brother Septimius Aper may have been disturbed more than most by what had happened: Sedatius Severianus had been his colleague in the consulship in the summer of 153.[1]

Marcus had to take rapid action on a variety of fronts. His brother Verus was to go to the east. In late 162 he arrived in Asia Minor after a somewhat leisurely journey. One of the outstanding generals of the day, Statius Priscus, had been appointed to take over Cappadocia and the war in Armenia. He had just been sent to govern Britain, where the situation was also disturbed, and had to be replaced there. The man chosen was Calpurnius Agricola. At the same time one of Marcus' closest friends, Aufidius Victorinus, son-in-law of his former tutor Fronto, was made governor of Upper Germany, to cope with an invasion by the Chatti. These were only part of a whole series of transfers, promotions and new appointments that were being put through when Septimius arrived in Rome. A change of emperor might in any case have brought some such measures in its train, but Marcus had long been sharing Pius' power, so continuity in commands would have been perfectly possible. As it was, the crisis made drastic changes necessary.[2]

Men from Africa soon came to the fore. Two compatriots of Fronto are found playing an active role in the east. Geminius Marcianus of Cirta, commanding X Gemina at Vindobona (Vienna) was directed to take reinforcements from the Danube. Antistius Adventus of Thibilis, already in the east in command of VI Ferrata in Palestine, took over the Aquincum (Budapest) legion II Adiutrix when it arrived at the front. The new governor of Britain, Calpurnius Agricola, was probably also from Numidia. But the wars which were to occupy the entire reign of Marcus saw men from virtually every province in the empire, as well as Italians, some of lowly origin, taking a prominent role. Statius Priscus, who won the first Roman victories in the east, and Pontius Laelianus, who seems to have acted as chief of staff to Verus at the beginning the the war, were probably both natives of Italy. Avidius Cassius, who won the final victories in the east, was Syrian, likewise Claudius Pompeianus, who played a leading role in the north. A general who played a distinguished role on both Euphrates and Danube, Claudius Fronto, came from proconsular Asia. Two men from western provinces prominent in high commands were Martius Verus and Julius Verus, from Gaul and Dalmatia respectively. One of the Praetorian Prefects, Macrinius Vindex, and his son, who held high positions as a senator, were from the north-west, perhaps from Cologne, or even Colchester. Valerius Maximianus, who had a meteoric military career, was Pannonian.[3]

When the imperial dynasty was itself provincial in origin, and so firmly entrenched, this was in no way surprising. Trajan and Hadrian sprang from colonial families that had been settled in Spain for hundreds of years. Trajan's wife Plotina came from Nemausus (Nîmes) in Gaul, the home of Antoninus' ancestors. Marcus himself, nephew by marriage of Pius, and thus linked with the Gallic provincial aristocracy, was from another Spanish colonial family, although his grandfather had married into the most blue-blooded Italian nobility. Leading men from Africa, as has been seen, had begun to rise to prominence even before Trajan's accession, and Trajan and Hadrian played a large part in promoting the wealthy from the Greek-speaking provinces to positions of power and influence. The long and peaceful reign of Pius had allowed the rise of the provincials to proceed gently and unobtrusively. When it ended, and the Antonine peace suddenly broke up, it was natural that men from all over the empire should take a leading part in its defence. Some were of Italian ancestry, others, such as Avidius Cassius and Claudius Pompeianus, descendants of men who had received the Roman franchise in the provinces.[4]

Thus it would be mistaken to view the arrival of the young Septimius at Rome, seeking senatorial rank, as anything but normal. On the contrary, with two close kinsmen who had already served as consul, and an elder brother already started on a senatorial career, it would have been strange if he had opted out. The broad purple stripe of senatorial rank, which, according to Statius, his grandfather could have had for the asking, was granted him by Marcus at the request of 'his kinsman Septimius Severus', that is, his 'uncle' Gaius, consul not long before.[5]

Septimius gained thereby no guarantee of a glittering career. The emperor had only one criterion in making appointments, merit. There is no sign that Septimius made his mark at the beginning of his career. He could not indeed enter the senate, as quaestor, until he had passed his twenty-fourth birthday, in April 169. One might have expected that he would obtain a commission as tribune with a legion. At latest by the summer of 164, when he reached his twentieth year, he may have hoped for such a post, may have canvassed by letter or through intermediaries. As it happens, his kinsman was governor of one of the German provinces in the early 160s and might have been expected to offer Septimius a commission. But Lower Germany, which was probably the province in question, had only one legion at this time, XXX Ulpia. The other, I Minervia, was in the east. In any case, if Septimius was *vigintivir* in 164, his kinsman may have almost completed his German command before Septimius was available. Meanwhile, Septimius' slightly older contemporary from Lepcis, Silius Plautius Haterianus, was serving in the Parthian war, probably under Antistius Adventus, and was to earn military decorations.[6]

However this may be, Septimius 'omitted the military tribunate', in the laconic phrase of the *HA*, derived ultimately perhaps from his autobiography. His brother Geta did obtain a tribunate, with II Augusta in Britain. It was based at Isca (Caerleon), but in the 160s, when Geta was there, it may have operated for some time in the north of the province. It seems likelier, although there is no proof, that Geta was the elder of the two brothers. In that case, he was probably in Britain with Calpurnius Agricola. This would be an interesting link between the Septimii and Numidia, Agricola's probable home. Geta's military service in Britain is important in two other ways for his brother's future. There is a strong possibility that he became acquainted with Helvius Pertinax who served in two posts there in the 160s. Geta's experience in Britain can hardly fail to have made an impact on him, and when he next saw his brother he must have given him some account of the province. Calpurnius Agricola's governorship was a time of considerable activity on the frontier. The territory re-occupied by Lollius Urbicus twenty years before was now definitively abandoned. Hadrian's Wall and its hinterland were strengthened and refurbished. Not all the men on the spot may have approved. Events in Britain in the 160s must not be forgotten when considering Septimius' own campaigns there forty years later.[7]

Septimius' omission of a tribunate may have been his own choice. But even if he tried for a tribunate and failed, this is not surprising. Although there were more legions than the twenty candidates who might seek a commission each year, other factors complicated the picture. Some young men with inclination or aptitude, or with influential relatives or patrons, served for more than one season and sometimes in more than one legion. Such cases must have been especially frequent when there was warfare on several fronts. The young *tribunus laticlavius* normally had little real responsibility, although in theory he was second in command of the legion. But in time of war too frequent changes of personnel must have been unwelcome to those in command. And, after all, when the fighting was fierce, the death of a general might make it necessary for the tribune to assume his latent powers as deputy-legate.[8]

Geta had gone to Britain after the mandatory year in the vigintivirate. He was one of the *decemviri stlitibus iudicandis*, who made up half of the young men thus designated as potential senators each year. The *HA* does not record any service in the vigintivirate at all for Septimius. This silence, combined with a confused story elsewhere about his early career, has led to the view that he did not occupy any such post, which is unjustified. One may be confident that soon after his arrival in Rome Septimius did spend a year as a *vigintivir*, either as *decemvir* like his brother, with duties in the courts, or in one of the other groups. He may have been *triumvir capitalis* or *quattuorvir viarum curandarum*, but hardly *triumvir monetalis*, to judge from his background and later career. This function, involving its three holders in some titular authority over the workings of the mint, was reserved in the first instance for patricians. Other vacancies went to plebeians with powerful patrons.[9]

The year 164 seems the most likely for Septimius to have served as a *vigintivir*. His formal duties must inevitably have brought him into touch with the leading men in Rome. But even the granting to him of the *latus clavus* on his arrival at Rome in 162 placed him on the threshold of public life. In his early years Septimius must have forged contacts with some of the men who would later play an important part in the fateful year 193. During this period in Rome he may have first met two men from Spain, Cornelius Anullinus and Fabius Cilo. Anullinus, ten years or more his senior, was from Iliberris (Granada) and Cilo, a year or two younger than Septimius, came from Iluro in the same region. Anullinus must have become praetor in 163 or soon after. Septimius may also have met his near contemporary Clodius Albinus from Hadrumetum in Africa, and Pescennius Niger, an Italian of equestrian family. Much senior to Septimius and with connections at the palace was Didius Julianus, a man of Milanese family, whose mother came from Hadrumetum and was a close relation of the great jurist Salvius Julianus.[10]

Consideration of what men of influence the young Septimius may have met can only be speculative. The letters of the younger Pliny show how Pliny himself in his youth relied on his links with the great men of the day, and then, as he climbed higher, exerted his influence to further the careers of his protégés at all levels. Such was the normal duty of a Roman senator. In the case of Septimius the direct evidence is lacking. The Pliny of the Antonine age, Cornelius Fronto, was still alive and flourishing when Septimius came to Rome. Some of his correspondence with his friends— and with his imperial pupils—has been preserved, and must be glanced at presently for the light it throws on Rome in the 160s.

The only information preserved about Septimius' life at this time concerns omens which gave him hopes of future greatness. In his autobiography he recorded numerous episodes and dreams which at various stages in his life led him to hope that he would become emperor. Some were even depicted in works of art after events had seemed to prove their accuracy. The *HA* has several anecdotes, some of which—perhaps all—derive from Septimius' own account. Dio likewise includes a number in his *History*. He was a fervent believer in omens and signs of all kinds. Soon after Septimius' accession he wrote his first historical work, an account 'of the dreams and omens that caused Severus to hope for the imperial power'. It is all too easy to comment that omens were only seen to be significant when they had already been fulfilled. Septimius was probably only one of numerous senators who convinced themselves that supernatural powers were showing them signs of future eminence. The age was highly superstitious. Even the emperor Marcus, with his lofty Stoic beliefs, was not altogether free from faith in the irrational. Belief in, and practice of, astrology was on the increase and Septimius was a prominent addict. But it was not new: had not Hadrian been a devotee?[11]

At the moment when Septimius first set foot in Rome, his host at the house where he was to stay happened to be reading a life of Hadrian— presumably reading aloud as was then the custom. The young man may have decided in advance that he would take as an omen the first words that he heard spoken at Rome. It is easy to guess at some particular phrase that could have given him special hope. It must be conceded that the *HA* would have found it amusing to invent the story. This note of caution must apply to all omens that otherwise unattested. But it would be unwise to neglect the ones authenticated by Dio. Their historical importance is small—they merely add a little colour—but they exemplify Septimius' extreme superstition. The biographer gives four more omens, only two of which are in Dio. The first, if authentic, would neatly illustrate how the young *laticlavius* was being prepared for public life. He was invited to dine at the Palace, and came incorrectly dressed, wearing the pallium or Greek cloak instead of the formal toga. To remedy his mistake one of the emperor's togas was given him. This may be an invention to introduce the next omen, which Dio also records. The same night, after the banquet (Dio does not have this detail), Septimius had a dream, in which he was sucking the teats of a she-wolf, like Romulus. Dio sets his dream at the time 'when he was enrolled in the senate'. The context of the story in the *HA* would place it earlier, and it may be that Dio's phrase should be understood as referring to the award to the *latus clavus*. The third omen, also in Dio, is not specifically assigned to this occasion in the *HA*, although it could have occurred at the same banquet. One of the emperor's servants inadvertently offered the imperial chair to Septimius, who promptly sat down on it, 'not knowing that this was not permitted'. The *HA* rounds off the account with the story that 'once when he was asleep in a stable a snake wound itself round his head. The members of the household were alarmed and shouted, and the creature went away without harming him'.[12]

However ill-informed about Septimius' life in these years we may be, it is fair to assume that he had already displayed some of the traits that were to impress Dio and Herodian. Dio describes him as small but physically powerful, a man of few words but with an active and original mind. Herodian calls him a born administrator, a man of great energy, used to living under rough conditions and capable of hard physical effort, quick to understand a problem and to act on it. The *HA*'s character-sketch, including plausible details about his tastes in food and African accent, betrays itself by the claim that he was 'huge' in stature. Dio, who saw him many times, will hardly have distorted the truth to say the opposite. Thus the 'African accent' may arouse suspicion. It may be a guess: if so, an informed one. After all, Septimius' grandfather—who had been brought up in Italy—had been complimented by Statius for not having an accent. Hadrian, as quaestor in 101, was laughed at in the senate for 'his somewhat rustic pronunciation'. He took steps to remedy it by intense application to eloquence in Latin. Hadrian's accent was unlikely to have been much affected by the speech of his family's home in southern Spain. He was born at Rome and had only spent a few years in Baetica, in his 'teens. In his case, prolonged army service—a record three military tribunates—had perhaps had an effect. His older contemporaries Tacitus and Pliny may have had a Celtic inflection, however, to judge from Pliny's story of a Roman knight at the races asking Tacitus: 'Are you Italian or provincial?', and then: 'Are you Tacitus or Pliny?' In Septimius' case, his upbringing in the still Punic or Libyphoenician society of Tripolitania very probably left its mark on his pronunciation. But the Roman senate now had plenty of members from all over the Mediteranean. Africans like Fronto may have made sure that their Latin was perfect, even if Fronto, in jest, liked to call himself 'a Libyan of the Libyan nomads'. But Fronto was the leading Latin literary man at Rome. Many others would have been less inclined to worry.[13]

Septimius' grandfather had had literary learnings. He himself 'received less education that he would have liked'. But it is not unreasonable to wonder whether he may have gained entry to the literary salon of Cornelius Fronto. Certainly there is no sign that he had philosophical leanings. One would not expect him to have joined the emperor and his admirers at the lectures of Sextus of Chaeronea. He is unlikely to have attended dissections performed by the young doctor from Pergamum, Galen, which attracted an audience of scientifically minded senators. But the chance of hearing Fronto converse or discourse may well have attracted him, even if Fronto's way of life in the 160s may not have resembled the halcyon days of twenty years before, when enthusiasts for learning would call on the great man simply to hear the flow of conversation and repartee. The times were no doubt long since gone by when a man going through the entrance-hall of the Palace could listen in as Fronto and his friends discussed the various Latin words for dwarf. Marcus Aurelius had given up this sort of thing more than fifteen years before; Lucius Verus was away in the east.[14]

Fronto continued to correspond with the emperors, sending off a flow of comfort and advice to Marcus, weighed down by his responsibilities, and to Verus, clearly in danger of neglecting his, in favour of high—or low—living. Fronto's other favoured pupil was now his son-in-law. While Victorinus was away in Germany, Fronto and his wife looked after their young grandson. A letter written soon after Victorinus went to Germany conveys a picture of the old orator blissfully happy responding to the boy's constant '*da!*' 'give', by supplying him with 'pieces of paper and writing tablets—things that I want him to ask me for'. This child, M. Aufidius Fronto, is next heard of over thirty years later, as consul in 199, when Septimius was emperor; and a younger brother was to be consul the following year. Septimius might have first met the young Fronto at the orator's house.[15]

Fronto was still active enough to take an interest in other matters besides his health, his family and his imperial ex-pupils. His young compatriot Arrius Antoninus of Cirta, serving in northern Italy as one of the newly instituted *iuridici*, was flooded with firmly worded appeals, in the form of avuncular advice, to look after the interests of various of

Fronto's clients. One Caelius Optatus received a letter in which Fronto warmly, though in terms long conventional, recommended another friend, Sardius Saturninus, whose sons 'are constantly in my quarters'. One of these sons was recommended by Fronto to his kinsman, the influential Petronius Mamertinus, son or nephew of Pius' Guard Prefect. This man had a link with a family of Septimii, perhaps the one from Lepcis. This is the nearest one can get to any hint that Septimius may have had access to a member of Fronto's circle.[16]

It was customary for young *laticlavii* who aspired to enter the senate to practise advocacy in the Roman courts at an early age. Pliny, for example, appeared (in the Centumviral Court) as junior counsel at the age of eighteen. There is every reason to believe that Septimius would have done likewise. The whole of his education will have been directed towards perfecting his ability as a public speaker: the only direct evidence comes in a phrase of Aurelius Victor. But at least he was competent enough, at the age of twenty-three, to plead a case (his own) before a magistrate. Fronto was the doyen of the Roman bar, and it is quite possible that Septimius, like the sons of Sardius Saturninus, sat at his feet.[17]

In 165 Fronto was preparing for a new role, as the historian of the Parthian war, now being brought to a successful conclusion. In the next year Verus returned as a conquering hero and in October 166, with Marcus, celebrated a triumph. Septimius is unlikely to have missed the occasion, the first of its kind for nearly fifteen years. The troops that had gone east to reinforce the eastern armies went back to their bases on the Rhine and Danube. Rome's victory in the east had apparently been sweeping: her generals crossed the Tigris into Media in 166, and in the previous year the twin Parthian capitals of Seleucia and Ctesiphon had been sacked. There was no doubt talk at Rome of reviving Trajan's policy of annexing Mesopotamia. Hadrian had rejected this, and Trajan's new eastern provinces had been hastily abandoned on his death in 117. Hadrian's whole policy of peaceful retrenchment was now being seriously questioned and some no doubt favoured a revival of Trajanic aims and methods in the east. But whatever may have been said or hoped by Verus and his staff or by circles in Rome, Marcus can scarcely have considered adding to Roman responsibilities in that quarter. The campaign of Calpurnius Agricola in Britain and of Victorinus in Germany would be sufficient to illustrate that serious problems elsewhere demanded attention. But these provinces were not the most crucial. The real threat to the Empire's security lay directly to the north of Rome itself, beyond the upper Danube. Pressure had been building up among the people of Bohemia, Moravia and Slovakia. The governors of the frontier provinces had instructions to refrain from military action until the eastern war was over. Meanwhile, two new legions were being recruited in Italy under the supervision of two generals, returned from the east before the war there was over. In 166 or 167 the first wave of barbarian invaders broke through into Pannonia. Much worse was to come.[18]

The festivities associated with the triumph gave a façade of public rejoicing. But the soldiers returning from the east, who included guardsmen, brought back the plague. Within a few months thousands had died, and the upper classes suffered with the rest. Senators and other men of wealth no doubt retired to the country estates. Even senators of moderate means, such as Pliny the younger had been, owned land in different parts of the peninsula. Senators of provincial extraction were required to have at least a proportion of their wealth invested in Italian land—Trajan had set the minimum at one third, Marcus reduced it to a quarter. Septimius must have had a place to go to, or else his property qualification for entering the senate would have been invalid. Later, except for an apartment in Rome, his only property was 'a single farm at Veii', clearly part of his grandfather's estate. But southern Etruria, however pleasant in normal times, was uncomfortably close to Rome. What is more, Lucius Verus had a pleasure villa on the Via Clodia, which must have brought sources of potential infection even closer to the country house of Septimius on the Cassia.[19]

It must have been an obvious decision to return for a time to Africa. Entry into the senate would still be assured. Septimius just had to wait until he entered his twenty-fifth year, on 11 April 169, or for the quaestorian elections in January of that year. In the meantime Africa was much healthier. Besides, his brother Geta had probably left Rome again, to be quaestor to the proconsul of Crete and Cyrenaica. Septimius may have gone home to Lepcis, and from there across the barren Syrtica to Cyrene, to visit him. After Rome Lepcis may have seemed a backwater. One may suspect that Septimius gravitated to Carthage in the year 167. There he could have heard the great Apuleius at last, if he had not already done so.[20]

His activities in Africa are revealed explicitly by one episode only, in the *HA*. He was a wild young man, the biographer records, hinting that he got into a lot of trouble. One instance is given. He was prosecuted for adultery, and pleaded his defence in person. The judge was either the proconsul Salvius Julianus, or his legate, Didius Julianus. The *HA* (misled by Aurelius Victor) found it difficult to distinguish between the two. However this may be, Septimius was found not guilty. There is no means of telling where the case came up—or where the lady in the case lived. It might have been at Carthage, perhaps even at Lepcis. The *HA* does not even put the case in Africa, and some have suspected the story as a fiction.

Now that Salvius Julianus is attested as proconsul for the year 168 to 169, with Didius as his legate, there is no longer any reason to doubt it.[21]

If there was any basis for the prosecution, it might be fair to construe any misbehaviour of Septimius as a last fling before attention to his future at Rome became necessary. By January 169 he should have been back at the capital, endeavouring to secure election as quaestor. The evidence suggests that the original minimum age of thiry had been modified to twenty-five. Hadrian, if not his predecessors, had then allowed a further reduction of one year: a man in his twenty-fifth year could count as qualified. Election was now the affair of the senate; to be elected quaestor meant being co-opted into the senate. Up till the end of the first century AD some genuine competition for the tribunate and praetorship may have continued. But there is no trace during the principate of competition for the quaestorship. Once a man had gained the *latus clavus* and had been *vigintivir*, it must have been automatic to proceed to the next stage: there were twenty quaestorships each year, one for each of the *vigintiviri*. But the *vigintiviri* would mostly be eighteen or nineteen-years-old, and would wait five or six years before becoming quaestors. A number of Septimius' fellow-*vigintiviri* may have been eliminated by war or plague. The same applies to his immediate predecessors. All things considered, it is highly unlikely that Septimius had any need to wait. It is probable that he was elected in 169, and took office on 5 December that year, for twelve months. Thus Septimius entered the senate, joining the venerable assembly, 600-strong, which constituted the élite of an empire containing some 60,000,000 people. He was *vir clarissimus*, the 'Right Honourable'.[22]

· 5 ·

INTO THE EMPEROR'S SERVICE

AT THE BEGINNING OF each year lots were cast in the senate for the proconsulships of the ten provinces still administered in the republican style. Ten of the twenty quaestors would be assigned to them: their duties would not begin until they left the city in the spring—at latest before 13 April—to go to their province. The other ten would serve in Rome. The *HA* does not specify where Septimius served. From its silence one may assume that it was at Rome. Equally, since nothing is said about it, one may assume that he was not one of the emperor's two personal quaestors. He may have been one of the two urban quaestors, whose residual duties, after the supervision of the state treasury had been taken away, were light. Otherwise he will have been assigned duties by the consuls. Only the two *ordinarii* and one suffect of 170 are known for certain. The *ordinarii* were Erucius Clarus and Gavius Cornelius Cethegus, the suffect Hoenius Severus. The latter was an Italian patrician, as was Cethegus, a pupil of Fronto. Fronto rated Cethegus' eloquence highly in a letter to his pupil's father: the satirist Lucian says the man was a fool—but the family was influential. The other consul, Erucius Clarus, was the son of a friend of Pliny who had eventually become Prefect of Rome, with a second consulship in 146. His own son was to be consul in the fateful year 193. The family had estates in Africa.

A major change had taken place during Septimius' absence. In spring 168 the emperors had left for the northern wars. They had inspected the Danubian front and returned to winter at Aquileia. Life in winter quarters on the Adriatic had irked Lucius Verus. His war in the east had been conducted from far pleasanter bases—Daphne on the Orontes and Laodicea on Sea. The presence of his dedicated elder colleague and adoptive brother demanded from him an attention to duty that he found difficult to maintain. In midwinter the spread of plague among the troops had provided a welcome excuse for the emperors to withdraw to more salubrious quarters. They began the return to Rome, but within a few days Verus died from a stroke. He had barely passed his thirty-ninth birthday. Septimius may have been back in Rome in time to witness the funeral and deification.[2]

The enforced return to Rome delayed Marcus' plans even more than he can have anticipated. He took the opportunity of raising funds for his projected campaign with a striking symbolic act, the auction of precious gems, clothing and furnishings from the palace. The sale went on for two months in the Forum of Trajan. A pressing concern for the emperor was what he should do about his widowed daughter Lucilla. She was a high-spirited and headstrong young woman, not lacking in physical charms. Some young senators of noble birth may have considered themselves eligible to be the second husband of a princess and stepfather to an emperor's child. But Marcus took no particular note of a man's origin, whether in appointing men to high office or in choosing husbands for his daughters. One was married to a man from proconsular Asia, Claudius Severus. As for Lucilla's two youngest sisters, one was to marry Burrus, from the family of the rising Numidian general Antistius Adventus, the other, Sura Mamertinus, possibly a kinsman of Septimius. It would be absurd to suggest that Septimius himself had any hopes—even in his dreams—of gaining the hand of Lucilla. But the choice of her husband is something that he must have watched with considerable interest. In the event almost everyone must have been surprised, not least Lucilla herself and her mother. The emperor married his daughter to a Syrian of equestrian background, Claudius Pompeianus. Indirectly this match was to affect the fortunes of Septimius. Pompeianus soon became the principal military adviser of his father-in-law, and was able to advance the career of a protégé, Helvius Pertinax.[3]

In October 169 Marcus returned to the northern front. As quaestor that year Septimius will have felt personally the effect of one of his measures. The emperor had conscripted gladiators into the army. This created difficulties for those who had to put on public games, including the quaestors. Septimius may have been able to use his connections at Lepcis to ensure a supply of wild beasts. But if the games were inadequate, there were soon more serious concerns. In spring 170 the emperor launched his long-delayed offensive across the Danube, evidently to prepare the way for the annexation of the Transdanubian lands. It was a disastrous failure. Roman losses were enormous. In the ensuing chaos a flood of northerners descended into the empire.[4]

The capital must have been thunderstruck by the news of the Roman defeat, on a scale not suffered since the disaster to Varus and his legions in AD 9. But that had taken place well beyond the Rhine, and the victorious Germans had failed to cross that river. This time the enemies of Rome were much closer to the heart of the empire. One group swept into

Greece, while two German tribes, outflanking the emperor's battered forces, broke into Italy itself. It was fortunate for Rome that Aquileia, the great trading city at the head of the Adriatic, acted as a magnet for the invaders. They could easily have pressed on southwards, crossed the Po and gone on to Ariminum (Rimini) and Fanum Fortunae (Fano), the roadhead of the Via Flaminia that led straight across the Apennines to Rome. Septimius, who was himself to lead an invading army by this route twenty-three years later, will have been impressed by the defencelessness of Rome. A force coming down on the city from Pannonia would find little in its path to oppose it. Through the efforts of Pompeianus and Pertinax in particular, Italy was cleared of the first foreign invaders for nearly three centuries. The situation was gradually restored in this and the following year, and the emperor was able to resume his offensive in 172. But many lives had been lost, not least among the officers. Many special measures were necessary. Septimius' brother Geta may have made a modest contribution. When land communications between Rome and the Danube were blocked or threatened, it was essential to maintain the sea-routes across the Adriatic, and the few Italian ports south of Ravenna were especially important. At about this time—the exact year cannot be fixed—Geta was made *curator* of Ancona. The appointment came after he had been aedile and was probably still under thirty. The *curatores* of towns in Italy and the provinces were normally concerned with the auditing of the municipalities' finances. This alone may well have been a vital matter when supplies were passing from Ancona across to Salonae (Split) in Dalmatia. As *curator* of Ancona in 170 or soon after Geta may have had added responsibilities.[5]

Although Septimius himself did not participate in any of the major actions of the 170s, his career was naturally affected. He was too junior to be given high responsibilities, but there were gaps to be filled at all levels. At some stage in 170 or early 171 it became clear that there would not be enough quaestors to serve in the provinces: Septimius was asked, or perhaps ordered to serve a second term, in the province of Baetica. It seems that the proconsul under whom he was to serve was Cornelius Anullinus. In 193 this man would emerge as a major supporter of Septimius in the struggle for the empire. It may be that the two were already acquainted. If the lot were operated strictly, the assignment of quaestors would be a matter of choice. But not infrequently personal choice was permitted. There is a chance that Septimius' second term as quaestor was the result of a request by Anullinus.[6]

Septimius will have been obliged to leave Rome for southern Spain before 13 April. But evidently before his departure he learned of his father's death, and he went first to Lepcis to settle the affairs of the family.

While he was in Africa events prevented him from taking up his appointment. Moorish tribesmen took ship and invaded southern Spain. It was only twenty years since their rebellion in Mauretania had been suppressed and the defences of western North Africa extensively reorganised. Now they were after a richer prize, and they could hardly have choosen a more favourable moment to attack. There was only one legion in the peninsula, stationed hundreds of miles from Baetica, at León. The single legion in Africa could not be safely transferred, especially as it was already weakened by sending men to the Danubian armies. Marcus again turned to his old friend Aufidius Victorinus. Baetica was temporarily taken out of the senate's control and joined to Tarraconensis, under Victorinus' overall authority. Cornelius Anullinus was made commander of the legion VII Gemina, sent down to Baetica from León. Victorinus' modest forces were strengthened by the despatch of a special force under the procurator Julius Julianus, who had just completed clearing-up operations in the Balkans.[7]

When the senate was obliged to hand over a province to the emperor—for only the elastic imperial administration could deal with an emergency situation and provide the military means of solving it—care was taken to avoid upsetting the system. The normal solution was for the emperor to surrender one of his own minor provinces to the senate. The province selected to compensate the senate for Baetica was Sardinia. Septimius thus spent the best part of twelve months in the island. Nothing is recorded about this stay there. If he was already as energetic and ambitious as he later showed himself to be, he must have wondered whether he would ever achieve greatness. Service in Sardinia can scarcely be said ever to have led that way before. One aspect of the island may have some interest for him: Sardinia in antiquity bore the stamp of Africa rather than of Italy. The Punic influence was still strong, and the Punic language still in use.[8]

The *leges annales* which still regulated the old republican magistracies apparently laid down that a *biennium* must elapse between each office. 'Two years' was interpreted liberally to mean anything over twelve months. But Septimius can have had little prospect of election as aedile or tribune of the plebs, the next obligatory stage in the *cursus honorum*, until the elections of January 173. This would have allowed him, as tribune, to take office on 10 December 174 (or 1 January 175 if he had become aedile). Of course, particularly at times of crisis, the rules could be adjusted to accelerate the careers of promising men. The procedure followed was *adlectio*: the emperor, in his censorial capacity, could enroll a man into a higher grade, allowing him to dispense with at least a year's service. Men needed on active service could not be held back by formalities. There were now senators who had been given their rank of *vir clarissimus*, and ex-praetor, at the front, and would not enter the *curia* in Rome for ten years—men like Helvius Pertinax. There is no sign that Septimius was deemed sufficiently vital to the state to be allowed such privileges.[9]

In the meantime employment of another kind was offered. C. Septimius Severus, by 173 a fairly senior consular—particularly as plague and war had thinned the ranks of the senate—was chosen by a lot to be proconsul of Africa. He selected Septimius as one of his *legati pro praetore*. They will have proceeded to Carthage in the spring or early summer. Septimius and the other *legatus* may have deputised for the proconsul on occasions. There would be some work of a judicial nature, on assizes—as with the memorable trial at Sabratha fifteen years earlier. The presence of proconsul and legate would be expected at a number of ceremonial occasions too. Ten years earlier the proconsul Salvidienus Orfitus had dedicated a monumental arch to Marcus and Verus at Oea, paid for by a local dignitary, Calpurnius Celsus. Apuleius' fulsome tribute to Orfitus, delivered at Carthage, suggests, combined with the evidence of this arch, that Oea was working hard to ensure favour in high places.[10]

Lepcis Magna was not to be outdone by her neighbour. A wealthy citizen, Avilius Castus, bequeathed 120,000 sesterces for an arch at Lepcis. The city provided additional funds and in 174, 'when the proconsul was C. Septimius Severus, and his legate was L. Septimius Severus, it was dedicated'. The arch was erected at the west end of Lepcis, on the Oea road. The proconsul himself may not have presided at the dedication, although he presumably did visit Lepcis during his year of office. He was also at the far north-western end of his province, it must be assumed: he was honoured with a statue at Thubursicu Numidarum, of which he was patron. During the year when the Septimii were in proconsular Africa, the army of Numidia was surprisingly active. A mixed force penetrated as far as 250 miles (400 km) beyond the frontier, to Agueneb. Proconsul and legates would not be formally involved—this was a matter for the commander of the legion, presumably instructed to exercise stronger control over the tribes. But Septimius must have heard of the venture, and approved. Two decades later he would be able to institute further measures of a more radical kind in this quarter.[11]

The inscription from the Lepcis arch provides good reason to accept as authentic the *HA*'s story of Septimius, as legate in Africa, returning to his home town. When he arrived there, preceded by lictors bearing the *fasces* which denoted his authority, and was embraced by an old acquaintance, he had the man flogged. The demonstration was followed up by an announcement by the legate's herald: no plebeian was to embrace a legate of the Roman people in this undignified way again.[12]

The arrogant and hot-tempered streak that this episode reveals is borne out in future occasions. His arrogance may have been encouraged by something else that happened during this spell of duty. In 'a certain African town', not specified by the *HA*, he consulted a *mathematicus*. When the details of his birth had been revealed, the astrologer was incredulous. He had seen a great future (*ingentia*) ahead, which he found incompatible with the young man he saw in front of him. 'Give me your real horoscope, not someone else's,' he told Septimius. He swore that it was indeed his own, and was then told 'everything that afterwards came to pass'. Dio records that Septimius later concealed the full details of his birth. It would not do for it to be widely known what was in store for him.[13]

By the end of his term as legate, Septimius had entered his thirtieth year and was still unmarried. It is probable that he took the opportunity during his return to Lepcis of finding himself a wife. The girl he chose was called Paccia Marciana. Her names reveal that she was ultimately of Punic or Libyan, rather than Italian origin: her ancestors had clearly derived citizenship from the first-century proconsuls Marcius Barea and Paccius Africanus. Her family was possibly linked distantly with that of Septimius' mother, the Fulvii. But a leading provincial family such as the Septimii, or the Fulvii, would inevitably have some marriage links with most of the other upper-class families in their own town. Nothing is known for certain of any of Paccia's relatives.[14]

If Septimius had first entered the senate in December 169, as has been suggested, he would now be ready and eager to set his foot on the next rung of the ladder. It seems that he had now attracted the attention of the emperor (or of his advisers—Marcus Aurelius was still far from Rome, at the front). He was chosen tribune of the plebs with the distinction of being one of the emperor's *candidati*. His year of office began on 10 December, presumably in 174. Paccia Marciana, if she did not accompany him back from Africa in the summer, must have followed soon after. The marriage took place during or immediately after his term of office. It lasted for some ten years, until Paccia's death. There were almost certainly no children—or none that survived infancy, unless credit is given to a suspect story in the *HA*. According to this, Septimius had two daughters old enough to be married in 193, hence born in the years 176–180. There is no other record of any daughters. He himself was silent about his first marriage in his autobiography, although he later had statues erected in memory of Paccia.[15]

The tribunate was in a sense even more obsolete than the other republican magistracies. The tribunes' once powerful position as initiators of legislation, and their right of veto, had quickly lapsed (after all, the emperors possessed the tribunician power). But their most ancient duty, to protect fellow citizens from injustice, remained, in theory at least. In practice this involved watching to see that other magistrates, especially the praetors, did not endanger the rights of Roman citizens. Some judicial functions may have been passed to them. Pliny as tribune refused to practise at the bar during his term of office, so that the dignity of his office should not be sullied. His sanctimonious reference to the course that he followed shows only too clearly that others rarely did this.[16]

However, Septimius is stated to have performed his duties 'with great rigour and energy'. And there may indeed have been the occasion, during the year 175, for the tribunes to take part in preserving public order. In the spring, following a false report that Marcus was dead, the governor of Syria, Avidius Cassius, proclaimed himself emperor. Once he had taken this step, he could not go back, even though it was soon confirmed that Marcus was alive and prepared to spare him. Cassius, one of the heroes of the Parthian war, had been endowed for several years with special overall authority over a large part of the east. He had support from the Prefect of Egypt and elsewhere. But Martius Verus, the governor of Cappadocia, remained loyal to Marcus. The rebellion was over by June: Cassius was murdered by one of his own officers. But there had been panic at Rome, and the emperor was obliged to send detachments from the northern legions to protect the city. Most of the Guard will have been at the front, and the forces available in the capital were minimal. The heir to the throne, Marcus' only surviving son, Commodus Caesar, was there. A boy of thirteen, he was still under the guidance of tutors. The emperor summoned him to the front, and he was invested with the *toga virilis* in July. Before his departure the young prince performed his first public act, distributing largesse to the people.[17]

These events must have made a deep impression on Septimius. He will have heard lively discussion of the upheaval in the east. There was gossip impugning the reputation of the empress Faustina: that she had written secretly to Cassius, encouraging him to make his coup, in the belief that Marcus was dying. Senators whose homes were in the east must have felt particular anxiety, and some, whether eastern or not, may have received messages from the pretender beseeching support. Cassius may have had many supporters among the senate. Septimius probably had no personal links with any of them. But he must have realised that Cassius' rising had more behind it than a piece of opportunism by an ambitious general. There was debate among the emperor's advisers concerning his war policy. Marcus was determined to annexe territories beyond the Danube. The eastern provinces will not have viewed this war with enthusiasm. It may not be fanciful to detect among Cassius' supporters elements that wanted a return to a purely Hadrianic policy. For all his philhellenism

Marcus was behaving in the manner of a Trajan, waging an all-out war of conquest. But in contrast to Trajan's Dacian wars, the northern campaigns of Marcus were bringing no profit to anyone, least of all to the wealthy east.[18]

There was something else for senators to gossip about in 175. Helvius Pertinax, the freedman's son and ex-schoolmaster, was made consul (in absence) with Didius Julianus as his colleague. The appointment was not completely unprecedented, but it caused a good deal of ill-feeling. Soon Pertinax, who went east with the emperor in the summer, returned to the Danube as governor, first of Upper, then of Lower Moesia. Septimius Geta was made legate of the legion I Italica, not long after this, and probably served under the command of Pertinax. Shortly before taking up his command Geta had been co-opted into one of the ancient priesthoods, the *fetiales*, whose task it was to make solemn declaration of war. The *fetiales* did not rank with the *pontifices*, *augures*, *quindecimviri* and *septemviri*, but they had great prestige—Aufidius Victorinus was a fellow-member. It is not known whether Septimius obtained a priesthood of any kind; but his kinsman C. Septimius Severus was both a *quindecimvir* and a *sodalis Hadrianalis* and is likely to have made efforts to have Septimius co-opted into one of the colleges.[19]

Septimius probably remained in Rome during 176, awaiting the next stage in his career. He was designated praetor at the beginning of the year. But he did not achieve the honour of being *candidatus* of the emperor again. Marcus returned to Italy in the autumn, after an absence of seven years. On 27 November Commodus was granted *imperium* and celebrated a joint triumph with his father on 23 December. On 1 January he was consul and was given the tribunician power, soon followed by the title Augustus. There were thus once more two emperors, the younger being only fifteen years old. Marcus Aurelius' intention was plain: his death would no longer place the succession in jeopardy. Commodus would need no further powers, all he lacked was the priestly dignity of being *pontifex maximus*. Doubtless Septimius was deeply influenced by this act, which he witnessed at close quarters as a magistrate of the Roman people. He was to follow this precedent, in a more extreme form, with his own elder son.[20]

Some of the eighteen praetors each year had additional titles and specific duties—the praetor *urbanus*, *peregrinus*, *hastarius*, and so on. The remainder presided over the permanent courts manned by the *iudices*. The *HA* does not specify any particular praetorship in Septimius' case. He may have presided at one of the courts where his grandfather had served as a simple juryman. The praetors had to work hard—in comparison with the tribunes—for the courts were in session for well over half the year.

Marcus had increased the number of days when legal proceedings could be carried on, to two hundred and thirty. Presumably November and December were still vacation periods, so for the first ten months of 177 Septimius will have been kept busy. And he will have needed to take his duties seriously. Marcus supervised the praetors with especial care.[21]

In the course of 177 Septimius' 'uncle' C. Septimius Severus had the honour of serving on the *consilium* of the emperors, when they considered a request forwarded by the procurator of Mauretania Tingitana on behalf of a Moorish chieftain. Marcus and Commodus duly granted citizenship, to the wife and four children of Julianus of the Zegrenses, on 6 July. An impressive extract from the imperial archives was despatched to the province, backed up by the names of the twelve imperial counsellors. C. Septimius Severus is listed in fourth place, after three more senior ex-consuls. This is the latest record of Septimius' kinsman. Whether or not he survived much longer, his young protégé was now well launched on his senatorial career. The praetorship was the springboard to posts of some responsibility.[22]

Praetors were liable to heavy expenses, for they were expected to put on games, as were the quaestors. If this had been unusually expensive when Septimius was quaestor, it must have become even more so now. All over the empire men whose holding of office obliged them to put on public spectacles were finding the task increasingly difficult. The supply of gladiators had become increasingly limited. In the course of 177 the matter was raised in the senate, and a decree was passed to reduce the price. Septimius did not put on games during his praetorship: he was sent off to his next post—his first in the emperor's service—before his year of office was up. This would have obliged him to miss the games, which he gave in absence, according to the *HA*. The post was in Spain, in the province of Hispania Tarraconensis. No details are given by the *HA*, but it is practically certain that he was *legatus iuridicus*, with special responsibility for Asturia and Callaecia. The Moors were again causing trouble in southern Spain, and it is possible that Baetica had reverted to imperial control. The governor and the legionary legate in Tarraconensis no doubt had military duties at this time. In that case Septimius' role as *iuridicus* will have been of especial importance.[23]

The *HA* has nothing more to record about his stay in Spain, except for two dreams, one of which certainly belongs later. In the other he was told to restore the Temple of Augustus at Tarraco. (If there was any basis for this subconscious command, one must assume that Hadrian's restoration of the temple fifty years before had not lasted long.) His term as *iuridicus* would not normally have lasted for more than three years at the most. By the beginning of 180 he will have been hoping for promotion. It was to come in the shape of a legionary command in Syria. But, perhaps before Septimius had obtained this appointment, Marcus Aurelius died, on 17 March 180, at his northern headquarters. The fateful sole reign of Commodus had begun.[24]

The philosopher emperor had ruled nineteen years and ten days. The empire had been through a considerable ordeal: almost continuous warfare against external enemies, rebellion, plague. Yet, as Ammianus Marcellinus put it in the fourth century, 'after calamitous losses things were restored anew ... with unanimous ardour highest and lowest hastened, as if to a calm and peaceful haven, to an honourable death in the service of the republic'. Out of the whole empire, almost the only part that had not been directly affected was Septimius' homeland, Africa, already the richest part of the west, and now still further at an advantage. Septimius himself can hardly be said to have contributed much. But he and other senators will have noted the incredible devotion to duty shown by the emperor. Marcus spent more than half his reign away from Rome, with the armies. Septimius was to follow this example. Another and telling example was Marcus' unequivocal rejection of the 'adoptive principle'. Indeed, he may not have recognised its existence. The rebellion of Cassius may have forced his hand a little, obliging him to accelerate promotion of his son to a share in his powers. But he had no scruples in associating a fifteen-year-old boy with himself as emperor. This must have made a deep impression on Septimius.[25]

A CAESAR BORN TO THE PURPLE

No one had had any experience of an emperor like Commodus, a Caesar born to the purple. The seventeenth emperor of Rome, he was the first who had been born during the reign of his father. What is more, by the series of adoptions begun by Nerva, and continued by Trajan, Hadrian and Pius, the dynasty to which he belonged had now produced a sixth emperor (one more than the Julio-Claudians). Commodus could call himself 'son of the deified Marcus', but by virtue of those adoptions he could and did style himself 'great-great-great-grandson', *adnepos*, of Nerva as well. Not for nothing was he called 'most nobly born of all emperors'.[1]

It was indeed to the ill-starred Julio-Claudians that men will have turned their minds in 180. Since the accession of Nero in 54, there had been no emperor as young as this. Commodus was only eighteen when Marcus died, just two years older than Nero had been when he gained the throne. The omens now appeared more favourable. Commodus succeeded a father who had been almost universally popular, and who had been revered by the senate. The suspicion that Marcus had been poisoned by Commodus (as Claudius had been by—or for—Nero), if present as early as this, will not have been widespread.[2]

Commodus may have been a lonely figure. His mother had died when he was fourteen. His twin brother had died when he was only four, and a younger brother four years after that. There were five sisters, all but one considerably older than him. Lucilla, the eldest, who had been the wife of Verus, was an Augusta. She was twelve years older than Commodus, and detested her husband Ti. Claudius Pompeianus, who had been Marcus' principal military adviser, and was old enough to be Commodus'—and Lucilla's—father. He was with Commodus on the Danube. Other senior advisers from the imperial family were there too: Bruttius Praesens, the emperor's father-in-law, and Vitrasius Pollio, husband of a cousin of Marcus. One of Marcus' best friends, Aufidius Victorinus, was ruling the city of Rome as Prefect. These and their like were the foundations of

Marcus' hope that his son's reign would continue along the lines of his own.[3]

The new emperor needed no further powers. There was merely the need to adjust his name and titles. But in spite of an apparent continuity in the administration, it is fair to suppose that there was a rush of applications for jobs, at all levels. Those who had connections at the court will have sought to use them. It is just at this time that Septimius received his next post, the command of the legion IV Scythica in Syria. Some new appointments may have been set in motion already by Marcus or made on the advice of Pompeianus and other senior men. But Commodus will already have found other voices more persuasive than that of his elderly and plebeian brother-in-law.[4]

In the *Meditations*, which Marcus Aurelius had been writing during his last campaigns, he thanked the gods that he found good teachers for his children. Only three are named in the *HA*, and only one of these is more than a name, Aius Sanctus, Commodus' tutor in oratory, who had combined his instruction of the prince with a career in the imperial service. In March 180 he had been for several years in Egypt, as prefect; his teaching duties had clearly ended. Marcus had himself studied oratory with Fronto—and other tutors—until his twenty-sixth year. Besides, he was an ardent student of philosophy from boyhood until death. No philosophy teachers at all are recorded for Commodus. One is driven to the melancholy conclusion that Marcus may have overreacted against his own upbringing. Faced, as emperor, with nothing but continuous warfare, he may have decided that he had been overeducated—and in the wrong fields—for his role. For the last two-and-a-half years of his life he had Commodus with him at the front. Among other motives he must have wished his son to acquire military experience at first hand. Other instruction may have continued, but it certainly ceased for good when Marcus died. Commodus had no 'higher education'.[5]

There was another difference. Marcus had not entered the imperial family until the age of sixteen, after a boyhood closely supervised by a host of relatives. Commodus, born a prince, probably did not see his father at all—or only briefly—from the age of eight to the age of thirteen. Marcus was away on campaign. Commodus was by nature 'lacking in evil qualities', Dio was convinced. As his near-contemporary, Dio had ample opportunity to form a judgement. The *HA* biographer seems almost to be going out of his way to contradict Dio. The report may derive from another contemporary, Marius Maximus, the neo-Suetonius of the third century. Maximus, a little older than Dio, was serving in the northern armies at the end of Marcus' reign. The verdict of the *HA* is savage: 'From early boyhood cowardly, dishonourable, cruel, lustful, defiled in mouth and debauched.' A sarcastic aside is added, that he had some talent for pottery, dancing, singing and whistling—'qualities unsuited for the imperial station'.[6]

Herodian avoids speculation about Commodus' character, but reports the emperor's outward appearance: 'he was in the prime of youth and was most attractive to look at because of his well-proportioned body and the manly beauty of his face. His eyes had a commanding look and flashed like fire. His hair was naturally blond and curly. When he walked in the sunlight it shone like fire (so that some thought he sprinkled it with gold dust before coming out) while others regarded it as a sign of divinity, saying that a heavenly light shone out above his head. And the first down was just beginning to appear on his cheeks.' Later, the flashing eyes were dulled (by drink)—and the shining locks were no longer naturally shiny.[7]

His parents had been first cousins. Children of such unions sometimes tend towards extremes. Clearly, the sober and philosophical inclinations of his father were totally lacking. His grandmother, Faustina I, had had a reputation for levity. But there is no need to look for the influence of heredity. Marcus was not a particularly typical product of his age. His co-emperor Verus, with his love of the stage and the arena, also reflected prevalent fashions and sentiments. Commodus, only seven when Verus died, may nonetheless have wanted to ape the man whose original names—Lucius Aurelius Commodus—he bore. At any rate, there is no need to believe the stories raked up later, that Marcus was not his real father. It seemed natural that the man he became must have been the son of a gladiator and it seemed incredible that Marcus could have fathered a son like Commodus—hence the gossip that he was illegitimate.[8]

For a few months after his accession Commodus remained with the armies on the Danube. Then the exhortations of Pompeianus and the other *amici* proved insufficient. Peace was made with Rome's northern enemies. Commodus returned to a rapturous welcome at Rome. He was lazy. This was perhaps his chief characteristic (not simple physical indolence—for he was to show himself a superb athlete). The courtiers knew how to play on his weaknesses—those among them, that is, who were themselves unmilitary, and eager to return to the centre of the empire. Chief among these was his chamberlain (*a cubiculo*), Saoterus, a Bithynian like Dio, who seems to have regarded this man without hostility. He is mentioned merely *en passant* in what survives of the *History*. Herodian knew nothing about him. But the *HA*, true to form, records that, when Commodus celebrated the triumph for the German wars on 22 October 180, 'Saoterus, his *subactor*, was placed on the chariot behind him. Often Commodus turned his head round and publicly kissed him. He did the same in the orchestra as well.' Saoterus' function on this occasion was to hold the golden crown above the head of the *triumphator*. But the word *subactor* has a double meaning. Marius Maximus, and many others, were disgusted. Saoterus soon acquired paramount influence over Commodus. No Roman emperor had let favourites of this kind exercise such power since the dark days of Nero. To those who had served Antoninus and Marcus, it must have been sickening. For the members of the imperial family, it must have been equally unnerving. Yet given the quite exceptional dynastic claims of Commodus and the charismatic nature of his position, any action would be difficult. Five years earlier, Avidius Cassius had not hesitated to claim the throne on a false report of Marcus' death. The immediate collapse of his rebellion, and his murder following the news that Marcus was after all alive, will have served as a warning to impatient and ambitious army commanders. And things were now different. In 175 Commodus was still a boy. Now he was recognised as emperor. Any rival would need vast prestige to gain acceptance. Marcus had chosen husbands for his daughters with the apparent deliberate intention of preventing counter-claims from that quarter. Only one of Commodus' six brothers-in-law, the obvious source of a rival to his throne, could be described as an aristocrat.[9]

In spite of these difficulties, there was an attempted coup less than two years after Commodus' return to Rome. With the benefit of hindsight it is possible to view the entire twelve-and-a-half years of his reign as a long drawn-out battle for survival by an emperor who was nonetheless, for much of the time, seemingly unaware of the danger. A succession of favourites held the real power like Grand Viziers, and Commodus devoted himself to pleasure. Meanwhile, with the exception of a few unambitious and devotedly loyal men like Claudius Pompeianus, the most prominent among the ruling classes plotted incessantly and manoeuvred for his inevitable removal.[10]

The first attempt was made by Lucilla, the former empress. Not with her husband's connivance; but two of the other brothers-in-law were to be executed for conspiracy later in the reign. In a second conspiracy, uncovered immediately after that of Lucilla, the military men can be seen to have had a bid ready—and a cousin of Commodus, perhaps intended to be used as a pawn, was implicated. There were signs of unrest in different parts of the empire throughout the reign. The British army, for example, twice attempted to force the throne on nervous and reluctant generals.[11]

The hatred that Commodus brought on himself because of Saoterus gave a group centred around Lucilla its cue in 182. Her motive is alleged to have been jealousy at the loss of her privileges in favour of the new empress Crispina. It may be only Herodian's naivety that led him to believe that the loss of the front seat at the theatre caused her to act. But it could be that her resentment was used by others. Two men are named. One was her lover Ummidius Quadratus, adopted son of Marcus' nephew and stepson of Commodus' eldest sister. The other was Lucilla's prospective son-in-law, Quintianus, a nephew of her husband Pompeianus. He too was said to be Lucilla's lover. These two men, closely connected to the dynasty by marriage, were predictable claimants to Commodus' throne.

But they bungled the job. As Commodus entered the hunting-theatre, Quintianus, his trusted boon companion, appeared in the narrow passageway. He held out his weapon, proclaiming rhetorically: 'This dagger the senate sends you!' The little speech gave the emperor's bodyguards time to seize the assassin. *Fatuus* was the opinion that the *HA* has of Quintianus, no doubt echoing Marius Maximus, who may have been a derisive onlooker. Quintianus and Quadratus were executed, along with others. Lucilla was exiled to Capri at first. Later she too was killed. Her husband Pompeianus withdrew from public life, pleading the excuse of failing eyesight. He had not been involved, but others had been, including one of the two Guard Prefects, Taruttienus Paternus. For the time being he escaped undetected. And, perhaps in the confusion that followed the attempt, he and his colleague Tigidius Perennis had Saoterus murdered by the secret police.[12]

Commodus took the loss of his favourite badly. The ambitious Perennis took his chance. He instigated the dismissal of his more distinguished colleague, who was 'kicked upstairs' by the award of senatorial rank. A few days later evidence was produced implicating Paternus in another conspiracy, and he was executed. This second plot was potentially much more serious. Paternus' alleged involvement with the Lucilla affair suggests that he may have been trying to use her group to remove Commodus, leaving the throne vacant for his own candidate, Salvius Julianus, whose son was betrothed to Paternus' daughter. Julianus, son of the great jurist, was commanding an army at the time the plot was detected, perhaps that of Upper Germany. Dio asserts that the charge was false, but it is plausible. Salvius' kinsman Didius Julianus, who had been governing Lower Germany, was later charged with complicity. He cleared himself but was ordered to withdraw to his native Milan. Apart from Paternus and Salvius Julianus, two of the consuls of 182, two ex-consuls, the *ab epistulis* Vitruvius Secundus, and Vitrasia Faustina, were also put to death. The involvement of the *ab epistulis* is a hint that Paternus had been attempting to use the secretariat to contact the provincial armies.[13]

More heads were to roll. The Quintilii brothers, who had shared the consulship over thirty years before, were executed. Quintilius Condianus, son of one of them, was then in Syria. He was hunted down and killed.

The pursuit of Condianus was a dramatic affair. Pertinax the governor of Syria, and Septimius Severus as one of the three legionary legates, will have had to take a leading role in this distasteful task. Condianus did not submit tamely, as so many had in the past to the assassins of a tyrannical emperor. Dio, who was at this time in the neighbouring province of Cilicia, which his father was governing, gives a detailed account. Condianus feigned death, by drinking the blood of a hare, falling purposely from his horse and vomiting the blood out, after which he was carried in as if dead. While he made his escape, a dead ram was cremated in his coffin. The story got out and he was hunted everywhere. Many suspects who resembled him were executed and their heads sent to Rome. His eventual fate was never discovered.

Witnessing what was happening both in Rome and in Syria, and elsewhere, Septimius cannot have felt secure. Before the end of 182 the blow fell. Pertinax was dismissed from his Syrian command. At the same time, or soon after, Septimius himself was sacked.[14]

· 7 ·

THE GREAT MARSHAL

Septimius' journey to syria must have affected him in many ways. It was, for one thing, probably his first experience of the Greek-speaking part of the empire. One cannot of course exclude that he had been to neighbouring Cyrenaica from Lepcis, during his boyhood, or even to Alexandria. But travelling through Greece and the great cities of Asia, at this time at the peak of their prosperity, must have been an absorbing experience for anyone with an interest in antiquity, which Septimius certainly possessed. Perhaps more than this though, it may have been a curiously moving experience for a man from Punic Africa to visit the heartland of Phoenician civilisation, to see Tyre and Sidon, the mother cities of Carthage. Septimius will have found that the predominant language was Aramaic, a Semitic tongue related to the Punic that he and his fellow-Africans still used. Greek was the language of the state and of culture. Aramaic was the language of the people.[1]

The most immediately significant experience for Septimius in Syria would be that he would serve under the governor Pertinax. This contact was fateful for Septimius' entire future. P. Helvius Pertinax was one of the most remarkable figures of that or any age of Roman history. Born in north-west Italy, at Alba Pompeia in Liguria, he was the son of a freedman. That a man whose father had been a slave had even reached the eminence of the consulship had, some years earlier, attracted considerable surprise and comment, not all of it favourable. His future was to be even more remarkable. Yet his career in the imperial service had not begun until he was thirty-four, almost precisely the age of Septimius himself when he went to Syria. The great marshal's father, Helvius Successus, like other freedmen—the example that springs to mind is the father of the poet Horace—had determined to advance his son's career by giving him a good education. He was sent to Rome to study with the celebrated *grammaticus*, Sulpicius Apollinaris of Carthage. Entry to Apollinaris' classes was perhaps secured through the mediation of Successus' patron, the well-connected senator Lollianus Avitus, on whose estates the Helvii lived. When his tuition from Apollinaris ended, Pertinax became a teacher himself, for at least ten years. Finally, in 160 he became discontented with his low income and decided on a very different career. He asked his father's patron to get him a commission as a centurion. This would have assured him a steady job with reasonable pay and prospects for the rest of his working life. There had even been men, such as the great Marcius Turbo forty years before, who had risen to be Praetorian Prefect from such beginnings. Pertinax had left his application for a commission too late to hope for this. In any case, Lollianus Avitus, for all his prestige, seems to have failed to acquire a centurionate for Pertinax. Perhaps he did not try very hard, or possibly something made Pertinax change his mind. At any rate, he accepted instead an ostensibly more attractive post, as prefect of a cohort of Gauls in Syria. This was the first grade of the equestrian *militiae*. But as prefect of an infantry battalion 500-strong, of non-citizen soldiers, Pertinax had acquired only a short-service commission, with no fixed length of tenure. When he was replaced, there would be no guarantee of further employment.[2]

Dio appears to state that Pertinax began his army career through the mediation of another patron, whom he had met 'in the course of his teaching'. This was Claudius Pompeianus, a native of Antioch in Syria, later to be the second husband of Lucilla. Attidius Cornelianus, the governor under whom Pertinax was to serve, had been in Syria since 157. Pertinax's first meeting with him was inauspicious. He made use of the government posting-service to get to Antioch, without having the official pass (*diploma*). As a punishment the governor refused him transport to get to his unit: Pertinax had to walk.[3]

Unfortunately, the rigidity of Attidius Cornelianus over regulations was not made up for by military capacity. The following year the Parthian war broke out. In 162, after the defeat of Severianus in Cappadocia, Cornelianus attempted to restore the situation: he was ignominiously defeated. The Syrian army had been a slack and undisciplined condition. Before long the balance was redressed. The expeditionary force under Verus came to Syria before the end of the year, and in 163 a great victory was won by Statius Priscus in Armenia. Pertinax had the opportunity to show his talents, showing a capacity for 'hard work'. Perhaps the new governor Cn. Julius Verus sent in a favourable report on him to the *ab epistulis*. Pertinax was promoted to the second *militia*. It may seem surprising that from Syria he was sent to distant Britain. But the Roman government never hesitated to transfer men from one end of the empire to the other. The governor Calpurnius Agricola had probably asked Rome for battle-trained men—or perhaps specifically for men of high intelligence and maturity. It could even be that Julius Verus, himself a former governor of Britain, was asked directly to recommend an officer that he judged would be suitable for service in Britain.[4]

Pertinax became one of the five equestrian tribunes of the legion VI Victrix at Eboracum (York). Their duties were mainly administrative. An ex-schoolmaster with several years of military service behind him, and one who had probably seen some fighting, will have been a useful staff officer. Calpurnius Agricola was engaged on an extensive reorganisation of the British frontier in the face of hostility both in the Scottish Lowlands and in the Pennines. Hadrian's Wall was reoccupied in strength and became the frontier line once more. Pertinax's duties may have taken him away from York, closer to the frontier: legionary detachments were stationed at Coria (Corbridge). Pertinax then went to the Wall itself. He was given command of another unit, evidently the First Tungrians, probably already at Housesteads, at the central point of the Wall. Pertinax may have made the acquaintance of Septimius' brother Geta, who was tribune with II Augusta in the 160s. The legion's base was at Isca (Caerleon), but parts of the legion were out-stationed, at Coria and on the Wall.[5]

Before the Parthian war ended preparations were in hand for the inevitable war on the Danube. It was an indication that Pertinax continued to show promise that his next appointment was to command a cavalry regiment in Moesia. As *praefectus alae* he had now reached the third *militia*. His friend and patron Pompeianus was also serving on the Danube, in the much more exalted position of governor of Lower Pannonia, with his headquarters at Aquincum (Budapest). It may be coincidence, but Pertinax appears for the first time in the historical record in this province, adjacent to Upper Moesia. An altar has been found at Sirmium, dedicated to 'Jupiter Best and Greatest and Mars the Protector' by 'P. Helvius Pertinax, prefect'. Sirmium was soon to become an important military headquarters. It was also on Pertinax's route from Britain to Moesia. But one may suspect that his presence there was brought about by Pompeianus, and that his unit was transferred to reinforce the Lower Pannonian garrison. Pertinax will have been close to the first ominous outbreak of war, when Upper Pannonia was invaded by a force of 6000 Germans. The officer who repulsed them, Macrinius Avitus, was a little senior to Pertinax and, like him, had come to the Danube from the VIth legion in Britain.[6]

Pertinax had now reached a turning point in his new career. In normal conditions he might well have been obliged to retire from the service. There was only one further promotion open to him as an equestrian officer, the fourth *militia*. But the number of appointments available was so small as to make it out of the reach of most. The alternative was the administrative service. No doubt with the backing of Pompeianus, he was appointed procurator of the *alimenta* system for the district of the Via

Aemilia in northern Italy. Although it was on the lowest rung of the procuratorial ladder, with a salary of 60,000 sesterces a year, the area had key significance at this time, almost certainly the year 168, precisely when the emperors established their base at Aquileia. Pertinax was soon promoted again, his salary increasing to 100,000 sesterces with the command of the German fleet. This appointment cannot have lasted long, perhaps less than a year, for he was then given a special procuratorship in Dacia, with a salary of 200,000 sesterces. Within three years at the most he had climbed through all the grades of the procuratorial hierarchy. Within the 200,000 or 'ducenary' category there were, it is true, variations of prestige, and a new higher grade of 300,000 a year had just been established. But the rapid promotion is very striking. The people of Cologne, where the German fleet was based, erected a statue to him when the news of his Dacian post came through.[7]

His new appointment lay in the thick of the action. In 170 Italy was invaded while Marcus was trying unsuccessfully to launch a Roman offensive across the Danube. Roman losses were heavy, and they included one of the leading generals, M. Claudius Fronto, who was killed in battle. It is uncertain where Pertinax was at the moment of the invasion. But now his career took a backward turn. He was dismissed from his Dacian post, and not given any further appointment. This is all the more surprising in that his patron Pompeianus had now reached a new pinnacle of influence, having married the widowed Lucilla. Perhaps the removal of Pertinax was engineered by enemies of Pompeianus, too weak to attack the emperor's son-in-law in person. But Pompeianus was entrusted with the task of clearing the invaders out of Italy, and selected Pertinax as his aide. He performed well, and was rewarded with promotion to the senate. There was a desperate need for senators with military talent, and after a short period he was given the rank of ex-praetor and command of the Pannonian legion I Adiutrix. Marcus had been informed of his dismissal in Dacia, and wanted 'to compensate for the wrong done him'. With his legion he completed the rout of the invaders by clearing the provinces of Raetia and Noricum. Soon after came a mysterious episode, the Rain Miracle. The long-delayed Roman offensive had at last begun. A Roman force operating in enemy territory was surrounded, exhausted from the heat and with no drinking water. A sudden cloudburst revived them and stunned the enemy, who were further disarrayed by hail and thunder-bolts. The Roman victory which followed was commemorated on the coinage and in the sixteenth scene of the Aurelian Column. The followers of various religions claimed that their prayers had brought about the rain. Most versions of the story speak of the emperor's presence—and some credit him with the prayers that brought the rain. But one source states that Pertinax was in command of the troops saved by the miraculous storm. Circumstantial evidence suggests that this is correct and that Pertinax was there as legate of I Adiutrix in 172. The prestige gained among the troops must have been immense. His legionary command evidently continued until he became consul in 175, with, as his colleague, Didius Julianus. Julianus' connections would have ensured him the consulship as his rightful due. Pertinax's tenure of the *fasces* (*in absentia*) provoked some to quote Euripides: 'Things of this kind wretched war brings to pass.' The emperor, as if to answer critics, made a speech recommending Pertinax as consul, with 'a eulogy of him', and an account 'of everything that he had done or suffered'. Marcus frequently praised Pertinax both before the troops and to the troops, and 'publicly expressed regret that he was a senator and could not be made Praetorian Prefect'. In the spring of 175 Avidius Cassius proclaimed himself emperor, but was subsequently killed by one of his own officers. For the second time in the reign the east was in turmoil. Cassius was a Syrian, and had won considerable local support. Marcus went to the east, and Pertinax was among the *comites* who accompanied him, though his second visit to Syria was brief. He returned to the Danube, governing Upper and Lower Moesia and Dacia in rapid succession. But before the death of Marcus in 180 Pertinax was appointed governor of Syria.[8]

The significance of this appointment is manifest. In the year before his death Marcus had sensed that he had not long to live. He wanted to ensure the succession, and above all to ensure that Commodus continued to rely on Claudius Pompeianus. By placing a protégé of Pompeianus in this key province he could secure both the allegiance of the east and the maintenance of Pompeianus' influence after his death.

As governor of Syria, Pertinax had now, at the age of fifty-three, reached the summit of the senatorial career. In normal circumstances he would have looked forward to an honorouble retirement, with the option of serving for a year as proconsul of Asia or Africa some fifteen years after his consulship; perhaps a second consulship might be hoped for, or even the Prefecture of the City of Rome. The retirement that was forced upon him only two years after the death of Marcus must have seemed a cruel anti-climax.[9]

· 8 ·

JULIA DOMNA

As LEGATE OF IV SCYTHICA Septimius had been assigned to the most prestigious of the three Syrian legions, the closest to the capital, Antioch on the Orontes. XVI Flavia, which his 'uncle' Gaius had commanded twenty-five years earlier, was based at Samosata on the Euphrates, in Commagene, not far from the border with Cappadocia. III Gallica lay at Raphaneae, south of Apamea, between the Orontes and the sea. As for IV Scythica, it had long been stationed at or near Zeugma, 'the bridge' over the Euphrates, where the road from Antioch crossed the river into the client kingdom of Osrhoene, in north-western Mesopotamia. The *HA* states that Septimius 'was put in command of the legion IV Scythica near *Massilia*'. A simple emendation produces '*circa Massiam*'. Places or rivers called 'Massyas' or 'Marsyas' are found in various parts of Syria. Massyas was the fertile upper Orontes valley, called 'Hollow Syria', *Coele Syria*, by the Greeks, between the Lebanon and Anti-Lebanon mountains, north-west of Damascus. But there is no other evidence for IV Scythica being based so far south, although it is more than likely that Septimius visited the area while in Syria. More plausible perhaps would be the River Marsyas, a western tributary of the Euphrates between Samosata and Zeugma. The *HA* doubtless drastically abbreviated its source, Marius Maximus. He certainly reported another story that the *HA* uses about Septimius' Syrian command; and he had reason to know this province well.[1]

Septimius was certainly at Antioch on occasion. He may even have been acting governor for a short time, after Pertinax's dismissal and before the arrival of the new governor Domitius Dexter. According to the *HA* the Antiochenes made fun of him while he was there in an official capacity. No details or reasons are given; but Septimius did not forget the slight. Apart from his duties, Septimius may have attended the Antiochene Olympic games, held every four years for forty-five days, beginning in August. All public spectacles at Antioch had been abolished by Marcus a few years earlier, to punish the city for supporting the usurper Cassius. Commodus had allowed the games to be restored. His brother-in-law Claudius Pompeianus, himself an Antiochene, may have exerted influence: the Secretary of the restored games, held in summer 181, was another Pompeianus. Antioch's teeming population needed public entertainment as Verus had found, to his own satisfaction, in the early 160s. The great city may have had as many as half a million inhabitants, making it the largest in the east after Alexandria.[2]

There was much here for Septimius to reflect upon. He will have come across Parthians and others from across the frontier. The Euphrates, which marked the border with Parthia, is a mere 100 miles in a direct line from Antioch. Osrhoene was some kind of buffer, and Roman garrisons may have been left at certain points in Mesopotamia, such as Nisibis—as they were in the kingdom of Armenia—after the end of the Parthian war in 166, but Septimius may have perceived the vulnerability of the Syrian frontier. As legate of IV Scythica he guarded the central sector and the route by which invaders would aim for the Syrian capital. His military responsibilities may have taken him across the Euphrates on occasion, for example to Edessa, capital of Osrhoene. Here reigned the Roman vassal Abgar IX, who had recently succeeded Ma'nu VIII, 'Mannus Philoromaeus', as he was known to the Romans. Ma'nu had been deposed by the Parthians in the 160s and restored by the armies of Lucius Verus. The dynasty, in origin desert Arabs, had ruled in this part of Mesopotamia since the late second century BC over a population whose language was a form of Aramaic, the *lingua franca* of the entire region, alongside Greek.[3]

It may have been necessary for Septimius to inspect Roman garrisons south of Zeugma, along the Euphrates as far as Dura-Europus, captured in the 160s and now Rome's furthest outpost on the Parthian frontier. The desert was the land of the bedouin, traversed above all by the caravanserai from Palmyra. This country must have reminded him of the hinterland of his native Tripolitania. Whether or not Septimius saw Dura and Palmyra during his tour of duty as legionary legate, it is clear enough that he went to another city in southern Syria, Palmyra's western neighbour, Emesa. Like Edessa, Emesa had once been the seat of an Arab principality. But whereas Edessa was a Macedonian foundation on the site of an earlier city, there is no record of any settlement at Emesa before the first century BC, when an Arab sheikh named Samsigeramus played a notable part in the last years of the Seleucid kingdom of Syria. The luckless Antiochus XIII, who had been promised the Seleucid throne by Lucullus, was backed by Samsigeramus; his rival Philip relied on another Arab dynast, Aziz of Beroea (Aleppo). Then, in 64 BC, Pompeius Magnus arrived. He refused to recognise Antiochus, who was killed by his erstwhile ally. The rump of Seleucid Syria was annexed as the Roman province of Syria. But Samsigeramus retained Emesa, and the strongpoint of Arethusa to the north, with Pompey's blessing. No doubt he made some of his considerable wealth available to the great general, whose relations with the Arab ruler were before long made fun of by Cicero (he began to nickname Pompey 'Samsigeramus'). A few years later Cicero himself was in the vicinity, as governor of Cilicia, and wrote warmly of Samsigeramus' successor Iamblichus, 'phylarch of the Arabs', as 'a person that men reckon has the right ideas and is a friend of our Republic'. Iamblichus was soon to ingratiate himself with Caesar, sending much-needed military assistance when the dictator was trapped in Egypt in 47 BC. He survived for another fifteen years, only to be executed by Antony, whom he had supported, on the eve of Actium in 31 BC. After a gap, his son of the same name was reinstalled by Augustus in 20 BC, to reign at Emesa as one of the numerous petty princes of the east, among whom Herod is the best known. The Emesene dynasty, like many of the others, was to become closely intermeshed with the Herodian royal house. Iamblichus II reigned until AD 14, his successor Samsigeramus II until AD 47. The latter was married to Iotape, descendant of a Median princess of that name; his daughter, also Iotape, married Aristobulus, brother of Herod Agrippa I. Samsigeramus attended Herod Agrippa's 'conference of kings' at Caesarea in 43, and his successor Aziz married Drusilla, sister of Herod Agrippa II (while the marriage lasted he converted to Judaism).[4]

Another Emesene princess, Julia Mamaea, was married to Polemo, king of Pontus and of Cilician Olba, whose previous wife was the Jewish princess Berenice. The last of the Emesene dynasts, Sohaemus, outdid all his predecessors. He became ruler in 54, the year Nero succeeded Claudius. Rome was heavily engaged with Parthia throughout Nero's reign, and Sohaemus was given the chance to play an active part. He was granted a second kingdom in far off Sophene, near the source of the Tigris, where his mounted archers could ward off the Parthians. When the Jewish revolt broke out he was quick to lend support to Rome; when Vespasian was proclaimed emperor he was among the first to swear allegiance; and a few years later he brought troops to assist in the annexation of Commagene. At the Roman colony at Heliopolis (Baalbek) in the Bekaa valley, Gaius Julius Sohaemus was honoured as the 'great king, honorary *duumvir quinquennalis*, and patron'. Furthermore, he had been granted the *ornamenta consularia*, honorary consular status.[5]

Sohaemus was apparently the last king. It is uncertain exactly when he died, but it seems probable that Emesa was absorbed into the Roman province of Syria soon afterwards, in the Flavian period. This is what happened to Agrippa II's realm when the last Jewish king died in the 90s. After the kingship lapsed, descendants of the royal house are still found at Emesa. The names Samsigeramus, Sohaemus, Iamblichus, Aziz, Iotape, likewise Alexio and Alexander, appear on inscriptions frequently. Two particular Emesenes achieved wider prominence in the second century. Sohaemus, already a Roman senator of consular rank, was installed by Lucius Verus as king of Armenia in 163. His contemporary the novelist Iamblichus, himself 'descended from the ancient dynasts', says that Sohaemus reigned 'in succession to his ancestors'. This must refer to the first century Sohaemus, to whom Nero granted the kingdom of Sophene. Iamblichus also calls the king of Armenia 'an Arsacid and an Achaemenid': he was, after all, a descendant of the Median princess Iotape. Iamblichus' novel, the *Babyloniaca*, by its very name underlines Emesa's connections with the east. The Arab names of the Emesene dynasts and their descendants, derived from Semitic deities in several cases, recall Emesa's links with her founder's bedouin past.[6]

Emesa was unquestionably wealthy. The fertile volcanic soil of the Orontes valley favoured cultivation. It produced wheat, vines and olives. Its great lake, formed by a dam across the Orontes, south of the city, provided ample water. Its territory extended far to the east across the steppe, where it bordered the western lands of Palmyra. The trade route from the east, via Palmyra, passed through Emesa on its way to the coast. This was terrain that the ancestors of the first Samsigeramus had travelled again and again, before deciding to settle in the Orontes valley. The people of Emesa evidently spoke Aramaic and Greek. Knowledge of Latin was probably also common: Berytus (Beirut) on the coast, a Roman colony with a flourishing law school, was not too far distant; Heliopolis, another colony, was only some fifty miles south; Raphaneae, where the legion III Gallica had its base, was even closer, to the north-west.[7]

The coastal cities of this region were all Phoenician in origin: Aradus, Tripolis, Byblus, Berytus, Sidon and Tyre. They retained some consciousness of their ancient past, even though by the first century AD they carried a heavy veneer of Hellenic culture, and the Greek language predominated. By extension Arab Emesa considered itself, or was considered to be, a Phoenician city. One of its best known sons, the novelist Heliodorus, called himself 'a Phoenician from Emesa, from the race of the Sun'. Emesa was to become famous above all for its cult of the god Elagabal, thought by Herodian to be 'the Phoenician name for the sun-god'. In fact the deity was the god (*El*) of the mountain (*gabal*), worshipped in the form of a conical black stone. To the Greeks the name sounded like '*Helio*gabalus', and the Emesenes themselves seem to have happily accepted the identification: dedications are found overseas to 'the ancestral Sun God Elagabal'.[8]

The earliest coin issues from Emesa, under Antoninus Pius, celebrate the cult of Elagabal: they depict an eagle perched on the black stone. Later an elaborate monumental altar is shown. Two superimposed rows of niches, between two pilasters, stand on a massive base, with statues in each of the six niches. Above is a smaller altar, surmounted by the great stone itself, ornamented with mysterious markings. According to Herodian, who describes the cult when it had reached even greater renown, 'all the neighbouring princes and rulers sent generous and expensive gifts there every year'. The priesthood was held by a family that may be assumed to descend from the princely house of Samsigeramus and Sohaemus. At the time of Septimius' visit the priest was named Julius Bassianus, whose Latin-sounding *cognomen* was presumably adapted from the Semitic priestly title *basus*. Herodian portrays the priest of Elagabal as clad in 'barbaric' costume—in fact it sounds Parthian—with long-sleeved and gold-embroidered purple tunic reaching to his feet, gold and purple trousers, and a jewelled diadem on his head. Julius Bassianus had two daughters, Domna and Maesa. Both names are Semitic, Domna being close to the Arabic 'Dumayna', an archaic diminutive form of *Dimna* (related to the colour black). It was assumed often enough by Romans to be a contracted form of *Domina*. A few years later Septimius was to marry Julia Domna, allegedly having learned that 'her horoscope predicted that she would marry a king'. For the time being, Septimius was still married to Paccia Marciana, and, addicted though he was to astrology, he may not yet have consulted what the stars foretold for Julia.[9]

As daughter of the priest of Elagabal, from a royal line, Julia might not have regarded such a horoscope as far-fetched. It was not long since a Sohaemus had been crowned king in Armenia. Whether he was still on the throne at this time is unknown. Sohaemus had been a Roman senator and consul before he was made king of Armenia; Julia Domna's father was of less exalted rank—Cassius Dio calls her 'plebeian', meaning no doubt, non-senatorial. A person of the same names happens to be registered at this very time by the jurist Cervidius Scaevola: a woman called Julia Domna was declared the rightful inheritor of an estate left some years before by her great-uncle, Julius Agrippa, a *primipilaris*. There is nothing inherently implausible about the notion that a man from the family of the Emesene high priests should serve in a legion and rise to be chief centurion. The Emesenes were a warlike people, and sent men into the legions, as well as contributing their archers to the *auxilia* of the imperial army.[10]

It is attractive to imagine Septimius visiting Tyre and Sidon, the mother cities of the western Phoenicians. Whether he would have had the opportunity at this time is hard to say. At all events, Dio registers a visit to a city north of Emesa, Apamea on the Orontes, about halfway between Emesa and Antioch. Here he consulted the oracle of Zeus Belos, that is, the local Ba'al. The god's reply was a quotation from Homer's *Iliad*:

72

Eyes and head like Zeus who delights in thunder,
Like Ares his waist, his chest like Posidon.

Whether Septimius instantly took this as a prediction of future greatness is
not clear: it is a description of king Agamemnon. But he noted the
response carefully.[11]

Septimius' dismissal from his legionary command is not described in
explicit terms, nor indeed is Pertinax's removal from the governorship.
But the *HA* reports of Pertinax that after his return from Syria to Rome
and his attendance, for the first time, in the senate-house, 'he was
immediately ordered by Perennis to withdraw' to the family property in
Liguria. The 'exile' lasted three years and was ended by the fall of Perennis
in 185. Hence Pertinax's dismissal must belong to the aftermath of
Lucilla's conspiracy. As a protégé of Lucilla's husband Pompeianus—even
though Pompeianus himself was not involved—Pertinax would be
suspect. Furthermore, the Condianus affair had taken place in his province, and two senators from the province, Aemilius Juncus of Tripolis
and Velius Rufus of Heliopolis, were exiled after the Lucilla plot. It looks
as if Syria, which had supported the rebellion of Avidius Cassius only
seven years before, was still disaffected.[12] •

As for Septimius himself, there is no direct clue. He may have remained
at his post for a time after Pertinax's departure, long enough to serve the
new governor Domitius Dexter, later an ally of his. Likewise he may have
overlapped with Fabius Cilo, who commanded XVI Flavia in the early
180s. The *HA* does not state outright that Septimius was dismissed or that
he was told to withdraw from public life. But following his departure
from Syria he went to Athens 'to study, and for religious purposes and to
see the monuments and antiquities'. He was denied further advancement
for several years. Tourism was by this time in vogue. Less than twenty
years before Pausanias had published his guide to Greece to cater for it.
Plenty of wealthy Romans from the west went to Athens to study, as was
the case with Apuleius and Sicinius Pontianus of Oea. Septimius had left it
a little late, perhaps, to attend lectures by the great Hadrianus of Tyre,
foremost among the pupils of the celebrated Herodes Atticus. Hadrianus
was probably already professor of rhetoric at Rome, and his own pupil
Julius Pollux held the chair at Athens. Pollux was a man of mediocre
talent, known as the author of an *Onomasticon* and as composer of
Commodus' wedding hymn a few years before. One teacher that
Septimius may have met and liked was Aelius Antipater of Phrygian
Hierapolis, his exact contemporary. Antipater was later to be a close
associate of Septimius.[13]

The religious motives are not specified. One may suspect that he had himself initiated into the Eleusinian Mysteries, following the example of four emperors, Hadrian, Verus, and, most recently, Marcus and Commodus in 176. One of the teachers whose lectures Septimius could have attended, if he really devoted himself to study at this time, was Apollonius, a native of Athens, who was hierophant of Demeter at Eleusis.[14]

At best these activities can only have palliated the boredom and frustration that so ambitious a man must have felt. News from Rome in 183 and 184 will have occupied his attention. Commodus inaugurated 184 as consul for the fourth time, with Victorinus, still City Prefect, as his colleague. But the reins of government were in the hands of the Prefect of the Guard, Tigidius Perennis. The emperor took a new title, 'Pius', and victories in the north won him fifth and sixth salutations as Imperator. Fighting was also going on in Britain, following disaster there at the opening of the reign. The governor Ulpius Marcellus ruthlessly suppressed the north Britons, winning Commodus a seventh salutation and the title 'Britannicus'. But Marcellus' harsh character caused trouble with the legions. There was an attempted coup, when the troops tried to invest a legionary legate named Priscus with the purple. He wisely refused. But Perennis took reprisals: the legates of the British legions were all dismissed and their duties assumed by equestrian officers. This was an unprecedented blow against the system of cooperation between senate and emperor.[15]

Perennis' hostility to the senate was far-reaching, if the HA may be believed: many senators were put to death. Yet at the same time Perennis' own sons advanced rapidly to the heights of the senatorial cursus. One was given the principal credit for victories on the Danube. This gave plausibility to the rumour that Perennis was plotting to place his son on the throne. Since the beginning of the second century it had been the army of the Danube, rather than of the Rhine, which was predominant.[16]

The confused conditions in the western half of the empire provided the opportunity to overthrow Perennis in the following year. Herodian attributes his fall to the arrival of soldiers from Pannonia who revealed his secret plans. Dio has another story: the soldiers who came to Rome were 1500 men from the army of Britain—and Commodus actually allowed them to carry out Perennis' execution themselves. It is hard to understand why or how a contingent of troops from Britain should have turned up outside Rome. Dio gives no clue that it was anything other than a deliberate sending of a deputation. But it may be that a force from the British army was already operating on the continent for another purpose, the suppression of brigandage. The end of the Marcomannic wars had left bands of runaway slaves and deserters roaming through Gaul, Spain and Italy. The soldiers in Britain were already mutinous and discontented.

There was a powerful ally in the palace, the freedman Cleander, who may have urged Commodus to believe the accusations against Perennis.[17]

The death of the Prefect brought about many changes. Ulpius Marcellus, recalled from Britain, was tried and narrowly escaped with his life. There were other trials also. The place of Perennis as real master of the empire was now taken by Cleander. Brought to Rome from Phrygia as a slave, to be a pack-carrier, he had become an imperial freedman and succeeded Saoterus as chamberlain. Now Cleander bestowed and sold entry to the senate, army commands, governorships, procuratorships. The great Aufidius Victorinus, renowned for his incorruptibility, preferred not to remain and watch. He committed suicide. Others had less scruples, especially those whom the domination of Perennis had thrust to the side. Pertinax was brought back and appointed governor of Britain, with the mandate of eliminating the spirit of mutiny in the army there. Septimius too was recalled, and received his first governorship, of Gallia Lugdunensis.[18]

Here he had no military force under his command, with the exception of the Urban Cohort at Lugdunum, 500 strong. But he had a large province, stretching from its capital on the Rhône, which was also the meeting-place of the annual assembly of the three Gallic provinces, to the Atlantic and Channel coasts. His duties were those of any Roman governor: to keep the province quiet and peaceful, and to act as its Chief Justice. There may have been particular difficulties at this time, on account of the widespread and increasingly dangerous activities of the deserters. In 186 there was serious trouble in the southern part of the adjacent province of Upper Germany, and later one of the deserters' leaders, Maternus, is said to have been daring enough to try to assassinate Commodus at Rome itself.[19]

Soon after Septimius' arrival in Gaul, Paccia Marciana died. Virtually nothing is known of her—Septimius apparently did not even mention her in his autobiography, although he did subsequently commemorate her with statues when he became emperor. Now over forty and still childless, he was anxious to remarry. According to the HA, 'as a very skilled astrologer he enquired into the horoscope of potential brides. Since he had heard that there was a woman in Syria whose horoscope predicted that she would be married to a king, he sought her as his wife—it was, of course, Julia—and through the mediation of friends he gained her hand.' The story of Julia's horoscope, for which the HA gives Marius Maximus as the source, sounds plausible enough: Septimius was unquestionably an addict, and an expert. (It might however have been concocted as propaganda at a later stage, when Septimius was fighting to keep the throne.) Septimius had at any rate had the opportunity to visit the great temple at Emesa a few years before. He probably knew its high priest, Julius Bassianus, and had perhaps met his daughters too—Julia Domna's sister Maesa was to marry a man of Emesa, Julius Avitus Alexianus, an equestrian officer at this time. For a proposal of marriage to be sent from Lugdunum to Syria was straightforward. Syrian merchants were present in strength in the Rhône valley. It would be simple for Julia, too, to take ship off Aradus, a short distance from Emesa.[20]

Some time early in 187, at latest, the letter went to Syria. After the proposal was accepted Septimius had a dream: the empress Faustina, dead for more than ten years, was preparing the bridal chamber for himself and Julia in the great temple of Rome and Venus, near the imperial Palace. He had other dreams at Lugdunum, so it was later advertised, to one of which he attached a deep meaning. In one, water appeared to gush from his hand. In another, the Roman empire itself, personified, approached him and saluted. Most impressive of all, someone took him up to a high mountain, from which he could see Rome and all the world. 'As he gazed down on all the land and sea, he laid his hands on them as one might on an instrument capable of playing all modes, and they all sang together.' This is Dio's version. The *HA*, which has more or less the same story (though sets it during the time in Spain ten years earlier), has the variant that 'the provinces sang together to the accompaniment of the lyre and flute'.[21]

The marriage took place in the summer of 187. Julia was a striking, indeed beautiful woman, to judge from her later portraits, with fine and sensitive features. As Gibbon put it, 'she deserved all that the stars could promise her. She possessed . . . the attractions of beauty, and united to a lively imagination a firmness of mind and strength of judgement, seldom bestowed on her sex.' She and Septimius probably spoke to each other in Greek, at first at least. It is conceivable that they could also communicate in a mixture of Aramaic and Punic. The two languages, both from the 'north-west Semitic' family, were closely related. Julia 'at once conceived'. Her first child, a son, was born on 4 April 188, at Lugdunum, and was given the *cognomen* of his mother's father, Bassianus; the *praenomen* is not recorded.[22]

During his governorship of Gaul there were several opportunities for Septimius to form close associations with fellow-senators serving in the region. The aristocratic Lollianus Gentianus, son of Avitus, patron of Apuleius and of Pertinax, may have passed through Lugdunensis on his way to assume command of the legion XXII Primigenia at Moguntiacum. Fabius Cilo, whom Septimius may have had as colleague in Syria, was proconsul of Narbonensis, the neighbouring province, at about this time. If the deserters were still a serious problem, governors would have been obliged to cooperate closely. Indeed the *HA*, in its admittedly mainly bogus life of Pescennius Niger, claims that Niger was sent 'to hunt down deserters' while Septimius was governing Lugdunensis, and that the later rivals were at that time on very friendly terms.[23]

Septimius' governorship in Gaul ended in 188 and he returned to Rome, where his name went into the ballot for a proconsulship in the New Year. He received Sicily. Julia was pregnant again, and early in 189 a second son was born, named after Septimius' father and brother: P. Septimius Geta. In the spring or early summer the family went to Sicily. It is not impossible that Septimius' brother was his predecessor as proconsul. His career also may have suffered a setback while Perennis was in power. It is impossible to tell at what pace his rise in the *cursus* proceeded, but its stages were closely parallel to that of Septimius: a legionary command (in Lower Moesia), a provincial governorship (Lusitania) and a proconsulship.[24]

While Septimius had been in Gaul the pace had quickened in the murderous politics of Commodus' reign. In Britain Pertinax had been almost lynched by his own men when a legion broke into open mutiny. This may have been when he refused to let the British army set him up as emperor—'for they wanted to set up any one (other than Commodus) as emperor, preferably Pertinax himself'. While in Britain Pertinax took a surprising step. He wrote to Commodus, informing him that the emperor's brother-in-law Antistius Burrus was seeking the throne, in association with his fellow-Numidian Arrius Antoninus. Antoninus must have been well known to Pertinax, and Burrus' kinsman Antistius Adventus had served with distinction as a general in both Parthian and Marcomannic wars. It is fair to suppose that Pertinax had some evidence for his allegations. Perhaps the two men had approached him, by letter or through an intermediary, wanting the support of the three disaffected British legions and their commander-in-chief. It may therefore have been an act of self-preservation to unmask the plans of Burrus—who might have seemed to Pertinax incapable of the task, not *capax imperii*. There may have been another motive. Burrus is said to have been 'denouncing and reporting to Commodus' everything that was being done—by the freedman Cleander. As Pertinax himself had regained his influence thanks to Cleander, he may have been persuaded by the freedman to act against a man whose outspokenness threatened to end his power.[25]

How long it took before Burrus and Antoninus were disposed of is not clear. Burrus had powerful allies, including the Guard Prefect Atilius Aebutianus; and Antoninus survived long enough to be proconsul of Asia for the year 188–9. Well before this Pertinax asked to be relieved of his command: 'The legions', he said, 'were hostile to him because of his strict discipline.' He returned to Rome, and was given the undemanding charge of the *alimenta*.[26]

He had become something of a hero on account of his success in quelling the British mutiny. 'When a horse called Pertinax won—it was raced by the Green faction and was favoured by Commodus—its partisans raised a great shout: "It is Pertinax!" The others, their opponents—in disgust at Commodus—added a prayer, shouting out: "If only it was!", referring to the man, not the horse.' But now Cleander was beginning to feel more confident. In 188 he disposed of Burrus and his ally the Prefect Aebutianus, latest of the numerous successors to Perennis. Thereafter Cleander obtained direct personal authority over the praetorians, as 'Bearer of the Dagger', *a pugione*, with two colleagues as Prefects.[27]

In the summer of 188 Pertinax went to Africa as proconsul. His term of office is alleged to have been stormy, with rioting at Carthage provoked by prophecies from the priests of Juno Caelestis, the Punic goddess Tanit. Pertinax survived these difficulties, and on his return to Rome in 189 became Prefect of the City. His colleague in Asia Arrius Antoninus, who had been faced only by fanatical would-be Christian martyrs, was less fortunate. Whether because of Pertinax's intrigues, or perhaps, as the *HA* suggests, because he had offended a powerful personage in Asia, Attalus, Antoninus was put to death on Cleander's orders. It was to create a backlash against Cleander and contribute to his downfall.[28]

The following year, 190, had the record number of twenty-five consuls. Commodus, holding office for the sixth time, opened the year with Petronius Sura Septimianus (brother of his brother-in-law Mamertinus). The emperor obviously resigned the *fasces* after a matter of days, his successor served as suffect with Sura Septimianus for the rest of January, and a new pair of suffects must have taken office in each of the remaining eleven months of the year. It was a scandalous climax to Cleander's selling of offices. Septimius was one of the twenty-five consuls, who, Dio specifically states, were 'appointed by Cleander'. But before Septimius' proconsulship in Sicily ended, Cleander had fallen. The death of Arrius Antoninus had made him intensely unpopular with the volatile plebs. In addition, he had made a dangerous enemy, Papirius Dionysius. This man, after a distinguished equestrian career begun under Marcus, had been serving as Prefect of the Annona. He was then appointed Prefect of Egypt, a normal promotion. But he may not even have reached Egypt, or, if he did, his promotion was rapidly cancelled, and he was recalled to be prefect of the grain-supply again. Back in his old position he was well placed to hurt Cleander. He deliberately created a corn-shortage, a sure way to arouse unpopularity against any government.[29]

The discontent broke out during a performance in the Circus Maximus. This vast stadium, capable of seating 150,000 spectators, was a standing source of danger if the mob got out of hand. As Prefect of the Annona, with his offices a few yards from the Tiber end of the Circus, Dionysius probably controlled the seating for the shows. It would have been easy to arrange favourable positions for his agents.

As the horses were about to start the seventh lap, a crowd of children ran into the Circus, led by a tall maiden of grim appearance—who, afterwards, because of what happened, people thought must have been a goddess. The children shouted out in unison, long and bitterly. The people took up the chant, and then began to shout out every conceivable insult. Finally the mob jumped down from their seats and went to look for the emperor, calling out many blessings on him and many curses against Cleander.

Commodus was at this moment at the villa he had confiscated from the Quintilii, a few miles out of Rome along the Via Appia. Cleander sent a few soldiers against the mob, but it was undeterred, especially, Dio records, 'because it was encouraged by the strength' of some other 'troops'. Who were these troops? Dio's abbreviated account gives no clue. But in disturbances at the theatre and on other occasions, the official whose duty it was to keep order was the City Prefect with the 1500 men of the Urban Cohorts. Pertinax clearly took no action, nor did Cleander's 'colleagues', the other Guard Prefects, to prevent the crowd streaming out of Rome. Finally Commodus' mistress Marcia told the emperor what was going on. He was terrified and at once ordered Cleander to be put to death.[30]

Pertinaxs' change of front vis-à-vis Cleander is not difficult to explain. For one thing, he had had the chance to observe the man at close quarters. Besides this, both Dionysius and another key figure, Julius Julianus, who were keenly interested in getting rid of Cleander, were men whom Pertinax is likely to have known well and trusted. It seems that Julianus was serving as Prefect of the Guard, with one Regillus, under Cleander. When Cleander was killed, they acquired substantive control, if only briefly. Julianus' career had begun many years before as prefect of a cohort in Syria at precisely the time when Pertinax himself was there in that rank. He too, like Pertinax, had commanded vexillations in the Marcomannic wars. Dionysius, although not primarily a military man, had had an administrative post during the second Marcomannic war at the end of Marcus' reign. Pertinax could have felt solidarity with people of this kind.[31]

The overthrow of Cleander may be dated with some plausibility to 19

April, when the *ludi Ceriales* took place. At this time of year a corn-shortage was quite likely and it would have been a master-stroke for Cleander's opponents to mount their attacks at games honouring the corn goddess. It was probably in the immediate aftermath of these events that Septimius returned from Sicily, and at once faced trial, according to the *HA*: 'he was accused of consulting seers or astrologers about the imperial position.' The charge could be constructed as treason; but the case, which was heard by the Guard Prefects, was dismissed, and his accuser cruci-fied.[32]

Julius Julianus' colleague Regillus was soon removed. By 15 July 190 Julianus was sole Prefect. He may have been given another colleague after the fall of Regillus: one Motilenus is mentioned as Prefect after Cleander's death. Nothing was done to alter the arrangements for the consulship: too many were involved. Septimius duly held office, with the otherwise unknown Apuleius Rufinus as his colleague. After his month as consul, no appointment was offered. A period of waiting in the background was in any case desirable: a new bloodbath was about to begin. Septimius was 'without employment for about a year after his consulship'.[33]

· 9 ·

THE CONSPIRATORS

THE FALL OF CLEANDER HAD inevitable repercussions among the ruling élite. Julius Julianus did not long enjoy his position at the pinnacle of the equestrian order, the reward for more than thirty years' service. The veteran general was embraced in public and called 'Father' by Commodus. But he had to submit to indignities at the emperor's hands. Being pushed into a swimming-pool when clad in the formal toga and in the presence of his own staff, could be laughed off, perhaps. But it was another matter when the Prefect of the Guard was made to dance naked before the emperor's concubines, clashing cymbals and making grimaces. The charade did not last long. Julianus was murdered.[1]

Other executions followed. One of these must have been noted with anxiety or at least particular interest by Septimius and Julia. A prominent Emesene, who may well have been a kinsman of Julia, was the victim, one Julius Alexander. The motive for this murder as given by Dio sounds surprising but may well be plausible: it was because 'he had brought down a lion with his javelin, from horseback'. The emperor who prided himself on his gladiatorial skill could not endure competition: Commodus' mania for the arena was soon to become further intensified. The HA states that Alexander was executed for rebellion. That may well have been the official version, justified by the man's behaviour when he learned that the assassins had arrived at Emesa. He somehow contrived to kill both them and his enemies in the city, and set off for the Euphrates, hoping for asylum with Parthia. 'And he would have escaped,' says Dio, 'if he had not taken a boy-favourite with him, for he was an excellent horseman himself. But he could not bear to abandon the boy, who was exhausted. So when he began to be overtaken, he killed both the boy and himself.'[2]

This was only the beginning of a bloody purge. The HA gives the names of fifteen senators, at least twelve of whom were ex-consuls, who were put to death in the last two and a half years of the reign. They included Sulpicius Crassus, proconsul of Asia, Commodus' brother-in-law Mamertinus and the latter's brother Septimianus. Another victim was first cousin of Marcus, Annia Fundania Faustina. Her daughter Vitrasia had been murdered after the conspiracies of 182 and she herself was living in Achaia at the time, no doubt in deliberately chosen retirement. As for the fifteen senators, the *HA* notes with all of them that they were killed *cum suis*, 'together with their kin'. And the biographer adds, after recording the death of Annia: *et alios infinitos*. It may be an exaggeration that 'innumerable others were put to death'. But there can be no doubt that many more than the fifteen senators and one noblewoman lost their lives. The panic that was thereby created must have been accentuated by the recurrence of plague, the greatest outbreak that Dio—too young at the time to remember the great plague of 166–7—ever experienced: '2000 people often died at Rome in a single day'. He added a curious story. 'Also at this time, many others, not only in the city but throughout most of the empire, died at the hands of criminals who smeared deadly drugs on tiny needles and were hired to infect people with them.' Whatever the facts, this peculiar anecdote reveals a great deal about the climate of the time.[3]

Cleander's removal had left a vacuum which Julius Julianus had not filled. In 191 unmistakable signs appeared that Commodus himself, now twenty-nine, was at last asserting his own authority. Coins of late 190 had proclaimed a new 'Golden Age of Commodus'. Now, in 191, Commodus changed his names. Abandoning 'Marcus' and 'Antoninus', that he had assumed on his father's death, he reverted to his original names, Lucius Aelius Aurelius Commodus. He was finally sloughing off any allegiance, even token, to the memory of Marcus. It could be that it showed merely that Commodus was now going to be 'his own man'. Or perhaps it was intended as deference to the memory of Lucius Verus, after whom he had been named originally. The coinage now began to identify Commodus with Hercules, and his devotion to oriental cults was intensified, to Isis and Sarapis, and to Mithras, in particular.[4]

Whatever the legends on the coinage, something else had changed. From 190 the silver content had been further debased. The wars under Marcus had necessitated a reduction in the fineness of the denarius, first in 161–6; then, after an improvement, from 170–80. On Commodus' accession the silver content had gone down further. Now it reached a new low. Clearly revenues were not keeping pace with spending. Meanwhile a new Guard Prefect had been appointed, Q. Aemilius Laetus. He came from Thaenae on the coast of Byzacena in Africa, where the old 'royal ditch' had marked off the first Roman province and the Numidian kingdom. There was also a new chamberlain in succession to Cleander. This was Eclectus, who had started in L. Verus' service, and then moved to the household of Ummidius Quadratus. When Quadratus was executed in 182 he entered the palace again, together with Marcia, the freedwoman who had been Quadratus' mistress. She became the concubine of Commodus, and after Cleander's death acquired immense influence over him. Laetus, Eclectus and Marcia between them now had the task of controlling Commodus, if it should be possible.[5]

Laetus' origin is another sign of the advance of Africans. Even the Christian leader at Rome at this time was from Africa, Pope Victor. It is no surprise to find the *HA* claiming that Commodus intended a visit to Africa, probably in early 191. The project was abandoned: it had only been a pretext to get an extra grant of funds voted. Commodus may, however, have been aware that he should conciliate the African elite, potentially alienated after the murders of Burrus and Arrius Antoninus. The province supplied a large part of Rome's food supply.[6]

Laetus soon began to exercise power. His brother Pudens, a former legionary centurion, was attached to the emperor's personal bodyguard. In the summer of 191 Laetus put through a surprising appointment. Septimius was made governor of Upper Pannonia 'on Laetus' recommendation'. With its three legions, this province could be of vital importance. No large army lay nearer to Italy. Yet Septimius was an unlikely choice. Few men were given command of so large an army unless they had had some experience of post-consular provincial government or, in the case of Upper Pannonia, unless they had governed the Lower province immediately before their consulship. Septimius had done neither, and his previous military experience was limited to his legionary command in Syria. He had never served on Rhine or Danube. The imperial government did not favour specialisation, and it was rare for a man to serve two terms in the same province. But this was not carried to extremes. Service somewhere on the northern frontiers was generally a prerequisite for a governor of one of the major provinces there.[7]

Septimius may not have been made aware at first of the reasons for his selection. But his star was in the ascendant—and no doubt his credit rating improved also. Up to this moment his property in Italy had consisted of a house in Rome and the 'single farm' at Veii. Shortly before his departure for his province he purchased elaborate gardens, *horti*, in the city.[8]

At the same time or a little later, his brother Geta was also appointed governor of a Danubian province, Lower Moesia, with two legions, and Clodius Albinus of Hadrumetum was made governor of Britain. The result was that men from Africa controlled eight of the northern legions. It may be that some of the other northern provinces were placed in the hands of Africans, or at least assigned to men whom Laetus and Pertinax could trust. The governor of Dacia, appointed at latest in 192, was one Q. Aurelius Polus Terentianus. Study of his nomenclature suggests, although it cannot prove, that he too derived from Africa. In any case, he had almost certainly served under Pertinax in Britain a few years before; as a *fetialis* he was a fellow-member of the same priestly college as Septimius

Geta. Another *fetialis*, incidentally, was sent to Lower Moesia to command one of the legions. This was Marius Maximus, the future biographer of the Caesars, whose younger brother Perpetuus had perhaps served
under Pertinax and Septimius in Syria: the Marii, too, were African.[9]

Legionary legates were appointed directly by the emperor. At a lower
level, provincial governors had wide powers of patronage. The influence
wielded by Septimius, Geta, Albinus and Polus Terentianus would be felt
in many areas. They could give commissions to officers up to and
including the rank of *tribunus laticlavius*. Septimius alone could offer
positions to three *tribuni laticlavii* and fifteen *angusticlavii*, and had in his
army seven auxiliary cohorts and five *alae* of cavalry (one of them an élite
milliary *ala*), in command of which he could place his own nominees.
One of the *tribuni laticlavii* that he appointed sounds like a kinsman: C.
Julius Septimius Castinus.[10]

In 191 Commodus decided to hold the consulship for the seventh time,
for 192. Pertinax was chosen as his colleague—the *HA* says that Commodus was pleased with the sixty-five-year-old Prefect of the City. No
reason is given for his satisfaction. Pertinax is said to have performed his
duties as Prefect 'with extreme gentleness and consideration'. Unfortunately the text of the *HA* is defective at this point, making it unclear
whether this had anything to do with Commodus' feelings about him.
However this may be, either in 191, or soon after Commodus and
Pertinax inaugurated the year 192, Pertinax was approached by Laetus
and Marcia to participate in a conspiracy to murder the emperor. He
accepted. Without doubt he was already Laetus' choice as successor to
Commodus.[11]

There had been many attempts against Commodus' life. The entire
reign is a story of miscarried conspiracies. This time careful steps were
taken to ensure success. The packing of the major northern provinces with
safe men has already been described. Egypt was always of crucial
importance. In the second half of 192 the Prefect Larcius Memor, who had
been in office for less than two years, was replaced by one Mantennius
Sabinus. No explicit connection has been recorded between Sabinus and
the conspirators. But it was perhaps no coincidence that his wife came
from Praeneste, where Pertinax's father-in-law Flavius Sulpicianus had
estates. No doubt Pertinax and Sabinus were well acquainted. As
important as Egypt was Syria. Events in Parthia had created a delicate
situation there, but one which reduced the potential threat to Rome. The
Parthian King Vologaeses III had been either challenged or was about to
be deposed after reigning for over forty years. Laetus and Pertinax may
have been unable to control the selection of the governor of Syria. The
post went to Pescennius Niger. Dio says that he was given the job

1 **Above** *The theatre at Lepcis Magna*

2 **Below** *Inscription from the theatre: the Latin text honours Caesar Augustus (AD 1–2) and records the benefaction of Annobal Tapapius Rufus; lines 3–5 are repeated in Punic below (IRT 322; IPT 24)*

3   *Aerial view of Lepcis Magna. The massive*
rectangle west of the Wadi Lebdah is the
Severan Forum. North-west of this is the old

Forum, to the south-west the theatre, to the
south the Hadrianic Baths. The circus and
amphitheatre complex is at the far right.

4 · Stele commemorating the paving of the old Forum at Lepcis in AD 53. The bronze letters of the Latin text have been removed. In the first sixteen lines the emperor Claudius is honoured and the proconsul and legate named; the last nine record the benefactor Gaius Anno and his family (possible ancestors of the Septimii); these details are repeated in Punic at the foot (IRT 338; IPT 26)

5   *Pertinax*
(BMC *V*, Pertinax 26)

6   *Didius Julianus*
(Roman Imperial Coins in the Hunter Coin
Cabinet, *III*, *Didius Julianus 10*)

7   *Pescennius Niger*
(BMC *V*, p. 74* n.)

8   *Clodius Albinus as Caesar to Septimius*
(*the reverse shows the African deity Ba'al
Hammon, with his Latin name favoured at*

Hadrumetum, Saeculum Frugiferum)
(BMC *V*, *Wars of Succession 103*)

9   *Septimius*
(BMC *V*, *Wars of Succession 582;* AD *196*)

10   *Julia Domna*
(BMC *V*, *Septimius & Caracalla 767*)

11   *Antoninus (Caracalla)*
(BMC *V*, *Wars of Succession 613;* AD *196–7*)

12   *Antoninus (Caracalla) and Geta*
(Roman Imperial Coins in the Hunter Coin
Cabinet, *III, Septimius 44*)

13   *Antoninus (Caracalla)*
(BMC *V, Septimius, Caracalla, Geta 205;* AD
210)

14   *Geta*
(*ibid. 313;* AD *210*)

16   The Berlin Tondo: Septimius, Julia and
their sons portrayed in Egypt. (Geta was
defaced after his murder by his brother)

15   **Left**   The Arch of Septimius Severus in
the Forum at Rome

17 *The central scene of frieze* D *from the Severan Arch at Lepcis Magna, a* dextrarum iunctio, Septimius and Antoninus *joining* hands. *The head of Geta is restored, the original having been stolen by an allied soldier during the Second World War*

18 *Julia Domna, shown looking towards her
husband and sons on frieze* D *of the Severan
Arch at Lepcis*

19　*A portion of the frieze* D *from the Severan Arch at Lepcis. These two figures, belong to the right of the* dextrarum iunctio *(plate 17) and are clearly important, perhaps Plautianus (left) and Septimius' brother Geta, the consuls of* AD *203*

20　*Septimius, flanked by his two sons, shown in a triumphal chariot on the Arch at Lepcis Magna*

21   *The fort at Gholaia (Bu-Ngem), blocking
the eastern route from the Sahara to the
Tripolitanian coast*

22   *The Severan Basilica at Lepcis*

23   *Carved marble piers from the Severan*
Basilica at Lepcis

24 **Above** *Zinchecra: the original promontory stronghold of the Garamantes, looking out over the Wadi El-Agial*

25 **Below** *Carpow, Septimius' new base in Scotland, from the north. The Tay is in the foreground and the north rampart is marked by the line of trees*

precisely because of his mediocrity. This may have made him seem harmless. The *HA* alleges that he owed the appointment to an athlete with whom Commodus trained, Narcissus. The two consular proconsulships, Asia and Africa, were given to Asellius Aemilianus and Cornelius Anullinus. Aemilianus was a kinsman of Clodius Albinus; hence perhaps African. He had also been Niger's immediate predecessor as governor of Syria. It may have been thought that he could exert some influence over the eastern legions if need should arise. Anullinus, a Spaniard, may have been a friend of Septimius Severus already—he was certainly a close friend later.[12]

Towards the end of the year 192 Commodus' pathological inclinations became even more extreme. He now identified himself completely with Hercules. As the Roman Hercules the emperor wished to become the divine founder of Rome, and the city was renamed *colonia Commodiana*. All the months of the year were now to bear his own extravagant nomenclature—which had conveniently expanded to make up the exact number required: *Amazonius Invictus Pius Felix Lucius Aelius Aurelius Commodus Augustus Hercules Romanus Exsuperatorius*. Places and institutions of all kinds throughout the empire were to exchange their original names for that of Commodus.[13]

Marius Maximus, source for some of the more reliable parts of the *HA*, was already serving on the Danube in 192, and did not witness these bizarre events to their final conclusion. This may be why there is no trace or mention in the *HA* of an event in that year which deeply impressed both Dio and Herodian. 'A fire that began at night in some house leaped into the Temple of Peace and spread to the Egyptian and Arabian warehouses. From there the flames were carried up into the Palace and consumed very extensive portions of it, so that nearly all the state records were destroyed.' Dio took it as an omen. This in particular—the destruction of the archives—made it clear to Dio that the calamity portended by this fire would not be confined to the city but would extend over the entire world. The great doctor Galen had particular cause for regret. Many of his writings, housed in the Palace libraries, perished. Herodian also describes the fire in dramatic terms, as a portent of impending disaster. It was preceded by a slight earthquake, and the Temple of Peace, which he calls 'the largest and most beautiful building in the city', was according to him totally destroyed—'and some conjectured that the destruction of the Temple of Peace was a prophecy of war'. He adds that the fire consumed the Temple of Vesta and exposed the sacred Palladium to public view for the first time since its legendary journey from Troy to Italy. The Vestal Virgins hurriedly carried the statue along the Sacred Way into the Palace.[14]

85

Herodian and Dio give detailed accounts of Commodus' last display in the arena. Probably at the Plebeian Games, which lasted fourteen days in November—unless it was at new, specially founded games—people came to Rome from all over Italy and the neighbouring provinces to see the emperor shoot down deer, roebuck, lions and leopards. On one occasion he shot down 100 lions with 100 javelins. On another he shot off the heads of ostriches with crescent-headed arrows—and the birds continued to run around. These performances won him some admiration for his marksmanship, says Herodian. Dio gives even more details: he killed 100 bears on the first day, 'shooting down at them from the railing of the balustrade'.

> For the whole amphitheatre had been divided up by means of two intersecting cross-walls, which supported the gallery that ran its entire length. The animals, divided into two groups, could thus be speared more easily from any point, at short range. In the middle of the 'contest' he became tired. He took some chilled sweet vine in a club-shaped cup from a woman, and drank it in one gulp. At this both we and the people all shouted out straightaway the words so familiar at drinking-sessions: 'Long life!'

Dio hastens to defend himself against anyone who might think that he was 'sullying the dignity of history' by recording such details. These were the events that dominated life in the capital, and he was obliged to watch.

In the mornings the emperor shot down wild beasts. In the afternoons he fought as a gladiator—fighting with shield in right hand and sword in left, 'indeed he took great pride in the fact that he was left-handed'. 'Standing beside him as he fought,' Dio continues, 'were Aemilius Laetus the Prefect and Eclectus the chamberlain. When he had fought his bout— and, of course, won—he would then kiss them just as he was, through the visor of his helmet.' Whenever Commodus himself was fighting, the senators and knights were obliged to watch. 'Only Claudius Pompeianus the elder never appeared, but sent his sons, and did not come herself, preferring death rather than see the emperor, the son of Marcus, do such things.' The rest of the senators were not only made to attend but to join in chorused chants of admiration: 'You are Lord and you are first and most fortunate of all men! You are victorious, you will be victorious! From everlasting you are victorious, Amazonian!' The common people, according to Herodian, flocked in large numbers. They may have done so on the first day. But Dio notes that many did not come and others left after a brief look. For one thing, a rumour had got about that Commodus intended to pursue his self-identification with Hercules to the extent of shooting some of the spectators, who were thus to play the role of the

Stymphalian birds. Dio and his fellow-senators were made to feel the danger themselves: 'Having killed an ostrich and cut off its head, he came up to where we were sitting, holding the head in his left hand and raising the bloody sword in his right. He said nothing, but he wagged his head with a grin, showing that he would treat us likewise.'

Dio's reaction may be described as verging on the hysterical: 'Many of us would have been killed on the spot, for laughing at him—for it was laughter rather than the fear that took hold of us—if I had not chewed some laurel leaves that I took from my garland, and persuaded the others sitting next to me to do the same. By moving our jaws steadily we could thus conceal that fact that we were laughing.' During these games Commodus displayed the old champion racehorse from the Green stable, now put out to grass in the country. It was shown to the people at the last race of the year in the Circus Maximus, its hooves gilded, and a gilded skin on its back. A great shout went up: 'It is Pertinax!' On the last day, when he was about to begin his bout as a gladiator, Commodus handed his club to the like-named Prefect. Whether these things seemed as significant, at the time, as Dio suggests is another matter. But if Dio was superstitious, the urban plebs as a whole will not have been less so, and superstitions could be worked on. The episode of Pertinax the racehorse may have been engineered.[15]

According to Dio, Commodus' behaviour began to worry Laetus and Eclectus, and they tried to restrain him. Commodus replied with threats. Terrified, they formed a plot against him to preserve their own lives. It seems, still following Dio, that Commodus intended to kill both the new consuls on New Year's Day 193, and to take their place as sole consul, garbed in the costume of a gladiator. 'Let no one doubt this statement', he concludes. As corroboration he cites the fact that Commodus cut off the head of the 100-foot high statue of the Sun god outside the Colosseum and replaced it with his own portrait. He added a club and a bronze lion at its foot to give the composite figure the appearance of the new Roman Hercules. After taking Marcia into their confidence, Laetus and Eclectus chose New Year's Eve to carry out the murder, while the people were celebrating the holiday. (The court was at this time in the Vectilian House on the Caelian Hill; Commodus said he could not sleep in the Palace.) Marcia administered poison. Commodus vomited but did not succumb. He became suspicious and began to look threatening. The athlete Narcissus was then sent in to strangle him in his bath.[16] Even more explicitly than Dio, Herodian indicates that the decision to murder Commodus was taken suddenly, only a few hours before it was carried out. Neither suggests that Pertinax, who was at once offered the throne, had any inkling in advance. The *HA*, or its source Marius Maximus, knew better: Pertinax was involved in the conspiracy, which had its origin some while before, and was consumated when the moment was ripe.[17]

How many of the men set in positions of power by Laetus and Pertinax had been warned is another matter. The conspirators had chosen their time supremely well—during a festival, when even the praetorians were to a large extent unarmed and unprepared. One may suspect that in some of the excesses perpetrated by Commodus in the last weeks of his life he was egged on, not restrained, by Laetus and Eclectus. One may even wonder about the poisoned needles rumour—and the fire. It would have been a risk to encourage an autocrat who was already demented to indulge his megalomania further, to increase the fear and hatred with which he was regarded. But this would have made his murder more palatable to those who might otherwise have reacted with suspicion or sorrow. The only hint of this kind is provided by the *HA*: Commodus' 'insane wish that Rome should be named the "Colony of Commodus" was put into his head while listening to the blandishments of Marcia'. Perhaps the conspirators merely took the easier course, acquiescing in the behaviour of their insane master. It is still reasonable to conclude that they had been waiting for many months for the moment when they could kill him. After the murder, they naturally put out a detailed story to justify their action. It is hard to believe that Dio was really deceived: devotion to the memory of Pertinax must have obliged him to suppress the latter's participation. His urgent insistence that no one should disbelieve the plot to kill the consuls surely betrays him.[18]

It was probably already dark when Commodus was murdered. Laetus and Eclectus at once sent word to Pertinax. To make sure that it was not a trick, he sent his 'most trusted companion' to see the body. When this man had confirmed the report, Pertinax left for the camp of the Guard, in secret. His arrival caused some alarm at first, but Laetus and his agents allayed the troops' fears. Pertinax made a speech that Commodus had died a natural death and that Laetus and Eclectus had thrust the imperial power on him. He promised a donative of 12,000 sesterces per man. The end of his speech upset them: ' "There are many disturbing features about the present situation, fellow-soldiers, but with your help the rest of them will be right again".' What was intended, probably, as no more than a vague and generalised reassurance seemed to the men like a veiled threat. 'He was a mediocre orator', the *HA* records, adding that he was 'smooth [*blandus*] rather than good-natured, and was never regarded as straightforward [*simplex*].' The response was neither immediate nor unanimous. When a few, no doubt primed by Laetus, finally shouted out the acclamation, the rest followed. He was now *imperator*. It was not yet midnight.[18]

88

· IO ·

THE YEAR 193

PERTINAX WENT STRAIGHT FROM the praetorian camp to the senate house. It was still pitch dark and a mist was rising rapidly from the low ground around the Circus Maximus. He ordered the doors of the *curia* to be opened, but the janitor could not be found. Pertinax walked over to the Temple of Concord close by, and sat waiting while arrangements were made. Claudius Pompeianus then arrived to see him, lamenting the fate of Commodus. The old man had not been seen at Rome by Dio for at least the past ten years: he had been living in retirement. Had he been forewarned and asked to come to Rome to lend moral support to his former protégé? It is impossible to believe that news of the murder of Commodus could have reached his estate at Tarracina sixty miles away in time to get him to Rome before the night ended. His appearance so soon after Commodus' death is yet another indication that the story told by Herodian and in the surviving excerpts from Dio is propaganda. Pertinax urged Pompeianus to take the throne. Pompeianus could see that Pertinax was already invested with the *imperium* by the soldiers, and refused. It was no doubt a purely formal gesture.[1]

The *curia* was now opened and the consuls and magistrates with the other senators entered. It was still night. Pertinax did his best to greet them, although there was such a jostling throng that it was difficult for anyone to approach him. In 'an off-hand way' he announced to them that he had been chosen emperor by the soldiers, but 'I do not want the office and I shall resign it today, because of my age and poor health and the distressing situation'. His health was excellent, except for slight lameness: and he was a little overweight. The stated unwillingness to serve was another gesture. He was unanimously acclaimed as emperor. The consuls Clarus and Falco made speeches in his honour. Then a remarkable scene took place. The senators poured out a savage chanted litany of execration against the fallen tyrant. Marius Maximus gave the acclamations in full, and they are reproduced by the *HA*. The recurring theme came with the words *unco trahatur*, 'let him be dragged with the hook'. 'Put it to the vote! We all call for him to be dragged with the hook.' Pertinax intervened to inform them that Commodus had already been buried. At his orders, the procurator of the imperial estate, Livius Larensis, who had been guarding it, had handed the body over to the consul designate, Fabius Cilo. No doubt in his capacity as *sodalis Hadrianalis* Cilo had it placed in the Mausoleum of Hadrian. In due course a purely factual tombstone was placed there, giving Commodus his full name and titles, with his ancestry back to Nerva, and styling him as he had preferred to be known in his last two years, L. Aelius Aurelius Commodus, instead of M. Aurelius Commodus Antoninus. It will have cost no effort to deprive him of the names Marcus and Antoninus, that he had rejected and had so little deserved. The extravagant titles of the last months, Hercules Romanus, Amazonius, and the rest, were also left out, likewise Pius and Felix.[2]

Pertinax's report caused an outcry: 'Let the buried murderer be dug up and dragged by the hook!' One of the *pontifices*, Cingius Severus, gave it as his opinion, speaking as *pontifex* on behalf of the college, that Commodus had been wrongfully buried. The office of *pontifex maximus* was of course momentarily vacant; Cingius was no doubt the senior *pontifex* present. At least, he added, his statues must be overthrown and his name erased from all public and private records—and the names of the month should return to what they were before. The motion was evidently accepted. Renewed shouting broke out. Dio comments that 'all the shouts that they had been accustomed to chant in rhythmic fashion, in the theatres, to flatter Commodus, were repeated with certain changes that now made them sound ridiculous'. Pertinax finally spoke again. He expressed his thanks to the senate, and also, especially, to Laetus. At the mention of Laetus the consul Falco interjected: 'We can tell from this what sort of emperor you will be—the fact that we can see Laetus and Marcia, the instruments of Commodus' crimes, behind you.' Pertinax made a gently sarcastic reply. 'You are a young man, consul, and you do not know the necessity of obedience. They obeyed Commodus against their will, and as soon as they had an opportunity they showed what they had always been wanting.'[3]

The customary titles and powers were voted. Exceptionally, the title *pater patriae*, 'Father of his Country', which by tradition previous emperors had not accepted until a decent interval had elapsed, was granted as well, and Pertinax revived in his official style the title of *princeps senatus*. He then went to the Capitol to pay his vows to the gods. Meanwhile the senate voted his wife Flavia Titiana the title of Augusta, and that of Caesar for his son. These titles Pertinax rejected on their behalf. Finally he entered the Palace. When the tribune of the guard asked for the watchword, he replied *militemus*, 'let us be soldiers'. This did nothing to allay the nervousness that the praetorians had already begun to feel when he spoke to them in the camp. He had chosen it without thinking—it was the same watchword that he had given in all his commands. On the first day he entertained the magistrates and leading men at a banquet.[4]

The following day, 2 January, the statues of Commodus were over-thrown. And Pertinax gave the same watchword. The soldiers reacted unfavourably. In any case, they disliked the prospect of service under a sixty-six-year-old emperor. On 3 January the annual oath of loyalty had to be taken. During the ceremony some of the praetorians attempted to stage a coup, and dragged a senator named Triarius Maternus into the camp. Maternus fled, naked, came to Pertinax in the Palace, and then left the city. No action was taken against him.[5]

The lesson was not lost on Pertinax. 'He ratified the concessions that Commodus had made to the soldiers and the veterans', no doubt on 7 January, the normal day when time-expired men serving in the capital received their discharge. At the same time he introduced a whole series of proposals in the senate. Treason trials were abolished, the exiles were restored, and the good name of those who had been unjustly executed was restored. The imperial treasury was virtually empty, and the donative to the troops, coupled with a bounty to the plebs, made matters worse. An obvious way to raise funds rapidly lay to hand: an auction of Commodus' luxury goods, including the extravagant costumes in which he had performed, and the imperial carriages. These were 'the very latest masterpieces of the art': some had seats that could be moved round into the shade or the breeze, others were equipped with mileometers and clocks, or were designed 'for the indulgence of his vices', as the *HA* puts it. The imperial household included large numbers of concubines, buffoons and other non-essential personnel. These too were sold, bringing in immense sums. Some of them, the *HA* adds maliciously, 'found their way back to minister to the old man's pleasure'.[6]

Pertinax was clearly determined to attack the economic crisis by drastic means. The change of policy that he instituted was dramatised by the auction. It can be observed in the change he made in the coinage. After the drastic debasement of 190–2, the silver content was pushed up to the standard of Vespasian. The aim must have been to restore confidence where he thought it mattered. But if that meant a short-term belt-tightening, there were risks. Herodian outlines a programme designed to improve agriculture and to remit newly instituted customs tariffs. He also tried to regulate the senate. Cleander's corrupt regime had upset seniority. Pertinax ruled that those who had held the praetorship should take precedence over those adlected. Ironically, he himself had been adlected *inter praetorios* by Marcus. The *HA* reports that there was ill feeling, doubtless reflecting the opinion of Marius Maximus, one of those affected; one reason for the slightly mixed verdict on Pertinax in the *HA*. During

January Pertinax made arrangements for the next year's magistrates. Cassius Dio (wholeheartedly in favour of Pertinax in his *History*) was designated praetor.[7]

One of the first steps taken after the new emperor had been installed must have been to inform the provincial governors of what had taken place. Some may not have been surprised. But many were suspicious that it was a trick, a test of their loyalty by Commodus, and imprisoned the couriers. The season of the year did not facilitate rapid transmission of messages. Still, in 69 the news of the revolt of the Rhine on 1 January, sent by the procurator at Trier, reached Rome in less than nine days. There is no reason to believe that the news of Pertinax's accession took any longer than this to get to the northern armies. It may have taken longer to reach overseas provinces. In 68 the freedman Icelus had reached Galba at Tarraco with the news of Nero's death after only seven days' journey from Italy. But that was in the summer. Nonetheless, this time the news reached Novius Rufus, the governor of Hispania Tarraconensis, by the beginning of February at latest. A decision that he made settling a dispute was issued under the new emperor's authority on 11 February. In Egypt the news was not issued until 6 March. Mantennius Sabinus may not have received word until shortly before making the announcement, for winter navigation from Italy to Alexandria was not easy. When his proclamation was issued, the wife and son of Pertinax were given the titles which Pertinax had rejected. It will be remembered that Sabinus' wife was a neighbour of the wife of Pertinax. Some provincial governors may have waited for quite some time before announcing what had happened. They will have wished to make absolutely certain that it was true, in their own interests: it had been Commodus' practice to keep the children of provincial governors at Rome as guarantees of fidelity.[8]

Septimius reacted to the news characteristically. After making sacrifice and administering the oath of allegiance to the new emperor, he returned to his quarters in the evening, fell asleep and dreamed a portentous dream. In his dream he saw a large and noble horse carrying Pertinax along the central portion of the Sacred Way. But when the horse reached the *comitia* at the far end of the Forum, it unseated Pertinax and threw him to the ground. While Septimius stood there, the horse slipped under him, took him up and carried him on its back. Then it stopped, in the middle of the Forum, lifting him up high so that he was seen and cheered by all. This dream, according to Herodian, was the climax of the long series of supernatural signs that had fed his burning ambition. It finally confirmed him in the belief that he would get everything that he hoped for.

Meanwhile, he was already a key figure. Pertinax 'did not remove any of those whom Commodus had put in charge of affairs'. He said that he was waiting for the anniversary of the founding of the city, 21 April. Considering that most of those holding office had probably been appointed with the approval, if not by the direct nomination, of Laetus and Pertinax himself, this is not surprising. But there were vacancies to fill. The obvious one was the City Prefecture, which he had held himself. He appointed his father-in-law Flavius Sulpicianus. The only other recorded promotion that he made was 'a favour to Septimius'. A man whom Pertinax himself, when proconsul of Africa, had condemned for corrupt practices, was given some unspecified post. The name is given in an extract from Dio as 'Fluvius'. This will be one of the Fulvii, Septimius' mother's family, almost certainly its best known member, Fulvius Plautianus. According to Herodian, he had in fact been condemned for certain offences before 193. Plautianus was soon to enter the stage at Rome. It is plausible that he was now given some post by Pertinax. He may have become *praefectus vehiculorum*, 'prefect of vehicles', that is, supervisor of the imperial posting-system, a vital role at this time.[9]

Pertinax relied a good deal on Aemilius Laetus, the Guard Prefect. At the beginning, Laetus was full of praise for the new emperor. It was no doubt with pride and pleasure that he despatched couriers to overtake a barbarian delegation, on its way back home with a subsidy in gold that Commodus had handed over. The gold was demanded back. The envoys were to tell their people that Pertinax was now ruler. Laetus knew that the name of Pertinax carried weight beyond the Danube. As governor of the principal military province on the Danube, Septimius had no doubt been responsible both for the original passage of the envoys to Rome and for their return.[10]

A new foreign policy was implied by this episode. At home a vital matter was the safeguarding and improvement of the corn supply. If this should fail, the urban plebs, which had shown in 190 that it was still a force to be reckoned with, might get out of hand again. In early March Pertinax visited Ostia to inspect the arrangements. The organisation of Rome's food supply, the Annona, was a vast and complex operation, directed from the city by the Prefect, the third most senior equestrian official in the empire. It is not known who occupied this key post in 192–3. But the procurator responsible for the safe arrival of the Annona at Ostia was a man from Emesa, the brother-in-law of Julia Domna, C. Julius Avitus Alexianus. Pertinax doubtless met him at the port.[11]

In his absence a second attempt was made to stage a coup, again by the praetorians. This time their candidate was the consul Falco, and again the attempt fizzled out. Falco was declared a public enemy by the senate, but Pertinax asked that he should be pardoned. 'May it never happen that any senator should be put to death, even for just cause, while I am emperor,' he said, jumping to his feet. At the same meeting of the senate he spoke bitterly of the soldiers' ingratitude, claiming that he had given them as much as Marcus and Verus at their accession, in spite of having far smaller funds available. This was not quite the truth. Pertinax's donative was not all that large. There were many soldiers and freedmen present in the *curia* and they reacted unfavourably to the exaggerated claim. Pertinax had long had a reputation for meanness. But, whether or not this was deserved, what he was now trying to do was to restore 'sound money'. His restoration of the denarius must inevitably have meant a reduction in the number that could be struck, and a lack of funds.[12]

The Falco affair is mysterious. Dio asserts that Laetus and the praetorians were behind it, and selected Falco. One may doubt this, especially in view of Falco's bitter attack on the Prefect at the senate's meeting on 1 January, unless Laetus engineered the coup, with the deliberate intention of suppressing it, for purposes of his own. The *HA* is of some help, although the text is fragmentary: the biographer reports that, according to many people, Falco did not know that he was being put forward as a candidate for the throne. In other words, he was framed; and show trials followed. Some soldiers were executed, but Falco himself was spared. Laetus had this done, but in the name of Pertinax, whose unpopularity with the Guard increased sharply. Laetus' own relations with Pertinax are said to have deteriorated—the emperor found fault with him because of 'the foolish advice he had given'. This may be true, but it is hardly sufficient as a motive for Laetus to have launched the final attempt to remove Pertinax, which soon followed.[13]

The successful coup came on 28 March. Pertinax had planned a visit to the Athenaeum for a poetry recital, but changed his mind and sent his escort back to the barracks. The rest of the Guard was there that day. A disturbance broke out—what started it is not recorded. Pertinax apparently had time to send Sulpicianus, his father-in-law, to the camp, and to summon a special meeting of the senate. But while he was returning to the Palace some two or three hundred men were on their way with drawn swords. They arrived just as Pertinax was inspecting the Palace slaves in the portico. The *HA* states that the troops were urged on by the Palace staff, who hated Pertinax. The emperor, informed of their entry by his wife, sent Laetus to meet them. But the Prefect covered up his head and went to his own house. Dio says that Pertinax could have ordered the *vigiles*, 'the night watch', and *equites singulares Augusti*, 'Horse Guards', who were in attendance, to kill the mutineers, or at least could have locked himself inside the Palace. Instead, he went out to confront them in person. The men were overawed at first when he spoke to them, at length and in a serious tone, and sheathed their swords. Then a Tungrian named

Tausius, shouting out, 'This sword the soldiers have sent you!', fell upon him. He covered his head with his toga, with a prayer to Jupiter the Avenger, and was struck down. Only Eclectus defended him, and even managed to wound two of the assailants before being killed. The soldiers cut off the emperor's head and stuck it on a spear. That was the end of Pertinax: he had reigned eighty-seven days.[14]

In contrast to the coup of 31 December, no successor was ready. Laetus may perhaps bear some negative responsibility for his refusal to make any resistance. But the fact that he did not produce a new candidate and did not participate in what followed, shows that he was not the moving spirit this time. It can only be explained as an act of mutiny. Only eight years before Perennis had fallen victim to a band of mutinous troops from the British army. Subsequent events in Dio's lifetime were to prove that the possibility of such outbreaks was constantly increasing. By the mid-third century no emperor was to be safe from his own troops for more than a few years.[15]

When Sulpicianus heard the news he at once began a move to have himself declared emperor. As City Prefect he commanded the Urban Cohorts, and may have hoped for their support. Convincing promises might have won over the praetorians as well. But all the City troops will have been wary of accepting as emperor the father-in-law of one who had just been murdered. Two tribunes of the Guard recognised the difficulty and went to look for an alternative candidate. They waited outside the senate-house, and there they found their man. Didius Julianus, with his son-in-law Cornelius Repentinus (whose father had been Guard Prefect thirty years before), had come to attend the meeting that Pertinax had summoned; but the doors of the *curia* were closed. The tribunes urged him to seize the throne. He pointed out that another man was already in possession, but they overrode his objections and took him to the camp. Sulpicianus' followers refused to let him through the gates.[16]

There ensued one of the most notorious episodes in the history of Rome. Two rival candidates bid for the throne, as if at an auction. Eventually Julianus got up on the wall. He warned the men not to choose an emperor who would avenge the death of Pertinax and gave written promises that he would restore the good name of Commodus. When Sulpicianus reached the figure of 20,000 sesterces per man, Julianus raised his bid by 5000, shouting it out in a loud voice and holding up his fingers as well as to indicate the amount. This won him the throne.[17]

Towards evening he came to the Forum to meet the senate in the *curia*. He had appointed two new Guard Prefects. Laetus' career was at an end. Julianus was escorted by a vast number of praetorians carrying their standards as if prepared for battle. The senators were nervous, not least

Dio, who had successfully prosecuted Julianus in court on several occasions. Julianus told the senate that the throne was vacant, and that he was the best qualified to fill it. The claim was not as boastful or empty as Dio makes it sound. He was possibly the senior consular living, with the sole exception of Claudius Pompeianus. He had had a long career in the imperial service, having commanded a legion and governed four imperial provinces. He was well-connected. During the reign of Commodus he had been in trouble several times—almost a guarantee of acceptability to the senate. (On the last occasion he had been protected by Laetus.) Pertinax had respected him also. The two men's careers had indeed been closely parallel since 175, when they had been colleagues in the consulship. Shortly before his death Pertinax had been guest of honour at the betrothal ceremony of Julianus' daughter. Pertinax had told the girl's fiancé to respect Julianus, 'my colleague and successor'—not only had they shared the *fasces* but Julianus had succeeded Pertinax as proconsul of Africa in 190. Pertinax's remark seemed like an omen, in retrospect. A comment by Julianus at this meeting of the senate was viewed in a similar light later on. When the consul designate formally proposed the motion 'That Didius Julianus be declared emperor', Julianus said, 'Add "Severus".' His full names were M. Didius Severus Julianus.[18]

Julianus had no fears about either the British or Danubian armies. He had connections through his mother with Hadrumetum, the home of the governor of Britain Clodius Albinus. Furthermore, his son-in-law Repentinus' origin was Simitthu in Numidia. These African links may have served to inspire his confidence in the reaction of Septimius and other northern commanders to his accession. But whatever his relations had been with the governor of Syria, he soon had cause to fear him. On 29 March the plebs shouted insults at him as he went to the senate-house and even threw stones at him. Dio records that 'they all began shouting, as if by preconcerted plan, calling him a thief and a parricide'. At first Julianus took it coolly and promised them money. But this failed to pacify them and he had to use force. A mob then poured into the Circus Maximus, where they spent that night and the following day. They changed slogans, calling on Pescennius Niger and the Syrian army to come to their support.[19]

Julianus' prospects were slim. He could rely only on the praetorians, to whom he had paid a donative even higher than he had promised. But the Guard had not succeeded in imposing an emperor of its choice for more than a century and a half, since the accession of Claudius. With the death of Nero 'the secret of the empire was made public: that an emperor could be made elsewhere than at Rome'. The provincial armies had learned this lesson in 68–9 and again in 97. Beside, the Guard had done no fighting since the Marcomannic war ended in 180.[20]

The news of the attempted coups of Maternus and Falco will have prepared Septimius and his fellow-governors for rapid action. It is not hard to believe that a contingency plan had been concerted by 28 March, if indeed Laetus had not made arrangements with Septimius and others in 192 in case something were to go wrong on 31 December. The news of Pertinax's murder had to be taken some 683 Roman miles from Rome to Carnuntum—if Septimius was still at the Pannonian capital. He might well have moved to the south-western borders of his province to await developments, when the news of the Falco coup reached him. He had allies in Rome, his kinsman Fulvius Plautianus for one. His brother-in-law, husband of his sister Octavilla, may have been at Rome. There were also various relatives of his wife, including her sister's husband Avitus Alexianus. Fabius Cilo, who had perhaps by now held his consulship, will have been another supporter. Someone must have rushed the news to him. He may have known the fate of Pertinax by the evening of 1 April. It would take little time to ensure the support of the legates of the three legions in his province and the governors of Raetia, Noricum and Lower Pannonia. The governor of Lower Pannonia, C. Valerius Pudens, later to receive high office from Septimius, must have given him unstinted backing at the time. He could rely on Geta in Lower Moesia. But he will have sent messages to the two German provinces and to Dacia and Upper Moesia as well. It is impossible to tell how long he had to wait for replies from all these provinces. By 9 April, the twelfth day after the murder of Pertinax, he felt secure enough to act. The Carnuntum legion XIV Gemina, and no doubt some other troops, were summoned, and he was saluted as emperor. The *HA* states that he tried to resist—*repugnans*. This was the conventional display of reluctance. He had no intention of refusing. Septimius depicted himself to the troops as the avenger of Pertinax. One of his three Upper Pannonian legions, I Adiutrix, had been commanded by Pertinax twenty years before. Some of the men still in the legion would have served under Pertinax. The same applied even more strongly to the six legions in the Moesias and Dacia. Septimius emphasised his attachment to the murdered emperor by adding that name to his new style: 'Imperator Caesar L. Septimius Severus Pertinax Augustus.' He will have refrained from laying claim to the tribunician power, which could only be conferred in Rome. There is one other thing for which Septimius may have waited before he acted on 9 April: news that his sons were safe. At any rate, one of his first actions on deciding to bid for the throne was to send a secret message for them to be brought to him. Fabius Cilo may have been the man who ensured their safety.[21]

Preparations for the march on Rome would already have begun before the proclamation. But there would still be much to do. A particular concern was the attitude of Clodius Albinus. Since Albinus was from Hadrumetum, the home of Julianus' mother, he could not be regarded as reliable. With his three legions and the enormous number of auxiliary regiments in Britain, he could pose a serious threat to Septimius's western flank. Septimius sent emissaries offering the title of Caesar, which carried with it the prospect of succession, if anything should happen to himself. Since his own elder son Bassianus was barely five, the offer was surely genuine, worth Albinus' while to accept. He now styled himself 'D. Clodius Septimius Albinus Caesar', and remained in Britain.[22]

Before Septimius began his march, news may have reached him that Niger had proclaimed himself emperor at Antioch, and that the east, including Egypt, had gone over to him. Niger thus had a force of ten legions at his disposal, against Septimius' sixteen from the Rhine and Danube armies, as well as, in theory, the three from Britain. In the meantime Septimius' agents will have been soliciting support from Novius Rufus, the governor of Hither Spain, who had one legion, and from the legate of III Augusta in Numidia, Naevius Quadratianus. It was forthcoming in both cases. Niger's move cannot have come as a surprise. Reports of the murder of Pertinax must have been followed almost at once by news of the riots in his favour by the Roman plebs. Septimius' prime concern was to seize Rome. The east could wait; but a force was sent from Geta's Lower Moesian army down into Thrace.[23]

Inscriptions provide details about two men who played a vital role in the *expeditio urbica*, as the march was styled. M. Rossius Vitulus, a former equestrian officer who had served in both Germany and Pannonia, was appointed quartermaster-general, *praepositus annonae*. He was probably a native of Tergeste (Trieste), hence would have personal knowledge of the territory through which the march was to go. L. Valerius Valerianus, a former equestrian officer and procurator, possibly of Pannonian origin, was given command over the cavalry. The advance guard was led by Julius Laetus, who had undoubtedly been serving in one of the northern provinces, if not as a legionary legate in Upper Pannonia, perhaps as governor of Raetia or Noricum.[24]

While Septimius and Niger were seizing control of most of the empire, Julianus blithely had coins issued proclaiming himself 'ruler of the world', *rector orbis*, and asserting the 'unity of the armies', *concordia militaris*. Septimius was declared a public enemy by the senate, at his request (as Niger no doubt was also), when the news of the revolt reached Rome. The soldiers in his army were offered an amnesty if they withdrew their support before a certain date. One Valerius Catullinus was designated

Septimius' successor. Envoys of consular rank were selected to take Julianus' appeal to the northern armies. They included Vespronius Candidus, a former governor of Dacia. A more practical step was the assignment of a former officer in the secret police, *frumentarii*, M. Aquilius Felix, to the task of assassinating Septimius. The 'murder of senators' had been this man's speciality.[25]

According to Herodian, Septimius and his army appeared on the borders of Italy before it was known that he had been proclaimed. At all events, Julianus failed to block the passes. The best he could manage was to send one of the Guard Prefects, Tullius Crispinus, to take command of the Ravenna fleet and lead some resistance with it. But Septimius, proceeding via Emona (Ljubljana) and Aquileia, met no resistance in taking Ravenna, and Crispinus fled.

Meanwhile Julianus was attempting to construct fortifications at Rome. The city became an armed camp. Even elephants designed for performance at the games were conscripted for military use. But, according to Dio, who watched the proceedings, Julianus' preparations were futile and ineffective: 'At times we were overcome with laughter.' The praetorians were loth to undertake the kind of military engineering at which the legions were so skilled, and some of them hired substitutes to do the work for them. The marines summoned from the Misenum fleet could not drill properly. And the elephants could not be trained to carry towers and threw their drivers. At this stage, Julianus had Laetus and Marcia murdered—he reckoned that Laetus was going to support Septimius.

However, Septimius was continuing to move at speed. The senatorial envoys went over to him, not before the unpopular Vespronius Candidus had nearly been lynched by the troops. The news that a senatorial deputation was on its way had at first caused Septimius some anxiety, but as it turned out he managed, by bribing them, to induce the envoys to address the troops in his favour and then to desert to him. Likewise Aquilius Felix adroitly changed sides. Julianus began to panic. He proposed to the senate that the priests, Vestal Virgins and senators should go to meet the advancing army as suppliants. But his authority was already negligible: the motion was rejected after a speech by Plautius Quintillus, himself an augur and a son-in-law of Marcus Aurelius. After contemplating a mass purge of the senate, and then abandoning the idea, Julianus had a decree passed making Septimius joint ruler with himself. He sent Tullius Crispinus to announce this to Septimius, and meanwhile nominated a third Guard Prefect, Veturius Macrinus, who he knew had already been appointed to this post by Septimius. Crispinus was intercepted by the Septimian advance guard under Julius Laetus, whose recommendation to put him to death was authorised by Septimius.

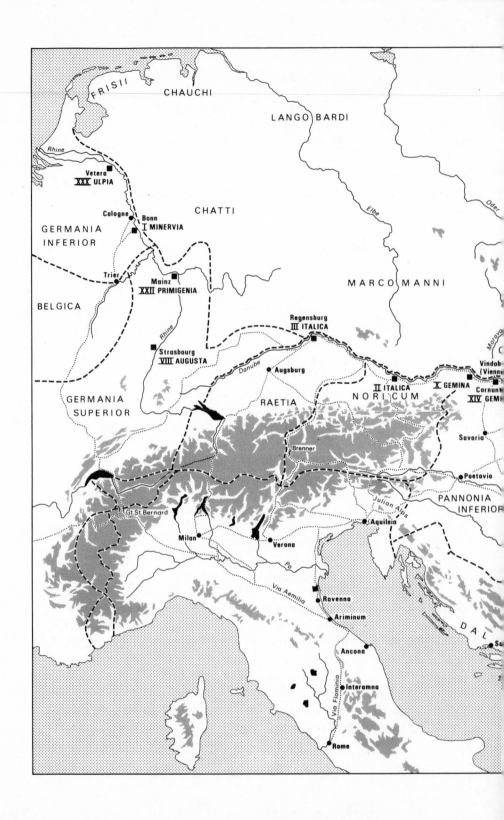

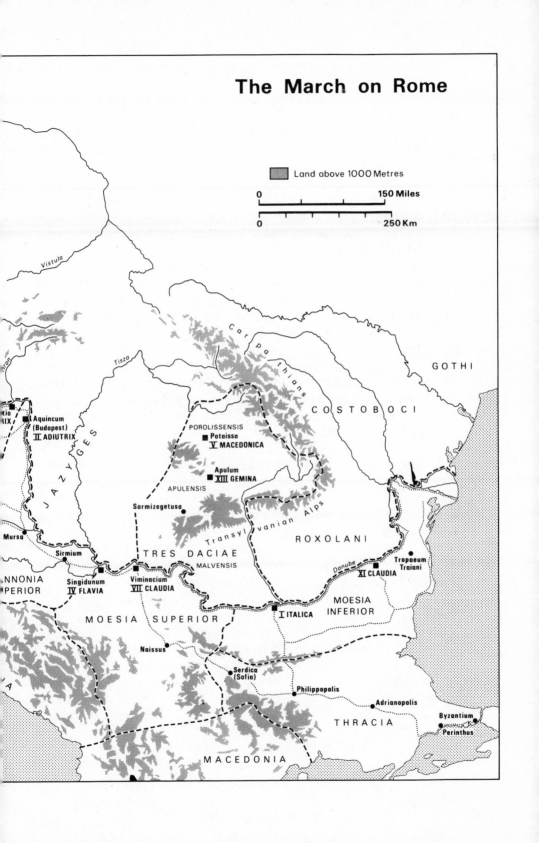

The March on Rome

Land above 1000 Metres

| 0 | | | | 150 Miles |
| 0 | | | | | 250 Km |

Vistula

Tisza

Carpathians

GOTHI

COSTOBOCI

RIX

**Aquincum
(Budapest)
II ADIUTRIX**

J A Z Y G E S

POROLISSENSIS
**Potaissa
V MACEDONICA**

APULENSIS

**Apulum
XIII GEMINA**

Sarmizegetusa

Transylvanian Alps

ROXOLANI

Mursa

Sirmium

Danube

**Tropaeum
Traiani**
XI CLAUDIA

**NNONIA
PERIOR**

**Singidunum
IV FLAVIA**

T R E S   D A C I A E

MALVENSIS

**Viminacium
VII CLAUDIA**

I ITALICA

MOESIA
INFERIOR

M O E S I A   S U P E R I O R

Naissus

**Serdica
(Sofia)**

Philippopolis

Adrianopolis

T H R A C I A

Byzantium
Perinthus

M A C E D O N I A

Julianus replaced him with Flavius Juvenalis, presumably, like Veturius Macrinus, thought to be acceptable to Septimius. Septimius' agents were now active in Rome itself, posting placards which announced his programme.[26]

Julianus had reached the end of the road. He again summoned the senate and demanded advice, but no one would commit himself. As a final despairing gesture he appealed to Claudius Pompeianus to share the rule with him, but Pompeianus revived the excuses that had kept him out of public life under Commodus, old age and weak eyesight. The praetorians received a direct order from Septimius, to keep the murderers of Pertinax under arrest. It was obeyed, and the fact was announced to the consul Silius Messala. He summoned the senate to the Athenaeum: Julianus was condemned to death, Septimius proclaimed emperor, and Pertinax deified. Julianus was killed by a common soldier in the Palace, deserted by all except his son-in-law Repentinus and the Prefect Flavius Genialis. He had been emperor for sixty-six days. It was 1 June. Septimius was at Interamna, just over fifty miles (80 km) to the north. Seven and a half weeks had elapsed since his proclamation and he had won Rome without a battle. The march must have been exhausting. Surrounded day and night by a picked bodyguard of 600 men who did not take off their breastplates, and sharing their hardships himself, he had delayed at no city in his path except to address a few words to the people and make sacrifice.

Messengers from Pescennius Niger were now beginning to appear, bearing proclamations to the people and letters to the senate. Septimius had them intercepted, and at the same time sent Plautianus to search for and seize Niger's children. The children of Asellius Aemilianus were also taken into custody. Reports indicated that the proconsul of Asia, after some hesitation, had thrown in his lot with Niger.[27]

Immediately after the meeting of the senate a deputation of 100 senators went to greet Septimius, who remained encamped at Interamna 'as though moving through enemy territory'. When they arrived they were searched for concealed weapons and he remained armed in their presence, with armed guards standing round. The next day the entire Palace staff—slaves and freedmen—appeared. They may have brought a supply of ready cash with them, for Septimius now presented each member of the senatorial delegation with seven hundred and twenty gold pieces. Those who wished were invited to remain in his entourage for the final stages of his journey.[28]

Septimius' next and most pressing concern was the Guard. First he formally reappointed Flavius Juvenalis Prefect. The only other record of a man with these names is of a centurion in the Numidian legion III Augusta in the year 162. It would have made an appropriate choice for

Septimius to have put an African who had risen through the centurionate in command of the Guard. The other Prefect, Veturius Macrinus, cannot have been a young man either. He had served as Prefect of Egypt at the beginning of Commodus' reign, but had received no further promotion. He must have been out of the service for ten years.[29]

Meanwhile Septimius issued secret instructions to the Guard tribunes and centurions. To the troops he issued a proclamation: they were to put on parade uniform, leave their weapons in the camp, take the oath of allegiance and assemble to greet him outside the city. Its language conveyed the implications that obedience would ensure their continued service, and the officers paraded the men. Septimius mounted the tribunal for what was expected to be a speech of welcome. But a detachment from his expeditionary force was on its way to the *castra praetoria*, where they seized the armoury and manned the gates. As the praetorians waited for the emperor to speak, other Danubian soldiers surrounded the parade ground. Then Septimius began. He attacked them bitterly for their treachery to Pertinax, telling them that even if they had not actually killed him, their failure to kill the assassins made them guilty. He formally discharged them, and ordered them to remove themselves beyond the hundredth milestone from the City on pain of death. They were to take off their uniforms and ceremonial daggers, inlaid with silver and gold. Most complied, those that hesitated had their belts and uniforms ripped off. The mounted men were told to let their horses go. One horse refused to leave his rider, but kept following and neighing. The man killed the horse and then himself; 'And,' says Dio, 'it seemed to those that watched that the horse too was glad to die.'

This was the end of the old élite corps of the Roman imperial army. The praetorians, nearly all Italians and from provincial families of Italian stock, had had a disproportionate influence on the course of events for over two hundred years. Service in the Guard was regarded with envy by the legionaries. The pay was much higher, conditions were more favourable and the length of service was shorter. Septimius began at once, during June, to form his new Guard, larger than the old one and manned by soldiers who had served in the northern legions. In partial compensation for the exclusion of Italians from the Guard, he increased the size of the Urban Cohorts and the *vigiles*.[30]

There had been panic at Rome among the civilian population, as well as among the guilty praetorians, as Septimius approached, not without reason. Septimius himself, after advancing as far as the gates uniformed and on horseback, dismounted and changed into civilian dress. But the entire expeditionary force, both infantry and cavalry, escorted him fully armed. Dio's account of 'the most brilliant spectacle of any that I have seen', fails to give an objective impression. It was written only a few years after the event, as part of the history of the civil wars that he presented to Septimius, and later incorporated, with some changes, into his complete work. He describes how the whole city was decked with garlands of flowers and with laurel branches and shone with the light of torches and burning incense. (Tertullian implies that only the Christians failed to participate: Dio, if he knew or cared, in accordance with his practice does not mention them.) This much of Dio's account is no doubt factual. But when he goes on to add that the white-robed citizens were radiant-faced as they uttered shouts of good omen, one may suspect that his language is disingenuous. When he says that the soldiers 'stood out conspicuously in their armour as they moved about like participants in some holiday procession', it is clear that tact has triumphed over accuracy. One must turn to the *HA* for a truer version. Septimius went first to the Capitol to make sacrifices. Then to the Palace, preceded by his legionaries trailing the standards of the disbanded Guard, a sign of his bloodless victory. The soldiers were quartered all over the City, in temples and porticoes and even in the shrines on the Palatine. Septimius' entry inspired 'hatred and fear', the biographer concludes, for the soldiers seized goods without paying for them and threatened to lay the city waste.[31]

The following day Septimius came to the *curia*, once more escorted by an armed guard. In a speech he justified his seizure of power, claiming that his coup had been made in self-defence: Julianus had sent men 'notorious for assassinating generals to murder him'. Most will have known that Julianus took this step only after Septimius' march had begun. Still, he was under no necessity to be apologetic: as he told them, he had come to avenge Pertinax, whom the senate had clearly preferred to Julianus. But to make it clear that no purge was to begin, he asked that a decree be passed, 'that the emperor shall not be permitted to put a senator to death without consulting the senate'. One Julius Solon, who had bought his senatorial rank from Cleander, had the honour of introducing the formal motion. While the session was in progress the soldiers began to create a disturbance outside, demanding that the senate grant them a bounty. The sum that they named was 10,000 sesterces—2500 denarii—the equivalent of eight years' pay, per man. They claimed as a precedent the grant to Octavian's soldiers in 43 BC. It is remarkable that the soldiers should have had knowledge of an event 235 years before. No doubt this colossal donative had become part of legionary folklore. Septimius was eventually able to pacify them with a tenth of what they asked, and then sent them away. It cannot have been easy to raise funds after two emperors had given out donatives. One may wonder whether steps were taken to recover the money Julianus had lavished on the praetorians—150 million sesterces. It was probably to pay the donative to Septimius' troops that a special issue of coins was struck. They bear the names of all but one of the Rhine, Danube and Dacian legions.[32]

His next public act was to order the state funeral and deification of Pertinax; and at his request, the senate formally bestowed the name Pertinax on him. Dio's elaborate description of the ceremonies has been preserved by Xiphilinus. A wooden platform was built in the Forum near the Rostra and on it a shrine surrounded by ivory and gold columns. A funeral bier, likewise of ivory and gold, was placed within, on which lay a wax effigy of Pertinax in triumphal dress. The emperor, with the senators and their wives, approached, wearing mourning. Then busts of famous Romans were carried past the bier, followed by male choirs singing a funeral lament, symbolic bronze representations of the provinces and the city guilds. More portrait busts were then carried past, of famous men from all nations. The troops rode and marched past and finally funeral gifts were laid before the bier. Then Septimius mounted the Rostra and delivered the customary eulogy, to shouts of approval from the senators. When it was over the bier was taken down by the priests and magistrates—including those designated for the following year, of whom Dio was one. They handed the bier to pall-bearers from the equestrian order, who proceeded to the Campus Martius, followed by the senators, 'some of us beating our breast and others playing a dirge on the flute'. Septimius came last of all. A three-storey funeral pyre had been built, surmounted by a gilded chariot that Pertinax had once driven. The offerings and the bier were placed in it, Septimius and the relatives of Pertinax kissed the effigy, and then withdrew to a safe distance. Magistrates, *equites* and soldiers paraded round the pyre and then the consuls fired it. When it began to blaze, an eagle flew out and upwards, symbolising that Pertinax had been deified. The worship of the new god was to be supervised by the *sodales* appointed for the cult of the Antonine Emperors, and Pertinax's son was made *flamen Helvianus*.[33]

The ceremony was an important gesture, which would give some credence to his claimed intention of modelling his administration on that of Pertinax—and that of Pertinax's own exemplar, Marcus Aurelius. Now there were more practical matters to attend to, first and foremost the preparation for the campaign against Niger. Septimius refused for the time being to make any public reference to his rival. But one of the first acts, before he reached Rome, must have been to despatch his friend Fabius Cilo to take command of a force at Perinthus, to prevent Niger's troops advancing any further into Thrace. Another army, under Marius Maximus, was already besieging Byzantium.[34]

The mint began striking coins in the names of Septimius and of

Albinus. These first issues stressed the generosity of the emperor, presumably indicating that he had issued a *congiarium* to the plebs, and the 'fertility of the age,' as well as the 'loyalty of the legions'. The *saeculum frugiferum* had already been advertised on the coinage of Pertinax. Its reappearance now is interesting. It was also the Latin name for an African god, the patron deity of Hadrumetum, home of Albinus. The Caesar's own coins stress the 'divine foresight' by which Septimius provided against future eventualities with his choice of successor. The first coins struck for Julia Domna celebrate the goddess Venus, both Venus Victrix who had won Caesar his Civil War victories, and Venus Genetrix, the divine ancestress of the original Julian family.[35]

Meanwhile Septimius and Albinus were designated to hold the consulship jointly for 194. Septimius had little time for civilian matters. He left Rome less than thirty days after his triumphant entry. He did find time on 27 June to give an adjudication on a point of law, preserved as the first of over 150 rescripts from him in the Code of Justinian. Interpretation of the law was to be a major feature of his reign. In the capital, particularly in the emperor's absence, the Prefect of the City played a preeminent role in the administration of justice. Immediately after his arrival he had appointed a friend named Bassus to the office. Just before the expedition departed, Bassus resigned. Perhaps Septimius had decided to take him to the east, or possibly he had been intended merely as a stop-gap, until a suitable man was available. At any rate, the person now appointed was C. Domitius Dexter, once the successor of Pertinax as governor of Syria, and hence perhaps Septimius' own commanding officer there for a short time. Undoubtedly the City Prefect would have exceptional importance during the absence of a new emperor. The same applies even more strongly to the commanders of the Guard—for some of the Guard at least would be left in Rome, with one of the Prefects. But no certain information is available. All that can be said is that the sources give scarcely any hint of trouble for Septimius in Rome during his absence, in spite of the earlier support for his rival.[36]

There were others besides the City Prefect left behind to watch his interests. The ex-centurion Aquilius Felix was one. He was placed in simultaneous control of three important bureaux, public works, Crown property (*patrimonium*) and the private property of the Antonine family (*ratio privata*). This would be a strategic role; and he could use it as a cloak for other activities. Steps were also taken to put new men into the senate. Ti. Claudius Claudianus, an African from Rusicade in Numidia, was made praetor. He had been serving as equestrian officer in Septimius' army, and was soon to take up a legionary command in Dacia. Another new senator was Claudius Gallus, perhaps a kinsman of Claudianus. He too was shortly to have an important position. A third was Julia's brother-in-law, the Ostia procurator, Julius Avitus Alexianus. Septimius' kinsman Plautianus, no doubt already promoted to a high equestrian post, was to accompany the expedition. He soon became the dominant figure in the new emperor's entourage, almost constantly at Septimius' side.[37]

The prime consideration at this time must have been the raising of new troops. Septimius had perhaps already decided to create three new legions, although he could hardly have formed them before his departure. His stated pretext for these military preparations may have been an expedition against the Parthians: the new legions were to be called I, II and III Parthicae. But it is probable that the *HA* is correct that Septimius officially set out 'to set eastern affairs in order', *ad conponendum orientis statum*. This terminology will have deceived no one, even though news from the east was still being suppressed. Septimius held a trump card. In his custody were the children of all those in official positions in the east, except for those of Niger himself. Plautianus was still hunting down Niger's children. Septimius doubtless hoped that when they fell into his hands he could use them as a bargaining counter. Meanwhile he ordered 'a legion to Africa', according to the *HA*, apparently fearing that Niger would send forces through Egypt and Cyrenaica to seize the province. This would cut off Rome's food supply. Further, Septimius' home town would fall into his rival's hands. Septimius' anxiety may have been lessened by the confidence that Mantennius Sabinus would try to swing Egypt out of Niger's camp at the first opportunity. For the time being it may be assumed that the legate of III Augusta was instructed to send detachments to Tripolitania. But it is not impossible that elements from the northern legions were shipped from Italy. Africa was worth defending.[38]

The vast palace household now had, in Septimius, their fourth new master in less than six months. He may have known some of the principal freedmen already and must have selected some of them and of the imperial slaves, to go with him. At the higher level of the secretariat and the great departments of state—*a rationibus, a libellis*, and the rest—he may have made changes now; but was probably obliged to take over most of the personnel. The *familia Caesaris*, certainly, was a major element in continuity, coups d'état or civil wars notwithstanding. Septimius' elevation gave him a further privilege of which he probably availed himself at once. Galen, the doyen of the medical profession, was at Rome and readily prescribed for Septimius the medicine he used to give Marcus (Commodus had done without), from the cinnamon-like cassia twigs. The best quality ones had perished in the Temple of Peace (with much of Galen's writings) when it burned two years earlier, and he had to use an old stock, stored up since Hadrian's day. Septimius was to recommend the treatment enthusiastically; Galen was much gratified.[39]

THE WAR AGAINST NIGER

THE EXPEDITION LEFT ROME by the Via Flaminia, the route by which Septimius had arrived only a month before. He soon ran into difficulties. At Saxa Rubra, less than ten miles north of the city, the troops mutinied, allegedly over the choice of camp site. The trouble was evidently overcome without difficulty, perhaps with a rapid distribution of the new coins struck in the legions' honour. The quartermaster on the 'city expedition', *expeditio urbica*, Rossius Vitulus, now had charge of the 'war-chest for the expedition', *arca expeditionalis*, proof that Septimius was continuing to cement the loyalty of his troops by disbursements of money.[1]

Septimius' departure from Rome by the northern route indicates that he travelled east by land. It might have been risky to cross from Brundisium to Dyrrachium and follow the Via Egnatia when Niger's forces were still in Europe. Indeed, Niger, who had apparently made Byzantium his headquarters, inflicted heavy casualties on Fabius Cilo's force in an attempt to seize Perinthus. This battle induced Niger to advertise a victory on his coinage, and made him conceited. His followers called him a new Alexander, Dio records. Niger clearly had every intention of fighting for the empire. But it was he who had opened hostilities. Now Septimius could take the step which he had so far avoided. The senate was asked to declare Niger and Asellius Aemilianus public enemies. Septimius was particularly incensed about Aemilianus, who had temporised for a time before accepting a major position under Niger. Since he was a kinsman of Clodius Albinus, Septimius may have hoped that he would back them rather than Niger.[2]

In spite of the support that had been shown to Niger at Rome, and his initial success at Perinthus, Septimius was confident. He believed in his destiny. Apart from the astrologer's forecast, and other omens, there had been a sign given to him while he was still at Carnuntum. The priest of Jupiter—at the shrine outside the town—had told him how he had seen, in a dream, a black man forcing his way into Septimius' camp and then being put to death. The 'black man' was Niger, so it was interpreted. No doubt Septimius' officers and agents broadcast this and other dreams and omens. They greatly impressed Cassius Dio.[3]

Septimius' route to the east presumably took him via Aquileia and the R. Save to Singidunum (Belgrade) on the Danube and down the river to Viminacium. From there he probably struck south, on the road to Naissus (Niš). Before he himself, with his wife and sons, and strong elements of the new Guard among other forces, reached Thrace, he must have sent another army drawn from the Pannonian legions, the *exercitus Illyricus*. The command was assigned to Ti. Claudius Candidus. This man, probably a Numidian from the Cirta region, had begun as an equestrian officer late in the reign of Marcus. He had become a senator, after holding a procuratorship, in the early 180s, but his career had stagnated. One of the few posts he obtained was that of legate to a proconsul of Asia. Conceivably he had been holding it under Aemilianus and had fled to join Septimius. At all events, he had some useful recent experience of the likely theatre of war.[4]

At some point in Septimius' journey east, probably soon after he reached Naissus, his brother Geta came to meet him. Septimius 'told him to govern the province that had been entrusted to him'. This may mean simply that he was ordered back to Lower Moesia. More probably Geta was transferred to Dacia, replacing Polus Terentianus. His successor in Lower Moesia was Pollienus Auspex, who had been in Dalmatia at the moment of the coup. Geta had 'hoped for something else', according to the *HA*. Some have deduced from this cryptic statement that he hoped for a share in the imperial power. It is more likely that he hoped for a field command. The *HA* undoubtedly derives the story from Marius Maximus, Geta's subordinate as legate of I Italica—the legion that Geta himself had commanded more than ten years previously. Geta may not have taken favourably to the prospects of Maximus and others acquiring glory in battle, while he remained far behind the front. Maximus had been given command of an army corps drawn from the Moesian legions, and the assignment to capture Byzantium.[5]

Niger had done his best to defend the coast of Asia Minor, giving the command to Aemilianus. But as he watched first Maximus' army settling down to besiege him in Byzantium and then Septimius himself arrive to make his headquarters at Perinthus, less than fifty miles (80 km) away, he began to lose his confidence. Besides, Septimius would have had Niger's children brought to Perinthus. Niger now made an offer to Septimius to share the empire. It was rejected out of hand. Septimius was prepared to spare Niger's life if he submitted and went into exile. But he refused to pardon Aemilianus.[6]

In the autumn Claudius Candidus took the Pannonian army across the Sea of Marmara. He defeated Aemilianus, who fled to Cyzicus, no doubt trying to reach Niger at Byzantium. But he was captured and executed by Candidus. His army fled eastwards, out of the province of Asia into Bithynia. Candidus pursued on both land and sea. Two great Bithynian cities reacted predictably. Nicomedia responded to the Septimian victory by an immediate change of side, sending offers of support. Candidus sent his troops ahead there, outflanking the enemy. Nicomedia's rival Nicaea gave a welcome to Niger's army. Niger himself managed to make his way there from Byzantium to take personal command.[7]

Candidus led his troops against Nicaea from the north. The battle took place in the narrow passes west of the city, leading past Lake Ascania to Cius. Dio gave a detailed account. As a native of Nicaea, he knew the terrain and was able to hear from eyewitnesses. Candidus had stationed his troops on the high ground and at first they had the advantage, although the fighting was confused. Some of the enemy were shooting arrows from boats on the lake. When Niger himself appeared, the Septimians began to give way. At this point Candidus displayed outstanding qualities of leadership. 'He seized hold of the standard-bearers and forced them to turn round to face the enemy, rebuking his men for taking flight.' This saved the day, and Niger's forces only escaped complete destruction through the onset of darkness. The battle must have taken place in December, or early January at the latest. News of Septimius' victory reached Rome by 31 January, and by 13 February Egypt had gone over to him. Niger's army retreated rapidly, and Niger hurried ahead to Antioch.[8]

Septimius now took possession of Asia as well as Bithynia. Fabius Cilo was made governor of the latter province. Claudius Candidus took at least part of his victorious Pannonian army into the province of Asia, where he pursued 'public enemies of the Roman people on both land and sea'. Claudius Xenophon, formerly procurator in Moesia and Dacia, and sub-prefect of the Annona, became procurator of Asia. Although there were no executions of prominent figures, except of Aemilianus, there will have been large scale confiscations and other penalties imposed on the cities that had supported Niger.[9]

The two victories had caused Septimius' army to acclaim him as *imperator*. He was able to add first 'Imp. II' and then 'Imp. III' to his titles, which, from the opening of 194, included *pater patriae*. Unlike Pertinax, he had allowed at least a token interval to elapse before he accepted this distinction. The mint of Rome hastened to strike new coins following each victory. After Cyzicus, as well as 'the emperor's victory' and the 'spirit of the Roman people', the ancestral gods of Lepcis Magna, the *di auspices*—Hercules and Father Liber—were invoked, making their first

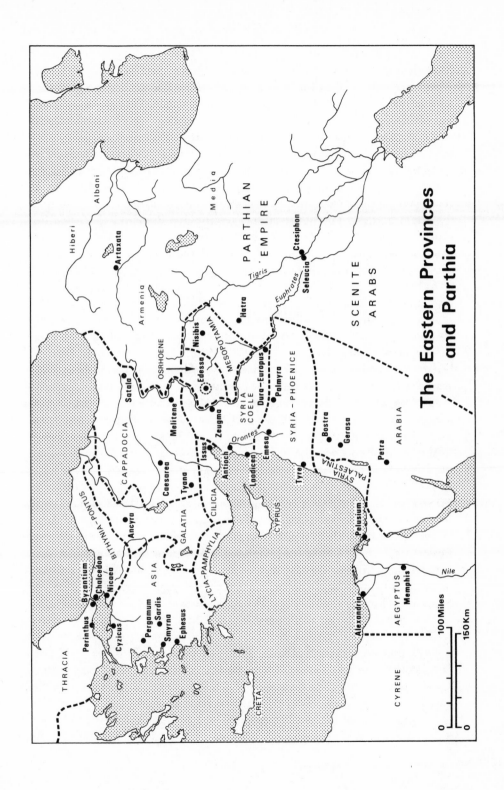

The Eastern Provinces and Parthia

appearance on the Roman coinage. Nicaea-Cius produced reverses of Mars the pacifier and Peace herself, and Septimius is shown clasping hands with Jupiter. Eternal Rome is figured on the bronze coinage from Rome, another issue of which shows Africa, with elephant-skin headdress and a lion at her feet, and corn-ears in her bosom. The exceptional prominence given to the province on the coinage was no doubt caused in part by its importance in supplying Rome with cereals. But in this and the following year the coinage of Albinus repeatedly shows the African deity called in Latin *saeculum frugiferum*. On one particularly fine *aureus* the god is represented seated with sphinxes on either side of his throne, wearing a fez-like headdress. The figure closely resembles a Punic relief of the fifth century BC found in the shrine of Ba'al Hammon at Hadrumetum, home town of Albinus. This coin, and those of the *di auspices*, suggest that Septimius, or the controller of the mint, thought it proper and desirable to advertise very specifically the African backgrounds of the Augustus and his chief ally, the Caesar.[10]

A new commander-in-chief for the Septimian army had now arrived, Cornelius Anullinus. He had been in Africa, as proconsul, when Septimius gained power, and may have been summoned to join him in Thrace before completing this year of office. Septimius had probably been well acquainted with Anullinus for over twenty years. He was a trusted friend, whom he was to honour and enrich. Niger had clearly valued the seniority and prestige of Asellius Aemilianus. Now Septimius could put a man of equal standing against Niger.[11]

While Anullinus began advancing through Galatia and Cappadocia in pursuit of Niger, Septimius may have remained at Perinthus. Before long he will have begun to follow. The only certain stage on his journey is Prusias ad Hypium, some sixty miles east of Nicomedia. Niger was making frantic preparations, fortifying the Taurus passes and raising further troops. But his support was dwindling further. The defection of Egypt was followed by that of Arabia: the governor of that province was a native of Perinthus. One of the two legions in Palestine, VI Ferrata, also defected, and even some of the cities of Syria itself showed support for Septimius. Two of these, Laodicea and Tyre, were punished by Niger. It may be that Emesa also abandoned Niger for the husband of Julia Domna well before the war was over.[12]

Only Herodian records a battle at one of the passes fortified by Niger. His account appears to indicate that the Septimians forced the pass during the winter or spring, for he speaks of a fall of snow. The decisive battle was to come near Issus, where Alexander had defeated Darius more than five hundred years before. Niger came out to meet the enemy as they moved down into the Gulf of Alexandretta. Dio gives a convincing account of the manner in which the victory was gained. Anullinus' men were helped by a heavy thunderstorm and rain from behind them driving at the faces of the enemy. But the decisive factor was Anullinus' move in sending Valerius Valerianus round with the cavalry to take Niger's army in the rear. They were already retreating, their morale lowered by the thunderstorm, when Valerianus appeared, and they were trapped. According to Dio they lost 20,000 men. Niger fled to Antioch. Anullinus followed and soon after captured the city. Niger apparently intended to flee to the Parthians, but he was caught on the outskirts and killed. His head was cut off and sent to Septimius, who sent it to the army besieging Byzantium, to induce that city to surrender. (It had no effect.) The defeat and death of Niger can hardly have been much later than the end of April.[13]

Pescennius Niger must remain a shadowy figure. On his proclamation as emperor he had assumed the additional name 'Justus', as if to announce the main theme of his rule. But he had little chance to put it into effect. Whether he would have succeeded is another matter. Dio notes that he was of equestrian origin. In a fragment of his account of the reign of Commodus there is a mention of Niger winning military renown, together with Albinus, in a war against the Dacians in the early 180s. Dio says that he was appointed governor of Syria because of his negative qualities—'he was remarkable for nothing, good or bad'. In other words, a grey figure who could be safely appointed to the key province of Syria during the confused last years of Commodus—especially as the Parthian empire was racked by civil war in 191. His coins portray him with long, narrow head, rather thick lips and a tense expression. The legends and reverse types represent him as the favourite of numerous gods. Herodian sneers at his vanity—and the anecdote about the 'new Alexander' recorded by Dio, already quoted, might seem to confirm this. The author of the HA, in a frank prelude to his biography of Niger, noted that it was an unusual and difficult task to record the lives of those 'who through the victories of others remained pretenders to the throne only'. This did not deter him from concocting a curious farrago that passes for a factual biography, based on the thin substratum of fact—the tale of Niger's 'presumption, the battle in which he was overcome, and the punishment that he suffered'—that he found in his source's account of Septimius Severus.[14]

How long it took before Septimius himself arrived in Syria is uncertain. Over thirty years later the Palmyrene garrison on the Syrian frontier at Dura still celebrated a Severan victory each year on 21 May. That could have been the day in the year 194 when the last of Niger's soldiers capitulated and Septimius' authority over the whole eastern empire was established.

It may have been in the aftermath of this take over that a decision of far reaching importance was taken. Niger had been minting silver coinage at a standard markedly inferior to that of any previous Roman denarii, below even those of Commodus' last three years. Septimius' first eastern issues followed suit. At the end of 194 the mint at Rome began issuing denarii which were only a little finer. They were still considerably inferior in silver content even to the late Commodan issues. Septimius was prepared to spend, on a massive scale: he was undertaking the ancient equivalent of 'printing money'.[15]

In honour of Issus Septimius took a fourth acclamation as *imperator*. He still refrained from exacting full vengeance against the senators who had supported Niger. It would have been foolish to do so, when disaffected senators had a potential rallying point in the person of Clodius Albinus. Dio records how one Cassius Clemens defended his behaviour: ' "I did not know either you or Niger," he said, "but since I was surrounded by his followers I had to look to the moment, not to fight against you but to depose Julianus." ' Septimius 'admired his frankness', and allowed him to retain half his property. Presumably the other prominent men, including most of the eastern governors and legionary legates, lost everything. One of the senators affected was a certain Flavius Athenagoras. Septimius later returned a million sesterces out of his confiscated property to the man's daughter as a dowry.[16]

An important step was to replace these men with his own nominees. The names of some new governors are recorded. Q. Venidius Rufus, a kinsman of Marius Maximus, who had been commanding the Bonn legion I Minervia, was assigned to Cilicia. Syria was treated drastically—it was divided into two. Syria Coele, northern or 'hollow' Syria, with the legions IV Scythica and XVI Flavia, remained consular. Syria Phoenice, with III Gallica, was now governed by the legate of the legion. The capital of the new province was Tyre, mother-city of Carthage and the western Phoenicians. Tyre was also given the *ius Italicum*, exempting its citizens from the tribute paid by provincials. The first governor of Phoenice was Ti. Manilius Fuscus, who had been legate of the Dacian legion XIII Gemina. Rewards and punishments were distributed to other cities which had taken a positive stance for either side during the war. Antioch was severely punished. Septimius now had the opportunity to get his own back on the people who had made fun of him when he was a legionary legate. The city was entirely deprived of its civic status and relegated to being a parish of its rival Laodicea, which replaced it as capital of Syria Coele and also acquired the *ius Italicum*. Similar measures were taken with other cities. Funds were raised on a massive scale by 'merciless' exactions. The immediate purpose may have been concealed. Septimius and Julia must have derived enormous pleasure from their triumphal tour of Syria. He had left twelve years before, abruptly removed from his legionary command and obliged to abandon his career for some time. Julia had left seven years earlier, to take ship for Lugdunum. There can be no question but that she revisited Emesa on this occasion, and that her fellow-Emesenes acclaimed their Augusta.[17]

But Septimius had other matters to prepare for during the rest of 194. A fair number of Niger's troops had taken refuge beyond the Euphrates, and various rulers in northern Mesopotamia had shown active support to Niger. Besides this, Septimius had some justification for taking action beyond the frontier. Nisibis, although far beyond the Euphrates and only fifty miles (80 km) from the Tigris, was in some sense dependent on Rome—it may even have had a token Roman garrison. When it was attacked by three peoples that had given aid to Niger—the Osrhoeni, Adiabeni and Scenite Arabs—Septimius took his opportunity. He rejected the claims of an embassy, that the attack on Nisibis had been made in his interest, against 'soldiers that had favoured Niger's cause'. In the spring of 195 he mounted an invasion of Mesopotamia. Dio, the only one of the three main sources who give any details, is scornful: it was done 'out of a desire for glory'—the same motive that he had imputed to Trajan. Considerations of this kind may have entered into the decision. It would have been politic to gain some success over a foreign enemy after more than a year of civil war. Besides, with Byzantium still unconquered, it may have seemed premature to return to the west. A campaign was opportune: it would allow legions that had taken opposing sides at three battles to fight together against a common enemy, and, besides, the Parthian empire was now weak. But Septimius had already formed a serious, long-term design to extend the eastern frontier. His own experience fifteen years earlier as legate of IV Scythica and Julia's personal knowledge of Syria, may have led him to believe that the Euphrates was seriously defective as a line of defence. The time was now ripe. He presumably crossed the frontier at Zeugma, his first objective being Osrhoene. The kingdom was annexed, and a procurator governor, C. Julius Pacatianus, was at once installed. However, its ruler Abgar was allowed to retain his capital, Edessa, and a small territory surrounding it. He evidently ingratiated himself with Septimius and was later to visit Rome with a large retinue. His dynasty's origins closely resembled that of Emesa: both sprang from the bedouin of the desert, had installed themselves in a fertile district, and adopted the use of the Aramaic or Syriac language.[18]

Julia was at Septimius' side, and on 14 April 195 was honoured with the title *mater castrorum*, 'Mother of the Camp'. It was just twenty years since Marcus Aurelius had awarded the same title, for the first time, to his wife Faustina. She had died, in Cilicia, less than a year later. Julia was to earn her title by her presence with Septimius and then with her elder son all over the empire during a quarter of a century. Early in the campaign Septimius assumed new titles, 'Arabicus' and 'Adiabenicus'. Surprisingly, they appear on the coinage before any addition to the number of his acclamations. Some great achievement early in the campaign must be commemorated—an achievement won before serious fighting had taken place. The answer must be that the Arabs and Adiabeni had offered submission soon after Septimius entered Mesopotamia. In their fullest form the titles are 'Parthicus Arabicus', 'Parthicus Adiabenicus', emphasising that the peoples who had surrendered were vassals of the Parthians. Apparently, Septimius rejected the title of Parthicus on its own to avoid offence to the Parthian king. In any case, there was no fighting with the Parthians themselves. In the course of 195 three victories were won, which brought successively the titles *Imperator V*, *VI* and *VII*. The coins display two captives, seated back to back, on round shields, wearing pointed hats and with their hands bound. If the Arabs and Adiabeni did offer submission early in the campaign, they soon caused more trouble— otherwise there would hardly have been three further battles. The victories were probably hard won. The senate decreed a triumph to him. But this he rejected—'in case it should appear that he was celebrating a triumph for his victories in the civil war'. A triumphal arch was, however, accepted.

The desert conditions, including a dust storm and shortage of drinking water, caused severe hardship among his troops. When water was found, it was rejected by the troops until Septimius called for a cup and drained it. He will have been familiar with desert wells from his boyhood in Tripolitania. Did he also recall the trouble Cato had had over drinking-water on his epic march through the Syrtica, as portrayed in Lucan? At all events, Septimius successfully conducted his army to Nisibis.[19]

Dio's account is too fragmentary to be really informative, but he gives the names of five generals. The first move out of Nisibis was made by three army corps, commanded by Claudius Candidus, Lateranus and Laetus. It is surprising to find Lateranus among them. T. Sextius Lateranus was a member of an Italian patrician family. But he was not the only man of his kind with Septimius. Lollianus Gentianus, son of Pertinax's patron, was serving as *comes* of the emperor. Laetus is probably the same as the Julius Laetus who had led the advance guard in the march on Rome. After the completion of their mission, 'laying waste the barbarians' land and capturing their towns', a second sweep was made, with the three corps commanded this time by Cornelius Anullinus, Laetus and a certain

Probus, otherwise unknown. Herodian's account is unfortunately worthless, as he has confused this campaign with the later eastern war; and the *HA* reports it in one sentence. Further light comes from a Syriac source, the Msiha Zkha, which indicates that Vologaeses of Parthia had fomented revolt or agression by the Osrhoeni and Adiabeni against Rome, but that he himself was distracted from active participation by the need to crush a rebellion in Persis and Media. His absence may have been decisive.[20]

Soon after his first victory, Septimius took a remarkable step. He proclaimed himself to be the son of Marcus Aurelius. In the first bronze issue which give him the titles that celebrate his victories, one sestertius describes him as 'Son of the deified Marcus Pius'. This title is repeated later in the year. Simultaneously, or soon after, he took another step. His son Bassianus, now seven years old, was renamed after Marcus, and from then on was known as 'M. Aurelius Antoninus.' He also received the title 'Caesar'. The title *mater castrorom* which Julia now had recalled the empress of Marcus. It has been plausibly suggested that the rainstorm, to which the Septimian success at Issus seems to be attributed by Dio, may have been exaggerated as part of a programme to associate Septimius with his new 'father'. After all, it recalled the two weather-miracles of the northern wars in the early 170s, which were at this very time newly commemorated in gleaming marble on the Aurelian Column at Rome. Indeed, a fragment of Dio even registers a northern 'weather-miracle' which supposedly took place while Septimius was in Mesopotamia. The 'Scythians' were about to invade, when their three chiefs were killed by thunderbolts. This must refer to the Goths, by now established on the Black Sea and beginning to eye the eastern empire hungrily. Septimius seems to have turned the episode to Rome's advantage. A few years later Goths are found serving in the army of Arabia.[21]

His victory beyond the Euphrates for the time being led to the annexation only of 'Osrhoene'. The new province may at first have extended as far as Nisibis and indeed to the Tigris. Nisibis was 'entrusted to a knight', perhaps the successful cavalry commander Valerius Valerianus. His inscription appears to credit him with the 'completion' of the *felicissima expeditio Mesopotamena*.[22]

There can be little doubt that Septimius had already decided to make a break with Albinus. He must have been supremely confident of the eventual outcome, may indeed have already taken steps to dispose of his temporary ally. Herodian records that Albinus was 'acting more and more as if he were emperor' and was receiving numerous letters from influential senators, 'who were trying to persuade him to come to Rome while Severus was absent, engaged on other matters'. Albinus, 'belonging to a noble family and regarded as being a good-natured man', was preferred to

Septimius by the 'aristocrats'. Septimius was kept informed of these developments. He therefore sent to Britain his most trusted couriers. They were to give despatches to Albinus openly, and then to request a private meeting to hand over 'secret instructions'. Once they were alone with him they were to strike him down. In case this failed, they were given poison, 'so that if the opportunity arose they could persuade one of Albinus' cooks or cupbearers to administer a dose of it in secret'. Albinus' advisers were suspicious and warned him to be on his guard. The couriers were seized, and revealed their instructions under torture. The HA has the same story in the mainly bogus Life of Albinus. Further details are probably derived from the author's own imagination: the number of messengers—five—and the place where they asked for the private conference—a distant portico.

The whole story may have been put out as anti-Septimian propaganda. Certainly, it was not long before Septimius himself inspired anti-Albinian propaganda. It was probably now that it was first alleged that Albinus had instigated the murder of Pertinax. Since Didius Julianus' mother came from Albinus' home town of Hadrumetum, the story may have seemed plausible. The fact that Julianus himself had had no part in the murder of Pertinax would have been conveniently ignored.[23]

Herodian has perhaps preserved some portion of the truth: that Septimius was unwilling to initiate hostilities against Albinus. Yet he must have known that his self-adoption into the house of the Antonines and the renaming of his son were actions of which Albinus could not mistake the implications. There was no longer any question of the title of Caesar that he had accepted in 193 giving him any rights of succession. Indeed, Dio says that Septimius 'would no longer give him even the rank of Caesar'. Dedications were being made to Septimius ascribing to him divine ancestry back to Nerva and, incidentally, calling him the 'brother of the deified Commodus'. His son 'Antoninus' was now his Caesar. Albinus was superfluous. Albinus' only recourse was to gamble for the highest stakes. During 195 he must have sent troops across into Gaul and proclaimed himself emperor. Septimius will have been ready for the move. Some of the troops brought east for the campaign were on their way back to Europe before the end of the summer. A soldier of the Pannonian legion X Gemina died at Ancyra in Galatia on 3 September, 'returning from Parthia'. He must have been in Claudius Candidus' army. The general himself may be on record at an earlier stage of the return march, between Samosata and Melitene. On a high ridge in sight of the Nemrud Dag a man called Candidus rebuilt a 'primeval altar', with a statue of 'Zeus, mighty king', in accordance with 'Apollo's deathless oracles'—and in passable hexameter verse.[24]

The rapid bringing to an end of the eastern campaign cannot have been forced on Septimius by events in the west. It must have been conceived from the start as a short-term punitive war. The assumption of the Antonine ancestry and the associated dynastic claims, probably in the spring of 195, were an open challenge to Albinus, which, if accepted, would make Septimius' return to the west necessary. Still, he did not leave Mesopotamia until he heard that Byzantium had fallen, news that gave him exceptional pleasure, according to Dio.[25]

The siege had lasted for more than two years, and Dio's detailed account is preserved in full—it naturally interested his epitomator Xiphilinus, whose eleventh-century Byzantine readers must have found this one of the most entertaining parts of the entire work. The late second-century Byzantines were evidently brave and resourceful, and the city only fell to Marius Maximus' besieging army when the people were starving—even then many escaped by boat, and the rest almost succeeded in getting away also. The city was treated in predictable fashion. Its walls were demolished, and its civic status annulled. It was annexed to its neighbour Perinthus. Dio, who had seen the city in its glory, with 'the seven towers extending from the Thracian Gates to the sea' that would pass on an echo from one to the other, comments sadly on what he later observed. The place 'looked as if it had been captured by some other people rather than by the Romans'.[26]

In recognition of the victory, Septimius now became *Imp. VIII*. An inscription preserves a letter that he wrote to the magistrates, council and people of Aezani, a city in Phrygia, in the eastern part of proconsular Asia. They had sent on to him the text of an honorific decree:

> I have clearly understood from your decree the pleasure that you take in my success and in the rise of my son Marcus Aurelius Antoninus with good fortune to the hopes of the empire and to a position alongside his father. And I am pleased that you celebrated a public festival and made sacrifices of thanksgiving to your local gods, since you are a famous city and one that has been of value to the Roman empire from of old. And when I saw that news of the victory had come to bear witness to my success, together with your decree, I was pleased. I sent my reply to you to be placed with your local gods. . . .

Septimius' titles are those of 195, except that he is already *Imp. VIII*. Clearly the embassy from Aezani had arrived in Mesopotamia at the same time as the news of the capture of Byzantium. *Imp. VIII* is not otherwise recorded until the beginning of 196. Thus the fall of Byzantium must belong late in the year 195. Antoninus' 'rise . . . with good fortune . . . to a position alongside his father' must refer to his having been made Caesar.

The only direct record from 195 which gives him the title, as well as the new names, come from Ulcisia Castra just north of Aquincum in Lower Pannonia. It is a dedication to Septimius, 'Arabicus Adiabenicus' and *Imp.* *V* by the garrison, the First Cohort of Syrians. On the coinage of 195 Antoninus is not yet called 'Caesar'. No doubt the Danubian armies were in close touch with their emperor.[27]

The journey back to the west began at once, along the route taken the previous year. Meanwhile at Rome the senate was obliged to declare Albinus a public enemy. This evidently took place on 15 December, to judge from Dio's reference to the 'last chariot-races' before the holiday. The realisation that another civil war was imminent—which can only mean that the breach had just been made open—caused dismay.

> We senators kept quiet [says Dio], but the people of Rome showed their feelings in no uncertain fashion. An enormous crowd had assembled to watch the last chariot-races before the Saturnalia, in the Circus Maximus. When the six-chariot races were over, there was a demand for silence and then a sudden clapping of hands. There were a series of shouts, prayers for the welfare of the state. Then the people began to shout appeals to the goddess Roma, addressing her as 'Queen' and 'Immortal', and crying out: 'How long are we to endure such things?' 'And how long are we to go on waging war?' After shouting out further things of this kind, they finally ended, as suddenly as they had begun, with the cry 'So much for that'—and turned their attention to the horse-race.[28]

Dio was there, as guest of one of the consuls, who was a friend of his. He attributed the behaviour of the crowd to 'some divine inspiration'. It may have been organised by supporters of Albinus. Dio noticed other omens, a 'great fire in the northern sky' and 'a fine rain resembling silver which fell from a clear sky on the Forum of Augustus'. He admits that he did not witness the silver rain in person, but 'after it had fallen I plated some bronze coins with it; they retained the appearance of silver for three days but on the fourth the substance had disappeared'. He does not expound the omen himself, but it has been shrewdly observed that silver, a white metal, could be taken to symbolise Albinus, whose name derived from *albus*, 'white'. And his appearance of power for three years was to be ended in the fourth.[29]

· I2 ·

THE WAR AGAINST ALBINUS

SEPTIMIUS WENT RACING BACK to the west—according to Herodian—
with the same breathless speed he had shown in three campaigns. But this
seems to be imaginative history, or fiction. In reality he proceeded with
thoroughness, making careful preparation. If the story of the unsuccessful
attempt to assassinate Albinus, also reported by Herodian and embroi-
dered by the *HA*, is true, Septimius' opponent would have been alerted to
what was coming long before the final encounter. And Septimius in any
case could foresee how his former ally would react to the news of
Bassianus' transformation into 'Antoninus Caesar'. Dio makes the se-
quence of events clear: 'Septimius would no longer even give Albinus the
rank of Caesar ... but Albinus was seeking the imperial eminence.'
During 195 Septimius abrogated the agreement made in the spring of 193.
Albinus was no longer to be 'Caesar'—though what powers, if any, had
been granted with the name is obscure. Septimius was to claim that 'he
had intended Albinus as his successor if anything should happen to
himself', in other words, if he were to fail against Didius Julianus or
Niger. Once these two were disposed of, Albinus' role could lapse. But
Albinus would not step down. He proclaimed himself Augustus. At the
end of 195 he was declared a 'public enemy'.[1]

Septimius began the march back before the end of 195. Others had
gone ahead to ensure his hold on Rome, Italy and the northern provinces;
the east and Africa were in firm and trusted hands. Some names can be
registered. Fabius Cilo moved from Bithynia, which he had been
governing since the victory at Nicaea, to take over Upper Moesia; and, it
seems likely, Julia's brother-in-law, the newly ennobled Emesene Avitus
Alexianus, became legate of the Singidunum (Belgrade) legion IV Flavia.
At Rome itself Septimius' own kinsman, the ruthless Fulvius Plautianus,
had been installed as Prefect of the *vigiles* by early summer 195. Candidus
began moving his Pannonian army back west, and Marius Maximus led
his Moesian army from the captured Byzantium to the Danube. A third
special force was formed from the vast Dacian army, under Ti. Claudius

Claudianus, the Numidian ex-equestrian officer. He had been serving as legionary commander with Geta. Steps were under way to recruit new legions and replenish the ranks of the old, particularly in northern Italy. The year 196 opened with the trusted Domitius Dexter as one of the *consules ordinarii*. Soon he was to be replaced as City Prefect by Septimius' senior marshal, Cornelius Anullinus.[2]

On his way back Septimius stayed again at Perinthus, where he dedicated a temple that he had vowed during his first stay. One of the legionary commanders in the recent compaign, T. Statilius Barbarus, was appointed governor of Thrace. During the journey westwards Pollienus Auspex, governor of Lower Moesia, greeted Septimius with a sarcastic comment on his self-adoption into the Antonine dynasty. ' "I congratulate you, Caesar," he said, "on finding a father." ' Dio explains the point of the story: the emperor's real father had been so obscure that it had seemed that he did not have one.[3]

Only one point on his journey is recorded after Perinthus. A ceremony took place at Viminacium on the Danube, the base of the legion VII Claudia. The *HA* says that Septimius 'named his son Caesar' there, 'to deter his own brother Geta from the hope of imperial power which he had conceived'. The new Antoninus had already become Caesar, in the east, presumably in spring 195. At Viminacium, it may be that he was displayed to the army; and no doubt Geta was present. As governor of Dacia he may have accompanied Claudius Claudianus' *exercitus Dacicus* to an agreed rendezvous. There it would join the forces gathering 'to suppress the Gallic conspiracy'. That was what they were calling Albinus and his followers. Marius Maximus, conducting the *exercitus Moesiacus*, was no doubt an eyewitness and the source of the *HA*'s anecdote (garbled a little in the transmission).[4]

Meanwhile in Noricum, Claudius Candidus, on his way west with his *exercitus Illyricus*, had to engage in a hunt for 'public enemies'. Albinus must have supporters in that province. Elsewhere too Septimius' rival was beginning to look more dangerous. He probably gained the support of the governor of Hispania Tarraconensis, Novius Rufus, and had seized Lugdunum, which became his headquarters. He expelled the governor, T. Flavius Secundus Philippianus. An attempt to occupy the Rhineland failed, although he did defeat the governor of Lower Germany, Virius Lupus. His forces besieged Trier in Gallia Belgica, but the city held out, defended by part of the Mainz legion XXII Primigenia under its legate Claudius Gallus. Septimius had naturally taken steps to secure the Alpine passes. One of the new legions was stationed in the Cottian Alps, under the command of Julius Pacatianus, recalled from the governorship of Osrhoene. Pacatianus, as a native of Vienne on the Rhône, will have been a useful man for this campaign. The commissariat was again entrusted to Rossius Vitulus.[5]

There was, it is clear, an atmosphere of confusion, as is illustrated by an episode in Dio. A schoolmaster named Numerianus set out from Rome for Gaul, 'pretending to be one of the senators appointed by Septimius to recruit troops'. After collecting a small force he entered Gaul and in a skirmish killed some Albinian cavalrymen. Septimius heard of his exploits. Under the impression that he was actually a senator, he sent a message of congratulations and instructions to increase the forces under his command. Numerianus thereafter managed to capture the impressive sum of seventy million sesterces. It was only after the war was over that he revealed his identity—and spent the rest of his life in retirement on a pension from the emperor.[6]

Septimius now proceeded to Rome, escorted by detachments under Fabius Cilo. Coins commemorate his 'most fortunate advent'. Other coins record distribution of largesse and the holding of lavish games. The behaviour of the urban plebs the previous December will not have gone unnoticed. Other issues emphasise war and peace—the martial prowess of the emperor and the peace that he would bring. During the first three years as emperor Septimius struck no fewer than 342 different issues. Coins struck for Antoninus advertised the 'perpetual security' and 'perpetual hope' that his proclamation as Caesar had brought. The boy now received the traditional title of heirs to the throne, *princeps inventutis*.[7]

The coinage of Albinus for the most part echoes that of Septimius: Jupiter who brings victory, Mars, Minerva the peace-bringer and Peace herself announce his confidence in the forthcoming struggle. The 'spirit of Lugdunum', his capital, is honoured, but there is no allusion to Africa. Septimius no longer felt the need to claim the loyalty of the army, but Albinus' coins proclaim the *fides legionum*. Two reverses emphasise Albinus' *clementia* and *aequitas*. Neither quality was claimed by Septimius. The *aequitas* reverse of Albinus closely matches one of Pertinax. These were the qualities that gained Albinus support among the senate. Some issues continue to give him the name Sep. or Sept., which appeared on his coinage as Caesar, the abbreviated form of Septimius. No doubt he had taken the name as a compliment to Septimius in 193. Why did he retain it? There seems to be no logical explanation.[8]

How long Septimius spent in Rome is not recorded. While there he made a dedication to 'the deified Nerva, his ancestor', on 18 September. It was the centenary of Nerva's accession. The Code of Justinian preserves a large number of rescripts from 196. Whereas there is only one from 195 (early in March), one from 1 January 196 and one from 30 June, there are ten from the period 1 October to 29 December of that year. It is reasonable to infer that Septimius' return produced a spate of legal business. Or at least, while in Rome he was able to give it his personal attention.[9]

Septimius cannot have remained at Rome long. Once again he went to Pannonia, then through Noricum and Raetia into Upper Germany. From here he moved south on Lugdunum with his army. The roads in the region through which his armies had passed that year and through which he now went himself had been repaired in the previous year, further evidence that he had begun preparing for the campaign against Albinus in 195. Cilo probably escorted Septimius as far as Pannonia, remaining there as governor of the Upper Province. Septimius' elder son was left in the care of Cilo. This passage through Pannonia was the occasion for Septimius to be assured of success by a prophecy. 'Anxious about his generals having been defeated by the Albinians [this will refer to the defeat of Lupus], he learned from Pannonian augurs that he would be the victor. His adversary would, in fact, neither come into his power nor escape, but would perish next to the water.'[10]

Dio records that 150,000 men were engaged when the decisive encounter came. Albinus had, it is true, the largest provincial army in the empire at his disposal. In the mid-second century, at least, for which detailed calculations can be made, the garrison of Britain had had some 35,000 auxiliary troops, including nearly 10,000 cavalry, in addition to its three legions. It is difficult to be sure if any of the *auxilia* had been withdrawn during the subsequent half century. But Marcus Aurelius had sent 5,500 Sarmatians to Britain in 175 and there had been a major war against the Caledonians in the 180s, so the British army very probably still amounted to over 50,000 men. Albinus no doubt endeavoured to ensure that the northern tribes which submitted to Ulpius Marcellus in 184 kept the peace, but he must have left a holding garrison behind him when he shipped his expeditionary force across the Channel. His British force in Gaul is unlikely to have numbered more than forty thousand. He may have hoped for the support of VII Gemina, the Spanish legion, and the modest *auxilia* in the peninsula. Whether his ally Novius Rufus, governor of Tarraconensis, could deliver is doubtful. Otherwise, he doubtless raised extra cohorts and *alae*, perhaps even legions, in Gaul. But he hardly had time to make them effective. Finally, there was the single Urban Cohort at Lugdunum, 500-strong, detached from the Rome garrison to police the Gallic metropolis.[11]

Septimius, by contrast, could draw on the entire forces of the empire other than those in Britain and Spain. The Rhine and Danube armies alone constituted an army of over 200,000. He also had his new legions—one guarding the Cottian Alps—and the praetorians. As the inscriptions of

Candidus, Claudius Claudianus and Marius Maximus witness, it was to be the Danubian-Balkan armies, once again, which bore the brunt of the fighting. The Rhine armies, already worsted in the opening encounter in 196, were probably assigned to cut off any attempt by the Albinians at retreat to the Channel ports.[12]

It was still winter when Septimius entered Gaul, early in 197, from Upper Germany. The first clash took place at Tinurtium (Tournous), sixty miles north of Lugdunum. Albinus was obviously trying to head his attackers off. But his forces were pushed back south to the outskirts of Lugdunum itself, where the final battle took place on 19 February. At first the Albinian left wing was defeated and fled back to its camp. But then the Septimian left fell into a trap. The Albinians had dug a series of concealed pits—the so-called *lilia*, which the British army must have been skilled at making from their experience on their northern frontier—and the Septimians were lured into them by a feigned retreat. Septimius himself came up on horseback with the praetorians, but instead of saving the situation got himself into extreme difficulties and was thrown from his horse. Then, 'tearing off his riding cloak and drawing his sword', he rushed after his retreating troops and shamed them into making a stand. That at least was the official version. According to Herodian, he simply fled with the rest—and flung off the purple cloak which revealed his identity. At this critical moment, while the pursuing British troops were already raising the chant of victory, Septimius' general Laetus appeared with the cavalry and routed the Albinians. It turned out subsequently—or so it was alleged—that he had been waiting to see which side was winning before making a move, hoping that both leaders would be killed so that he could gain the throne for himself.[13]

Albinus' troops were pursued into Lugdunum, which was sacked and burnt by the victorious army. Albinus himself was trapped in a house beside the Rhône and committed suicide. His body was brought to Septimius, who 'feasted his eyes on it', according to Dio. The version in the *HA* is that Albinus was half alive when brought to Septimius and that the prophecy of the Pannonian augurs was thereby fulfilled. The head was cut off and sent to Rome. The *HA* adds that 'the corpse was, by Severus' order, laid out in front of his own home, to be exposed to view, for a long time. Besides which, he himself rode over the body, and when the horse shied he spoke to it and loosened the reins, to make it trample boldly.' Finally the body was thrown into the Rhône, with the bodies of Albinus' murdered wife and sons. The *HA* also records that the bodies of senators who had fought for Albinus were mutilated by Septimius' orders.[14]

A whole series of administrative moves now had to be made. Claudius Candidus was sent into Spain as governor of Tarraconensis, with the added mission of hunting down supporters of Albinus. It was a task for which his similar operations in Asia and Noricum had given him ample qualifications. Novius Rufus, who had been governor since at least 192, was put to death. But the legion VII Gemina must have changed sides, or at least failed to join Albinus. It was rewarded with the title *pia*, 'loyal'. In Spain and Gaul numerous members of the local aristocracies were executed. They had clearly given Albinus financial backing. Their estates were confiscated, and in southern Spain much of the olive oil production thus fell into the hands of the state. In Gaul the factories that produced *terra sigillata*, Samian pottery, were either destroyed, or went out of production when their owners were killed and their property forfeited. Septimius' aristocratic supporter Lollianus Gentianus was made governor of Lugdunensis with power to conduct a new census—it would be badly needed.[15]

These were not the only parts of the empire that were affected. The procurator Claudius Xenophon returned to the west from Asia to become *procurator ad bona cogenda in Africa*, 'to confiscate the property of the condemned'. Albinus had had allies in his native province, even though less powerful than those of Septimius. Three procurators are later found administering such property, evidently at Rome. Septimius was to institute a drastic purge of the senate when he returned to Rome from Lugdunum.[16]

First, urgent measures were taken in the north-west. Marius Maximus was made governor of Belgica and Valerius Pudens of Lower Germany, replacing Virius Lupus, who became governor of Britain. The defeated British legions were sent back, no doubt heavily reinforced with new manpower, necessary to restore losses—and their loyalty. Lupus faced an appalling situation. In the absence of the Roman garrison, the northern part of the province had been plundered by the Maeatae, probably joined by other tribes closer to Hadrian's Wall and some of the Brigantes within the province. The destruction caused was far from total, but must have been serious; and they had taken captives. Lupus was obliged to buy off the Maeatae, who were on the point of bringing in the Caledonii when he arrived: the latter 'had not kept their promises', an excerpt from Dio records, 'and were preparing to assist the Maeatae . . . Lupus was obliged to buy peace from the Maeatae for a great sum of money, receiving back a few prisoners'. Inscriptions show Lupus carrying out rebuilding in the north; but for the moment Britain was a sideshow.[17]

Septimius did not go straight to Rome. Once more he seems to have travelled via Germany and Pannonia. In Germany envoys came to him from the senate, no doubt bearing congratulations and protestations of loyalty. One of these was a young man from Cirta in Numidia, from which so many of Septimius' henchmen had already been drawn. The senate's choice of such a man was undoubtedly politic. The embassy went on into Pannonia to take messages of a similar nature to Antoninus. While in Germany Septimius ordered Claudius Gallus, the deserving legate of the legion XXII Primigenia, and another Numidian, to muster an army corps drawn from all four German legions and set out with it for the east. Laetus, the man who had saved the day at Lugdunum, was probably sent post-haste to Mesopotamia. Reports must have already reached Septimius—and they cannot have surprised him—that the Parthians had invaded.[18]

The senate awaited Septimius' return with justifiable anxiety. Those who had had any dealings with Albinus must have trembled—Septimius had taken possession of Albinus' correspondence. Once again populace and senate came out to greet him, as they had done four years earlier, with laurel branches. Once again, he made sacrifice in the Temple of Jupiter on the Capitol and went to the Palace. His first speech before the senate caused dismay and terror. He now demanded the formal deification of Commodus, whose 'brother' he was constantly calling himself, as well as 'son of Marcus'. It is, however, unlikely that he carried out the ornate and elaborate rituals that had been performed for Pertinax in 193. He openly praised the severity and cruelty of Sulla, Marius and Augustus, and criticised Pompey and Caesar for their clemency (the very quality that Albinus had claimed for himself on his coinage). He defended the character of Commodus and attacked the senate for dishonouring him unjustifiably—since many of them lived worse lives.

> 'For if this was disgraceful, that he slew wild beasts with his own hands, yet only the other day at Ostia, one of you, a consular and an old man, was performing in public with a prostitute who imitated a leopard. Did Commodus fight as a gladiator, by Jupiter? And does not one of you fight as a gladiator? If not, how and why is it that some of you have bought his shields and those famous golden helmets?'

At the time he was making this speech some sixty-four out of the 600 members of the senate were under arrest. Thirty-five were then released, but the remaining twenty-nine were executed. There were some famous names among them, including Sulpicianus, the father-in-law of Pertinax, and Erucius Clarus, one of the consuls of 193. Clarus had been offered a free pardon if he would act as informer. He preferred death. Another man was easily found to play the role, in return for his life, but was obliged to submit to torture so that his evidence could be verified.[19]

A striking passage in Dio well conveys the atmosphere in Rome either before or after the battle of Lugdunum. Everyone did their best to pretend to be loyal, but sudden news would catch men off their guard and their faces revealed their true feelings. 'And some, because they exaggerated their pretence, were recognised more easily.' It was ironic that one of the senators executed was Julius Solon. Four years earlier he had introduced the decree of the senate that the emperor should not put his peers to death without trial. Analysis of the names of the senators put to death reveals that more than a third were closely connected by birth or by property-ownership with proconsular Africa, and others were linked with Gaul and Spain.[20]

A natural corollary of this ruthless purge was the inflow of substantial funds to the Treasury. The procurators specially appointed to administer the property of the proscribed have already been mentioned. A more permanent step was taken with the transformation of the Privy Purse (*res privata* or *ratio privata*). Its operations were greatly extended by the setting up of regional offices throughout Italy. At this time the sinister Aquilius Felix was given the special task of revising the lists of Roman knights. Many changes will have been necessary—some sixty or more *equites* must have been serving as officers in the British army under Albinus. Few of these will have retained their rank, even if their lives were spared. This influx of funds, coupled with debasement of the silver coinage, made it possible for Septimius to grant a major pay increase to the army, the first, indeed, for over a century. He also made a dramatic concession over terms of service: for the first time since Augustus soldiers were permitted to marry. The loyalty of the whole imperial army to himself and his dynasty was now secure.[21]

On 8 June 197 three troopers of the imperial House Guard (*equites singulares Augusti*) celebrated 'the return of the unit'—undoubtedly from the campaign in Gaul—by a dedication to 'Unconquered Hercules and the other gods and goddesses', for the safety of Septimius, of Antoninus, and of C. Fulvius Plautianus, Prefect of the Guard. Plautianus also had the title *clarissimus vir*, 'right honourable', and hence had been granted honorary senatorial rank. Septimius' energetic and strong-willed kinsman had been at his side during most of the last four years.[22]

Antoninus was now frequently called *imperator destinatus*, 'emperor designate', and at the same time he was co-opted into the great priestly colleges. Septimius was awaiting an auspicious moment before making his son his full colleague. Measures were taken to ensure the favour of the urban populace at Rome with more lavish games and further distribution of largesse. Then he departed for his second war with Rome's eastern enemies.[23]

· I 3 ·

PARTHIA AND EGYPT

THIS TIME SEPTIMIUS WENT east by sea. Embarking at Brundisium he sailed directly across to Asia Minor, probably landing at the Cilician port of Aegeae and completing the journey to Syria by road. The bulk of the expeditionary force, including two of the new legions, had been sent on ahead. The other new legion, II Parthica, was left in Italy, garrisoned at a new fortress thirteen miles south of Rome on the Via Appia, at Alba. Together with part of the Guard and other elements of the enlarged Rome garrison, this would be sufficient insurance against possible trouble during his absence. II Parthica was given an equestrian rather than a senatorial commander, as were the other new legions. Septimius' friend Anullinus was City Prefect. Other close associates of Septimius were in strategic positions. Fabius Cilo ruled the key province of Upper Pannonia during the entire period of his absence, Geta was still governing Dacia and a high proportion of the other military provinces were entrusted to men of African origin or connections. Septimius was to be away from Rome for five years. There is no hint of any trouble in this period.[1]

He was accompanied by Julia and their sons and by his kinsman the Prefect of the Guard, Plautianus. On arrival in Syria he immediately mustered his forces and crossed the Euphrates. Abgar of Edessa handed over his children as hostages and provided archers, and the king of Armenia, fearing that he would be attacked, likewise sent hostages, money and gifts, in return for which his status was recognised by a treaty. Septimius pushed on to Nisibis, which Julius Laetus had managed to rescue. The Parthians withdrew before Septimius arrived. These successes may have led him to accept a new imperatorial acclamation, his tenth, before returning to Syria to prepare for a much more ambitious undertaking.[2]

His plan now was to attack the Parthian capital itself, in person, unlike Lucius Verus thirty years earlier, who had remained in Syria while his generals, above all the Syrian Avidius Cassius, took Roman armies to the Tigris. He constructed a fleet on the Euphrates and began moving his forces south when the summer was over, probably in late September. He was accompanied by a brother of the Parthian king. Dissension in the

Parthian empire gave an ideal opportunity to neutralise Rome's major enemy in the east once and for all. Babylon, in any case a largely deserted city, had been abandoned by the enemy when Septimius' forces reached it. They pressed across to the Tigris and found the once great city of Seleucia, ruined by Cassius' troops in 165, likewise undefended. Across the river stood Ctesiphon, the royal city. Quite when the Roman army reached this point is unclear, but Parthian resistance was minimal. The king escaped and Septimius did not trouble to pursue him. Ctesiphon was sacked and plundered: 'vast numbers were killed', Dio says, 'and 100,000 prisoners taken'. Herodian adds that 'the royal treasury was captured and all the king's jewels and valuables'.[3]

On 28 January 198 Septimius proclaimed that he had conquered Parthia, and took the title Trajan had first held, 'Parthicus Maximus'. The date was carefully chosen: it was the exact centenary of Trajan's accession. He was now the equal of the 'best of emperors', whose great-great-grandson he claimed to be. On the same day he conferred on his elder son, now nine years old, the title of Augustus and the status of co-emperor to which he had been clearly designated for the past year. His younger son Geta received the name of Caesar. Septimius was once again following the example of Marcus Aurelius, the first to take a colleague as co-emperor, as he had already done by making his wife *mater castrorum*.

Whether he had intended to annexe the whole of the land between the two rivers down to the Persian Gulf, when he set out the previous autumn, is unclear. Trajan had tried this and failed. Dio suggests that he departed 'as if his sole purpose had been plunder', but that his real reason for abandoning Ctesiphon was 'lack of supplies' and inadequate military intelligence: 'ignorance of the country'. He took the army back by a different route, up the Tigris. But he had a further military objective, the great desert city of Hatra. Like Edessa, Palmyra and—once—Emesa, it was an Arab caravan city, with powerful military forces of its own. Its ruler Barsemius had offered support to Niger and had not yet been punished. He could, if left alone, interfere with the passage of Roman troops along the Tigris. Furthermore, Trajan had failed to capture the city. Herodian, indeed, seemed to believe that the prime purpose of the entire expedition was to capture Hatra, and places the siege before the attack on Ctesiphon. Dio was much better informed, even if his accounts, as preserved by Xiphilinus, is hostile. Only Dio reveals that Septimius attacked Hatra twice. The first attempt, presumably in February or March 198, soon after the invasion army left Ctesiphon, is dismissed curtly as a failure: Septimius 'crossed Mesopotamia to Hatra, which was not far off, but achieved nothing, in fact his siege engines were burned; many soldiers perished, a great many more were wounded'. Septimius withdrew and moved elsewhere.[4]

During the siege there were two unpleasant episodes. A tribune of the Guard, Julius Crispus, was overheard quoting some lines of Virgil which expressed the army's disgust at the apparent pointlessness of the siege. He was reported to Septimius and executed; and, Dio adds, the informer, a soldier named Valerius, was appointed to Crispus' tribunate. The second episode was much more serious: this time the victim was Julius Laetus, who had been with Septimius in the march on Rome, had served in Mesopotamia in 195, had carried the day at Lugdunum in 197 and raced off from there to rescue Nisibis from Parthian attack the same year. He had become too popular with the troops. Dio says that they were refusing to fight unless Laetus led them. After his death, no doubt, the story was put out that he had planned to seize the throne himself at Lugdunum and had held his men back deliberately. Laetus had presumably remained with Severus as a *comes* after the relief of Nisibis the previous autumn, but not given a field command. Septimius became unpopular with his army, and tried to disclaim responsibility. It may well be, indeed, that the initiative for the act came from Plautianus, who, according to the *HA*, was at this time engaged in a hunt for surviving supporters of Niger. A number of Septimius' close associates lost their lives. Another prominent victim, now or a little later, was Claudius Candidus: his names were erased from the base of a statue in his honour at Tarraco. Plautianus could not brook any rival, and was well on the way to creating for himself a position of unmatched power. But besides this Plautianus could exploit Septimius' superstition. The *HA* also reports that 'many who had consulted astrologers or prophets about his survival were put to death'; especially suspect were 'any who seemed capable of being emperor'.[5]

After mentioning the death of Laetus, the *HA*, somewhat incongruously at first sight (no doubt because the author has drastically abbreviated his source), inserts an anecdote about Septimius' sister Octavilla. 'His sister, a woman of Lepcis, came to see him. She was scarcely capable of speaking Latin and the emperor was greatly embarrassed about her. He awarded her son the *latus clavus* and gave her many presents, and ordered her to return home [presumably to Lepcis], together with her son, who died shortly afterwards.' There is no obvious connection with what precedes or follows this story in the *HA*: its source had presumably supplied the context. Septimius was by now, no doubt, back in the north, perhaps at Nisibis or in Syria. The fact that his sister's son had to be given senatorial rank indicates that her husband was a non-senator. It may be that he was serving in the east, perhaps as a procurator. When

Octavilla herself died, before Septimius, she was commemorated with the title *clarissimae memoriae femina*, indicating that her husband had by then been made a senator. Octavilla's poor Latin is generally taken to mean that she was more used to speaking Punic; it could be that her husband was a Greek-speaker and that her Latin had become rusty from lack of practice.[6]

During the spring and summer of 198 Septimius must have devoted attention to reorganising the eastern frontiers. Above all, he created a further new province, Mesopotamia. Osrhoene was retained as a province too, with its capital probably now at Carrhae, which was given the rank of a Roman colony. The territory to the east of Abgar's residual kingdom of Edessa, which had perhaps been included in the province of Osrhoene when it was established in 195, now became Roman Mesopotamia, thus reviving the shortlived Trajanic province. This time it was to be permanent, 'a bulwark for Syria', Septimius claimed. Dio was later to be sceptical: Septimius was merely motivated by 'a desire for glory', he believed, and it was 'a drain on Roman resources'. Nisibis became the capital of the new province, and it was placed under an equestrian Prefect, on the model of Egypt, with a legionary garrison formed by the newly raised I and III Parthica. The former was stationed at Singara, close to the Tigris, the latter at Resaina in the west of the province. Both these cities, and Nisibis, became *coloniae*. The first Prefect was a man from Numidian Cuicul, Ti. Claudius Subatianus Aquila. As if to underline the ascendancy of the Africans, another man from the same town, L. Alfenus Senecio, is found shortly afterwards governing Syria Coele.[7]

The failure at Hatra still rankled. It was only just over sixty miles (100 km) from the new frontier along the Jebel Sinjar, and the only remaining strongpoint between the two rivers not under direct Roman control. The eastern provinces were now more strongly garrisoned than ever before and a powerful expeditionary force from his Danubian armies and Guard were still with him. He had the services of the engineer Priscus, who had done much to frustrate the besieging forces of Marius Maximus at Byzantium before the city surrendered (Dio notes with some pride that the man was a fellow-Nicaean). He could not resist making a renewed attempt. But Hatra was defended by a massive double wall, four miles in circumference. In spite of Septimius' massive preparations—Dio writes of great supplies of food and many siege engines—the second attack on Hatra apparently also failed. 'He lost a great deal of money', Dio writes, 'and all his engines except the ones built by Priscus, and many men too. Considerable numbers perished when foraging, from the rapid and violent attacks by the barbarian cavalry (that of the Arabs, I mean). The long-range archery of the Hatrans was also effective, and their artillery.'

The defenders also used bituminous naphtha to set fire to the Roman siege engines.

Septimius observed proceedings from a lofty tribunal. The Romans broke through the outer, earth wall and were ready to press the attack, but he ordered the retreat to be sounded, expecting that the Arab defenders would sue for peace to escape capture and enslavement. Dio draws attention to the great wealth of the sun god's temple, implying that the defenders were likely to make terms rather than see it destroyed. During the night, however, they rebuilt the gap in the outer wall, and Septimius was obliged to renew the assault. At this point, according to Dio, the European troops refused to obey orders, enraged that they had been obliged to withdraw on the previous day. The Syrians who were sent in were wiped out. 'One of Septimius' officers told the emperor he could finish the job if he could have a mere 550 European soldiers. "Where could I get so many?", Septimius replied, within the hearing of all, referring to the soldiers disobedience'. After only twenty days from the beginning of the second siege, Septimius 'left Hatra and went to Palestine', Dio concludes.[8]

In spite of the negative impression conveyed by Dio, Septimius may well have achieved his main objective at Hatra, the submission of king Barsemius. He seems to have claimed this operation as the culmination of his Parthian campaign, and may well have been able to impose a Roman garrison on the city. Some decades later the Ninth Cohort of Moors was stationed there; it may have been installed shortly after Septimius' apparently abrupt departure.[9]

The sources are largely silent about Septimius's activities during the next few months, when he remained in the east. Xiphilinus' version of Dio jumps from Hatra, in the autumn or winter of 198, to Septimius' entry into Egypt via Palestine late in the following year. Another excerptor of Dio refers to Septimius coming 'into Arabia from Syria, and into Palestine'. It is clear enough that he would need more time in Syria, now divided into two provinces, Coele in the north with two legions, at Samosata and Zeugma—his old command, IV Scythica, had been busy in the past few years strengthening the military links with the new province of Osrhoene—and Phoenice in the south, governed by the legate of III Gallica at Raphaneae, with its chief city, Tyre, raised to the rank of *colonia*. Two prominent Syrians must by now have obtained positions of influence, both distinguished lawyers. Domitius Ulpianus, of Tyre, the younger of the two, was perhaps in a rather junior post at this stage. Aemilius Papinianus, a kinsman of Julia, may have already been holding the powerful position of *a libellis*, chief of the Petitions Bureau. It may have been on this visit to Syria that Septimius once more consulted the oracles of Zeus Belos at Apamea which gave him a promise of greatness when he was a legionary legate. This time, Dio records, the god's answer was a quotation from Euripides: 'Your House will utterly perish in blood.' The city of Apamea itself was now connected to the imperial family. One of the two young daughters of Julia Domna's sister Maesa, Julia Soaemias, was married to a young man from this place, Sex. Varius Marcellus; he had been made a junior procurator. Maesa's husband Julius Avitus Alexianus, made a senator by Septimius, was at this time probably governing far off Raetia and soon would be consul. But her sons-in-law, Marcellus, and Gessius Marcianus, from another southern Syrian city, Arca, husband of Julia Mamaea, remained equestrian.[10]

Whatever else Septimius did in these parts during 198–9, it seems clear that he reorganised the frontiers. Parts of southern Syria Phoenice were detached and added to Arabia. That province, which a fragment of Dio indicates that he visited himself, received substantial strengthening: a burst of military construction has been identified from this time. Milestones attest work all along the Trajanic road, the great north–south trunk route. Further, a chain of forts was built or reinforced to control the Wadi Sirhan, the 300-mile-long depression from Basie (Qasr al Azraq in Jordan) to Dumata (Jawf in Saudi Arabia), Rome's gateway to the Persian Gulf. The emperor born on the edge of the Sahara was doing his best to extend and solidify Roman control of the eastern deserts over a vast area. He and his wife, it may be argued, had a keener realisation of the importance of the eastern frontiers and a shrewder perception of how they should be controlled, than any previous Roman ruler. As for Syria, now two provinces, there was some redeployment of the legionary force of Syria Coele. The two legions, at Samosata and Zeugma, on the Euphrates, were no longer on the frontier, shielded by the new provinces of Osrhoene and Mesopotamia. Detachments from both were soon assigned to Dura, far down the river. Dura itself, which had only been added to the empire after Verus' war in the 160s, was no longer the limit of Roman control on the lower Euphrates. Within a decade or so Roman garrisons were at Anatha, over eighty miles (130 km) further downstream, and at Kifrin a little beyond it. Another modification, of a different kind, was soon to follow. The great desert city of Palmyra had long had its own defence forces to protect the caravans that plied between the Parthian empire and the Mediterranean. For some years, at least since Hadrian's day, they had supplied troops to Rome, including a garrison for Dura. Following the division of Syria in 194, Dura was assigned to Syria Coele, but Palmyra itself was controlled by or responsible to the governor of Phoenice. It may be only now that Palmyra became formally part of the empire. Its troops became regular regiments of the Roman army, such as the *cohors XX Palmyrenorum* at Dura, rather than just 'Palmyrenes' and the great *emporium*, the 'desert harbour', became a Roman *colonia*.[11]

In what survives of Dio's account no details are preserved of Septimius' stay in Palestine, although in the context of the first Parthian war of 195 he mentions trouble with a brigand named Claudius who was overrunning Judaea and Syria. The *HA* has a brief remark about his 'granting many privileges to the Palestinians on his journey', and adds an implausible statement that 'he banned conversion both to Judaism and Christianity.' A few sentences earlier, in a thoroughly garbled section of the *vita*, the *HA* claims that Septimius' son Antoninus was later granted a 'Jewish triumph because of Septimius' own achievements in Syria'. This may be an invention by the *HA*, but Jerome in his *Chronicle* does list the outbreak of a 'Jewish and Samaritan war' in Septimius' fifth year, which should be 197. Later chroniclers, Michael Syrus and Bar-Hebraeus, explain this as a violent outbreak of fighting *between* Jews and Samaritans. Some Roman intervention may have been necessary to restore the peace, but whether Septimius and his ten- or eleven-year-old son were involved remains uncertain. The 'privileges granted', may be reflected in the assumption by the cities of Eleutheropolis and Diospolis-Lydda of titles taken from Septimius' names. At all events, the period was a favourable one for the Jews, whose privileges were protected in imperial rescripts. The Talmud reports pro-Roman activity by the Rabbis Eleazar and Ishmael, and Jerome, indeed, insists that Septimius and Antoninus 'very greatly cherished the Jews'.[12]

Sixteen years earlier, Septimius had gone from Syria to Athens, when he was in disfavour. His expressed motives were study and interest in antiquities and religion. Then, as a senator, he would not have been permitted to go to Egypt. Now this was an obvious goal. The great province had supported his rival Niger, as it had earlier backed Avidius Cassius. There had been active discontent there during the reign of Commodus, when there were as many as ten prefects in thirteen years, hence an obvious need for reform. The *HA* and Dio both attest Septimius' fascination with Egypt. Afterwards, says the *HA*, 'he always indicated that he had enjoyed this tour, because he had taken part in the worship of the god Sarapis, had learned something of antiquity and had seen unfamiliar animals and places'. Dio reports that 'he enquired into everything, including what was totally secret. For he was the sort of man to leave nothing, whether human or divine, uninvestigated. Accordingly, he removed from almost all the temples all the books he could find containing any secret lore; and he closed the tomb of Alexander. This was to prevent anyone else looking at the body of Alexander or reading what was written in those books.' Fear of the myth of Alexander, the potency of which had still not reached its peak, is understandable in an emperor who had campaigned on the Tigris, but had gone no further. Besides, his rival Niger had briefly posed as a new Alexander. As for the secret lore of Egypt, Septimius' superstitious nature will have made him both fear and be fascinated by it. Well before he entered Egypt he sent instructions to the prefect denouncing divination and magic. Simple and ignorant people must be protected from 'dangerous inquisitiveness into the future', whether practised by private consultation or oracles or through the magic arts. One year's grace was offered: thereafter the penalty would be death, also applicable to any who harboured such criminals. The proclamation was to be posted by the *strategi* in their nome capitals and all the villages; and they were to exercise constant vigilance, and 'send in fetters for judgment anyone found acting contrary to these regulations'.[13]

Septimius entered Egypt by land, stopping first at Pelusium, where he sacrificed at the tomb of Pompey, murdered there nearly two and a half centuries before. Reverence for the dead was a special characteristic of the Libyans in Septimius' homeland. Besides, he was following the example of Hadrian, who had rebuilt the tomb on his visit in 130. But in Septimius' case there may have been an additional motive for this act of piety. Pompey had been murdered by treacherous Egyptians commanded by a renegade Roman. According to Dio, their act 'brought a curse upon themselves and all Egypt', which he explains by their own deaths not long afterwards and by Egypt coming under the rule of Cleopatra, then of Rome. As it happens, the Roman who killed Pompey was a certain Lucius Septimius. The emperor could not have failed to know this detail. He may even have remembered Lucan's chilling lines about the murderer:

> Inmanis, violentus, atrox nullaque ferarum
> Mitior in caedes ...
>> Qua posteritas in saecula mittet
> Septimium fama?

> A monster, violent and savage, a killer worse
> than a wild beast ... What verdict will posterity
> pass down the ages on Septimius?

Even if there were no tie of descent to perpetuate any blood-guilt, he may have felt the need for a personal act of reconciliation with the dead. Ironically, Marcus Aurelius, whose son Septimius now claimed to be, had been a remote descendant of Pompey. This act at Pompey's tomb was loaded with overtones.[14]

The imperial party made a festive entry into Alexandria. It was marred a little, according to an anecdote in the late chronicler John Malalas. Septimius spotted an inscription on the city gate, which the Alexandrians had imprudently omitted to remove: 'Niger is the Master of the City'. His irritation may not have been assuaged by the excuse that, after all, he was the master of Niger. Apart from inspecting the embalmed body of Alexander, and sealing up the tomb, Septimius is said to have donated baths, a gymnasium and a temple of the Mother Goddess, Cybele, to the city. He also undertook a major programme of reform. The principal change was the granting of a council to Alexandria and the other major cities of Egypt. This right had been denied to them, alone among the cities in the empire, from the time of the conquest by Rome in 30 BC, because of imperial suspicion of the country's volatile population. The Alexandrians, in particular, had been petitioning the emperors for a council almost continuously ever since. Septimius' action was thus the rectification of an anomaly. Egyptians were also permitted to enter the Roman senate for the first time. The first beneficiary was to be a certain Aelius Coeranus, described as a hanger-on of Plautianus.[15]

Plautianus' power was highly visible during this visit. Soon after arriving in Egypt the prefect of the province, Q. Aemilius Saturninus, was promoted to be Plautianus' colleague in command of the Guard. Plautianus took extreme exception to receiving a colleague, and before long apparently had Saturninus murdered. He also took steps to reduce the powers of the Guard tribunes, to remove the possibility that one of them might become eligible for the Prefecture, so Dio reports. 'Already he wanted to be Prefect for life, not merely sole Prefect', Dio adds, with two further stories to illustrate his ruthlessness and arrogance, which resulted in his acquiring 'much more' in the way of plunder from the provinces 'than was sent to Septimius himself. Finally, he stole horses with tiger-like stripes [presumably zebras] sacred to the Sun, from the islands in the Red Sea [perhaps the Persian Gulf] sending centurions' for the purpose. It was later discovered, Dio went on, that 'at home [this presumably refers to Rome rather than Lepcis Magna] he had castrated a hundred Romans of noble birth, to give his daughter Plautilla an entourage of eunuchs, especially as teachers in music and the other arts'. He was no doubt already planning to marry his daughter to Antoninus. He and his brother Geta were meanwhile under the tuition of the sophist Aelius Antipater of Hierapolis. Septimius had made this man his Greek Secretary, *ab epistulis Graecis*. Philostratus claims that Antipater fulfilled his duties brilliantly. 'No one composed letters better: like an outstanding tragic actor ... whose phraseology was always in keeping with the imperial *persona*.' Antipater used his influence with Septimius to find a husband for his own unattractive daughter. He also composed a *History*, exalting Septimius' achievements. 'We used to call him "Tutor of the Gods" when we applauded his lectures', Philostratus recalls.[16]

When Septimius was in Egypt it was inevitable that he would receive innumerable petitions, *libelli*. Some of the decisions of the emperors—for his son was his equal colleague—have been found on papyri. One particular papyrus preserves a whole series of imperial responses, *apokrimata*. Ulpius Heraclanus, also called Callinicus, was reminded that penalties imposed on the Alexandrians (no doubt for their support of Niger) had been revoked. Cronius son of Heraclides was told that transient sickness did not exempt him from compulsory public services (liturgies). Dioscorus son of Hephaestio and others were told that the emperors had forbidden the payment of money in lieu of grain. One Isidorus was referred to Plautianus: 'Floueios Plaudianos [*sic*: the scribe had difficulty with the name] the Distinguished Prefect of the Guard and Our Kinsman will investigate' an accusation against an official called Como; 'as for the tax–collector Apio, if he is not involved in the charge against Como, the governor of the province will be your judge.' Aemilius Saturninus had not yet been replaced as prefect; it seems that a man called Alfenus Apollinaris was acting-governor for the time being. Septimius was still at Alexandria on 9 March 200, when delegations from communities in the Egyptian countryside (*chora*) appeared before him in the court-house.[17]

The emperor was a devotee of Sarapis, the god whose cult the Ptolemies had fostered, indeed invented, or adapted from that of the god of Memphis, Osor-Hapi. The massive temple at Alexandria constructed by Ptolemy III had been rebuilt under Roman rule in the Corinthian style. Its priests and rituals were largely Greek, and this was no doubt what was familiar to Septimius from early youth, when, no doubt, he had worshipped the god at Lepcis. In Egypt he would be identified by many with the god himself: he was often enough portrayed with Sarapis' corkscrew curls and forked beard, and appears in this guise in a painted portrait found in Egypt, showing him with Julia and their sons (pl. 16). It may be the Alexandrian Sarapeum to which the *HA* refers when it recalls the emperor's 'pleasure in taking part in the worship of the god'.[18]

He had an opportunity, if he wished, to see the original Egyptian cult at Memphis, which he visited. At the Pharaohs' old capital Osor-Hapi remained strictly Egyptian. Greeks from Egypt and other foreigners left some mark, for example with statues of philosophers and poets; but Memphis, with its pyramids and shrines of animal gods, the bull of Apis and the ibis of Thoth, remained truly Egyptian, as had been ordained under Ptolemy V that it should. Apuleius had referred, in his *Metamorphoses*, to the 'secrets of Memphis'. Here, if anywhere, Septimius might have tried to collect and suppress 'hidden lore', such as the Ptolemaic *Oracle of the Potter*, foretelling the destruction of the foreign rulers, the 'belt-wearers' [Greeks], and the 'desertion' of the alien city by the sea. Apuleius, on trial for magic in Tripolitania, had laughed off the accusation that he had a mysterious cult-image of an emaciated Mercury. It may have been a figure of 'Thrice Greatest Hermes', the strange amalgam of Egyptian Thoth and Greek Hermes, a powerful source of occult power. Apuleius had been planning a visit to Egypt when he fell ill at Oea; and Septimius' contemporary and fellow-African, the Christian Tertullian, knew something of this cult.[19]

At Memphis he saw at any rate the pyramids and visited the statue of the Sphinx, which the prefect Saturninus had thoughtfully had repaired shortly before. A little further upstream he diverted to see the great Labyrinth on Lake Moeris, with its twelve covered courtyards and three thousand chambers. The next recorded stop was Thebes in Upper Egypt, where he saw the colossal statue of Memnon, the sitting figure of the Pharaoh Amenhophis III. Generations of Roman tourists had recorded their presence at dawn, when the statue 'sang'. Septimius pressed on and on, stopping only 'at the frontier of Ethiopia because of a plague', Dio says. Since the Pharaohs, the ruler of Egypt had been a god, and the Nile was a sacred river. Every year at the end of May a ceremony was held on the Upper Nile, at which the monarch cast gold and silver gifts down into a rock cave near the river. Under Roman rule the ritual was performed by the prefect, as Viceroy, unless the emperor was in Egypt. There is little doubt that the deeply superstitious, or religious, Septimius took the opportunity of carrying out the *sollemne sacrum* in person, at Philae (Aswan), presumably in late May of the year 200. This visit will also have enabled him to inspect the defences of Egypt. Roman garrisons may have stretched as far south as Primis (Qasr Ibrim); and north of Philae the routes across the eastern desert to the Red Sea, especially the Berenice Road, and those linking the Nile valley with the other ports, such as Myos Hormos, with the porphyry quarries on the way, may have claimed his attention.[20]

If he returned northwards by the river, Septimius must have left in early June at latest: a religious taboo debarred the ruler of Egypt from sailing on the Nile while it was in flood. The coins of Alexandria indicate that he was still in Egypt after the beginning of his ninth year, which in the Egyptian calendar started on 29 August in 200. He left Egypt by ship for Syria, but neither the exact date nor his precise whereabouts during the year 201 are on record. Early in 201 he decided to hold the consulship again, with his son Antoninus as his colleague, in the following year. Before this the boy, who had his thirteenth birthday in April, was invested with the *toga virilis* and formally entered man's estate. None of the sources comment on the anomaly that Antoninus was already Augustus as a *puer*. Nor has any trace of criticism survived at the implied insult to tradition in making a thirteen-year-old consul. There was little difference, perhaps, from the action of Marcus who had given the *fasces* to his son when Commodus was only fifteen. But Marcus had at least invested Commodus with the toga of manhood before he was either Augustus or consul.[21]

The ancient supreme magistracy was now an empty façade. But to be one of the two *consules ordinarii* was a highly prized distinction: not least, it meant that the year was known by these consuls' names. Septimius adhered to tradition. The ordinary consuls of his reign were either members of the imperial family, City Prefects holding office for the second time—such as Dexter in 196, Anullinus in 199, and, before long, Fabius Cilo in 204—or members of long established senatorial families. Within these limits the choice of those after whom the year was named allowed the emperor a useful means of patronage and of signalling his favour. Thus in 197 one consul was the aristocrat Sextius Lateranus: this could be construed as a gesture to the past but was also a sign of how those who supported Septimius could be rewarded. Albinus had been said to enjoy the backing of the aristocracy; Lateranus had thrown in his lot with Septimius and had served in the first Parthian war. His colleague was Cuspius Rufinus, a Greek senator from Pergamum, whose selection might conciliate the eastern notables. In 198 one consul was Martius Sergius Saturninus, a member of the recently decimated Gallic aristocracy and son of Marcus Aurelius' marshal Martius Verus. In 199 and 200 the sons of Marcus' friend Victorinus, who were also grandsons of Fronto, held office. These two represented both the Marcan tradition and Septimius' strong reliance on Numidia. Deference to Marcus' memory was also underlined by the other consul of 200, his grandson Ti. Claudius Severus Proculus, whose wife was Marcus' grand-niece.[22]

Septimius and Antoninus inaugurated the year 202 as consuls at Antioch. It was by now not uncommon even for *consules ordinarii* to hold office away from Rome; but it was rare for both to be absent. What is more, with the exception of 161, when Marcus and Verus were colleagues, there had never been an occasion when two emperors were consuls together; and in any case Marcus and Verus had not become emperor until after their consulship began. This made 202 a very special year and the honour shown to Antioch all the greater. Septimius had clearly decided to revoke the punishment inflicted on the city seven years previously. But it was announced that he did so at the request of Antoninus, thereby bringing his son into greater prominence and gaining him a fund of good will.[23]

The time had now come to return to Rome. On 9 April the tenth year of his reign would begin and Septimius would celebrate his *decennalia*. He and the court probably left Antioch soon after the ceremonies on New Year's Day. Only two stages in the first part of his journey, before he reached Europe, are recorded. Dio has two more anecdotes to illustrate the unchecked increase in Plautianus' arrogance and power. At Tyana in Cappadocia he had fallen ill. Septimius went to visit him, but the soldiers guarding the Prefect made the emperor enter alone, without his escort. Septimius apparently 'tolerated seeing Plautianus lodge in better quarters than himself, and have better and more abundant food than he did'. Dio confirms the latter point by relating how 'at Nicaea, my native city, when Septimius once wanted a mullet—and the lake there produces large ones—he sent to Plautianus for one'. Dio adds that Plautianus had become a complete sensualist, gorging himself at banquets and freely indulging his lusts with both girls and boys. Yet his wife was kept more or less in purdah, and forbidden to see or be seen by anyone, even Septimius and Julia. Septimius' authority was indeed being seriously undermined. When the *a cognitionibus* was asked to bring forward one of the cases due to be heard before the imperial tribunal, he told Septimius: ' "I cannot do that unless Plautianus orders me to do so." ' Meanwhile Julia was treated by Plautianus with scorn and hatred; he often abused her violently to Septimius.[24]

Julia took refuge in the company of sophists and the study of 'philosophy'. One sophist whom she had perhaps already met, was Philostratus, a pupil of Aelius Antipater. He was later, at her request, to compose a biography of the wonder-working philosopher Apollonius of Tyana. Julia's interest in the legendary sage may have been awakened in the course of this journey. Another literary figure who was in contact with the court was Cassius Dio. He had sent Septimius a copy of his first work, a little book 'about the dreams and omens which led Severus to hope for the imperial power'. Septimius liked it, and thanked Dio in a long and complimentary letter. Dio received the emperor's reply one evening and soon afterwards fell asleep. Then he himself had a dream, in which 'the Divine Power commanded me to write history. He at once decided to write an account of the disturbances [*staseis*, i.e. civil wars] and wars which followed the death of Commodus.' He covered, in other words, the events of the years 193–198, from the murder of Commodus to the end of the second Parthian war, clearly following the 'official' version. This work 'also won great approval from Septimius, as well as from others'.

Therefore [Dio wrote] I decided not to leave my first historical work as a separate composition, but to incorporate it in the present narrative, so

that in a single work I might write down and leave behind me an all-
embracing history, from the beginning down to the moment that shall
seem best to Fortune.

Quite when Dio wrote his first two works is not clear, but his motives are
not difficult to divine: the wish to conciliate the emperor. His home town,
Nicaea, had made the mistake of supporting Niger in 193–4 and had been
severely punished. It had always been obliged to play second fiddle to its
rival Nicomedia, but under Commodus it had gained some imperial
favour when the favourite Saoterus, a native of Nicomedia, was over-
thrown. Now Nicaea was denied even the title 'first in the province' with
which it had sought to emulate Nicomedia, 'the metropolis and first city
in the province', and 'temple-warden' of the imperial cult. Shortly after
the imperial visit in 202, Nicaea proudly called itself 'the most glorious,
the most great, loyal Friend and Ally of the Roman People, from the time
of our ancestors close to the Imperial House, Aureliana Antoniniana, most
pious City of the Nicaeans'. Nicaea had no doubt won imperial favour
through the efforts of Antoninus, or at least, as at Antioch, he could be
given the credit. Byzantium too was to gain benefits, thanks to the
intervention of Antoninus, and took the title 'Antonina', when its status as
a city was restored and the public buildings that had been demolished after
its capture were rebuilt.[25]

Cassius Dio may have played a part in gaining favour for Nicaea. Since
his praetorship in 194 he had doubtless been holding a number of official
posts. He was to become consul a few years later, c. 205, and at the time of
the imperial journey through Asia Minor may have been serving in the
east. He reported in an early part of his *History* one further act by
Septimius, which must have greatly interested him. He may even have
witnessed it, but, if not, he will certainly have seen the result. The great
Carthaginian opponent of Rome, Hannibal, had died an exile, in 183 BC,
taking poison when the king of Bithynia planned to betray him. He died
at a place in Bithynia called Libyssa, fulfilling the misleading oracle that
had promised he would die 'on Libyan soil'. Septimius erected a white
marble tomb to his great fellow-countryman, for he too was 'a Libyan by
race', as the Byzantine writer Tsetzes, whose information derives from
Dio, expressed it.[26]

After the stay in Bithynia, Septimius and the court crossed to Thrace.
The governor of this province, who will have received them, was a
Tripolitanian, from Oea: Q. Sicinius Clarus Pontianus. He was clearly a
close kinsman, perhaps the son, of Sicinius Pudens, Apuleius' loutish
stepson. An inscription from Lepcis Magna may allude to the favour that
Clarus Pontianus had enjoyed at the hands of the Lepcitane emperor. It is a

metrical dedication to Septimius, by one Pudens, in gratitude for his son's advancement. An imperial instruction carried out in Thrace by the governor Pontianus was the establishment of an *emporion* at a place called Pizos, with a hundred and seventy-one settlers. 'Moved by concern for the road-stations,' the governor's edict proclaims, 'and wishing that their province should remain in the same state of prosperity throughout their lifetime, our Great and Most Divine Lords the Emperors gave orders that existing *emporia* should be improved and new ones established'.[27]

A great many dedications and building inscriptions from the time of Septimius' visit have been preserved throughout the Danubian and Balkan region; but they do not prove that he visited the places in question. The coming *decennalia*, and the marriage between Antoninus and Plautilla, and indeed the successful conclusion of the Parthian war not long before, would have been ample occasion for most of the dedications, even without an imperial visit. Even if he did not set foot in a particular town, his presence somewhere in a province would result in the setting up of statues, altars and other marks of honour. Any who sought the emperor's favour would hasten to meet him, armed with letters of recommendation which would refer to the petitioner's loyalty to the imperial house as shown by the endowment of this or that monument.

It is highly probable that the route followed was along the Danube. The welfare of the armies that had won him the throne would never be closer to Septimius' heart than when the anniversary of his proclamation was approaching. It is plausible that he visited Lower and Upper Moesia, perhaps Dacia also, and then the two Pannonian provinces. It may even be that he chose to be at Carnuntum on 9 April, the *dies imperii*, and that his journey from there back to Rome was timed to repeat the stages and the timing of his march on Rome nine years before. But this is purely speculation. As he passed through these key military provinces he will have had the chance to confer with some of his most trusted adherents. In several of them new governors seem to have been installed in 202: they may have arrived with Septimius. In Lower Moesia L. Aurelius Gallus, who had commanded one of the Upper Pannonian legions under Septimius in 193, began his governorship in that year. Likewise a new governor was his neighbour in Upper Moesia, Q. Anicius Faustus, an African from Uzappa near Mactaris, who had just completed a lengthy term as commander of the Numidian legion III Augusta and as such had made sweeping changes to the whole frontier of Africa. Septimius will have especially welcomed the opportunity to hear from Faustus' own lips about the defences of their homeland. Faustus had been extending the frontiers of Africa, where Septimius was being accorded the title *propagator imperii*. It is possible that Septimius extended Rome's dominion beyond the Danube at this time, although firm evidence is lacking. He may have ordered the eastward extension of the Dacian frontier from the line of the river Aluta (Olt) for some twenty-five miles or a little more (40–50 km) to the *limes Transalutanus*. At Carnuntum, perhaps the final stage of this northern journey, there was another new governor. Ti. Claudius Claudianus, from Numidian Rusicade, who had been an equestrian officer in Septimius' army in 193, and had served him well in the civil wars, was now the consular. The trusted Fabius Cilo, who had ruled this key province from 197 to 201, had been appointed to the City Prefecture.[28]

The return to Rome after five years' absence was celebrated in high style. First there was a distribution of largesse to the urban plebs and the Guard, ten gold pieces a head. Dio says that 'Septimius took particular pride in this generosity; indeed, no emperor had ever before made such a large donation to the entire population of the city. The total sum amounted to 200,000 sesterces.' Next followed the imperial wedding. Antoninus, the reluctant fourteen-year-old bridegroom, received as his wife and indeed empress—she took the title Augusta—Fulvia Plautilla, the Prefect's daughter. Dio was among the guests: 'Plautianus gave as much for his daughter's dowry as would have sufficed for fifty women of royal rank. We saw the gifts as they were being carried through the Forum into the Palace. Then came the banquet, partly in royal and partly in barbaric style. We were given not only the usual kind of cooked meat, but raw meat too, and live.' (Does he just mean oysters and other seafood?)

Then came the main events, the ceremonies to mark the *decennalia* proper, certainly involving public sacrifices, and victory games and spectacles. None of the sources explicitly call the celebrations a triumph. The *HA* actually says that Septimius 'was offered a triumph by the senate, but refused it: the disease in his limbs [apparently gout, from which he suffered] made it impossible for him to stand up in the triumphal chariot'. Be this as it may, games of the most spectacular kind imaginable were put on to honour *decennalia* and Parthian victories. Again, Dio has a full account. 'At these spectacles sixty wild boars of Plautianus fought together at a signal and among other wild beasts that were slain were an elephant and a corocotta. This animal is Indian, and as far as I know was brought to Rome then for the first time. It has the colour of a lioness and tiger combined and the general appearance of those animals, as well as of a dog and a fox, in a curious mixture.' The corocotta, which the *HA*, contrary to Dio, thinks had already been shown at Rome under Antoninus Pius, was probably a striped hyena. 'The entire receptacle in the theatre', Dio goes on, 'had been constructed so as to resemble a boat . . . as it suddenly fell apart there came pouring out bears, lionesses, panthers, lions, ostriches, wild asses and bison . . . so that seven hundred beasts in all, both wild and domesticated at the same time, were seen running about and then slaughtered'. Coins issued to commemorate the occasion show the great boat in the Circus Maximus rather than theatre. 'To correspond with the duration of the festival, which lasted seven days, the number of animals slain was likewise seven times 100.' Septimius, whose own name derived from *septimus*, seventh, seems to have been influenced by the magic of numbers. He would soon have an even more striking opportunity to commemorate the number seven: the time was approaching, two years hence, when he could celebrate the seventh in the series of *ludi saeculares*.[29]

· 14 ·

RETURN TO AFRICA

SEPTIMIUS CAN SCARCELY HAVE remained much longer at Rome on this occasion than on the previous three flying visits: the triumphant entry in 193, when he stayed less than thirty days, and the brief periods in 196 and 197, before and after the war with Albinus. This time he planned a journey that should have been the most satisfying of all, a return to Africa. The stage was set for a celebratory passage of the African Emperor through the land of his origin. Only one predecessor had been before, Hadrian in 128. Septimius himself and Antoninus were consuls in this year. For the following year the designated consuls were two more sons of Lepcis, his brother Geta, holding his second consulship, and Plautianus— and he too was anomalously to be called 'consul for the second time', even though he had not really been consul before. Plautianus' 'honorary consulship', *ornamenta consularia*, were thus made equivalent to actual tenure of the *fasces*. (Dio, and no doubt others, strongly disapproved.)[1]

Once again the entire imperial family appears to have gone with Septimius: Julia, both their sons, Plautianus and Plautilla. Indeed, it may be supposed that this time his brother Geta was of the company, at least in Tripolitania, likewise various cousins, Septimii and Fulvii, such as L. Septimius Aper, perhaps a grandson of Septimius' 'uncle' Aper, who was to be consul in 207. The route chosen can only be guessed at. They might have gone first to Lepcis, but it is more probable that they landed at Carthage. The great *metropolis*, now well over 200 years old in its revived Roman form, was given a great privilege, the *ius Italicum*, carrying with it exemption from provincial taxation. This was something of an empty honour. The Caesarian colony had been assigned a vast 'measure', *pertica*, of land, and considerable if not complete tax-exemption, and was responsible for settlements, *pagi*, of Roman citizens and native communities far inland, at least as far as Thugga, over sixty miles (100 km) to the west. Now Thugga and two other communities in the region, Thignica and Thibursicum Bure, were granted the status of *municipium*, and were thus removed from Carthage's territory. At least eight or nine other 'peregrine' communities were similarly treated. Carthage had been cut down to size. The move may have been in response to canvassing by prominent persons from these areas—the Marii brothers, for example, probably from Thugga, and the family of the Gargilii Antiqui from that place, long established in the senate. Other measures were taken in the north-east of the province—the only part, other than Lepcis, so treated. Abitina in the Bagradas valley was made a *colonia*, promoted from *municipium*. Vaga, further west, which had already been promoted in this way early in the reign, actually received new veteran settlers, reviving the ancient custom: it was the first *deductio* for generations. Elsewhere in the old province, Utica, original capital of Roman Africa and by tradition the earliest Phoenician settlement in the continent, was given *ius Italicum* to match Carthage, and it may well be that she too lost territory in a similar manner.[2]

As would be expected, there is record of the imperial presence at Lambaesis, where the legion had its fortress. A few years after Septimius' visit, Numidia, which the legionary legates had in effect governed for more than a century and a half, is on record as a province *de iure*. It is reasonable to suppose that the decision was made during the imperial visit. The newly appointed legate, Claudius Gallus, who had served with Septimius against Albinus and in the second Parthian war, was himself from the Cirta region. It is likely enough that Septimius visited the old royal capital of Syphax and Massinissa, perched on its rock, a site said to make it one of the most beautiful cities in the world. But he certainly went to Lambaesis, where the III Augusta had been since Trajan's day, and may well have inspected the new frontier posts far to the south. During the preceding five years the legate Anicius Faustus had undertaken a whole series of measures designed to improve the security of Roman Africa. From Castellum Dimmidi in the west, some 190 miles (over 300 km) south of Algiers, to Cydamus and Gholaia (Bu-Ngem) deep in the desert south of Tripolitania, the frontiers had been extended and newly fortified. Dimmidi, founded in 198, lies on the same latitude as Agueneb, where a Roman patrol had been based briefly in 174, the year Septimius was in proconsular Africa as legate to his 'uncle' Gaius. A quarter of a century later he was to order the advance of Roman garrisons to this line on a permanent basis.[3]

Among the troops that constructed the fort of Dimmidi was a detachment from the Syrian legion III Gallica. It might seem at first sight surprising that men from the Syrian army should have been sent away from their base at the time of the Parthian war. But the deficiency was more than made good by the despatch of legionaries from III Augusta to Syria. A fruitful interchange of experience, it could be called. The lessons learned by the Syrian legion in controlling a desert frontier would be invaluable when a new desert frontier was being established in North

Africa. The notion was not new: Palmyrene and Syrian auxiliary units had long served in the Numidian army. As the same time, as a disciplinary measure for men who had supported Niger, a tour of duty in the Sahara could hardly have been bettered. The task assigned to the Numidian commanders was a formidable one: the line of military posts stretched from Dimmidi to Gholaia for a distance of nearly 1000 miles (over 1500 km). All this, a distance comparable to that of the entire Danube frontier, with only one legion and an auxiliary force that had amounted in the mid-second century to some 6000 men, a total of some 12,000. The threat, it must be conceded, was of a different order, no teeming hordes of 'barbarian' peoples, as there were beyond Rome's northern frontiers. Nonetheless, the semi-nomads could cause serious trouble, as they had in Africa under Tacfarinas long before, and, more recently, when the Moors had risen under Pius, and had broken out to ravage Spain under Marcus (a foretaste of what was to happen five centuries later). Septimius had cause to remember that well—it had deprived him of his quaestorship in Baetica. The Moors had continued to give trouble and it is no surprise that the two Mauretanian provinces also received attention from him, whether or not he went in person. A new frontier line (*nova praetentura*) was established south of the Tell in Caesariensis. The work began in 198 under the procurator governor Octavius Pudens, himself a native of the province (his home town Auzia was promoted to *colonia* by Septimius, the only such change in Mauretania). Tingitana, cut off by mountains from the other Mauretania, shows no clear evidence of an advance of this kind, although there may have been campaigning precisely in the Taza Gap and upper Moulouya valley between the two provinces. A Victory monument was set up at Bou Hellou, fifty-five miles (90 km) east of Volubilis, perhaps the outcome of actions by the procurator Haius Diadumenianus, in office precisely in 202, or his probable successor Sallustius Macrinianus. Both these men were given the exceptional joint command over both Mauretanias, a sign that there was fighting going on.[4]

Then to Lepcis: perhaps directly from Lambaesis, east to Theveste, then south-east to Thelepte, down to Capsa, where Jugurtha's treasure had been captured, and across to the coast at Tacape. From there, along the road he must have known well, the Carthage–Alexandria highway, through Sabratha and Oea, to reach his *patria*. It may have been nearly thirty years since he had been at Lepcis, as he would be reminded by the arch on the Oea road.[5]

There were new things for him to see. The baths had been restored, for one thing, under Commodus, but the inscription had already been revised: first Commodus' name had been deleted after his death and *damnatio*, then Septimius' own name and titles substituted. But this was only one small item. The whole of Lepcis was now full of statues and dedications to Septimius, Julia, Antoninus, Geta, Plautianus, Plautilla, and indeed of Septimius' father and mother, his grandfather and his first wife, Paccia Marciana (a woman of Lepcis, it will be remembered). The process had doubtless begun in the summer of 193, although the first dated examples belong to 197, with a statue in the shrine of Liber Pater in the Forum. It was dedicated to him with all his titles and the additional grandiloquent label *conservatori orbis*, 'defender of the world': the Lepcitani put it up, from public funds, because of his *pietas* 'loyal affection' in his public capacity (*publicam*) and, 'towards them, in his private capacity' (*et in se privatam*). Thus the emperor's home town tactfully asserted their special relationship to the seat of power. A statue of Antoninus was alongside, calling him '*M. Aurellius Antoninus Caes. imp. destinatus*'. The Aurelian name, already very widespread after numerous grants of citizenship by the emperors from Antoninus Pius to Commodus, is spelt with a double L, an apparent attempt, which seems to have been officially inspired, to distinguish the new Antoninus from the common mass of Aurelii. A dedication to Geta has survived, set up at Lepcis by the *colonia* of Tyre, 'mother-city of Phoenicia and of other cities'. The old links were remembered: at Tyre the Lepcitani reciprocated.[6]

In the years that followed, from 198–202, a mass of further such displays of loyalty appeared, by the Lepcitani as a community, by *curiae* and by zealous individuals. No doubt many more have vanished. A procurator, M. Ulpius Cerealis, 'most devoted to his divine spirit', *devotissimus numini eius*, put up a statue to Septimius in the south-east angle of the Forum in 198, and another to Geta Caesar (no doubt to Antoninus as well, but the inscription has not survived). Cerealis, like Plautianus, is presumably a Lepcitane beneficiary of Septimius' rise to power. Two other procurators, M. Junius Punicus and D. Clodius Galba, who honoured Septimius at Lepcis may also be Lepcitanes, although they could be men from other cities who took steps to honour the emperor at his *patria*. A further procurator, Flavius Celer, who erected a statue to Fulvia Plautilla as the fiancée, *sponsa*, of Antoninus, did so with the freedmen and slave clerks attached to the tax bureau which he headed, presumably the Tripolitanian branch of the revenue, *IIII publica Africae*. Punicus styled himself procurator *ad Mercurium* (at Alexandria) on the dedications of his statues to Septimius and the rest of the imperial family set up in the theatre in 201. Clodius Galba put his statues up in the portico behind the theatre the year after the imperial visit, when he had just been promoted, from running imperial estates in western proconsularis, to an Italian district of the 'privy purse', *ratio privata*. The promotion may have resulted from the imperial visit.[7]

In 202 the people of Lepcis erected further statues to Septimius, Antoninus and Geta in the baths, 'on account of the extraordinary and divine favour towards them' by the emperors; and the Lepcitani now call themselves Septimiani. Septimius may have waited until his arrival in the city before announcing the grant of *ius Italicum*: like Carthage and Utica—and indeed like Tyre and certain other cities he had already favoured—Lepcis Magna was to be treated as if it were part of Italy, and exempt from tax. It is perhaps fanciful to imagine Statius' lines to the first Septimius Severus echoing in the emperor's ears—*sermo non Poenus, non habitus tibi: Italus, Italus!*—as he made the announcement, perhaps to an assembly of the *curiae* in the theatre. The *curiae* now, in some cases at least, added the name 'Severa' or 'Severiana' to their style. Apart from these private and public tokens of devotion the people of Lepcis honoured Septimius with a monumental quadrifrons arch over one of the major crossroads in the city, just where Aelius Lamia's forty-four miles road was commemorated. It seems that the arch was already standing. It was now adorned with reliefs depicting the imperial family, with a scene of triumph evoking the celebrations of Parthian victory the previous summer and another showing Parthians being defeated.[8]

The benefit which Septimius conferred on Lepcis may have led the city notables, perhaps in response to his prompting, to offer something in return. At all events, Septimius is said to have provided free oil rations to the people of Rome in perpetuity. In other words, what was given with one hand, the exemption from tribute conferred by the *ius Italicum*, may have been taken away with the other. The quantities involved were very substantial, requiring considerable organisation. It is probably no coincidence that Tripolitanian oil containers begin to be stamped at precisely this time. Among the suppliers thus identified are, not surprisingly, the emperors, the Guard Prefect and L. Septimius Aper, further the family of the Silii Plautii. Equally, it was appropriate that a few years later the post of prefect of the Annona was to be held by one of the Lepcis Marcii, Q. Marcius Dioga.[9]

The only direct mention of Septimius' stay in Africa in the literary sources comes in Philostratus' *Lives of the Sophists*. Two rival sophists, Heraclides of Lycia and Apollonius of Athens, had competed with declamations before the emperor. Heraclides, who came off worst, 'spread a false report about Apollonius, that he was about to set out straightaway for Libya, when the emperor was there and gathering the talented together from every country'. Whether sophists or poets accompanied the imperial party is not attested. It is not impossible that leading actors or other performers came from Rome, to Carthage and to Lepcis, to put on displays. But the archaeological evidence certainly suggests that leading sculptors were commissioned. Septimius had ambitious plans for the embellishing of his native city. Work was begun shortly after his visit on a huge new Forum and Basilica, in the area between the Hadrianic Baths and the old Forum. Alongside the west bank of the Wadi Lebdah, once liable to flooding, a monumental colonnaded street was laid out, running from the Baths to the harbour, which was now reconstructed on a vast scale. Work on the new Forum and Basilica was not to be completed until 216. Expensive marble had been imported from the eastern Mediterranean on a grand scale, some of it marked 'on the order of Fulvius Plautianus, *c.v.*, Guard Prefect and Kinsman of our Lords, to be sent to the Most Splendid *colonia* Leptis Magna'. Apart from this, the city water supply was improved and the Circus enlarged and restored.[10]

On the far side of the new Forum from the Basilica was a great temple. It is generally assumed that it was dedicated to the Septimian house, as once Augustus and then later emperors had been so honoured here, in the old Forum and elsewhere. Dio refers acidly at one point to Septimius' building activities: 'he also wasted a great deal of money by repairing other buildings and building new ones: for example, he built an excessively large temple to Bacchus and Hercules.' No Severan temple to Bacchus and Hercules has been identified at Rome. Perhaps, as was suggested long ago, it was this shrine at Lepcis to which Dio referred. He could have seen it not long after its completion, as proconsul of Africa about the year 223. Septimius' devotion to the *di patrii*, Shadrapa-Liber or Bacchus and Melqart-Hercules, was to be displayed at Rome in 204.[11]

The imperial party probably wintered at Lepcis and it was no doubt there that Septimius' brother Geta and Plautianus inaugurated the Roman year as the consuls for 203. Septimius had more to do. He wanted to put the finishing touches to the defence of his *patria*. Much had been done already in the later second century to give Tripolitania protection. Under Commodus military posts were established at Vezereos, west of Gigthis, where the western route from the Sahara, between the Great Erg and the Hamada el Hamra—the 'red rock'—comes up from the south, at Tisavar, and Tillibari. Under Anicius Faustus' command there was activity at Vezereos and Tillibari. In 198 he 'ordered a garrison to be placed' south of Tillibari (at the modern Si Aioun), and, far down the road to the Garamantian country, at Cydamus (Ghadames), the first oasis which caravans from the Sahara could use after a journey of over 300 miles (500 km) from the nearest Garamantian settlement. On the Gebel road there was also a line of military posts. A dedication to the Syrian deity, Sol Hierabolus, at Auru, midway between Tillibari and Lepcis, was made for the welfare of Septimius, his sons and Julia and 'the whole divine house' by 'a detachment of III Augusta and the men from the cohort of Syrian archers'. At Thenadassa (Ain Wif), south-west of Mesphe (Medina Doga), fifty miles (80 km) south of Oea, over sixty miles (100 km) south-west of Lepcis, Caninius Adiutor Faustinianus, prefect of the Second Cohort of Hamii (raised at Hamath-Epiphania not far from Emesa) and acting commander of another detachment of the Third legion, set up an altar to Jupiter of Doliche for the 'welfare and victory' of Septimius and his sons and Julia. Just under fifty miles (75 km) south of Thenadassa, on the southern edge of the Gebel and at the western end of the Sofeggin valley (the modern Bir Tarsin) there was another post. Others may be postulated at this time, particularly on the road that went due south from Oea and, after being joined by the Lepcis–Thenadassa road, crossed the Gebel on its way to the Sahara skirting the east side of the 'red rock'. Over 180 miles (nearly 300 km) south of Lepcis, two military posts at the Gheriat oases now guarded the approaches to the Sofeggin and Zem-Zem valleys, the Gebel and the *emporia*. Finally, in January 201 'a detachment of III Augusta came to build the fort Ghol(aia)'. The centurion C. Julius Dignus consecrated the site to the 'Spirit of Gholaia' (*Genio Gholaiae*), for the health of the emperors, 'on the first day of coming to the place where our three Lords ordered a fort to be built'. Gholaia (Bu–Ngem), the most easterly of these forts, was sited by Faustus in the last year of his command to cover the main route from the eastern end of the Garamantian oases across the Black Mountain, leading caravans, or raiders, either north-west, past Gheriat to the Gebel, or north-east, across the Bei el-Kebir valley, to the Syrtica. From Gholaia to Lepcis is over 150 miles (some 250 km) as the crow flies, rather longer by the shortest passable routes.[12]

The three great valleys of the pre-desert zone between the Cinyps and Gholaia, Sofeggin, Zem–Zem and Bei el-Kebir, running parallel to the Gebel towards the sea, are at first sight arid and barren. The wadi beds are dry for all but a few days and annual rainfall is as low as two inches (50 mm) in the southern and eastern zone. Yet during the two centuries before Septimius' return to Africa settlement had developed to a surprising extent. It was the native Libyan population, presumably elements of the great Macae tribe known to Herodotus, which had managed to cultivate olives and other crops and rear some stock in this unpromising territory, as the discovery of olive-presses and other remains have demonstrated. The people were strongly Punicised. It is they who provide the latest examples of the Punic language in this part of Africa, on inscriptions in the Latin alphabet, with names like 'Julius Masthalul ben Chyrdidry', a remarkable blend of the three elements in their culture. There were major settlements such as that overlaid by the modern Mizda, immediately south of the Gebel in the upper Sofeggin basin, or Ghirza, the largest such centre, in the even more arid Zem–Zem valley. What the legal status of these territories was is unclear. The Macae, or subdivisions of that people, may have had institutions of self-government. It is not impossible that they were 'attributed' to Lepcis and controlled from there. Further, it is not known who owned the land. Some of it may have been in the hands of the major olive-growers of Lepcis; they are, at the least, likely to have played a major role in marketing the modest camel-loads brought up from the valleys, and to have shared in the profit from their sale.[13]

In the winter or early spring Septimius launched a campaign. It is hard to believe that he himself went right down to the heartlands of the Garamantes, the three parallel lines of Saharan oases, running east–west. The nearest oasis south of Gholaia was some 100 miles (160 km) away, and the total distance from Gholaia to Garama a good 300 miles or more (500 km). Yet Septimius had been as far as Ctesiphon, he was to go to the limits of North Britain. His restless energy may have impelled him to follow in the path of Balbus and Valerius Festus. At least it may be supposed that he went as far as Gheriat or Gholaia, and then entrusted the new legate of the Third, Claudius Gallus, and Plautianus with the final stage. Elements of the legion must have been involved, and the Syrian auxiliaries, presumably some of the Guard, if the Prefect was there (they will have been ill-adapted to the desert conditions). At all events, Aurelius Victor says unequivocally that Septimius 'freed Tripolitania, the region from which he came, from fear of attack, by crushing most warlike tribes'. The Nasamones of the Syrtica may also have been on the receiving end—Gholaia was so sited as to be able to watch them too.[14]

If Septimius waited for some weeks at Gholaia he will have found baths ready for use, as an inscription of 202 records. Shortly after this time the legionary centurion Q. Avidius Quintianus set up an acrostic dedication in the bath-building, thirty-six lines of verse with the letters of his own name forming the first letter of every other line. He 'found at last the name and spirit (*nomen et numen*) of the goddess', and 'hallowed her name as best he could'. In the baths 'the true waters of health' allowed all to 'soothe their bodies by swimming in tranquillity', to counteract the 'scorching flames of the south wind . . . in these ever sandy hills', an evocative description of the *ghibli* at Bu-Ngem. On 11 April, Septimius' birthday, T. Flavius Marinus, a legionary centurion, dedicated an altar beside the Severan harbour, in front of the temple of Jupiter Dolichenus, 'for the health and victory of our three Lords the Emperors [and—later deleted—of the prefect Plautianus] and for their return to their city'. It is not dated to a precise year, but it seems plausible that it was set up in 203, and that Septimius and his sons were not yet back at Lepcis.[15]

A few weeks earlier, on 7 March (which was the fourteenth birthday of

Geta) Carthage saw the worship of a god very different from the ancient Hittite storm-god of Commagene—a *conservator mundi* that appealed to the soldiers, with his thunderbolt, double axe, royal cuirass and sword. A young Christian called Vibia Perpetua was gored to death by a heifer in the arena, after trial and sentence by the acting governor, the procurator Hilarianus (the proconsul had died in office). A few years later Tertullian told the proconsul Scapula that Septimius had protected Christians of high rank against the fury of the mob. He gives no details, and the story may be suspect. But Tertullian also relates that Septimius had the services of a therapist—perhaps a masseur, to relieve his gouty limbs—called Torpacion or Proculus, a Christian all his life ('nurtured on Christian milk'). 'Antoninus knew this man', he told Scapula. But it is doubtful whether Septimius and the imperial party took note of Perpetua's martyrdom. Such events, not always spectacular, were becoming routine, and were certainly not the result of a change of policy initiated by Septimius.[16]

It was perhaps while the imperial party was at Lepcis that a rift was caused in Plautianus' immense power. For some reason Septimius became displeased with him. Dio and the *HA* differ about the details, but what happened is clear enough. According to Dio, Septimius was annoyed at the number of statues that were set up to Plautianus. The *HA* specifies that he was angry that 'Plautianus had placed his own statue among those of his kinsmen and relatives.' There can hardly have been another city where images of the imperial house and the whole clan were so omnipresent as at Lepcis; and the Prefect and his daughter were included. Dio says that Septimius had some bronze statues of Plautianus melted down: from this act a rumour spread that he had been overthrown. Some in official positions took appropriate action and themselves demolished Plautianus' statues. One was the governor of Sardinia, Racius Constans, who later paid the penalty. He and others who had acted similarly were tried and punished. The *HA* asserts that Septimius actually declared Plautianus a public enemy, and then relented. It is easy to understand that Septimius might have tolerated affronts from Plautianus elsewhere. At Lepcis Magna, the Lepcitane emperor would wish it to be clear that he, not Plautianus, was the city's greatest son. At all events, for the time being the breach was healed, and the imperial party departed for Rome after a stay of many months. Shortly before 10 June 203 the Horse Guards, *equites singulares Aug.*, made a dedication at the capital on their return from *expeditio felic(issima)*, as the African year could fairly be called.[17]

· 15 ·

THE YEARS IN ITALY

SEPTIMIUS' ENTRY INTO ROME on his return from Africa will certainly have been festive. It may be that he held a 'minor triumph', *ovatio*, for his military successes in Tripolitania. According to the *HA*, he entered the city, after his reconciliation with Plautianus, 'as if celebrating an ovation'. (The author has drastically abbreviated his source: his notice about Plautianus is inserted, out of place, immediately before the mention of Septimius' departure for the east in summer 197.) Septimius did receive one public honour. A magnificent arch, probably voted at the end of the first Parthian war, was dedicated in 203. It was set up in the north-east corner of the Forum, between the Rostra and the senate-house, in front of the temple of Concord. The monument towered more than seventy-five feet (22 m) above the level of the Comitium, adorned with reliefs commemorating the *victoria Parthica*. It was placed on the spot where, in his dream in early 193, Septimius had seen Pertinax fall from his horse, and himself being taken up on it. The imperial vision had already been commemorated by an equestrian statue. Now the massive arch, the first major addition to the architecture of the Forum for eighty years, gave the place more dramatic emphasis. Commemoration of the dream was not the sole reason for putting the arch there. The Comitium was the site of the legendary encounter between Romulus and Titus Tatius, and then the meeting place of the *comitia curiata*, the oldest assembly of the people. The Rostra, the *curia* of the senate, the temple of Concord, all had immense symbolic significance. Looming over the meetings of the senate, but next to the temple of Concord, the arch was a powerful reminder of the emperor's power but also perhaps a pointer to reconciliation. What is more, it stands diagonally opposite the arch erected to celebrate Augustus' diplomatic success over the Parthians in 20 BC. Thus Septimius would be linked with the first emperor and perhaps subtly be shown to have surpassed him. Besides all this, the arch gave final definition to the architectural design of the Forum.[1]

The inscription in gilded lettering on the arch, honouring Septimius and his sons, states that the senate and people of Rome set it up to them, 'on account of the restoration of the Republic and the extension of the

Empire of the Roman People by their outstanding virtues at home and abroad'. The 'restoration of the republic' can only refer to the defeat of Didius Julianus, and perhaps the other rival claimants. 'Extension of the Empire' acclaims the new provinces of Osrhoene and Mesopotamia, perhaps also the advance of the African frontiers. Further extension of the boundaries of Rome was yet to come.[2]

The year 204 was inaugurated by Fabius Cilo, consul for the second time, and Annius Libo, grandson of Marcus Aurelius' cousin. Cilo's second consulship was the payment of a debt to a friend who had served Septimius well. Septimius' gratitude also took tangible form. Cilo was among the emperor's friends whom he endowed with substantial wealth, according to a late fourth-century writer. His palatial mansion, the 'domus Cilonis', became a city landmark. The choice of Libo as the other consul once again marked Septimius' proclaimed membership of the Antonine dynasty.[3]

In the course of 203 arrangements had begun to mark the following year with ceremonies and celebrations of the most striking kind known to the Romans, Saecular Games. Their origin was cloaked in legend and uncertainty. Augustus, renovator of the Roman state and the Roman religion had chosen to celebrate them in 17 BC, which suited his political needs. It was possible to assert that these were the fifth in a series held at intervals of one hundred and ten years, the Etruscan era or *saeculum*. All were ready to agree that the establishment of his rule marked a new age. With the ending of the civil wars, the final conquest of Spain, the fruitful marriage of his daughter Julia, the recovery of the legionary standards from the Parthians, Saecular Games could fittingly denote the close of one era and inaugurate a new golden age. For three nights and three days, from 1–3 June, sacrifices and games were conducted by the *quindecimviri sacris faciundis*, the Board of Fifteen for performing sacrifices.

The next games, the sixth, should have been celebrated in 94. Claudius found an excuse for holding his own in 47, which marked the eight hundredth year of Rome. Domitian ignored the Claudian games and held the sixth in the series, six years early, in 88—unless his reason was that the Augustan games had been postponed (as well as they might have been) from a date originally set in 23 BC.[4]

Now 220 years, two *saecula*, would have passed, by the summer of 204. What is more, by happy chance the time had come to celebrate the seventh in the series: Septimius was surely attached to the planetary number. That the celebration of these games was by tradition the task of the *quindecimviri sacris faciundis* may also have been of special interest to him. His kinsman C. Septimius Severus had been one, and he himself could have been co-opted before becoming emperor. Members of the great priestly colleges generally did their best to secure a priesthood for their relatives or protégés when vacancies arose. Or if a deceased priest had been respected by his colleagues, the man's own nominee would be given the place that he had vacated. Septimius may have replaced his kinsman. Certainly, during Commodus' reign there must have been a higher turnover than usual, as the number of victims continually rose.[5]

To the *quindecimviri* was entrusted the care of the Sibylline oracles and of foreign religious rites of which the worship was licensed at Rome, including the cult of Isis and Sarapis. If Septimius had indeed become a *quindecimvir* as a senator, he would have relished both aspects of his duties. It would not have required especial skill in sacred lore to establish that Saecular Games would soon be due. Under Commodus the *quindecimviri* may well have pondered what form the deranged emperor would impose on the solemn ceremonies. The oracles in their guardianship were those carefully vetted by Augustus and housed in the temple of Palatine Apollo. Other oracles circulated under the name of Sibyl, in the Greek east, composed by Jews. One prophesied the return of Nero and the fall of Rome in the year 195. That year had safely passed. The civil wars were over. The Parthians had been defeated and a new land added to the empire of the Roman people. The emperor had ruled for more than ten years, his elder son was his colleague, there were now hopes, with Antoninus' marriage to Plautilla, of a third generation in the divine imperial house.[6]

At a meeting of the senate in 203—the exact date has not survived on the inscription, but it was March, June or July—the *quindecimviri* stood before the consuls' raised bench, and the Master of the College, Manilius Fuscus, read out a prepared speech. He recalled to the senate that the time was at hand for holding the Saecular Games. He spoke of the Sibyl's prophetic song, that the longest span of human life reached the hundred and tenth year. It was the duty of the senate, in view of the happiness and joy of the human race, to render thanks for present benefits and to ensure their future continuance, by providing for the holding of these games.

'You should, with all worship and veneration of the immortal gods, for the security and eternity of the empire, frequent the most sacred shrines, for the rendering and giving of thanks, so that the immortal gods may pass on to the future generations what our ancestors have built up and the things which, after previously conferring them on our ancestors, they have granted to our own times as well.'

A motion was then formally introduced by Calpurnius Maximus: that the emperors and Septimius Geta the most noble Caesar should be requested to hold the Saecular Games, which were customarily held at intervals of 110 years, in the following year: that the games should be held at public expense; and that there should be public holidays on the days when the games were held. Lawsuits should be postponed for thirty days, likewise mourning by women should be prohibited for a similar period, and to commemorate the proceedings a record should be inscribed on marble.

Further arrangements were made at a meeting of the *quindecimviri* on the Palatine on 11 November, and in February or March 204. On 15 April the members of the College received a letter from the emperors, read to them by the Master, Pompeius Rusonianus. They were to assemble in the temple of Apollo on the Palatine on 25 May, 'to choose by lot the places in which the members, seated on tribunals, are to distribute means of purification to the people'. A second letter was also read out, informing them that if they decided on which days and nights the games should be held, and the matrons should offer prayers and incense, the emperors would so decree. The College duly met and drew lots on 25 May, and on the same day issued an edict announcing the arrangements.

On 26 May the *quindecimviri* took up their allotted positions on the Capitol, Palatine and Aventine hills, and distributed the incense and other purificatory materials. Probably three days later they took up their positions again, this time to receive symbolic offerings of first-fruits from the people, after prayers to Jupiter Best and Greatest, Juno Queen of Heaven and Apollo Good and Beautiful, led by Septimius. On 31 May the solemn purificatory rites were undertaken. The Master, Pompeius Rusonianus, purified the spot known as Terentum or Tarentum, on the edge of the Campus Martius, where the Saecular rites, once a private ceremony of the Valerian *gens*, had always had their focus. It was sacred to the gods of the underworld, whose share in the ritual had largely been taken over by heavenly deities. The purification of the people followed, then preparatory sacrifices, in the presence of the *quindecimviri* and two senior Vestal Virgins, on the bank of the Tiber.

The next night, after midnight when the Kalends of June began, the Saecular rites proper were inaugurated, with sacrifice and prayer to the Moerae or Fates, on the Campus Martius. At the second hour of the morning were staged performances on a specially erected stage. Meanwhile Julia Domna, with one hundred and nine other married women, one for each year of the *saeculum*, held sacred banquets (*sellisternia*) on the Capitol in honour of the goddesses Juno and Diana.

Through the three days and two nights following Septimius and his sons performed all the traditional rituals of sacrifice and prayer, with games at intervals. On each occasion Septimius presided, Antoninus led the prayer and Geta carried it on. The traditional formulas used by Augustus in 17 BC were faithfully followed. The god or goddess was invoked by name, then came these words:

'let all good fortune attend the Roman People, the Quirites, let sacrifice be made to you with [the appropriate sacrifice for the particular deity]. I beg and beseech you that just as you have increased the empire and majesty of the Roman People, the Quirites, in war and in peace, so may the Latin always be obedient; that you may grant everlasting safety, victory and health to the Roman people, the Quirites; that you may protect the Roman People, the Quirites, and the legions of the Roman People, the Quirites; that you may keep safe and magnify the republic of the Roman people, the Quirites; that you may be favourable and propitious to the Republic of the Roman People, the Quirites, the College of the Quindecimviri, to me, my house, my household.'

As in 17 BC, the final games in the Circus were preceded by a hymn, the *Carmen Saeculare*, sung first on the Palatine and then again on the Capitol, by two choirs of twenty-seven boys and twenty-seven girls. Augustus could call on Horace to compose the hymn. The name of the poet of 204 has not been preserved, and cannot be conjectured. Little of the hymn itself has survived, either. There is an invocation of Apollo and Diana, as in the Horatian *carmen*. There is reference also to the shores and cities of the empire, to Bacchus and the golden fields, to ships sailing the seas, to the camps of the army, and, at the end, a prayer to protect 'our Leaders'. Bacchus is the same god as Liber Pater, one of the two guardian deities of Lepcis Magna. However traditional the prayers and rituals may have been, there was clearly some modification in honour of the *di patrii* of Septimius, Hercules and Liber. The surviving portions of the commentarium do not contain any mention of them, apart from the name of Bacchus in the *carmen*. But the coins issued in commemoration of these games convey the impression that the two gods of Lepcis were the presiding deities of the whole occasion.

Again in the tradition of the Augustan celebration, the three-day ceremony was followed by seven days of games, both stage performances and circus races. On the last day came the 'Troy Game', performed by boys of senatorial family. One of the boys, who bore an historic name, being a Calpurnius Piso, was severely injured. There were still a few surviving descendants of the Republican nobility. They were kept well in the background. Augustus, mindful of the origin of the Saecular Games as a rite of the Valerii, had given two distinguished members of the *gens* a role in 17 BC, as *quindecimviri*. There were two men alive in the reign of Septimius who advertised descent from the patrician Valerii, L. Valerius Messalla Thrasea Priscus, consul *ordinarius* in 196, and L. Valerius Messalla, who was to hold the same distinction in 214. Neither was a *quindecimvir*.[7]

The composition of the College is an interesting study in itself, not least for contrasts and comparisons with 17 BC. Then, together with Augustus himself, two Valerii Messallae, an Aemilius Lepidus, a Licinius Stolo and a Mucius Scaevola, noble names, balanced the *novi homines*, great soldiers and politicians such as Agrippa, Sentius Saturninus and Cocceius Nerva. The bearers of great names among the *quindecimviri* of 204 had acquired them not from descent but from grant of citizenship to their ancestors—a Cassius, a Fabius, two Fulvii, a Manilius, a Pompeius. Some of the other *nomina* were redolent of provincial Italy: Gargilius, Ofilius, Pollienus, Vetina. But of the twenty-six *quindecimviri* recorded only one, Nonius Arrius Mucianus of Verona, is known to have been the son of a consular. Few besides Mucianus were even Italian. Pollienus Auspex, the sarcastic friend of Septimius, was probably one. The emperor, his sons and the Praetorian Prefect, had several fellow-Africans in the College, perhaps as many as nine. The *magister* in 204, Julius Pompeius Rusonianus, whose *cognomen* is otherwise recorded only at Lepcis, was given a special role to play in the rites—the purification on 31 May. It would not be surprising if he was another Lepcitane.[8]

In the list of married women and boys and girls who participated in the rites provincial names seem also to be dominant. Unlike the Augustan *commentarium*, which speaks only of the hundred and ten *matronae*, that of the year 204 specifies Julia Domna, *mater castrorum*, with 109 others who took part. Ninety-one were wives of senators. The remaining eighteen equestrian ladies were headed by Julia's niece, Julia Soaemias, wife of Varius Marcellus of Apamea.[9]

Of the three narrative sources only Herodian contains any mention of these games. Dio's account has obviously been omitted by his epitomator. The author of the *HA* gives up any pretence at detailed narrative after the first six years of the reign. Herodian is brief and inaccurate, but one sentence does strike a true note: 'Heralds were sent out in Rome and Italy, calling all to come and see what they had never seen before and would never see again.' As it turned out, no one was ever to see Saecular Games again. These were the last in the series.[10]

In the course of 204, probably early in the year, Antoninus and Geta were designated to the consulship for the year 205. Thus the first year of the new *saeculum* would bear the names of Septimius' sons. Geta, who had probably received the *toga virilis* the previous year, was by now known generally as 'most noble Caesar'. For the past few years there had been some variation in his nomenclature: he had sometimes the *praenomen* Publius, sometimes Lucius. From now on he remained Publius officially. There must have been some reason for the change, although none of the ancient sources discusses it. It may be that when his elder brother changed his name to M. Aurelius Antoninus, Geta took Antoninus' original *praenomen* Lucius. Antoninus' original *praenomen* is however unknown. Such a change of name would recall the action of Marcus Aurelius and Lucius in 161, when Marcus took the name 'Antoninus' and gave his original name 'Verus' to Lucius. Or perhaps Geta's name was changed to Lucius to avoid confusion with the emperor's brother. Geta the elder remained in the background after his Dacian command. The inscription from the base of his statue at Lepcis does not even mention his relationship to Septimius. Another inscription apparently in his honour, from Ancona where he had once served as curator, calls him *cognatus* of Septimius and *avunculus* of Antoninus and the younger Geta. *Cognatus* means 'relation by marriage' and *avunculus* means 'maternal uncle'. It may be that the people of Ancona—and indeed everyone else—were forbidden to call Geta the brother and paternal uncle, *patruus*, of the emperors. The inaccurate description of Ancona may be the result of an evasion by people determined somehow to indicate that a man linked to their city was a kinsman of the imperial family. However this may be, in 204 the elder Geta died. On his deathbed, no longer restrained by his fear of Plautianus, he revealed all the facts about him to his brother. Septimius set up a statue to him in the Forum. And his attitude to Plautianus began to change. He stripped him of much of his power.[11]

The urban plebs, which had hardly had a chance to observe Plautianus during the years when he was building up his power, had soon commented on the Prefect's extraordinary preeminence. At the Circus on one occasion, Dio records, there was a shout: 'Why do you tremble? Why are you pale? You possess more than the Three!' 'Plautianus', says Dio, 'was in fact always pale and trembling because of his hopes and fears.' Dio was much stirred by an event that he took to be an omen of impending change at the highest level, an eruption of Vesuvius. The blast could be heard at Capua over twenty miles away, where Dio was living on his estate.[12]

The marriage of Antoninus and Plautilla was not a success. In spite of this, some have deduced that Plautilla may have borne a child in 204. But the evidence thought to refer to such an event may indicate no more than pious hopes. The language of Dio allows one to doubt whether the marriage was even consummated. As the bridegroom was only fourteen at the time of the ceremony, this would not have been surprising, especially as he loathed his wife and her father.[13]

Dio's account of the denouement has been preserved in some detail. In January 205 Antoninus felt confident enough to try a bold stroke. He persuaded the freedman Euodus, who as his *educator* had supervised his early boyhood, to enlist the services of three centurions. The plan was carried out without a flaw. On 22 January, while the imperial family was about to begin dinner, after the *ludi Palatini*, the three centurions presented themselves to Septimius. They informed him that they and seven others had been ordered by Plautianus to kill both emperors, and read out a letter which appeared to confirm their story. Septimius believed them, not least because of the dream he had had the previous night that Albinus was alive and plotting against him. He immediately summoned Plautianus. When the Prefect arrived at the palace, his followers were not permitted to go in with him—as had once been the case with Septimius at Tyana, as Dio notes. He was alarmed at this, but could not withdraw. When he entered Septimius spoke to him in a mild tone, but reproachfully, merely asking him why he wanted to kill them. He intended to give him the chance of making his defence. Antoninus could not endure the suspense. As Plautianus began to express his innocence in tones of amazement, he rushed up, seized the Prefect's sword and struck him with his fist. He wanted to kill him with his own hands, but Septimius restrained him. Antoninus then ordered one of the attendants to do the deed.

Someone plucked some hairs from Plautianus' beard and took them to Julia and Plautilla, who were together in another room and had not known what was happening. 'Look at your Plautianus', the man said. Julia was delighted, Plautilla griefstricken. The body was flung out into the street, and only later buried at Septimius' orders.

The senate was summoned to a special sitting. Septimius did not accuse his fallen favourite. He merely lamented the weakness of human nature. The honours given to the Prefect had been excessive. He blamed himself for loving and honouring the man so much. The three centurions were called in to testify, after some senators whom Septimius did not fully trust had been removed from the *curia*. Many who had enjoyed Plautianus' friendship were now endangered. Some were put to death. One of his satellites, a procurator of Mauretanian origin, Opellius Macrinus, was saved by the intercession of Cilo. Septimius restrained the senate from voting a decree in praise of Euodus. It would be shameful, he told them, for an imperial freedman to be mentioned in a decree of the senate in this way. The senators, many of whom must have been in a state of panic, chanted out Septimius' praises, even shouting, 'Everyone does everything well because you rule well'. Plautilla, presumably after being divorced— although this is nowhere stated—was banished to the island of Lipara with her brother. The names of Plautianus and his family were sedulously erased from all public monuments and his statues defaced. The immensity of his wealth, now confiscated, required the appointment of a special *procurator ad bona Plautiani* to administer it.[14]

At a meeting of the senate, or soon afterwards, a detailed account of the 'plot' against the emperors by Plautianus must have been circulated. Herodian shows that he for one swallowed it, although some of the details in his account are so implausible as to have been the product of his imagination rather than imperial propaganda. He is good at external description, however, and his picture of the Prefect of the height of his power conveys a vivid impression that is worth quoting. 'He alone had the outward appearance of all-powerful authority. When he went out in public he was an object of fear. No one would approach him, and even those who came upon him by chance turned aside. The guards who preceded him did not allow anyone to stand near him or even look at him. They ordered people to step out of his path and keep their eyes fixed on the ground.' The effort made to suppress Plautianus' name from the record was largely successful, although a considerable number of inscriptions in his honour survive. A list of soldiers from Rome seems to show one deriving from a city named after him; its location is unknown. Dio says 'that his power was equal to that of the emperors themselves. . . . All the soldiers and senators took oaths by his Fortune and all publicly prayed for this health.' This was the fault of Septimius himself, 'who yielded to Plautianus to such a degree that the latter occupied the position of emperor and he himself that of Prefect'. He knew everything the emperor did, no one knew his secrets. Septimius 'as good as prayed to have him as his successor, and once wrote in a letter: "I love the man so much that I pray that I die before he does".' Another fragment of Dio adds 'that . . . someone actually dared to write to him as to a fourth Caesar'.[15]

There had never been a man like Plautianus among the ministers of the Caesars. Even Sejanus had not reached the same heights. Besides, Sejanus had built up his power when Tiberius let the reins of government slip out of his hands. Plautianus had been constantly at the side of Septimius. This was indeed the source of his strength. Alone among Septimius' generals and ministers he had been continuously with him since 193. But the hold that Plautianus had over Septimius up till the last minutes of his life may have had its origin in the Lepcis of their youth. Herodian reports the story that he had been Septimius' 'boy-lover'.[16]

Little is recorded about the three years that followed the fall of Plautianus. During his reign Septimius did much to improve the appearance of the City of Rome, but most of his work had probably been done before 205. The Temple of Peace, destroyed at the end of Commodus' reign, was restored and a new version of the marble plan of the city, the *forma urbis*, was attached to the outside wall of its library. The Pantheon was restored in 202. The arch in the Forum has already been mentioned. Another striking arch in honour of Septimius and his family was erected in 204 by the *argentarii*, to form a monumental new entrance to the Forum Boarium. No trace now survives of a striking new building erected in 203, at the corner of the Palatine that faced the Via Appia, the Septizodium. Nearly 100 feet (30 m) high and more than 300 feet (90 m) long, it resembled a nymphaeum, or theatrical *scaenae frons*, and perhaps contained statues of the seven planetary gods, Saturn, Jupiter, Mars, the Sun, Venus, Mercury and the Moon. The central statue of the Sun was quite probably depicted in the likeness of Septimius himself—looking south towards Africa, and welcoming travellers coming from Africa. The symbolism behind this great monument can only be guessed at. In the Palace itself, Septimius also undertook rebuilding. New *thermae* were constructed and the front of the palace facing the Circus Maximus was extensively altered. Dio gives an interesting account of the interior decoration of part of the palace: the emperor had 'the ceilings of the rooms where he heard lawsuits painted with the stars under which he had been born'. They were visible to everyone—'except that portion of the sky which "observed the hour", as they call it, when he first saw the light of day'. This vital section was painted in different ways in two different rooms. Septimius did not want too much to be known about what the stars had ordained for him.[17]

The murder of Plautianus made necessary a new appointment. Septimius now reverted to previous practice by giving command of the Guard to a pair of Prefects, Q. Maecius Laetus, who had been Prefect of Egypt from 200–03, and Aemilius Papinianus. Maecius Laetus was the senior. Little is known of him except that he enjoyed favour with Antoninus throughout the next ten years, which could be said of very few. He no doubt had considerable military experience. Papinian was not a military man but a jurist. His experience went right back to the reign of Marcus when he had been a legal adviser to the Prefects. More recently, he had been serving as *a libellis*. The *HA* states that he was a great friend of Septimius, 'and, as some record, related to him by marriage, through his second wife'. In that case, Papinian must have been a Syrian. Students of Roman law from the time of Justinian onwards have concurred in rating Papinian highest among all its great classical exponents. This was indeed a great age of jurisprudence. A younger contemporary of Papinian was Domitius Ulpianus, also a Syrian, from Tyre. The third great jurist of the age, Julius Paulus, may have come from the east as well. What these jurists and their colleagues may have lacked in elegance of style or clarity in comparison with their predecessors of the previous generation, like Salvius Julianus, they more than made up for by their voluminous output. During the Severan age they distilled an enormous quantity of earlier material to produce the basis of the law codified by Justinian.[18]

Septimius himself took a keen interest in the administration of justice. Dio, who as a member of the emperor's *consilium* could speak as an eye-witness, records with approval his patience in court: 'He allowed the

litigants plenty of time and he gave us, his advisers, full liberty to speak.'
Apparently he was particularly strict in enforcing the law against adultery,
to which he added. Dio says that during his own consulship, which was at
about this time, he happened to notice that there were as many as three
thousand cases pending. One piquant case is preserved in the *Digest*. A
senator named Claudius Gorgus accused his wife of adultery. He was then
discovered to have taken her back. Septimius did not wait for a
prosecution, and convicted the man of procuring. The *Digest* and other
legal compilations preserve numerous decisions of his, covering the whole
range of private and public law, including the rights of women, minors
and slaves, the obligations of *curatores* and *tutores*, or guardians, testamen-
tary laws, property disputes. No attempt can be made here to deal with
the legislative and juridical activity of the reign. Aurelius Victor called
Septimius *conditor legum longe aequabilium*, 'the establisher of thoroughly
equitable laws'. Now, to be sure, it was openly asserted that 'the emperor
is not bound by the laws', *princeps legibus solutus est*. But at the same time,
he and Antoninus in a joint pronouncement declared that 'although we
are not bound by the laws, nevertheless we live in accordance with
them'.[19]

As far as the vast majority of the inhabitants of the empire were
concerned, the doctrine held good. The senate, unfortunately, was still too
much feared as a source of possible danger to be treated in this way. The
murder of Plautianus did not bring to an end the execution of senators.
Dio speaks of 'many being put to death, some of them after they had been
formally arraigned before him, had made their defence, and had been
convicted'. Several instances are preserved in excerpts from his *History*.
Plautius Quintillus was the most eminent victim, a nephew of Verus and
son-in-law of Marcus. His only recorded political action had been in May
193, when he intervened forcefully against Didius Julianus' proposal that
the senate and Vestal Virgins should meet Septimius' advancing army as
suppliants. He was now 'at the gates of old age, living on his country
estate, interfering in nothing and doing nothing wrong'. Nonetheless he
was informed against, and forced to suicide. He called for his funeral
shroud, which had been made for him long before. It was by now tattered
with age. ' "What is this?", he said, "we are late!" ' Preparing to die, 'he
burned incense, and said: "I make the same prayer that Servianus made for
Hadrian" '—that is, that the emperor should wish to die, but be unable to.

The other case Dio records is that of the proconsul of Asia, Apronianus,
condemned *in absentia*. His nurse had once dreamed he would become
emperor: it was alleged that he had used magic to bring this about. A
remarkable scene occurred during the trial. Under torture, a witness had
been asked who had told the story about the dream, and to whom. The

witness said that he had seen 'a certain bald-headed senator peeping in'. When the report, prepared by the emperor himself, was read out, the senators were horrified. No name had been put down by Septimius, and everyone, even the ones who were only slightly bald and those who had never visited Apronianus' house, was frightened. No one could remain calm except those with plenty of hair. Dio gives a vivid picture of the humiliating and absurd position the senators were placed in.

> We all looked around at the men who were bald, and murmurs spread, 'It's So-and-So'—'No, it's So-and-So'. I will not disguise what happened to me, ridiculous though it is. I was so taken aback that I actually felt the hair on my head, with my hand. A good many others found themselves doing likewise. We took good care to stare at those who were more or less bald, feeling that this would divert the danger from ourselves onto them.

Then evidence was read out that identified the bald senator as a certain Baebius Marcellinus. He stood up, came forward and said: ' "The man will of course recognise me, if he has seen me." ' The informer was brought in and gazed around for some while. Then someone—Dio does not say who it was—gave an almost imperceptible nod towards Marcellinus, and the informer identified him. He was led out straight away, said goodbye to his four children in the Forum, and was executed—before Septimius had even learned of his condemnation.[20]

Septimius' behaviour in January 205, and during the trials that followed, was hardly characteristic of the calm and ordered routine he followed in his Italian years. According to Dio he was always up and busy before dawn, and then would take a walk, on which affairs of state would be discussed. Then he would hold court, 'unless there were some great festival'. Dio's description of his patient and fair conduct of cases has already been quoted. At noon he would adjourn for a ride, 'as far has his health permitted, and then would exercise in a gymnasium and take a bath'. This would be followed by a substantial meal, taken alone or with his sons, and a siesta. After more official business, he would once again take a *passeggiata*, walking about and conversing in both Greek and Latin. Towards evening he would bathe again and then dine with his intimates. 'He very rarely invited guests to dinner, and only on days when it was unavoidable did he arrange expensive banquets.' It must have been one of those rare banquets that was witnessed and described by the writer Sammonicus Serenus. A sturgeon 'was brought in by servants [who were] garlanded with flowers, moving in time to the music of flutes'.[21]

No doubt Septimius and his sons attended meetings of the senate regularly. In 206, as Ulpian, writing a few years later attests, Septimius and Antoninus made recommendations on the law regarding gifts between husband and wife: 'the greatest emperors advocated these proposals and the senate so decreed'. Elsewhere, at greater length he quotes from the speech made by Antoninus. The eighteen-year-old junior emperor, whose own wife was languishing in exile, was able to adopt a mature and compassionate approach: 'It is wrong for him who made a gift to change his mind; but for the heir to seize the property against what may be the last wish of the donor is hard and avaricious.' As likely as not the speech was written for him by Ulpian himself or one of the other imperial advisers. Ulpian sums up the speech as advocating 'some relaxation in the rigour of the law'.[22]

Another matter which presumably concerned the senate in 206 was the trial of Pollienus Sebennus, nephew of Septimius' friend Auspex, accused of misconduct during his governorship of Noricum. Dio took some satisfaction in Sebennus' conviction: he had made the preposterous charges that led to Baebius Marcellinus' death. Sebennus was 'delivered up to the Noricans . . . and he had to endure a most shameful experience . We saw him lying on the ground and pleading piteously.' As once with the province of Africa and its rapacious governor Marius Priscus, it was still possible for Rome's subjects to seek redress. Sebennus was 'handed over to his accusers' by the new governor, Catius Sabinus, who had presumably made the prosecution possible. However, the influence of Pollienus Auspex was sufficient to rescue Sebennus from death.[23]

The fact that Sebennus was tried by his peers may seem a welcome concession to the senate's traditional prerogatives. Dio's description hardly gives this impression, even if this trial was less hysterical than that of the Apronianus 'dream' case. Septimius no doubt wanted to restore a calmer atmosphere and may have shown himself conciliatory during those years. But what he expected from the senate was acquiescence. Tertullian, writing ten years earlier, in defence of the patriotism and loyalty of Christians, insisted that they prayed constantly for all emperors. What they asked God to give them was 'long life, secure rule, a safe household, brave armies, a faithful senate (*senatum fidelem*), a well-behaved people, a quiet world'.[24]

It was perhaps during this period that Septimius composed his auto-biography. That he had not forgotten his struggle for power is proved by his dream about Albinus the night before the murder of Plautianus. The work dwelt on dreams and other portents that had told him of his destiny, and it vilified Albinus and Niger. No direct quotations are preserved. It is not even known whether it was in Latin or Greek. If it was in Greek, Aelius Antipater may have helped him with it. If in Latin, perhaps the African lawyer Messius Saturninus gave some assistance. Saturninus was the holder of the new post *a declamationibus* (and had a very high salary). In this capacity he clearly drafted Septimius' speeches for delivery in court. Ulpian, quoting a letter of Septimius (and Antoninus) which gives the imperial decision (in a case involving acceptance of presents by a proconsul), describes it as 'very elegant'. A Greek proverb is quoted and the emperor's judgement is pithily phrased.[25]

There were certainly plenty of literary figures at the court. For one thing, the empress liked the society of such men. She had turned to this for consolation when Plautianus ousted her from her position of influence with her husband. There is no reason to believe that she sent the sophists packing when Plautianus went. The intellectual curiosity was genuine. Philostratus, who was with the empress and her son in the east after Septimius' death, speaks of 'the circle around Julia'. The coherence of this 'circle' has perhaps been exaggerated. But Philostratus himself was encouraged by Julia to compose his *Life* of Apollonius, the wonder-worker of Tyana; and he calls her 'the philosopher'. Other members of the circle may be found. It would be uncritical, however, to assume that all the writers of the age, from Diogenes Laërtius to Alexander of Aphrodisias, must have at some time danced attendance at the salon of the philosophical empress. 'Philosophy' is in any case a courtesy term. To judge from the *Life* of Apollonius it meant a combination of religious superstition with somewhat pretentious erudition.[26]

Julia had another reputation, for promiscuity. Perhaps she did have lovers. Dio implies that she was slanderously accused of misconduct by Plautianus. Herodian had little interest in the subject. Hence the only explicit accusation comes from much later times. But it was plausible enough; the intellectual stimulus of sophists may not have been enough to console her for the treatment she got from Plautianus.[27]

During these years in Italy Antoninus and Geta reacted to the removal of Plautianus as if been released from the charge of an oppressive tutor. The two youths 'treated women shamefully, abused boys, embezzled money, hobnobbed with gladiators and charioteers'. What may have begun as harmless rivalry ended as mutual hatred—which the coin issues advertising their 'harmony' might have led one to suspect, even if Dio did not explicitly report it. During a fiercely contested chariot race Antoninus fell and broke his leg.[28]

In the meantime Italy was being subjected to a humiliating demonstration of how precarious was the recently re-established security and peace. A brigand named Bulla eluded capture again and again, and for two years 'ravaged Italy in the presence of the emperors and a great host of soldiers'. Perhaps as a pun on the similarity of his name to the great Sulla, he also called himself 'Felix'. 'He had a great many runaway imperial freedmen with him', Dio notes. 'Some of them had been paid very badly—and some had received no pay at all.' Dio had earlier mentioned that Septimius' strictness with his freedmen had won him praise—presumably from the senators. However, the ones who had joined Bulla would not have come from the Palace staff—they would be lowly employees on the imperial estates in Italy, now vastly increased in size by confiscation. Another element from which Bulla may have found support, although Dio does not specifically mention it, would be the several thousand Guardsmen discharged in June 193. But the men under Bulla's command did not number more than six hundred. He was eventually captured through a trick.

Brigandage was a problem that had probably become endemic. Tertullian, early in the reign, refers to 'military garrisons in all the provinces being assigned to tracking down brigands', and the *HA* calls Septimius 'an enemy of brigands everywhere'. The problem was not new, but the Marcomannic wars, the 'deserters' war' under Commodus and finally the civil wars of 193–7 had clearly made it more serious.[29]

Until 204, Septimius had not spent more than twelve months at a time in Italy for forty years. Apart from the Saecular Games, he cannot have found his life there in the years 204–07 very much to his taste. The restlessness and impatience that marked his character were certainly exacerbated by the behaviour of his sons. The murder of Plautianus, the political trials, the frustrating Bulla Felix, must have made him yearn to be back with the armies. He was now over sixty, convinced that he had not long to live. He wanted to end on a triumphant note.[30]

· 16 ·

EXPEDITIO FELICISSIMA BRITTANNICA

SEPTIMIUS 'WAS BECOMING ANGRY', says Dio, 'that in Britain he was winning wars through others while being worsted by a brigand in Italy'. After the lengthy account, in Xiphilinus' *Epitome* of Dio, of the two year campaign against the bandit chief Bulla and his 600 followers, from which this quotation is taken, comes the story of the British expedition. It was undertaken, even though Septimius knew from the stars that he would not return, 'because he saw his sons becoming undisciplined and the armies slack through idleness.' Herodian echoes Dio over the conduct of Antoninus and Geta: 'he wanted to get his sons away from Rome, so that they would behave better, under military discipline, after being removed from the life of luxury at Rome'. Herodian offers more. Just when Septimius 'was displeased by his sons' behaviour and indecent enthusiasm for the shows, he received a letter from the governor of Britain. He wrote that the barbarians there were in rebellion, laying waste the countryside, carrying off plunder and wrecking almost everything. Hence there was need either for more troops to reinforce the garrison or for the imperial presence. This was welcome news for Severus, being in any case a lover of glory by nature, and eager for a triumph against the Britons to add to his victories and titles won in east and north.'[1]

The governor to whom Herodian refers can be identified with a high degree of probability as L. Alfenus Senecio. He is recorded on no fewer than nine inscriptions in the north of England, four from the hinterland of the frontier, four from the forts along the line of Hadrian's Wall, and one from the outpost of Habitancum (Risingham) north of the Wall, on the old road into Scotland. Most of these stones record building (some are incomplete or not explicit). At Bainbridge in Wensleydale, where his predecessor Valerius Pudens had built a barrack block for the Sixth Nervians under their prefect Vinicius Pius in 205, Senecio erected a rampart, probably in the next year (the same prefect was there). At Birdoswald on the Wall the First Aelian Cohort of Dacians and the First Cohort of Thracians built a granary under his direction. The First Vangiones, a part-mounted milliary cohort, under their tribune Aemilius

Salvianus, rebuilt a gate and adjacent walls, which had 'collapsed from age', at Habitancum, 'by order of Alfenus Senecio, right honourable consular'—and, it is a surprise, 'under the supervision of Oclatinius Adventus, procurator of our emperors'. The involvement of the highest-ranking equestrian official in the province, side by side with the governor and commander-in-chief, is unexpected and unusual in this military context. It is matched by another stone, from Cilurnum (Chesters) on the Wall itself, which, although fragmentary, clearly indicates that Senecio and Adventus were both engaged on work there too. One explanation seems to be that Adventus was a specialist in military intelligence. The notoriety which he was to achieve at the end of his career, a dozen or so years later, prompted Dio to describe his background in some detail. He had started as a military policeman, *speculator*, been a centurion in the secret service, *frumentarii*, and had commanded that force's Rome head-quarters as *princeps peregrinorum*, before becoming procurator. It is plausible to suppose that he had been given the British appointment not least with the mission of reporting on the state of the frontier and indeed of gathering intelligence on the enemies of Rome.[2]

Alfenus Senecio was doubtless a trusted servant of Septimius, like his two known predecessors in this reign. The first, Virius Lupus, had taken over the province immediately after the defeat of Albinus and the British army at Lugdunum in 197. Work was done that same year at Verterae (Brough) on Stainmore and Verbeia (Ilkley) in the Yorkshire Dales; undated inscriptions show Lupus' hand at Lavatrae (Bowes) on Stain-more, where 'a bath-house, destroyed by fire, was rebuilt by the First Thracians', and at Coria (Corbridge), where a detachment of the Sixth legion was at work under his command. Dio reports how Lupus had to buy off the Maeatae with 'large sums of money', receiving 'a few prisoners back' in return. Clearly, in the absence of most of the British garrison in 196–7, Rome's northern enemies had invaded the province, and the Brigantes of the Pennines had perhaps risen in rebellion. The Maeatae, whose home was north of the Antonine Wall, were on the point of being joined by the Caledonians, from the Highlands beyond, when Lupus arrived. How much damage had been done is hard to estimate. But in any case, there had been trouble in Britain not long before 196–7, with the death of a governor in a barbarian invasion c. 182 or 183, and the campaigns of Ulpius Marcellus followed by discontent and mutiny in the British legions.[3]

In Septimius' boyhood and youth, Rome's north-west frontier, the limit of her rule in Britain, had been the Antonine Wall. By the early 160s, barely twenty years after it had been created by Lollius Urbicus, the Antonine frontier had been abandoned. Some strongpoints were retained north of Hadrian's Wall, it is true, but there had been a retreat. This will have been the impression that Septimius' brother Geta, as tribune in II Augusta, and Pertinax, as an equestrian officer in Britain, will have gained in the 160s, and no doubt transmitted to Septimius, years before. It is not certain who replaced Lupus as governor, but Valerius Pudens, who probably went to Britain c. 202, had been governor of Lower Pannonia in 193, in other words was a foundation member of Septimius' winning team. He had gone on to be Lupus' successor in Lower Germany and after his service in Britain was proconsul of Africa. As for Alfenus Senecio, it is known that he was Numidian, from Cuicul, and that he had been governor of Syria Coele in the year 200, at the very time of Septimius' lengthy stay in the east. Senecio's previous career is not known, unless he is identical with the procurator of the same names who after various junior posts was governor of Mauretania Caesariensis and then procurator of Belgica and the two Germanies. Otherwise the governor of Syria and Britain was presumably son of the procurator.[4]

Senecio seems to have done some fighting as well as building. As if to confirm Dio's remark about 'others winning wars in Britain', there is an altar from Condercum (Benwell) on Hadrian's Wall, dedicated 'to the Victory of the Emperors' by the cavalry regiment of Asturians based there, naming Alfenus Senecio as the consular. Julius Julianus, legate of II Augusta at this time, himself devoted an altar to Imperial Victory near Coria, while another, at Greetland in the southern Pennines, was set up by a private individual to the 'Goddess Victoria Brigantia' in the year 208. It might be possible to interpret these stray pieces of evidence as an indication that Senecio had fighting to do against Brigantians within the province as well as against external enemies beyond the frontier. It has to be admitted that the Condercum altar might quite well be a British commemoration, ten years on, of the Parthian victory of AD 198, and nothing more. Nonetheless, Dio's story about 'wars being won in Britain' cannot be dismissed. Herodian's report of the appeal from the governor of Britain is quite another matter. This writer's account of the reign is riddled with mistakes, omissions and inaccuracies. Further, Herodian is a devotee of the rhetorical *topos*. It can be observed that on two later occasions in his work imperial expeditions are ostensibly brought about following letters from provincial governors ('of Syria and Mesopotamia', and 'in Illyria', respectively) describing enemy invasions. In the first of these later despatches Herodian reports the governors telling the emperor, as if it were urgent news, about an event which had taken place at least five years before the supposed despatch. It is better to reject Herodian's story about the British governor's letter as pure invention.[5]

There may have been several changes of policy regarding Britain during the past few decades. It is quite possible that plans had been made to reoccupy southern Scotland in the later 170s and that the governor defeated early in Commodus' reign by tribes 'crossing the Wall'— unspecified, but mentioned by Dio in language similar to that used of the Antonine Wall—had been preparing to recommission the Antonine frontier. It is far from certain what orders Septimius had given to Virius Lupus or indeed to Valerius Pudens. They may conceivably have been told to move back into Scotland. On the other hand, the attention they were giving to forts in the Pennines makes it more probable that Hadrian's Wall was still envisaged as the frontier, and this is certainly the inescapable inference from Alfenus Senecio's activity at Birdoswald, Vindolanda, Cilurnum and Habitancum. One of Septimius' governors— the name has not been preserved—built a new granary at Coria (Cor-bridge), and the structural evidence from this base just south of Hadrian's Wall, on the River Tyne, suggests that a major new stores building was being constructed at this time. Further downstream, on the south bank of the river near its mouth, at Arbeia (South Shields), the fort which formerly housed an auxiliary cohort was totally converted into a supply depot. The normal accommodation had been demolished to make way for an extra twenty granaries, giving a total of twenty-two. Arbeia could now hold enough corn to supply more than 40,000 men for three months. But presumably, once the imperial expeditionary force reached Britain, supplies of food were shipped continuously from southern Britain and the Rhineland, and redistributed from Arbeia up the coast to Cramond on the Forth and up the Tyne to Coria. It is not unlikely that the 'Tigris bargemen' recorded at Arbeia in late antiquity were first based on the Tyne at this very time. After the conquest of Mesopotamia, Arab lightermen had very likely been drafted into Roman service, some, perhaps, whose loyalty was suspect, to the other end of the empire. They were evidently to give their name to the port where they were based, for 'Arbeia' is simply a version of 'Arabia'. It is fair to add that they would have found fellow-Arabs on the Tyne already, at any rate Palmyrenes. Barathes of Palmyra, dealer in ensigns, buried his young British freed-woman and wife Regina at Arbeia, giving her an ornate tombstone with epitaph in Latin and Palmyrene. Later he was to die at Coria.[6]

How soon orders were sent to prepare the great supply depots at Arbeia and Coria is uncertain. But once they came, the intention was surely clear: there was to be a massive imperial expedition, a Roman invasion of north Britain the like of which had never been seen before. Septimius had quite possibly read Tacitus' *Life of Agricola* and his *Histories*, in which the 'complete conquest of Britain' by the historian's father-in-law was immortalised—and its abandonment denounced. The governorship of Agricola was well known to Cassius Dio, and another contemporary of

Septimius, Tertullian, had also read some Tacitus. Septimius' grandfather, as a pupil of Quintilian, and as one who had perhaps known Tacitus personally when he and Pliny were prosecuting Marius Priscus, very much in the interests of Lepcis Magna, could well have had personal copies of his writings. About another literary work of that era there can be no doubt. The first Septimius Severus must have had his own copy of Statius' *Silvae*. His own family may, to be sure, have ignored everything in that work except the *Ode Lyrica ad Septimium Severum* in the fourth book. But there is a chance that Septimius also knew the *Laudes Crispini Vetti Bolani filiii* in the fifth book. Here he could have read how 'Crispinus' mighty father entered Thule, that sets a limit to the western waves, where Hyperion is ever weary, bearing the commands of Caesar.' Statius asks where the young Crispinus will serve:

> 'But if the land curbed by your mighty parent receives you ... what glory will exalt the fields of Caledonia! When some ancient dweller in that savage land shall tell you: "Here did your father dispense justice, from this mound did he address the cavalry ... these gifts, these weapons did he dedicate to the gods of war ... this breastplate did he himself put on when battle summoned, this one did he take from the breast of a British king." '

Dio certainly ascribes Septimius' Mesopotamian conquests to 'desire for glory'. As far as Britain is concerned, he explicitly states that Septimius 'intended to conquer it all'—at last, it might be added, or for the first time since Julius Agricola. Septimius also had an insatiable curiosity, a love of *peregrinatio*, foreign travel, and of novelties. He had been virtually over the entire empire, except for 'the great outermost island towards the west'. Now he would even see those 'parts of Britain inaccessible to the Romans' which Tertullian, shortly before, had claimed (Septimius would hardly have known this) were conquered by Christ.[7]

Whether driven by a remembered line of Statius (*quanta Caledonios attollet gloria campos!*) or by some more prosaic motive, Septimius will have consulted whatever British specialists were to be found before he departed. There would be the former governors, Lupus, if he was still alive, and Valerius Pudens. One Gaius Julius Asper, later *consul ordinarius* (in 212), was patron of the province of Britain, and may have had longstanding links and special knowledge. Polus Terentianus, Septimius' ally as governor of Dacia in 193, had been legate of II Augusta in the mid-180s, and could have been consulted. So too might Septimius' fellow-Lepcitane, Silius Plautius Haterianus, another former legate of the Caerleon legion. Then there was the *quindecimvir* Antius Crescens Calpurnianus, former *iuridicus* of Britain and acting governor at a moment of crisis under Commodus. None of these men, as it happens, are known to have accompanied the imperial party in 208. One or more may have been among the *comites* of the emperors. Only two *comites* are explicitly attested. One was Julia's brother-in-law, Julius Avitus Alexianus. He had held no office since the consulship, following his governorship of Raetia ten years before. It is probable that Plautianus' hostility to Julia had extended to her relatives. Now the Emesene clan was back in favour. Alexianus' own son-in-law, Sex. Varius Marcellus of Apamea, who had previously served only as procurator of the aqueducts at Rome, was made procurator of Britain, presumably as successor to Oclatinius Adventus. Another kinsman of Julia, Aemilius Papinianus, was of course still Guard Prefect, and he, rather than his colleague Maecius Laetus, was the Prefect who accompanied the expedition. The other senatorial *comes* was a man from proconsular Africa, C. Junius Faustinus Postumianus, who had recently governed Lower Moesia. Postumianus was to take over the governorship of Britain during the expedition, it seems, presumably as successor to Alfenus Senecio. A further high-ranking member of the imperial party may be postulated, Ulpius Marcellus, the son, it could be supposed, of the Commodan governor of that name who had battered the north Britons into submission twenty-five years earlier.[8]

Apart from these persons, Septimius will have taken a very considerable team with him. The whole business of the empire would have to be conducted from distant Britain for some while, and at the very least the head of the Secretariat, the *ab epistulis*, must have been of the company. Above all, a large number of the imperial slaves and freedmen from the *familia Caesaris* must have gone to Britain. Two are mentioned, Castor the chamberlain and *a memoria* and Euodus, Antoninus' old *educator* (neither would return). Inscriptions register two men involved in the expedition whose names are missing. One was the fleet commander, who, exceptionally, was assigned not merely the *classis Britannica*, but the Rhine and Danube flotillas as well, the *classes Germanica* and *Pannonica* and *Moesica*. No doubt they were involved in the laborious task of supply, as was another nameless official 'in charge of the granaries' at Coria 'at the time of the most fortunate expedition', *tempore expeditionis felicissi(mae) Brittanic(ae)*. The Rhine and Danube armies will also, it is clear, have contributed to the expedition, not merely the naval forces of those provinces. It may be that several whole legions were sent, although it is more probable that *vexillationes* only were detached. But the new legion II Parthica, effectively part of the Rome garrison, which now had the makings of a mobile field army, probably accompanied strong elements of the Guard.[9]

Before Septimius could leave Italy he had to take steps to ensure that

Rome and the rest of the empire remained loyal and secure in his absence. There are indeed hints of some kind of trouble at this time. Two inscriptions at widely separated places, Ephesus in Asia and Sicca in Africa, refer in very similar language to the defeat of 'insidious plots'. The first is not precisely dated, the second was set up in 208. Both suggest that some insurrection had been suppressed. There may have been an uprising in Gaul, for the legate of the Bonn legion I Minervia, Julius Septimius Castinus—a possible kinsman of the emperor—is known to have commanded at this time a force drawn from all four German legions 'against defectors and rebels'. Coins issued in 208 honour 'Jupiter the Victorious'; but they could refer to Senecio's campaigns. In 207 the governor of Upper Pannonia, Egnatius Victor, made a dedication at Arrabona to 'the Victory of the Emperors and of the legion I Adiutrix', which might mean there had been fighting on or near the middle Danube. Perhaps Antoninus was there and participated in some military action: the coinage of 207 gives great prominence to his martial prowess. Yet, as with the Victory dedications from Britain at this time, there remains the possibility that Victor was merely commemorating the Parthian war of 197–8. It has to be admitted that little is known about what was happening in 207. It is even possible that Septimius made a second visit to Africa: his silver coinage of that year depicts the personified province with her distinctive elephant-skin head-dress.[10]

It is possible to establish some of the arrangements made for the government of the empire during the imperial visit to Britain. Care was certainly taken to place reliable men in key positions. Syria Coele was in the hands of Marius Maximus, a legionary legate of the Septimian armies of 193, and later successful commander of the Moesian army corps at Byzantium and Lugdunum. He had gone on to govern Belgica and Lower Germany. One of Maximus' recorded actions in Syria was to arrange for the passage of a Parthian envoy to the emperors. Before Septimius' death in 211 Maximus had been replaced, but not by a senatorial governor: the financial procurator Minicius Martialis seems to have taken over as acting governor. Marius Maximus was hardly removed as potentially dangerous. He was certainly in high favour in the next reigns, and his brother Marius Perpetuus was governor of Upper Moesia at the time of Septimius' death. Of the other provincial governors one may note the prefect of Egypt. From 206–11 this office was held by Ti. Claudius Subatianus Aquila, who had previously been first ever prefect of Mesopotamia. At this very time his close kinsman Subatianus Proculus was governor of their home province Numidia. It will be recalled that Alfenus Senecio was a native of the same town as the Subatiani, Cuicul. Septimius Castinus, possible kinsman of the emperor, became legate of Lower Pannonia at about this time. Egnatius Victor, governor of the Upper Pannonian province, and Aiacius Modestus Crescentianus, governor of Upper Germany, are among the further holders of powerful positions who may be identified, like the Marii, the Subatiani, Senecio and Castinus, as natives of Roman Africa. Septimius, it seems clear, felt he could trust these men.[11]

The year 208 was inaugurated once more, as in 205, by a joint consulship of Antoninus and Geta, holding office for the third and second time respectively. Antoninus had now equalled his father's number of consulships and had been joint emperor for ten years. There was no sign that this brother, albeit less than a year younger, was destined for promotion: Geta remained 'most noble Caesar'. Tenure of the *fasces* during the last years of Septimius' reign was still reserved mainly for the high aristocracy, so it seems, men of old consular families, or for those with imperial connections. In 206 the consuls had been two Italians, Nummius Albinus, son of a stepbrother of Didius Julianus, and Fulvius Aemilianus. One of the consuls of 207 was a Septimius from Lepcis Magna, L. Septimius Aper, probably a grandson of Septimius' 'uncle' Aper. In 209, as in 200 and 204, a member of Marcus Aurelius' family held office: this time is was a son of old Claudius Pompeianus and Marcus' daughter, the Augusta Lucilla. What is more, he flaunted the name Commodus as well as Pompeianus. His colleague was Plautius Avitus, grandson of Pertinax's old patron Lollianus Avitus and also, through his mother, of Lucius Verus' sister Ceionia Plautia. Avitus' brother Gentianus was to be consul in 211. Their father had been an important early ally of Septimius and a *comes* in the wars of 193–7. Two daughters of Marcus Aurelius were still alive, who might have been potential figureheads for the disaffected: Septimius had effectively neutralised them by finding them husbands of humble status. Vibia Aurelia Sabina, widow of Antistius Burrus, murdered by Cleander in 189, was now the wife of L. Aurelius Agaclytus, son of a freedman of Lucius Verus. Cornificia, whose husband Petronius Mamertinus had lost his life in 190 or 191, was supposed to have had an affair with Pertinax. Now she was safely married to a Syrian procurator, Didius Marinus. The emperor's 'sisters' were safely out of reach.[12]

Coins of 208 show Septimius riding off to war. Herodian notes that 'for most of the journey he was carried in a litter'. He was increasingly troubled by a painful condition in his legs or feet, variously interpreted as gout or arthritis. But in spite of this, and in spite of his age—in 208 he reached what the ancients called the grand climacteric, his sixty-third birthday—'he was more vigorous in mind than any youth'. Herodian also claims that he and his sons 'completed their march to the coast with amazing speed'. This is part of his standard description of a Severan campaign; it is far from certain that it is true. There was no particular necessity for breakneck speed in 208. Herodian also claims that 'the Britons, thunderstruck by the sudden arrival of the emperor and hearing of the vast force assembled against them, sent embassies and proposed peace terms, and tried to make excuses for their offences. But the emperor was looking for reasons to delay, so as not to have to return to Rome again—for he still wanted to gain a British victory and title. He dismissed their envoys, who achieved nothing, and prepared for battle.'[13]

It may be assumed that Septimius established himself initially at Eboracum, where lay the fortress of VI Victrix and a sizeable town often used as a residence by governors of Britain. The governor's *praetorium* would, for the duration, become the imperial *palatium*. Its location is unknown, but it was presumably somewhere in the civil town, now boasting the rank of *municipium*. One feature of Eboracum which will have pleased Septimius was a temple of Sarapis, erected not long before by a legate of VI Victrix, Claudius Hieronymianus.[14]

Dio and Herodian both introduce their accounts of the British campaigns with fanciful-sounding travellers' tales, or indeed tall stories, about the remote and watery north and its barbarous inhabitants. Dio, whose original version is missing, has the merit, in the epitome of Xiphilinus, of making it clear that he is referring to the free Britons 'beyond the cross-wall which cuts the island in half', whose 'two main tribes' were 'the Maeatae, next to the Wall and the Caledonians beyond them'. Dio, here as elsewhere, plainly regarded the Antonine Wall as the limit of Roman territory in Britain—even if Roman control over that Wall had not been effectively exercised for over forty years. 'Both tribes', according to Dio, 'inhabit wild and waterless mountains and deserted marshy plains; they have no walls, no cities and no agriculture, but live off their flocks, from hunting, and on certain fruits—for they do not touch the fish, of which there are vast and inexhaustible quantities.' He goes on to tell how they live 'naked and barefoot in tents', have their women in common, a mainly democratic form of society with war-leaders 'chosen from the boldest, because of their love of plunder'. They had no body-armour, a shield and short spear and daggers were their arms. It is only when Dio concludes with stories of the north Britons 'hiding themselves in their swamps for days on end with only their heads above water, and living off bark and roots', and in emergencies 'on a special food of which a small portion the size of a bean wards off hunger and thirst', that the modern reader becomes a little sceptical. Herodian, whose brief account survives complete, clearly derives some items from Dio. He stresses the marsh-like nature of the whole of Britain: 'most of the country of the Britons, being flooded by the continual ocean tides, is marsh'—which the more or less naked barbarians do not mind, either running or swimming in the swampy water. Mud does not bother them because they do not know about clothes, having iron belts and necklaces and tattoes all over their bodies (the reason for dispensing with clothes, which would cover the tattoes). After describing their weapons, in a manner similar to Dio, Herodian explains that they dispense with breast-plates and helmets 'which would impede their movement through the marshes'. Finally, Herodian comments, 'the atmosphere in that country is always gloomy, because of the thick mist arising from the marshes'.[15]

Septimius' coinage in 208 shows a bridge, which it is tempting to associate with the efforts to cope with waterlogged country attributed to him by the two Greek writers. However the bridge is depicted as a monumental permanent structure. It could be at Eboracum, or indeed across the Tyne, at Pons Aelius. In the year 209, a bronze As or small medallion of Antoninus shows a bridge of boats with the legend TRAIECTUS. This may well commemorate what is described by Herodian as 'putting pontoons across the marshy places' or by Dio as 'filling up the swamps and bridging rivers'. Dio opens his story of the fighting by depicting Septimius invading 'Caledonia, wishing to subjugate the whole of it' [i.e. Britain], and as he advanced running into immense difficulties because of the terrain, and failing to get the enemy into battle. They indeed enticed the Roman soldiers into danger by leaving sheep and cattle for them to seize, and luring them into swamps where they attacked them. Those who could not walk after this would be killed by their own men in preference to being captured by the Caledonians. As a result, says Dio, 'up to 50,000 perished', surely an exaggeration. But Septimius

> did not desist until he had approached the furthest limit of the island, where he observed most accurately the variation of the sun's motion and the length of days and nights in summer and winter respectively. Having thus been conveyed through practically the whole of the enemy country—for he actually was carried in a covered litter for the most part because of his weakness—he returned to the friendly part of the island, having forced the Britons to come to terms, namely that they should surrender no small part of their territory.[16]

Herodian devotes a mere two sentences to this first campaign, but he prefaces his brief remarks with the statement that Septimius left his younger son Geta in the Roman part of the island 'to administer justice and carry on the civil government of the empire, giving him for this purpose a council of senior advisers'. He specifically adds that Septimius took Antoninus with him on the expedition. The only conceivable trace of independent activity in Britain by Geta, during the absence on campaign of his father and brother, may be preserved in the earliest manuscript of the *Passio* of Britain's first Christian martyr, Albanus. St Alban's death has generally been placed later, during the so-called Great Persecution under Diocletian and his colleagues. Yet it seems clear that at that time there were no martyrdoms, thanks to the protection afforded by Constantius Chlorus. Geta may thus be the 'most impious Caesar' who, after the saint had been put to death, called a halt: 'Without an order from the emperors the most impious Caesar ordered the persecution to cease, reporting to them that slaughtering the saints was causing Christianity to flourish, rather than suppressing it.' Geta is at any rate the only Caesar who could have operated in Britain at a time when there were also emperors, if Constantius is ruled out.[17]

Geta is also recorded, with his brother, on an inscription from Aenus in Thrace which reveals that on 12 September in one of the years that the imperial family was in Britain they heard an embassy from this town, at Eboracum. The decision made by the brothers, after hearing Diogenes, son of Theocharis, and his fellow-envoy, the *defensores* of the people of Aenus, was presumably favourable, hence the copy inscribed on white marble at Aenus, from the original in the imperial *commentarii*. It may be suggested that the year was 208 and that Antoninus and Geta, at Eboracum, received delegations and dealt with imperial business, while Septimius was inspecting the frontier.[18]

The evidence of Dio and Herodian suggests that there were two campaigns, the first, in 209, undertaken by Septimius and Antoninus jointly, leading to the submission of the Caledonians and their surrender of substantial territory. Early in 210 the emperors assumed the title Britannicus, and the coinage celebrated the Victoria Britannica; furthermore, VI Victrix, and perhaps the other legions, became *B(ritannica)*. The scope and direction of the expedition is now better understood in the light of archaeological discoveries. Two series of marching-camps have been traced by air photography over a large part of Scotland, both perhaps from this time. One series is of camps some 63 acres (25 ha.) in size, while the other series is of much larger camps, mostly 120 acres (48 ha.) but the southernmost examples are even larger—165 acres (66 ha.). The first of these massive camps is at Trimontium (Newstead) in the Eildon Hills, close to the fort which had been a Roman base, at intervals, since Julius Agricola's day. Its vast extent makes it large enough to have included a major part of the army of Britain within its ramparts. No doubt other camps were set up further south, in which the army and its supply-train could halt on the way from Coria, a distance of over fifty miles (80 km), passing on their way Habitancum, where Senecio and Adventus had carried out repairs shortly before. But no camps as large as that at Trimontium have yet been identified along the road from Coria and Hadrian's Wall. Trimontium was perhaps the point where Septimius and his generals concentrated their forces for the big push into hostile territory. Three more of these giant-sized camps, with perhaps one more at Inveresk on the south side of the Forth, show the line of advance, slow but menacing. Beyond the Forth more have been detected, now reduced in size by a quarter to some 120 acres, perhaps because part of the army had been detached to proceed by ship. The 120-acre camps begin at Ardoch, a few miles south of Agricola's old legionary base at Victoria (Inchtuthil) on the Tay. More have been detected for miles further north, showing the expeditionary force swinging on across the Earn and Tay, around the foothills of the Grampians into the Dee valley, then right up as far as the Pass of Grange, a little way south of the Moray Firth.[19]

Septimius must be envisaged as going at least to the Moray Firth, where he could reasonably enough claim to have reached the 'extremity of Britain'. The scale of these camps is such that they can only be associated with his expedition, confirming Dio's evidence for 'the great sums of money' brought to Britain by Septimius and the indications of major troop reinforcements in Herodian and other sources. The smaller series of camps has been detected as far south as Kirkpatrick, some seven miles north of Aballava (Burgh-by-Sands) close to the western end of Hadrian's Wall. Two possible examples to the north-east of Kirkpatrick suggest that there was an advance into Scotland by the western route as well, which then moved across, skirting the Pentlands, towards the Forth. Further examples have been picked up beyond the Forth, the first at Ardoch, where it is evidently earlier than the 120-acre camp there. Beyond Ardoch there seem to be two parallel lines of 63-acre camps, perhaps representing a single army, setting out for the north and returning, by slightly different routes. From Ardoch the westerly line goes north-eastwards across the mouths of the glens running south-east out of the Highlands. The other line, first detected at Auchtermuchty in the Ochil Hills, goes on to Carpow on the south bank of the Tay, which must have been crossed here by a bridge of boats. Here perhaps was the TRAIECTUS on the coin or medallion of Antoninus from the year 209. A polygonal enclosure some seventy acres in size, bounded on the north by the steep descent to the river, presumably represents a base where the army could link with the fleet, and could be supplied by vessels plying from Tyne and Forth. On the north side was a small fortified post, no doubt to guard the bridge. From here the route went northeast via Longforgan, Kirkbuddo and Kinnell to Keithock, which also seem to be the goal of the 63-acre series beginning at Ardoch.[20]

That it was Septimius' intention to do more than merely ravage Caledonia might in any case be understood from the statement of Dio and from the scale and scope of these marching-camps. Proof that he planned a permanent occupation of north Britain, such as had not been attempted since the time of Agricola, is supplied by the evidence from Carpow. Within the polygonal enclosure already described a stone fortress was constructed, measuring 24 acres (9.6 ha.) internally and 27.6 acres (11 ha.) over the ramparts. It was of more or less orthodox plan, with *principia* of standard type and an elaborate *praetorium* adjacent, well equipped with baths. Its size made it too small for a legion, but it was probably intended for a special force including detachments from the two legions known to have participated in the building. VI Victrix is represented by over two hundred stamped tiles, on which it bears its new title *B(ritannica)*, while the emblems of II Augusta are carved on the side of a monumental inscription from the *porta praetoria*. Although the new base was never to be completed, the nature of its masonry alone shows that the occupation was intended to be permanent: the walls of the *principia* were over three feet (1 m) thick, and the floors were of high quality *opus signinum*. Troops stationed here would indeed need solid accommodation. However attractive the views across the river to the north, or westwards to the Highlands and south to the looming hills beyond Abernethy, the place was often damp and cold. Situated on a level shelf just east of the confluence of the Earn with the Tay, Carpow is well-drained, certainly, but there are reed-beds on the north side where the river floods from time to time at high water. It is not surprising that army rations included wine infused with horehound, recommended for chest complaints.[21]

The *HA* is almost useless as a source for these campaigns. Great emphasis is placed there—following Aurelius Victor—on Septimius' achievement in building the Wall. With no apparent knowledge that the work carried out under Septimius was merely a reconstruction of the Hadrianic frontier, the Wall is described as the greatest glory of the reign. Jerome's *Chronicle*, which has the same basic story, dates the work of building to the year 207—which is correct enough, for Alfenus Senecio had certainly still been at work on the Wall in that year. It looks as if later propaganda, after Septimius' death, asserted that the purpose of his expedition all along had been the strengthening of the existing frontier fortifications, in conjunction with a punitive campaign. But the evidence of Dio, combined with the archaeological record, shows that in Britain, as in the east and in Africa, Septimius showed himself to be a *propagator imperii*.[22]

Dio has one or two stories to illustrate the campaign. Antoninus evidently continued to cause Septimius anxiety because of his lack of self-restraint and his obvious wish to kill his brother if he could get the chance. He had a row with the freedman Castor, and burst out of his tent, yelling that Castor had 'wronged him'. The thing was a put up job—he had primed a group of soldiers beforehand to join in his shouts and raise an outcry. Another episode was more serious. Septimius and Antoninus were riding forward to meet the Caledonians to discuss terms. The two emperors were out in front, with the army following. The enemy was arrayed on the other side. Antoninus suddenly reined in his horse and drew his sword. It looked as if he was going to strike his father in the back. Their attendants shouted out a warning, and he refrained from making the attempt. It seems incredible that he should have been so senseless as to try to kill his father in the presence of thousands of Roman soldiers. If Dio gave no further details it would have been natural to assume that a movement by Antoninus had been misunderstood. But that was not the end of the matter. Septimius turned when he heard the shouts, and saw his son's sword, but remained silent. After the negotiations with the Caledonians were completed, and they had returned to headquarters—perhaps at Carpow—he summoned Antoninus, Papinian and Castor. He ordered a sword to be placed within easy reach and then reclining on a couch, gave his son a tongue-lashing—not only for daring to try such a thing at all, but for trying it in the face of both armies. Then his tone changed to sarcasm. ' "But if you really want to kill me, do it here. You are strong and I am an old man, and am lying down. If you don't shrink from doing this, but hesitate to kill me with your own hands, there is Papinian the Prefect standing besides you, and you can order him to put me to death. For he will surely do anything that you command, since you also are emperor." '

Nonetheless, Septimius refrained from taking any action against Antoninus, even though, according to Dio, he had now realised that his plans for the succession were less wise than he had thought. 'He had often blamed Marcus for not removing Commodus—and he had often threatened to do this to his son.' His love for Antoninus outweighed his love for his country—yet to spare Antoninus was to betray Geta, 'for he well knew what would happen'.[23]

Considering how superstitious Septimius was, his belief that his days were now numbered was presumably strengthened by a series of omens. In the version now preserved, Dio only has one of these, which occurred shortly before the departure from Rome in 208. Lightning struck an inscription on the gate through which Septimius planned to march out of the city, erasing the first three letters of his name. The remaining three formed the Greek word *(h)ero*. This was interpreted to mean that after three years he would die, and be deified. The *HA*, in its perverse fashion, after neglecting to give any details about the campaigning, records four omens that may be assigned to the end of the year 209, if they are not the product of the author's own imagination. The first purports to be a dream that Septimius had about his own deification. The second apparently took place at games in honour of the victory in the north. They will have taken place at the main base, perhaps Carpow. Three plaster figures of the goddess Victory were set up, one each for Septimius and his sons. The central one, bearing a globe inscribed with his name, was struck by a gust of wind, and fell down from the podium. The one honouring Geta was blown over and totally shattered, while Antoninus' Victory lost its palm and barely remained upright.

The third and fourth omens, which seem part of the same story, belong to Septimius' journey southward to winter-quarters. The beginning of this passage is difficult to translate and is perhaps corrupt. It has been variously emended, but can be understood perfectly well as it stands, in the light of evidence from Britain.

> After giving a Moor his discharge from the army, on the Wall (*apud vallum*) [this would be something quite normal at the end of a campaign] when he returned to the nearest *mansio* [halting-place], not merely as victor but having established eternal peace, and turning over in his mind what sort of man should meet him [or 'what omen he should meet with'] a certain 'Ethiopian' (black man) from the military *numerus*, with a wide reputation as a buffoon, and always noted for his jokes, met him with a garland made from cypress-boughs. When ordered that the man should be removed from his presence, in a rage, being upset by the man's colour and the ill-omened nature of his garland, the man is said to have called out, as a joke: 'You have overthrown all things, conquered all things, now be a conquering god!' When he reached the town and wanted to make sacrifice, by a mistake on the part of the rustic soothsayer, in the first place he was taken to the temple of Bellona, and then the sacrificial victims that were provided were black. Then, when he had abandoned the sacrifice in disgust, and had withdrawn to the Palace, through the attendants' carelessness the black victims followed him right up to its doors.

The story could be easily rejected as a feeble concoction. But curiously enough, at the fort of Aballava (Burgh-by-Stands), west of Luguvalium (Carlisle) on Hadrian's Wall, the garrison in the third century included a *numerus Maurorum*, a unit of Moors, which could well have had black soldiers in its ranks. That Septimius should have used Aballava as a *mansio* is perfectly plausible. The fort guarded two important fords across the Solway and the marching-camp at Kirkpatrick shows that the western route was used at this time by the army. As for the shrine of Bellona, a dedication to the goddess has been found at the fort of Maglona (Old Carlisle) some ten miles away. The town may have been Luguvalium itself, although Eboracum might seem likelier, in view of the mention of a 'Palace'.[24]

The *HA*'s anecdote, feeble or not, has the merit of locating Septimius *apud vallum*. It is not implausible that in 209, after his campaign, he traversed the western and central sectors of the old frontier. He may have instituted changes. Luguvalium, the largest town on the Wall, may now have become the administrative centre of the Carvetii, the tribe which inhabited the Solway plain and Eden valley. They had acquired the organs of self-government by the third century. Just outside Luguvalium was the base of Britain's largest auxiliary unit, the only double strength cavalry regiment in the province, the *ala Petriana*. He would have proceeded east, by Castlesteads and Birdoswald, to Carvoran, where the Wall climbs up to the crags. There he would have found a shrine of the Syrian Goddess, for the fort had been garrisoned by archers from Hamath, or Epiphaneia, not far from Emesa, the *cohors I Hamiorum*. An elaborate verse dedication to the goddess identified her, in the syncretistic fashion of the age, with the Great Mother, Peace, Virtue and Ceres, and with the African Juno Caelestis, the 'heavenly' Tanit. At Vindolanda, further east, the villagers outside the fort had set up a humbler altar, 'for the Divine House and Deities of the Emperors', *pro domu divina et numinibus Augustorum*, to Vulcan. Nearby, at Housesteads, Septimius may have recognised the fort where Pertinax had commanded the First Tungrians more than forty years before. His route to Eboracum should have taken him on to Coria, where the old north road crossed the Tyne. At the great supply base he would have seen further shrines which would evoke recollections of earlier days, including one to the Phoenician deities Ashtaroth, of Sidon, and Melart, of Tyre—and of Lepcis.[25]

He presumably spent most of his time, after the campaign of 209, at Eboracum. Certainly, on 5 May 210, if the heading of a rescript in the Code of Justinian is accurate, a reply written 'at Eboracum' was sent in the names of Septimius and Antoninus in response to the enquiry of a lady named Caecilia. (The case concerned the ownership of a slave.) There are eighteen rescripts from the years 208–10, all of which, except three from February 208, were no doubt issued from Britain. This is a salutary reminder that Septimius could not relax his attention. Once a man was emperor his subjects would constantly crave his attention. An inscription from Ephesus records how an ambassador from that city came to Britain to petition Septimius and Antoninus.

Dio has a pleasant story which shows that the empress found some intellectual diversion in the island. In conversation with the wife of a

Caledonian named Argentocoxus, after the treaty had been concluded, Julia joked with her about the sexual customs of her people, referring to their women's freedom in having intercourse with men. The Caledonian woman showed a biting humour in her reply: 'We fulfil the demands of nature in a much better way than you Roman women. We have intercourse openly with the best men—you allow yourselves to be seduced in secret by the worst.'[27]

The peace that Septimius had imposed did not last long. The Maeatae broke out into revolt, and were soon joined by the Caledonians. It may well be that Maeatae had one of their tribal centres very close to the fortress of Carpow: the later Pictish capital of Abernethy is only a mile or so away, and the Maeatae may be regarded as 'proto-Picts'. They may have taken some months to realise that the Romans were settling down permanently in their heartland. Septimius decided on a campaign of extermination, quoting the Homeric Agamemnon's exhortation to slaughter the Trojans:

> Let no one escape utter destruction,
> Let no one escape our hands, not even the babe in its mother's womb,
> If it be male—let not even this escape utter destruction.

The second campaign, in 210, was evidently conducted by Antoninus alone. Septimius, crippled by his illness, remained behind, probably at Eboracum. Once again a massive army was taken up into Scotland. Its route could be that indicated by one of the lines of camps already described. According to Herodian, Antoninus paid little attention to the war, but concentrated on winning the personal allegiance of the soldiers. Certainly Dio notes that Septimius began preparing to take over the command again in person after the Caledonians joined the revolt. But at last he must have realised that his life was nearly at an end, and that he must take a further step to protect the position of his younger son. He raised Geta to the rank of Augustus. An inscription from Athens happens to preserve the decree passed by the two Councils and the People of Athens in the month of Poseidon (December 210 or January 211) when they heard the news. They voted to hold a festival and public sacrifice, since 'the most sacred and perfect of all days, longed for by all, on account of the undying concord of the Sacred Emperors, Lucius Septimius Severus Pertinax Augustus . . . and Marcus Aurelius Antoninus Pius Augustus . . . has been announced by a joint proclamation to all men by the great Emperors, in which, by their heavenly decree and judgment, they have made the most divine Emperor Publius Septimius Geta Pius Augustus an equal partner in the imperial rule, establishing the rule of the world in their whole family.'

The promotion had been left surprisingly late, considering that Geta was less than twelve months younger than Antoninus. He had had to wait for more than twelve years to attain equal rank. Septimius clearly knew by 210 that he could not rely on Antoninus to make Geta his colleague.[28]

During the winter of 210–11, Septimius' illness got worse and on 4 February 211, at Eboracum, he died. Dio notes that Antoninus was said by some to have hastened his death and Herodian states outright that he had tried to bribe his father's doctors and nurses to bring this about. Septimius' last words of advice to his sons—Dio claims to 'give them exactly, without any embellishment'—were, ' "Do not disagree between yourselves, give money to the soldiers, and despise everyone else" '. Aurelius Victor, whose fault as an historian is simply incompetence—rather than fraud as in the case of the *HA*—reports that at the end of his life Septimius uttered the despairing remark that 'I have been all things, and it has profited nothing'. The *HA*'s attempt at originality in the description of his death is better disregarded. Dio hits a convincing note: 'He showed himself to be a man of such energy that even as he expired he gasped: "Come, give it to me, if we have anything to do".'[29]

AFTERMATH AND ASSESSMENT

THE BODY OF THE DEAD EMPEROR was cremated at Eboracum. His ashes were placed in an urn of 'purple stone', which he had ordered before his death, Dio says. After handling it he said, 'You will hold a man that the world could not hold'. Antoninus and Geta at once made preparations to leave Britain. In Antoninus' case this included the dismissal of Papinian from the prefecture and the execution of a number of members of the household, the freedmen Castor and Euodus among them, and the court doctors, according to Herodian, who 'had refused to obey his orders to hasten the old man's death'. Euodus, who had supervised Antoninus and Geta as boys, and had helped to dispose of Plautianus, and Castor, whom Antoninus hated, had 'continued to urge him to live at peace with Geta'. In secret, Herodian says, Antoninus began bribing the officers to induce the troops to 'accept him as sole emperor'. If Herodian's account may be trusted for detail, it appears that Antoninus wanted to have Geta killed, and made his overtures to the army in the north, having left Geta and Julia at Eboracum. For the time being he did not succeed: the soldiers' loyalty to Geta was partly inspired by 'his very close resemblance to his father'.[1]

In the face of this refusal, Antoninus made peace with the enemy, 'withdrawing from their territory and abandoning the forts'. For a short time the major new base at Carpow may have been retained, but the decision was now made to make Hadrian's Wall the frontier once more. A concerted attempt to claim that this had been Septimius' plan all along may have followed. If, as seems possible, the younger Ulpius Marcellus was now appointed governor, it may have been hoped that that name would inspire terror in the northern tribes which his father had crushed in 184. At Eboracum Julia made an attempt, backed by the imperial *comites*, to reconcile the brothers. Antoninus made a show of agreement and the imperial party hastily left the island. The outcome was obvious from the start. Even on the journey they had separate quarters; at Rome the palace was physically divided; and after the ceremony of deification for their father the two emperors led separate existences. The months that followed saw a battle for support, a majority in the senate supposedly favouring Geta, who at least gave the appearance of being a cultivated person. Antoninus had adopted the role of the rough, plain soldier.[2]

The end came over the Saturnalia holiday in late December. Antoninus may have been desperate to remove Geta before the oath of loyalty was renewed on 3 January. On 26 December, following the pattern of Plautianus' murder, Geta was stabbed to death—in his mother's arms: Julia had been persuaded to summon him for a 'reconciliation'. Antoninus went post-haste to the Guards barracks, claiming hysterically that he had escaped an attempt on his life. He told the praetorians to rejoice: 'for now I can do you favours'. In the senate the next day he proclaimed an amnesty, but there was a holocaust of Geta's supporters. Dio says that 20,000 were killed, men and women of all ranks. Papinian was a prominent victim, others included Pertinax's son, a sister of Commodus, and Antoninus' own cousin, a Septimius Severus. Fabius Cilo narrowly escaped, after an outcry from the Urban Cohorts, which he had commanded as City Prefect, and a section of the plebs. Antoninus appointed his cousin's husband, Sex. Varius Marcellus, as acting commander of the Guard and simultaneously acting City Prefect. He had briefly served as head of the imperial finances, a rationibus, after returning from Britain.

Geta's memory was sytematically obliterated. All his portraits were defaced, his name erased from inscriptions. Where the empty space would have been a constant reminder, new titles for Antoninus and for Julia—who was now styled not merely 'Mother of the Camp' but 'of the Senate and the Fatherland' as well—were inserted. It was as if Geta had never existed. Even inscriptions that merely presumed his existence by the abbreviation Auggg. to show three emperors and in some cases from the past year Augg. (for the two brothers) were doctored by the deletion of a g.[3]

Antoninus' sole reign lasted just over five years. History knows him as 'Caracalla' from the nickname the plebs gave him, a Celtic word for the hooded cloak he affected, not unlike the burnous. Dio also calls him 'Tarautas', after 'a gladiator who was very small and extremely ugly, and of most violent and bloodthirsty character'. Dio's hatred for him may render his account suspect, but there is little to set in the opposite scale. Herodian has one or two good words to say. He could grasp the essentials of a case and give a quick verdict. His attachment to the soldiers led him to share their burdens: 'If a ditch had to be dug, the emperor was the first man to dig ... grinding corn with his own hand, one man's ration, he made a loaf, baked it in the coals and ate it. He scorned luxuries and used what was cheapest and issued to the poorest of the soldiers.' He marched with the men, and sometimes even carried the legionary standards, 'a very heavy burden even for the strongest soldiers'. This won him the men's admiration: 'for a small man the performing of such efforts was praise-worthy', Herodian concedes. Dio also reports this soldierly conduct. The trouble was, in his view, that even if Caracalla was a good soldier he made a hopeless general.

True to his father's practice, Caracalla soon went to the armies. In 213 he campaigned on the upper Danube, where his British experience was perhaps put to good use. He may be responsible for the stone wall, less massive than Hadrian's in Britain, although longer, that was erected on the western part of the Raetian frontier, now threatened by the Alamanni. The next year he left for the east, taking the northern land route, and was never to return to Rome. There was conflict within the Parthian empire, of which he hoped to take advantage. The years 214–15 were spent in the eastern provinces, with a visit to Alexandria, during which some kind of massacre took place. In 216 he began a Parthian expedition: little had been achieved when one of the Guard Prefects, Opellius Macrinus, had him murdered, in April 217, in Osrhoene.[4]

One action of Caracalla's mentioned briefly by Dio, ignored by Herodian and barely alluded to in the *HA*, has won him praise from posterity. Some time after his brother's murder he issued an edict granting Roman citizenship to all free inhabitants of the empire. Dio includes it in a list of fund-raising measures: the motive was to increase revenue from taxes paid only by citizens, which were doubled. The taxes in question funded the military treasury, *aerarium militare*, to which his kinsman Varius Marcellus, now made a senator, was assigned as prefect. This institution paid bounties to veterans, and, given Caracalla's clearly attested favour to the military—he further increased pay—Dio's interpretation is plausible. The exact scope of the award may be debated. Some were evidently excluded, but in practice Dio's statement that 'he made all the people in his empire Roman citizens' scarcely exaggerates. The legal privileges attached to citizenship had by this time been much diluted, but the symbolic value of the measure cannot be denied. In the long term it gave a sense of unity to the empire: Rome became the 'common fatherland' of all, the *communis patria*. The lawyers, of whom Ulpian and Paulus were still in active service, may well have recommended the move.[5]

Caracalla had also taken measures in Britain. In 213 a new governor, C. Julius Marcus, had clearly ordered displays of loyalty. All over the frontier region—that is to say, along Hadrian's Wall and its outposts, once more the limit of Roman rule, and in the Pennine hinterland—dedications were made expressing the troops' devotion to the emperor, *pro pietate et devotione communi*. The army of Britain had seen more of Geta than any other and may have taken the news of his murder badly. Julius Marcus himself evidently failed to retain imperial favour: his name is deleted on some stones. As for the province and its enormous army, Caracalla split it into two, following his father's policy with Syria in 194. (Herodian mistakenly assigns the division of Britain to the aftermath of Lugdunum.) The commander of VI Victrix now became governor of 'Lower Britain', Britannia Inferior, responsible for the northern parts of eastern England, including the old Flavian *colonia* at Lindum. The civil town at Eboracum, already a *municipium* when Septimius died there, was elevated to the same status. The legions at Deva and Isca were in the Upper province, Britannia Superior, whose governor resided at Londinium, and, having two legions under him, was of consular status, whereas his colleague in Inferior was more junior. The identity of the earliest legate of Inferior on record is revealing: in the year 216 it was a certain M. Antonius Gordianus, an already elderly person of literary inclinations, whose home was in Cappadocia or Galatia. The army, or armies, of Britain, thus divided and with such commanders, would no longer be a threat. At the same time an adjustment was made in Pannonia. The Upper province, the army of which had put the dynasty in power, lost part of its territory and one legion, given to the other Pannonia. No province in the empire now had more than two legions.[6]

Italy, presumably accustomed by this time to seeing less of the imperial presence, submitted to treatment which foreshadowed its demotion to provincial status. One of Caracalla's most trusted senatorial friends—for he did have some—held a hitherto unknown appointment: Suetrius Sabinus was 'chosen to regulate the status of Italy'. During his brief sole reign Caracalla set many changes in train, it is clear. His further increase in army pay was coupled, not surprisingly, with monetary changes. These measures were to fuel galloping inflation, once it had been triggered by the instability which his own murder, and the events that followed, were to engender.[7]

Macrinus' action was taken for self-preservation: he had intercepted a letter which might have been in effect his own death-warrant. He had to conceal his role in the murder, for fear of the army. To appease it, he added the name 'Severus' to his own, 'Antoninus' to that of his son and Caesar, Diadumenianus, still a child. He did not wait for recognition from the senate, but assumed the titles and functions of emperor. His fellow-Prefect, the now aged Oclatinius Adventus, acquiesced. Julia Domna, who had been constantly with Caracalla and a close adviser, was treated with cautious respect by the usurper. Nothing is heard of his own wife, if still alive: she was probably a daughter of Haius Diadumenianus, procurator of Macrinus' native Mauretania fifteen years before. But Julia declined to remain in the background, began intriguing, and was ordered out of Antioch, where Macrinus had established himself. The sense of helplessness this brought, and shock at the news of rejoicing at Rome over Caracalla's death, led her to suicide.[8]

Her sister Julia Maesa was not so ready to surrender the high position she had enjoyed as sister of the empress for twenty-five years. She was back at Emesa, a widow: her husband Avitus Alexianus had just died, in Cyprus, 'from old age and disease'. After his return from the shadows in 208, when he went to Britain, presumably accompanied by Maesa, their daughter Soaemias and son-in-law Marcellus, he had been given several appointments by Caracalla, governing Dalmatia and Asia. Maesa had no doubt followed him there too. Now there was only one man left in her family—for Marcellus had died before Caracalla, as governor of Numidia: the other son-in-law, Gessius Marcianus, whose home was Arca Caesarea, not far from Emesa.

But Macrinus had difficulty in establishing himself. Dio speaks of him with studied contempt. He was the first emperor who had not even been a senator. He was a 'Moor', albeit a native of the great city of Caesarea, and had been a satellite of Plautianus. Worse, he was incompetent, in war—he made an ignominious peace with Parthia—and in administration. Dio was horrified by his flouting of the rules of rank and precedence. He alienated the troops, not surprisingly finding it difficult to pay them at the new high levels introduced by Caracalla. By the winter the men in the east were openly discontented.

A means of redress lay to hand. Maesa's eldest grandchild, Varius Avitus Bassianus, now about fourteen, was at Emesa, already fulfilling the function of hereditary priest at the great temple, which had been further enhanced and adorned in the past two decades. The youth closely resembled the murdered Caracalla, his mother's first cousin. A certain Eutychianus is credited with the proposal to present the boy-priest as Caracalla's illegitimate son, dressed in clothes his alleged father had once worn. This man, also called Gannys, had been brought up in Maesa's household, had some talent in acting and gymnastic exercises, had been made the guardian or tutor of young Avitus, and was the lover of his mother Soaemias. With a few freedmen and soldiers, some members of Emesa's council and perhaps a few Roman knights (Dio's text is fragmentary), he took Avitus by night to the fortress of the legion III Gallica at nearby Raphaneae. At dawn on 16 May 218 Avitus was displayed to the troops, who acclaimed him as emperor under the name 'Marcus Aurelius Antoninus'.

Macrinus had plenty of other troops, not just the two legions of Syria Coele, but the Guard and the Alban legion, II Parthica, not far north at this time, at Apamea, and Moors, fellow-countrymen, summoned by Caracalla for his war. His Guard Prefect Julianus rapidly had Gessius Marcianus' daughter and son-in-law, also in Syria at the time, put to death, and then Marcianus was killed too. Macrinus came down from Antioch to Apamea, and proclaimed his son co-emperor. But III Gallica repelled Julianus, Macrinus retreated and the revolt spread. It took less than a month to topple him: he was defeated near Antioch on 8 June and killed shortly afterwards. His reign of less than fourteen months could be regarded as a mere interlude. The dynasty had returned to power. At Rome the senate dutifully prayed that the new 'Antoninus', of whose bizarre nature they must have been quite unaware, should be like his alleged father, whom they had feared and loathed. The boy-emperor was to become known as 'Elagabalus', after his god: for good reason—he was a fanatical devotee. He quite literally brought him to Rome; the black stone, or betyl, was paraded all the way across Asia, and transported to the capital. From Nicomedia, where he wintered, a portrait of the new emperor in his exotic priestly robes, gold and purple long-sleeved *chiton* and trousers, and jewelled crown, was sent ahead to be hung in the senate-house, above the Altar of Victory. The magistrates were directed to call first on the new god in their official prayers.

In early autumn 219 'Antoninus' and Elagabalus, emperor and god, arrived. The two and a half years that followed were perhaps the strangest in Rome's entire history. Julia Maesa was evidently powerless. Gannys, who had been trying to impose restraint, had been killed by the boy's own hand at Nicomedia. Elagabalus' mother Soaemias pandered to his extra-ordinary tastes. After the—very real—religious fanaticism, foremost among these were his sexual deviations. Dio expatiates on them in detail. The *HA*, it is a surprise, has less; the author preferred to embroider with a string of fictional anecdotes. Herodian passes over the deviations in silence, but mentions the exhibitionist tendencies: 'he had no wish to sin in secret. He appeared in public with his eyes made up and rouged cheeks', adding, characteristically, that this spoiled a naturally handsome face. Dio indicates that he had several male lovers, selected after research in the public baths. But he did not shun the opposite sex, and in spite of his youth had three successive wives during his short reign. One was a Vestal Virgin, and this marriage was complemented by the summoning from Carthage of an image of Juno Caelestis, the Queen of Heaven, the Punic Tanit, as consort for the Arab Lord of the Mountain who had become a Sun god. Another empress was a descendant of Marcus Aurelius, whose name the emperor bore. This marriage, to Annia Faustina, came in 221, when the prestige of her name was desperately needed.

The troops at Rome were unimpressed by the new religion and

disgusted by the unRoman conduct. They and the senate watched with numbed horror as actors, dancers, charioteers and athletes were advanced to high office after gaining the emperor's favour by their sexual prowess. It could not go on. In reserve was another grandson of Julia Maesa, child of her other daughter, Mamaea. On 26 June 221 this boy, Gessius Alexianus Bassianus, was formally adopted by Elagabalus as his son and heir. His name was changed to 'Marcus Aurelius Alexander' and he became Caesar. He had been deliberately shielded by his mother from his cousin's excesses. Elagabalus soon became jealous when he saw his new Caesar's popularity and tried to have him killed. That was too much for the enraged guardsmen. The 'false Antoninus', as Dio calls him among other names, was murdered along with his mother Soaemias, on 12 March 222, and Alexander became emperor. He at once took a further name, becoming 'M. Aurelius Severus Alexander'. 'Antoninus', now irrevocably associated with Caracalla and Elagabalus, he shunned. Still, he too was proclaimed a bastard son of Caracalla—'the deified Antoninus the Great'—and 'Alexander' was a further echo: Caracalla's obsession with Alexander the Great had been pathological.[9]

Alexander was scarcely more than fourteen at his accession (he had assumed the *toga virilis* only the previous year, when he became Caesar). Still, he was to reign for thirteen years, a remarkable achievement given what had happened in the past decade. The opening of the reign seemed to augur well, when the great jurist Ulpian was appointed Guard Prefect. Alexander's colleague as fellow-consul in 223 was Marius Maximus, one of Septimius' marshals from the 190s, with an astonishing record of high office in the years 208–18 (proconsul of both Asia and Africa and City Prefect). He was now in his sixties and perhaps already at work on his biographies of the Caesars from Nerva to Elagabalus. Cassius Dio belatedly began an intensive period of public service, governing Dalmatia and Pannonia after holding the proconsulship of Africa, achieving his own second consulship as reward in 229. But by then things had begun to slide. Ulpian had been murdered by the Guard less than two years after assuming the Prefecture. Dio, who had offended the Pannonian army by his strict discipline, was in danger of similar treatment from the guardsmen as a result, and was advised by the young emperor to avoid Rome during his term of office. He soon withdrew to his native Bithynia, where he watched developments with some foreboding as he completed his great *History of Rome*. In the east there were ominous changes. Parthia, fatally weakened by the campaign of 197–8, was threatened by a revived Persia. The Parthian king Artabanus V was killed in 224, the Persian Ardashir, or Artaxerxes, was crowned in 226, as ruler of a reborn Persian empire. Submerged for five and a half centuries, the Persians re-emerged under the Sassanid dynasty, to be a new and far more dangerous enemy on Rome's eastern frontier.

Julia Maesa did not long survive the accession of Severus Alexander. For a while, as long as there was peace, Julia Mamaea and her son made acceptable rulers. But when Ardashir invaded Mesopotamia and threatened Syria in 230, diplomacy was not enough. Alexander accompanied an expeditionary force to the east in 231 and after further unsuccessful negotiations entered Mesopotamia in 232. Ardashir withdrew and the status quo was restored; but the northern frontiers were now in turmoil— the Germans took advantage of the removal of some army units to the east. Alexander was back at Rome in 233 and in 234 went to the Rhineland. Early in 235 all was ready for a campaign. Again he tried diplomacy first. The troops did not like it: diplomacy now meant payment to barbarian chiefs who swore oaths to keep the peace. The legions wanted to fight, and to keep the money themselves as a donative for victory. Alexander was murdered by his own men on 21 March 235. The Severan dynasty had lasted—with the interlude of Macrinus—for forty-two years, less nineteen days. What followed is generally labelled the 'third-century crisis', exactly half a century of upheaval, with repeated Roman defeats in north and east, civil wars becoming endemic and the empire almost breaking apart.[10]

The senate, indeed, continued to enjoy great prestige. Predictably, after 193–7 some families disappear and new fortunes were founded. Septimius' marshals, enriched and ennobled, formed the nucleus of a new aristocracy that was to be prominent for generations. Anicius Faustus is the most striking example. Septimius favoured his fellow Africans, that cannot be denied, likewise persons from Syria. His Guard Prefects Plautianus and Papinian were kinsmen of himself and Julia respectively. His brother Geta played a part at first, and Julia's sister's people, Avitus Alexianus and Varius Marcellus, were given influential, if minor posts. More significant, perhaps, are the governors of major military provinces, Alfenus Senecio in Syria Coele and Britain, the Marii, the Numidian Claudii (Candidus, Claudianus and Gallus), Subatianus Aquila and a good many more, all from North Africa. He could trust these men, he and they could understand each other. He was, after all, responsible for an important shift of military policy, and needed the right people to implement it. He did not, however, rely exclusively on his fellow-countrymen or on Syrians from Julia's orbit. Cornelius Anullinus, Fabius Cilo and probably Manilius Fuscus were from Spain, Sextius Lateranus and Lollianus Gentianus were Italians, all five in high favour.[11]

As for the equestrian order, it had an obvious boost, with the command of the three new legions and the governorship of the new eastern provinces all going to equestrian prefects rather than senatorial *legati Augusti*. He appears to have created new posts for procurators, and more of the procurators from now on derive from the provinces rather than from Italy—sixty per cent from Africa and the east, on one estimate. Neither senate nor equestrian order received many recruits from the Danubian-Balkan region, the source of his power. But from its armies he was to draw the men for his new Guard. The twelve legions that were based along and beyond the Danube remained the largest grouping, and their links with Italy and in particular with the Guard (and with II Parthica at Alba) were to play a vital part in keeping the empire together.

Septimius' military policy is indeed significant. His dying advice to his sons—'Give the soldiers money and despise everyone else', so Dio reports—seems to sum up his attitude. Dio and others shivered at the 'barbarous soldiery' that infested the streets of Rome. Herodian actually claims that he quadrupled the garrison, which cannot be substantiated. But the Guard itself, the Urban Cohorts and the *vigiles* were all considerably increased in size, and the legion at Alba was effectively part of the same force. There may have been further 'special forces', or specialist troops, based in the *castra peregrina*. The purpose may not have been merely to overawe the senate and people of Rome, but to create a larger and more effective central reserve than the old Guard had provided. Certainly, II Parthica as well as the Guard is attested on expeditions. The long wars under Marcus had demonstrated the dangers of shunting whole legions from one frontier to another: three at least had gone from Rhine and Danube to the east in the 160s, allowing the Marcomannic threat to develop. Septimius favoured the system pioneered in the 170s, of brigading detachments, *vexillationes*, from several legions into army corps. But that was still not ideal. II Parthica and the enlarged Guard provided further back up. His alleged 'barbarisation' of the Rome units must not be exaggerated. The Urban Cohorts, now 6000-strong, were larger than the old, mainly Italian, Guard; and the new *vigiles*, 7000-strong, formerly manned by freedmen, now accepted free-born recruits. Italians were not excluded from Rome's security forces. Furthermore, Italians continued to serve as legionary centurions and equestrian officers—but provincials had been well represented or even dominant in these categories fifty years before Septimius' accession. It is true that army officers from his time on were more often of lower social standing than before. More came from frontier areas and some were ex-rankers. Municipal notables or gentry were certainly not excluded.

The increase in pay and improvements in conditions of service—the right to marry particular—are held against him (by Herodian, for example, the only explicit source on the subject). Pay had been constant for over a century and it may be that he increased it to compensate for inflation—but the evidence for inflation before 193 is defective. Also significant, of course, was his desire to keep the men loyal. But he may have been anxious to ensure a ready flow of volunteers: he had witnessed in Gaul the problem of mass desertion in the 180s. Besides, he had expanded the entire army, not merely in the Rome garrison and by raising three legions: new auxiliary regiments were formed.[12] His frontier policy demanded more troops, for he was indeed a *propagator imperii*. In Africa there was a new forward line, in Mauretania, Numidia and Tripolitania; in the east two new provinces beyond the Euphrates, extension of Syria down the river and into the desert, extension of Arabia. Perhaps—it is now doubted—he pushed the eastern limits of Dacia out beyond the Aluta. He very decisively altered the shape of the empire, weighting it much more towards the east (and to a lesser extent his native 'deep South'). The long-term effects of this are not negligible. At the end of his life he was in the far west, trying to repeat the conquests of Agricola. That part of his policy was aborted by his death. Still, the British campaign, manifestly intended to conquer the whole island, could be dismissed as motivated solely by 'desire for glory' with more justice than the annexations beyond the Euphrates to which Dio applied this judgement. Mesopotamia and the other extensions of territory in the east were worth more to Rome than Caledonia, as Caracalla recognised. Caracalla also tried to tackle the Alamanni—perhaps his father should have dealt with the northern frontiers, rather than succumb to the lure of the fabled island.[13]

Given the chaos into which the empire descended in the third century, and the contrast, grim in many respects, between the Antonine era and the new world that was to emerge, it is not surprising that Septimius Severus has been pilloried. His was by far the longest reign of any emperor between the death of Marcus in 180 and the accession of Diocletian in 284. 'The contemporaries of Severus, in the enjoyment of the peace and glory of his reign, forgave the cruelties by which it had been introduced', wrote Gibbon. 'Posterity, who experienced the fatal results of his maxims and example, justly considered him as the principal author of the decline of the Roman empire.' Such a verdict, in the fifth chapter of the mammoth work, may seem over-hasty (Gibbon was to find other villains, such as Constantine, in later pages). But the decline set in soon enough, even if the fall was long postponed. Was it Septimius' doing?

His contemporaries, Galen, Tertullian, Dio and (perhaps) Herodian, are of differing value. The famous doctor, late in life (he seems to have died before 200), was delighted that the new emperor, unlike Commodus, swore by his patent medicine, with which Marcus Aurelius had regularly dosed himself. This mixture, once familiar only to a narrow circle around Marcus, was now generally known—for the greatest of emperors (Septimius and his young son) wanted all to benefit from improved health. Galen's prescription carried the imperial warrant; he was also gratified by an imperial summons to attend the eloquent Antipater, tutor to Antoninus and Geta, and *ab epistulis Graecis*, when he was suffering agonising kidney trouble. Various remarks of Tertullian in the *De pallio* refer to the flourishing state of Africa in Septimius' reign. Addressing the citizens of Carthage, he rejoices in their prosperity, and the leisure it gives them to be critical judges of dress. (The tone is unmistakably sarcastic.) He enlarges on the theme: 'What a great part of the world has been changed by the present era! What a great number of cities has the threefold virtue of the present emperors [i.e. Septimius and his two sons] created, amplified or restored!' God has shown the emperors favour, and 'in truth the world is the cultivated garden of this empire, all poisonous weeds of external hostility have been eradicated, the cactus and briar of conspiracy at home has been uprooted, and it is more pleasing than the orchard of Alcinous or the rose garden of Midas'. This does not really tell us anything about Septimius' policies.

One can find in Herodian gushing admiration of Septimius' success in civil war. No battles or victories of the past could compare with his, even Caesar against Pompey, Octavian against Antony or the son of Pompey, Sulla against Marius. 'Here is a single man who overthrew three emperors who were already in power, who gained control of the Guard by a trick, who succeeded in killing Julianus, the emperor in the palace, Niger who ruled the people of the east, and had been saluted as emperor by the people of Rome, and Albinus who had already the title and authority of a Caesar—this he did by virtue of his courage. One could not easily name his equal.' Similar sentiments are expressed by Aurelius Victor, 100 years later, who had the excuse of being a fellow-countryman, and devoted more space to the African emperor in his modest chronicle than to any other. Victor has his word of criticism, especially for the cruelty exhibited in the mass executions, but goes on to call Septimius wise as well as successful, especially in war, 'so much so that he left no battle except as victor'.[14]

Cassius Dio is the only witness who knew the emperor personally (Galen can scarcely have met him). Dio introduces Septimius as the most intelligent of the three army commanders of 193. The obituary notice with which he ends Book 76 is respectful, almost affectionate in tone:

He was a small man, but physically strong (although he did become very weak from gout). His mind was extremely keen and vigorous. He did not get as much education as he wanted, and because of this he was a man of few words, although he had plenty of ideas. He did not forget his friends, his enemies he treated with a very heavy hand. He took a great deal of thought over all his plans; but never gave a thought to what was said about him. For this reason he raised money from every source—except that he never killed anyone for this reason—and he met all necessary expenditures unstintingly.

As if to guarantee that he was writing quite freely, Dio goes on to criticise Septimius' wasteful building programme and habit of inscribing his own name on buildings that he had merely restored, 'as if he had erected them himself'. Suspicion about Dio's frankness is in any case removed by what is revealed in another passage. After Septimius' death Dio had a dream. He saw the entire Roman army lined up on a great plain. The emperor was standing on a tribunal addressing the troops. When he saw Dio standing nearby and trying to hear what was being said, he spoke to him: 'Come nearer, Dio, so that you can learn exactly what is being said and done, and write an account of it.' As has been pointed out, Dio could hardly have had a dream like this if the emperor had not been 'a respected and authoritative figure in his eyes'.[15]

Dio and the HA both stress, with more detail than any other sources, the number of senators put to death. Dio gives a figure for the purge after Lugdunum: twenty-nine executed, thirty-five pardoned (the HA gives a long list of names, a great many of them invented). 'Many' were killed a year or so later, for consulting astrologers about the emperor's life expectancy, the HA reports. Dio says that 'many other senators', as well as Plautius Quintillus, died, some of them after a formal trial, some time after Plautianus' death in 205—so Plautianus cannot be blamed for that batch, as he might be for earlier ones. There were times of terror—not surprising with civil wars—but perhaps, to senators like Dio, less horrific than what went on before and after, under Commodus and Caracalla.

The stigma of cruelty cannot be covered up, even if the first emperor, Augustus, in his earlier career, could be invoked, as he was by Septimius himself before the senate in 197. It was the happier times of Antoninus and Marcus, whom Dio and others wistfully remembered, that formed the damaging comparison. But the reign of Commodus and four years of civil war that followed had had a brutalising effect. At his first proclamation, Septimius proclaimed himself the avenger of Pertinax, who had promised to bring back the spirit of Marcus' rule. Septimius never dropped the name 'Pertinax', although it was squeezed out for lack of space as his titles proliferated. Indeed, his deference to that memory was even emphasised, it could be maintained, when 'Pius' was inserted between 'Severus' and 'Pertinax': that connoted loyalty. Septimius is an ambiguous figure. His grandfather, the Italianate man of Lepcis, at home in cultivated circles in Rome of the Silver Age, may seem worlds away. Septimius himself lacked this polish, may have remained closer to Lepcis' Punic past, at least until he reached manhood. But his early adult life was spent mostly at Rome, in the reign of Marcus. In many respects he seems to have emulated that paragon: making his empress *mater castrorum* and his son co-emperor; adopting an expansionist policy; spending long years with the armies. More damaging, perhaps, in the long run, was his monetary policy. He unquestionably debased the silver currency to a far lower level than Marcus or even Commodus had. His pay increase for the troops, made possible by this means, resulted in far greater quantities of money in circulation. During his lifetime there was sufficient confidence in the strength of his government for this to act as a stimulus to the economy, above all in the frontier regions. The instability which soon followed his death, coupled with further increases in the volume of coinage, was in due course to bring about the great inflation of the later third century.[16]

He can at least be assessed as a remarkable phenomenon, the first truly provincial emperor, for Trajan and his successors from the western colonial élite were not only descended from Italian settlers but themselves thoroughly assimilated to the metropolitan society, born and brought up at Rome, not at Italica, Nemausus or Ucubi. Antoninus probably never visited the Gallic home of his ancestors, Marcus and Commodus certainly never set foot in Spain. Septimius Severus was a product of Africa, and of an African city in which Italian settlement had been unusually meagre. It cannot be known whether, for example, the ancestral gods whom he honoured under their Roman names were also familiar to him as Shadrapa and Milk'ashtart. In any case, the sole other mention in the sources of his religious inclinations is of the Greco-Egyptian Sarapis. The African emperor who died in Britain has to remain an enigma.

Abbreviations used in Appendices and Notes

AE	*L'Année épigraphique* (Paris 1888 ff.)
ANRW	*Aufstieg und Niedergang der römischen Welt* (Berlin & New York 1972 ff.), eds H. Temporini & W. Haase
BAR	*British Archaeological Reports* (Oxford)
BMC	*Catalogue of Coins of the Roman Empire in the British Museum* IV. Antoninus Pius to Commodus (London 1940); V. Pertinax to Elagabalus (London 1950)
CIL	*Corpus Inscriptionum Latinarum* (Berlin 1863 ff.)
CP; Supp.	H. G. Pflaum, *Les carrières procuratoriennes équestres sous le Haut-Empire romain* (Paris 1960–1); Supplement (Paris 1982)
CRAI	*Comptes-Rendues de l'Académie des Inscriptions et Belles-Lettres* (Paris)
EE	*Ephemeris Epigraphica* (Berlin 1872–1913)
HA	*Historia Augusta*, ed. E. Hohl (Leipzig 1927; repr. 1955)
HAC	*Historia-Augusta-Colloquium* (Bonn 1964 ff.)
IG	*Inscriptiones Graecae* (Berlin)
IGLS	*Inscriptions grecques et latines de Syrie* (Beirut 1929 ff.)
IGRR	*Inscriptiones graecae ad res Romanas pertinentes* I, III, IV, ed. R. Cagnat (Paris 1901–21)
ILAfr	*Inscriptions latines d'Afrique*, eds. R. Cagnat, A. Merlin, L. Chatelain (Paris 1923)
ILAlg	*Inscriptions latines de l'Algérie* I, ed. S. Gsell (Algiers 1923); II 1 ed. H. G. Pflaum (Algiers 1958); II 2 ed. H. G. Pflaum (Algiers 1976)
ILS	*Inscriptiones latinae selectae*, ed. H. Dessau (Berlin 1892–1916)
ILTun	*Inscriptions latines de Tunisie*, ed. A. Merlin (Tunis 1944)
IPT	*Iscrizioni puniche della Tripolitania (1927–1967)*, eds. G. Levi della Vida and M. G. Amadasi Guzzo (Rome 1987)
IRT	*Inscriptions of Roman Tripolitania*, eds. J. M. Reynolds and J. B. Ward Perkins (London 1952)
JRS	*Journal of Roman Studies* (London 1910 ff.)
KAI	*Kanaanäische und Aramaische Inschriften*, eds. H. Donner and W. Röllig (2nd ed. Wiesbaden 1968)

PIR[1]	*Prosopographia Imperii Romani*. I. A–C, ed. E. Klebs (Berlin 1897). II. D–O, ed. H. Dessau (Berlin 1897). III P–Z, eds. P. v. Rohden and H. Dessau (Berlin 1897)
PIR[2]	*Prosopographia Imperii Romani*, ed. altera. I. A–B, eds. E. Groag and A. Stein (Berlin 1933). II. C, eds. E. Groag and A. Stein (Berlin 1936). III. D-F, eds. E. Groag and A. Stein (Berlin 1943). IV. 1. G. eds. E. Groag and A. Stein (Berlin 1952). IV. 2. H, eds. E. Groag and A. Stein (Berlin 1957). IV. 3. I–J. ed. L. Petersen (Berlin 1966). V. 1. L, ed. L. Petersen (Berlin 1970). V. 2. M, ed. L. Petersen (Berlin 1983). V. 3, N–O, eds. L. Petersen et al. (Berlin 1987).
RE	Paulys *Realencylopädie der classischen Altertumswissenschaft*, eds. G. Wissowa et al. (Stuttgart 1893–1978)
RIB	*The Roman Inscriptions of Britain* I. eds R. G. Collingwood and R. P. Wright (London 1965)
RIC	*The Roman Imperial Coinage*, eds. H. Mattingly, E. A. Sydenham et al. (London 1923 ff.)
RIT	G. Alföldy, *Die Römischen Inschriften von Tarraco* (Berlin 1975)
RMD	M. M. Roxan, *Roman Military Diplomas 1954–1977; 1978–1984* (London 1978, 1985)

APPENDIX I
Ancient Evidence and Modern Scholarship

A. ANCIENT EVIDENCE

1. Septimius wrote an autobiography, referred to or cited a few times. *HA Sev.* 3.2 mentions his marriage to Marci[an]a, 'de qua tacuit in historia vitae privatae'. Herodian 2.9.4–7, having mentioned the 'dreams . . . and oracles and other signs' that led Septimius to hope for the empire, says that he 'has given an account of many of them himself in his autobiography' and quotes the one about Pertinax's horse. Dio 75.7.3, reporting Albinus' suicide, says that 'I am not stating what Severus wrote about it but what actually took place'. *HA Nig.* 4.7–5.1 purports to derive from the autobiography ('in vita sua Severus dicit . . . si Severo credimus'), as also *Alb.* 7.1 ('ut . . . ipse in vita sua loquitur'): there may be some basis in the stories, illustrating Septimius' alleged claims regarding his rivals; but it looks as if the *HA* has mangled them. In any case, it is probable that the author took them from Marius Maximus. Finally, Victor, *De Caes.* 20.22 refers approvingly to the work: 'idemque abs se texta ornatu et fide paribus composuit'. Victor seems to have read his fellow-countryman. *HA Sev.* 18. 6 (in the section adapted from Victor, below, A.5) has 'vitam suam privatam publicam ipse composuit ad fidem, solum tamen vitium crudelitatis excusans'. The last phrase is an addition, reflecting the author's use of Marius Maximus, cited earlier (15.6): 'se excusabat [for the executions of 198] . . . quod de Laeto praecipue Marius Maximus dicit'. Hasebroek 8 has little comment, Platnauer 17f., noting that it is uncertain even what language, Greek or Latin, the memoirs were written in, stresses that only Victor took their author at his word. Rubin 26 n. 29 insists the work was in Latin; 130, 191f. argues that Herodian knew it second-hand; 133ff., 171ff., 190ff. discusses at length the relationship between the autobiography and the biography by Maximus (also a lost work).

2. Cassius Dio (often called 'Dio Cassius' in the Greek style), by his full names L. Cassius Dio Cocceianus (*PIR*² C 492; *praenomen: RMD* no. 133), a senator's son, from Bithynian Nicaea, born c. 165, himself a senator under Commodus, consul for the first time under Septimius (sometimes disputed, but clear), with Caracalla in Nicomedia; appointed curator of two Asian cities by Macrinus 217–8; proconsul of Africa c. 223, then—exceptionally senior—legate of Dalmatia and Upper Pannonia, finally *cos.II ord.* with the emperor Severus Alexander, in 229. His first historical work on Septimius' dreams, and other signs that forecast his rule, won favour; in a dream of his own, *to daimonion* told him to write about 'the wars and very great disturbances' that followed Commodus' death, which should mean the civil and Parthian wars from 193–8; this too was well received and he eventually (the timing is vague) decided to incorporate it in a complete history of Rome. He spent ten years in research 'from the beginnings down to Severus' death', and a further twelve in writing the work, which was extended from 211 to the moment of his own second consulship in 229. Opinion has varied over the interpretation of this passage, 72. 23.1–5. Millar 1964, whose monograph is an essential introduction to the man, his background and his work (see now also Ameling), unfortunately has a forced and unconvincing dating of its composition (G. W. Bowersock, *Gnomon* 37 (1965) 471). After various other proposals, by Eisman and Letta, Barnes 1984 argues convincingly that Dio began research in 211 at earliest, completed it 220 or a little later, and wrote his work over the twelve years 220–31 ('the actual dates, however, may be a little later', Barnes 1984, 252). Exactly when he had written his preliminary works remains largely a matter of guesswork. But there is no reason why he should not have sent either or both to Septimius, i.e. he need not have presented copies in person—but, if he did hand over the second work himself, it could have been in Bithynia, e.g. in 202. Rubin 9ff., 41ff., and *passim* has a series of valuable observations on Dio, in particular related to the civil war period. His detailed analysis goes a long way towards disentangling the uncritical dissemination of propaganda, incorporated by Dio from his earlier works, from the later rectifications. Dio's *History*, in eighty books, has not survived complete. Of the last part, covering the history of his own life-time, only the years 217–18 are preserved in full (with some lacunae). For the remainder we depend on excerpts and epitomes: standard edition by U. P. Boissevain (5 vols., 1895–1931); English translation in the last volume (IX) of the Loeb edition with parallel Greek text (E. Cary and H. B. Foster, 1927 and reprints), numbered one book higher than in Boissevain (e.g. Dio Book 72 is 73 in Loeb, and so on; Boissevain's numbering is cited here *passim*). Cf. also Bering-Staschewski; Šašel-Kos 18–48.

3. Herodian wrote a history of the period 180–238 in eight books, probably in the 250s, which has survived in full. He has always had his fanciers, or defenders, but he was careless, ignorant and deceitful, a self-conscious stylist who wanted to write a 'rattling good yarn' and happily adjusted the facts to achieve readability and excitement. Platnauer 2 has some trenchant remarks about his faults, including 'slovenliness'. Hohl 1954, 1956a and b, exposed his inadequacies on Commodus, Pertinax and the fall of Plautianus respectively. Alföldy, in a series of papers, especially 1971, a,b,c, 1972, 1973 and 1988, has further demonstrated Herodian's shortcomings and fraudulence, as well as illuminating his background. Kettenhofen shows up his untrustworthiness on the Emesene empresses (some details on Elagabalus are defended by Bowersock 1975, which does not persuade me, cf. **App. 2** n. 49), and, especially valuable, confirms, for the period 218 onwards, the use—or abuse—of Dio. This latter question is treated elaborately by Kolb, whose theories are too ingenious to convince completely (cf. **5**, below) in every case. Herodian preferred heroines, and ascribes leading roles to a variety of princesses and empresses at dramatic moments. He happily trotted out clichés, often taken seriously (for an example, Birley 1972 and chapter 16, p. 172, above, in addition to the works already cited). The defence attempted in the valuable

Loeb edition and translation by Whittaker does not convince. For a fuller introduction, not uncritical but more sympathetic than I can offer, cf. Šašel-Kos 276–318, with useful bibliography.

4. Marius Maximus wrote *Lives* of the Caesars from Nerva to Elagabalus, much read in late fourth century Rome (Ammianus 28.4.14). The life of Nerva is evidently cited by the scholiast on Juvenal 4.53, all other citations or references to his work come in the *HA*. He is assumed to be identical with L. Marius Maximus Perpetuus Aurelianus, whose career, spanning some forty-five years from c. 178 to his second consulship in 223, is known from a string of inscriptions, some papyri and a mention in Dio: *PIR*² M 308. He was presumably son of the procurator L. Marius Perpetuus (*CP* no. 168; *PIR*² M 313) and grandson or great-grandson of another L. Marius Perpetuus, *scriba* of a proconsul of Africa (*ILAfr* 591: *PIR*² M 190, perhaps (M. Vitorius) Marcellus, if so c. 120). The *scriba*, the family's tribe 'Quirina', the names 'Marius' and 'Perpetuus', among other indications, all point to African origin, see *PIR*² M 308; note esp. Jarrett 1972, who adds C. Marius Perpetuus, patron of Thugga (*CRAI* 1962, 55, AD 83–5): for the local origins of Thugga's patrons cf. the list in Harmand 274. Maximus was clearly an important source for later Latin writers, including the *HA* and the so-called 'Kaisergeschichte' (*KG*), a lost work composed in the first half of the fourth century on which Victor, Eutropius and others relied (**5–6,** below). However, Syme and Barnes, in a series of publications since 1967, following earlier arguments e.g. by Barbieri 1954, minimise the use of Maximus by the *HA* and postulate an unknown, 'good biographer', 'Ignotus': e.g. Syme 1971a, 30ff., 133ff.; 1983, 30ff.; Barnes 1978, 98ff. Their case is accepted e.g. by Rubin 63ff.; but Maximus is preferred by (among others) Birley 1971, 308ff.; Schlumberger 124ff.; Birley 1987, 229f. The question must remain undecided; but on Barnes' appeal to Ausonius, *De Caesaribus ... Tetrasticha* as evidence for Maximus' coverage, see the comments of R. P. H. Green, *JRS* 69 (1979) 228: Maximus need not be Ausonius' source. The mistake in the *HA, Sev.* 9.1, also in Victor 20.8 and Eutropius 8.18.4, that Niger was killed at Cyzicus, should not have been made by Maximus, who was commanding an army nearby at the time; but the author of the *HA* was about to plagiarise Victor (*Sev.* 17.5ff.) and could have taken over the error from him. The largely fictional character of *HA Macrinus* is odd if the *HA* could consult Maximus: the latter was actually made City Prefect by Macrinus: Dio 78.14.3, 38.1–37.3; 79.1. It is perfectly possible that Maximus deliberately declined to devote a separate life to a man treated as a usurper after his death, particularly since his own acceptance of high office was better passed over: Dio was perhaps concerned to draw attention to the behaviour of his contemporary. The two could have known each other's work, Maximus certainly Dio's monograph on the *Wars*, Dio some at least of the *Lives*.

5. The so called *Historia Augusta* is a celebrated problem of historical scholarship, a 'Serbonian bog' (Syme 1968, 220). Platnauer 4ff. displays the exasperation characteristic of the uninitiated who had to struggle with the often fanciful theories generated in the first wave of 'Augustan historiography', set off by Dessau in 1889. This work (Teubner ed. Leipzig, by E. Hohl, 1927, repr. with, corrigenda 1955; Loeb ed. with English translation by D. Magie and A. O'Brien-

Moore, 1921–32; English translation of first part, down to Elagabalus, Birley 1976) is a set of biographies of emperors, Caesars and usurpers, from Hadrian to the sons of Carus (AD 117–284: a gap from AD 244–60), ostensibly by six separate biographers, of which the lives of Didius Julianus, Severus, Caracalla, Niger and Geta are attributed to 'Aelius Spartianus', Pertinax, Albinus, Macrinus to 'Julius Capitolinus' Commodus, Diadumenianus, Elagabalus and Severus Alexander to 'Aelius Lampridius' (to mention only those most relevant to the present study). Since Dessau argued that there were not really six authors, but one and that the work was written at the end of the fourth century, not at different times during the reigns of Diocletian and Constantine (as purports to be the case), controversy has raged and theories proliferated (for the latest, slightly strange, Honoré 1987). But defenders of the ostensible date and multiple authorship appear to have capitulated, retired or fallen silent, thanks not least to the series of *Colloquia* held at Bonn under the auspices of A. Alföldi and J. Straub, which have generated not only the series *HAC*, but a splendid series of books by Sir Ronald Syme: Syme 1968, 1971a and b, 1983. One must note, further, the valuable monograph on the *HA*'s sources by Barnes 1978 (in spite of my doubts over his adherence to 'Ignotus', above A.4; and his excessive rejection of Kolb, whose case that the *HA* used Dio may not be defensible as it stands but cannot be dismissed completely. The answer may lie, in my view, in Marius Maximus having used Dio, in places; but the question is probably insoluble).

The *HA Sev.* is the most important portion of the work for this study. Hasebroek's monograph remains indispensible, even if requiring correction in detail. On the first four chapters, Birley 1970. As the author reached the second Parthian war, covered 14.11–16.7, he became bored and impatient (his source, as I believe Maximus, is later described as 'homo omnium verbosissimus', *HA Quad. tyr.* 1.2, and according to *HA Get.* 2.1 wrote several *septenarii* on Septimius, an obscure word, discussed Birley 1971, 322f.). The work had already gone to pieces with the insertion, out of order, of material from later parts of the reign, 14.4–10, most of it about the statues row with Plautianus, datable to 203. Now, after jumbled remarks referring to the visit to Egypt and the last stay at Antioch (in reverse order), 16.8–17.4, he suddenly remarks, 'And it is tedious to pursue minor details'; and summarises the entire reign, 17.5–19.3, in a passage closely based on Victor, *De Caes.* 20, written in 360, Dessau's major clue to the false date conveyed in the *HA*. The author then presumably decided that he had ended the work too abruptly, and added some more, much of it fiction (especially 20.1–21.12, cf. Straub), omens of death (22.1–7, Hasebroek 148f.; Mouchova) and some miscellaneous items, particularly on Septimius' death and burial.

The lives of *Niger*, *Albinus* and *Geta* are mainly pure fiction, although where the author was adapting or re-using material from his sources for *Sev.*, some of it is authentic, if often garbled. There is no simple yardstick. For some useful remarks, Barnes 1978, 48ff. Similar considerations apply to the lives of *Macrinus* and *Diadumenianus*, much of the *Elagabalus* and most of the *Severus Alexander* (the longest *vita* in the whole work, and one of the major sources of misinformation, still often disseminated, on the third century: Syme 1971a, 146ff. is a valuable antidote). Access to the web of *HA* studies is now facilitated by the copious three volume bibliography of Merten.

6. The fourth-century and later Latin 'chroniclers', principally Victor, Eutropius, and the anonymous author of the *Epitome de Caesaribus* cannot be ignored but are of minor importance for this study. On Victor: Bird. On the *Epitome*: Schlumberger. The *Epit.* does supply a few useful names, e.g. of the father of Julia Domna, 21.3, 23.2 and of the four friends enriched by Septimius: Anullinus, Bassus, Cilo and Lateranus (20.6), of whom only the second is not certainly identifiable. Later Greek writers, e.g. Zosimus, either add little or nothing; or simply reproduce or summarise Dio and Herodian. On the so-called 'Kaisergeschichte' on which the fourth century Latin writers depended, see Barnes 1978, 91ff. with further references.

7. The *Digest* and other legal compilations of Justinian reproduce a vast mass of Severan material, including numerous letters, rescripts, etc. of Septimius and his elder son. One cannot neglect the copious and controversial writings of Honoré on the jurists, particularly Ulpian, e.g. Honoré 1979; 1981; 1982; but Syme 1984, 863ff., 1393ff. is an essential corrective; also valuable Millar 1986.

8. Contemporary writers are naturally important, for stray facts or for background. Philostratus, biographer of the sophists and (heavily fictionalised) of the sage Apollonius, is probably the most important: dealt with admirably by Bowersock 1969, who also has useful comments on Galen, 59ff. Tertullian, as a fellow-countryman of Septimius, from Carthage, and the most copious Latin writer of the period other than jurists, requires the attention of all students of the period: Barnes 1971 offers the most accessible introduction (with addenda in the reprinted edition, modifying some of his chronology). Champlin has reconstituted a Latin author: Serenus Sammonicus merging with Septimius Serenus and Septimius the author of the Latin Dictys Cretensis, *Ephemeris Belli Troiani*, dedicated to Aradius Rufinus of Bulla Regia (cf. **App. 2** nos. 11; 51). The 'courtier and man of letters' Serenus Sammonicus, mentioned in the *HA* and cited by Macrobius, becomes 'a grand personage at the court of the first African emperor . . . by turns scholar, translator, and a poet.' (I hesitate to accept a few details, especially that he was tutor to Caracalla and Geta, 191; and cannot readily regard him as one of the Lepcis Septimii—after all, Tertullian also had the *gentilicium* 'Septimius'). More might be said, e.g. about Athenaeus and other *litterati* of the age (cf. above all Bowersock 1969, especially his cautionary comments on the 'circle of Julia Domna', 101ff.); or on other Christian writers of the age, apart from Tertullian. But that is too vast a topic for this purpose.

9. Finally, the evidence derived (in the broad sense) from archaeology. For the coinage, one relies still on Mattingly's *RIC* IV and *BMC* V, while noting the work of Hill: other numismatic contributions are cited in the notes. Much has been written on the question, important for the economic history of the period, of 'devaluation' or debasement, on which I have turned to Walker for guidance. Murphy's sketch of the epigraphic material has not been enlarged upon; for Caracalla and Geta there is now the excellent volume of Mastino. *IRT*, so important for Lepcis and the Septimii, remains indispensible; *IPT* at last provides convenient and authoritative treatment of the Neo-Punic material from Tripolitania. As well as the *apokrimata* which shed light on the visit to Egypt (some revisions offered by Merentitis) there is the remarkable Prefect's letter issued just before the imperial party arrived (Rea). The results of excavation and fieldwork in various parts of the empire are cited in the notes, particularly to chapters 1–3, 14 (Africa); 11, 13 (eastern provinces); 16 (Britain). On buildings and sculpture, apart from works cited in notes to chapters 14 (Lepcis) and 15 (Rome), McCann on the portraits is essential.

MODERN SCHOLARSHIP

It remains to list recent work of importance for this biography not referred to above. Since Birley 1971 the only monograph on Septimius is that by Kotula (inspected but not yet read: in Polish). Walser provides a survey. The prosopographical method employed in Birley 1971 and by others is attacked vigorously by Graham. Millar 1977 is a monumental treatment of what emperors did (at home; for foreign and military policy, omitted from the vast work, partial compensation in Millar 1982). Imperial travels are discussed and tabulated by Halfmann. Talbert's massive study of the imperial senate is now essential reading. Barbieri 1952, still irreplaceable, although naturally outdated in places, is now supplemented by Thomasson, a source of instant reference for all provincial governors; further volumes of PIR^2 (L–O); Raepsaet-Charlier on senatorial women; Schumacher on members of the priestly colleagues; and, above all, the two copious volumes, *Tituli* 4–5, the proceedings of the international 'colloquio' at Rome in 1981. For this reason it has been possible to dispense here with the attempts made in Birley 1971, 327–58, to provide a Severan 'Who's Who'. In particular, the African origins of many major figures are now better documented in that work, repeatedly cited in the notes here.

Alföldy, G. 1971a	'Herodians Person', *Ancient Society* 2 (1971) 204–33
Alföldy G. 1971b	'Cassius Dio und Herodian über die Anfänge des neupersischen Reiches', *Rheinisches Museum* 114 (1971) 360–6
Alföldy G. 1971c	'Zeitgeschichte und Krisenempfindung bei Herodian', *Hermes* 99 (1971) 429–49
Alföldy G. 1972	'Der Sturz des Kaisers Geta und die antike Geschichtsschreibung', *Historia-Augusta-Colloquim 1970* (Bonn 1972) 19–51
Alföldy G. 1973	'Herodian uber den Tod Mark Aurels', *Latomus* 32 (1973) 345–53
Alföldy G. 1988	'Cleanders Sturz und die antike Überlieferung', *Geschichte, Geschichtsbetrachtung und Geschichtsschreibung in der Krise des Römischen Reiches* (Heidelberg 1988)

(The first five items are reprinted with addenda in the 1988 publication.)

Ameling, W.	'Cassius Dio und Bithynien', *Epigraphica Anatolica* 4 (1984) 123–38
Barbieri, G. 1952	*L'Albo senatorio da Settimio Severo a Carino* (Rome 1952)
Barbieri, G. 1954	'Mario Massimo', *Rivista di filologia* 82 (1954) 36–66, 262–75
Barnes, T. D. 1971	*Tertullian. A literary and historical study* (Oxford 1971; reprinted with addenda 1985)

Barnes, T. D. 1978   *The Sources of the Historia Augusta* (Collection Latomus 155, Brussels 1978)

Barnes, T. D. 1984   'The composition of Cassius Dio's *Roman History*', *Phoenix* 38 (1984) 240–55

Bering-
Staschewski, R.   *Römische Zeitgeschichte bei Cassius Dio* (Bochum 1981)

Bird, H. W.   *Sextus Aurelius Victor* (Liverpool 1984)

Birley, A. R. 1970   'Some notes on *HA Severus* 1–4', *Historia-Augusta-Colloquium 1968–9* (Bonn 1970) 59–77

Birley, A. R. 1971   *Septimius Severus the African Emperor* (London 1971)

Birley, A. R. 1972   'Virius Lupus', *Archaeologia Aeliana*, 4th ser. 50 (1972) 179–89

Birley, A. R. 1976   *Lives of the Later Caesars* (Harmondsworth 1976)

Birley, A. R. 1987   *Marcus Aurelius: a biography* (London 1987)

Bowersock, G. W.   *Greek Sophists in the Roman Empire* (Oxford 1969)
1969

Bowersock, G. W.   'Herodian and Elagabalus', *Yale Classical Studies* 24
1975   (1975) 229–36

Champlin, E.   'Serenus Sammonicus', *Harvard Studies Class. Philol.* 85 (1981) 189–212

Dessau, H.   'Über Zeit und Persönlichkeit der *Scriptores Historiae Augustae*', *Hermes* 24 (1889) 337–92

Eisman, M. M.   'Dio and Josephus: parallel analyses', *Latomus* 36 (1977) 657–73

Graham, A. J.   'The limitations of prosopography in Roman imperial history (with special reference to the Severan period)', *ANRW* 2.1 (1974) 136–57

Halfmann, H.   *Itinera Principum. Geschichte und Typologie der Kaiserreisen im Römischen Reich* (Stuttgart 1986)

Harmand, L.   *Le Patronat sur les collectivités publiques* (Paris 1957)

Hasebrook, J.   *Untersuchungen zur Geschichte des Kaisers Septimius Severus* (Heidelberg 1921)

Hill, P. V.   *The Coinage of Septimius Severus and his Family of the Mint of Rome* (London 1964)

Hohl, E. 1954   *Kaiser Commodus und Herodian* (Sitzungsber. Berlin 1954)

Hohl, E. 1956 a,b   *Kaiser Pertinax und die Thronbesteigung seines Nachfolgers im Lichte der Herodiankritik, mit einem Anhang: Herodian und der Sturz Plautians* (Sitzungsber. Berlin 1956)

Honoré, T. 1979   'Imperial rescripts A.D. 193–305: authorship and authenticity' *Journal of Roman Studies* 69 (1979) 51–64

Honoré, T. 1981   *Emperors and Lawyers* (London 1981)

Honoré, T. 1982   *Ulpian* (Oxford 1982)

Honoré, T. 1987   'Scriptor Historiae Augustae', *Journal of Roman Studies* 77 (1987) 156–76

Jarrett, M. G.   'An album of equestrians from North Africa in the emperor's service', *Epigraphische Studien* 9 (1972) 146–230

Kettenhofen, E.   *Die syrischen Augustae in der historischen Überlieferung* (Bonn 1979)

Kolb, F. *Literarische Beziehungen zwischen Cassius Dio, Herodian und der Historia Augusta* (Bonn 1972)

Kotula, T. *Septymiusz Sewerus. Cesarz z Lepcis Magna* (Wroclaw 1987)

Letta, C. 'La composizione dell'opera di Cassio Dione: cronologia e sfondo storico-politico', *Ricerche di Storiografia greca e romana* (Pisa 1979) 117–89

McCann, A. M. *The Portraits of Septimius Severus AD 193–211* (Memoirs American Academy Rome 30, 1968)

Mastino, A. *Le titolature di Caracalla e Geta attraverso le iscrizione (indici)* (Bologna 1981)

Merentitis, J. 'Die neugefundenen Reskripte des Septimius Severus (*P.Col.* 123)', *Platon* 30 (1978) 31–43

Merten, E. *Stellenbibliographie zur Historia Augusta*. 1. *Hadrian-Didius Julianus* (Bonn 1985). 2. *Septimius Severus-Alexander Severus* (Bonn 1986). 3. *Maximini duo-Tyranni triginta* (Bonn 1986) (with corrigenda and addenda to 1–2)

Millar, F. 1964 *A Study of Cassius Dio* (Oxford 1964)

Millar, F. 1977 *The Emperor in the Roman World* (London 1977)

Millar, F. 1982 'Emperors, frontiers and foreign relations', *Britannia* 13 (1982) 1–23

Millar, F. 1986 'A new approach to the Roman jurists', *Journal of Roman Studies* 76 (1986) 272–80

Mouchova, B. 'Omina mortis in der Historia Augusta', *Historia-Augusta-Colloquium 1968–9* (Bonn 1970) 111–49

Murphy, G. J. *The Reign of the Emperor L. Septimius Severus from the Evidence of the Inscriptions* (Philadelphia 1945)

Platnauer, M. *The Life and Reign of the Emperor L. Septimius Severus* (Oxford 1918)

Raepsaet-Charlier, M.-T. *Prosopographie des femmes de l'ordre sénatoriale (Ier-IIe siècles)* (Louvain 1987)

Rea, J. R. 'A new version of P. Yale Inv. 299', *Zeitschrift fur Papyrologie und Epigraphik* 27 (1977) 151–6

Rubin, Z. *Civil-War Propaganda und Historiography* (Collection Latomus 173, Brussels 1980)

Šašel-Kos, M. *A Historical Outline of the Region between Aquileia, the Adriatic, and Sirmium in Cassius Dio and Herodian* (Ljubljana 1986)

Schumacher, L. *Prosopographische Untersuchungen zur Besetzung der vier hohen Priesterkollegien im Zeitalter der Antonine und Severer (96–235 n. Chr.)* (Diss. Mainz 1973)

Schlumberger, J. *Die Epitome de Caesaribus. Untersuchungen zur Heidnischen Geschichtsschriebung des 4. Jhdts n. Chr.* (Munich 1974)

Straub, J. 'Die *ultima verba* des Septimius Severus', *Historia-Augusta-colloquium 1963* (Bonn 1964) 171–2

Syme, R. 1968 *Ammianus and the Historia Augusta* (Oxford 1968)

Syme, R. 1971a *Emperors and Biography* (Oxford 1971)

Syme, R. 1971b *The Historia Augusta: a call for clarity* (Bonn 1971)

Syme, R. 1983   *Historia Augusta Papers* (Oxford 1983)

Syme, R. 1984   'Fiction about Roman jurists', *Roman Papers* III (Oxford 1984) 1393–1414 (reprinted from *Zeitschrift der Savigny-Stiftung* (Roman. Abt.) 97 (1980) 78–104)

Talbert, R. J. A.   *The Roman Imperial Senate* (Princeton 1984)

Thomasson, B. E.   *Laterculi Praesidum* I (Gothenburg 1984)

Walker, D. R.   *The Metrology of the Roman Silver Coinage III: From Pertinax to Uranius Antoninus* (BAR S40, Oxford 1978)

Walser, G.   'Die Beurteilung des Septimius Severus in der älteren und neueren Forschung', *Museum Helveticum* 30 (1973) 104–16

Whittaker, C. R.   *Herodian* (Loeb edition, Cambridge, Mass. 1969–70)

APPENDIX 2

The Septimii and Fulvii of Lepcis Magna, the Julii of Emesa and their Connections

Over sixty persons, some of them of unknown name, and a few whose existence is hypothetical, are shown on the stemma, pp. 216–217. In some cases (notably the Petronii Mamertini, nos. 57–9, and Julius Agrippa, no. 43), relationship to Septimius or Julia is highly conjectural and is shown on the stemma by broken lines, interspersed with question-marks. Attested or highly probable descent or kinship, which cannot be exactly tabulated, is shown by broken lines without question-marks. One case of adoption (Anno Macer and Balitho Commodus, nos. 3–4) is shown by dotted lines. The numbered list of 60 persons which follows summarises the evidence for each individual (the unnamed persons are discussed under their parents). They are grouped under five main headings: A. Possible Punic ancestors at Lepcis; B. Septimii; C. Fulvii; D. the Emesene dynasty; E. Others.

A. POSSIBLE PUNIC ANCESTORS AT LEPCIS

Evidence cited under no. 26 (L. Septimius Severus the *sufes*) makes it clear that the first known Septimius of Lepcis was of Punic origin, a Roman knight in the year 95 or earlier, taken to an estate in Italy as a child. The Septimii were enrolled in the tribe 'Quirina' (no. 25), an early member of the family was called 'Macer' (no. 23), and they used the *praenomen* 'Gaius' (nos. 16, 25) as well as 'Lucius' (nos. 14, 17, 27, cf. 22) and 'Publius' (nos. 15, 20–22). One family among the quite numerous Punic notables of late first century BC and first century AD Lepcis uses the names 'Macer' and 'Gaius'. They can be traced for four generations, the latest record being from the end of Claudius' reign (*IRT* 338). It seems logical to identify them as the likeliest ancestors of Septimius before the family acquired a Roman-style *gentilicium* and citizenship. See also Birley 1988.

1. Anno, known only from the filiation of no. 2 in *IRT* 338, *IPT* 26; he could be the same as the father of no. 5 in *IPT* 22. The name, Punic Ḥn', vocalised at Lepcis as 'Anno', although generally 'Hanno' in Latin authors, means 'give thanks'. It is also found in *IPT* 17 (date uncertain): Anno *ben Arishom Ygmʻk*; 18 (date uncertain): Candidus *ben* Candidus *ben Anno ben Abdmelqart*; 32 (date uncertain): Himilcho *Dryds*, 'descendant of Anno'; and in *IPT* 21, Punic version of *IRT* 319, of 8 BC, as father of Muttun, *sufes* that year.

2. C. Anno. Gaius Anno, *G'y ben Ḥn'*, paved the Forum and set up a portico in AD 53–4 'in the name of his grandson Gaius (*G 'y*) by his son Macer (*M'qr*)'; Macer's adoptive son Balitho Commodus supervised the work (*IRT* 338, *IPT* 26) and a statue-base records that 'senate and people of the Lepcitani' honoured the grandson Gaius, also called here 'Phelyssam' (*IRT* 615). The Punic *G 'y*, latinised as 'Gaius', might represent the Libyan *Gaia* (the name of Massinissa's father: Rössler 274ff.). 'Phelyssam' certainly seems Libyan rather than Punic (cf. *IRT* 698 for the form 'Felyssam' at Lepcis).

3. Anno Macer. Known from *IRT* 338 = *IPT* 26, *IRT* 615. The name 'Macer', meaning 'lean', is a fairly common Latin *cognomen* (Kajanto 244). It is rendered *M'qr* in Punic and occurs on the independent coins of Oea, apparently as the name of a *sufes* (Jenkins nos. 26–9: the colleague's name, *Pyln* or *Pylt*, remains unexplained, cf. *IPT* 21; it is missing from *IRT* 319, the Latin version), and in *IPT* 10 at Lepcis. It might be a Latinised version of a Libyan name. For names beginning 'Mac-' note the Macae tribe and *IRT* 886c, W. Sofeggin, *Macarcum* on a Latino-Punic inscription read in full by Elmayer 93f., who also produces *Machrus ben Rogate* on another stone from the same place. 'Macer' might also be linked with the god *Melqart*. Cf. the name 'Amicus', favoured at Lepcis and elsewhere in North Africa, very probably a Latin-sounding version of 'Amilcar' (*Abdmelquart*). See further Birley 1988.

4. Balitho Commodus. Adopted son of no. 3 (*IRT* 338, 615; *IPT* 26). 'Balitho', Punic *Ba'alyaton* ('Ba'al has given') is also found at Lepcis on *IPT* 22, 26.

5. Balitho G[.] Saturninus. Known only from *IPT* 22, recording him as *sufes* with *Bodmelqart ben Bodmelqart*, one of the Tapapii, when the statues of Tiberius and other members of the dynasty were set up around the Temple of Rome and Augustus c. AD 14–19. He is called son of Anno, perhaps no. 1. His second name, clearly very short and beginning with *G*, was probably *G'y* = 'Gaius'. 'Saturninus' is the favourite Latin name in Africa (Kajanto 213: 'Saturn' was the equivalent of the Punic *Ba'al*).

6. Gaius Phelyssam. Known from *IRT* 338, where he is 'Gaius, son of Anno' and its Punic version, *IPT* 26 (*G'y*). On *IRT* 615 he is 'C. Phelyssam', cf. under no. 2 on the latter name, Libyan rather than Punic.

B. SEPTIMII

7. (Septimia). Postulated mother of no. 59, on the sole basis of his second *cognomen* 'Septimianus' and the evidently African origin of the Petronii Mamertini. A sister of nos. 15 and 25 would be of the right rank and age as wife for no. 57.

8. Septimia Octavilla. Septimius' sister, named only on *IRT* 417, set up after her death by three of the Lepcis *curiae* in the lifetime of Septimius, not before 198 (he is 'Parthicus maximus'). Her title *c.m.f.* shows that she had been married to a senator, but as Chastagnol 1978, 111ff. indicates, as she had to ask Septimius to confer the *latus clavus* on her son, her husband cannot have been a senator at the time. The story comes in *HA Sev.* 15.7, in a context suggesting 198, although it may be misplaced. Barnes 1967, 96 doubts the story that Septimius was embarassed at her poor Latin and sent her home. She might have married a

Greek-speaker, which would also explain her presence in the east, regarded as suspect by Barnes. If no. 17 is her son, her husband was presumably an L. Flavius. 'Octavilla' suggests that there was an Octavius or Octavia in an earlier generation, perhaps her maternal grandmother. The name is unattested at Lepcis, but cf. *IRT* 921 (Bu-Ngem/Gholaia) and, much more promising, L. Plautius Octavianus (*IRT* 517, redated by Di Vita-Evrard 1981, 183ff. to the reign of Pius). The Lepcitane Plautii were certainly linked to the Fulvii (cf. nos. 29, 32–3). Barbieri no. 611; Birley 1969, 256f.; Corbier 1982, 724f.; Raepsaet-Charlier no. 697 (with further references).

9. Flavia Neratia Septimia Octavilla. Known only from *CIL* VI 1415, Rome, which she set up to her father, no. 17. Her mother was presumably a Neratia, cf. no. 55. She was still *c(larissima) p(uella)* herself. Barbieri no. 2237; Raepsaet-Charlier no. 372 (with further references).

10. Septimia Polla. Sister of Septimius' father (no. 20), who commemorated her at Lepcis with a silver statue, 'the most expensive . . . in Africa' (Duncan-Jones 68). Apparently unmarried. Her name 'Polla' evokes a lady in Statius' *Silvae*, from the circle in which her father moved (*Silvae* 2.2.10; 3.1.87, 159, 179; 4.8.14—the wife of Pollius Felix; 2. *praef.* and 7,—Lucan's widow (cf. Chapter 3 n. 1 below, p. 233).

11. Septimia Severa. Wife of an Aradius Saturninus (no. 52), who prepared their sarcophagus in their lifetime at Interpromium in eastern central Italy (*EE* VIII 132). Her names may only coincidentally reflect those of the Lepcis family; but her husband should belong to the Aradii of Bulla Regia. Champlin 1981 202f.; Corbier 1982, 713.

12., 13. (Septimius) If no. 14 is grandson of 13, and 24 a grandson of 25, an intervening generation must be supplied.

14. L. Septimius Aper *cos. ord.* 207. Known for certain only from his consulship, but probably identical with the cousin of Antoninus whom he murdered after Geta's death (*HA Carac.* 3.6–7, called 'Afer'). Presumably a grandson rather than son of no. 14, in view of the gap of fifty-four years before between their consulships. This man is likely to have been born c. 174. Unlikely to be the same as no. 17. Barbieri no. 466; Corbier 1982, 725; Torelli 380. For his being an olive oil producer, Manacorda; Di Vita-Evrard 1985.

15. P. Septimius Aper *cos.* 153. Called 'patruus' of Septimius in *HA Sev.* 1.2, but more probably cousin, 'frater patruelis', of Septimius' father Geta, and son of no. 16. Birley 1969, 258f.; 1970, 64f.; 1976, 63f. The first recorded consul from Lepcis. Corbier 1982, 723.

16. C. Cl(audius) Septimius Aper. Known only from *IRT* 316 a dedication at Lepcis in honour of Antoninus Pius, where his last name is read '[A]fer'. '[A]per', conjectured Birley 1969, 258; 1970, 64f., is confirmed by E. Birley's observation (cited Birley 1976, 63f.). He is presumably the 'Gaius' whose son was no. 25; and the *cognomen* of no. 15 surely indicates that this person was another son. He should thus be a brother of Septimius' grandfather the *sufes* (no. 26). On his name 'Gaius', cf. the remarks above under no. 2. His name 'Claudius' could derive from a marriage link with the family of Ti. Claudius Sestius, senior or junior (*IRT* 318, 347) or Ti. Claudius Amicus (*IRT* 590). His presumed father could have married a Claudia.

17. L. Flavius Septimius Aper Octavianus. Known only from *CIL* VI 1415, Rome, set up in his honour by his daughter (no. 9). It gives him the following senatorial career: *Xvir stlitibus iudicandis, sevir eq.R.,* quaestor of Cyprus, *sodalis Hadrianalis,* tribune of the plebs. Perhaps the unnamed son of Septimius' sister, for whom she obtained the *latus clavus* (*HA Sev.* 15.7, cf. under no. 8, above). If so, he did not die quite so soon as the *HA* suggests, since he should have been at least twenty-six as tribune. That is perhaps not a serious difficulty. Torelli 380 and n. 14 argues that the career is too modest for a close kinsman of the emperor; yet Julia Domna's kinsmen, nos. 36, 45, 50, were not given very exalted rank; the two younger ones were still equestrian when Septimius died. This man's wife was presumably from the Saepinum family (*PIR*² N 50ff., Barbieri nos. 2062–6), cf. no. 55 below. Barbieri no. 2237; Corbier 1982, 725.

18. (L.?) Septimius Bassianus = M. AURELIUS ANTONINUS = 'Caracalla'. Born 4 April 188, Platnauer 50ff., Barnes 1967, 93 n. 48. Named after his maternal grandfather (no. 46); original *praenomen* unknown. Renamed 'M. Aurelius Antoninus' and made Caesar in 195, as shown by Soproni. Further details in Mastino: co-emperor probably from 28 January 198, as argued by Guey 1948. Betrothed to Fulvia Plautilla (no. 29) from 200, married in 202, divorced in 205. No certain record of any offspring.

19. C. Julius Septimius Castinus *cos.* c. 211. His career is known from numerous inscriptions and, in its latter stages, from mentions in Dio. Tribune of I Adiutrix almost certainly under Septimius in 192–3, then of V Macedonica perhaps under Geta, then, after other posts, legate of I Minervia and *dux* of detachments from the four German legions against 'defectores et rebelles' c. 207, legate of Pannonia Inferior, consul, *comes* of Caracalla and his trusted friend (Dio 78.13.2, 79.4.3), governor of Dacia, removed by Macrinus and killed by Elagabalus in Bithynia in 218 (Dio 79.4.4,6). A possible kinsman of Septimius: Barbieri no. 308; *PIR*² J 566. 'Castinus' is very rare (Kajanto 252) but 'Castus' is popular in Africa (Kajanto 251) and 'Julius Castus' occurs there sixteen times, Alföldy 1968, 195. Alföldy 1967, 51; Thomasson 1984, 115f., 157.

20. P. Septimius Geta. Septimius' father, known from *HA Sev.* 1.2, *Geta* 2.1, the latter passage claiming that Marius Maximus had written at some length about his '*vita et moribus in vita Severi ... primo septenario*'; he died when Septimius was about to set off for Baetica as quaestor, *HA Sev.* 2.3, i.e. in 171. Known also from his inscription in memory of his sister Polla (*IRT* 607, cf. no. 10 above), and from commemorative inscriptions at Lepcis (*IRT* 414, AD 201) and elsewhere. None record any career, local or imperial. He was certainly not a senator, but might have held local positions and he might even be the aedile '[ ]s Geta', *IRT* 597, doubted by Torelli 385. For the name Geta, Kajanto 204 is inaccurate. See Birley 1988: there are only eighteen epigraphic examples (apart from senators) of free men, seven of them at or near Lepcis. It is conceivable that this Geta, the earliest at Lepcis, was named after C. Vitorius Hosidius Geta, son of the first Septimius

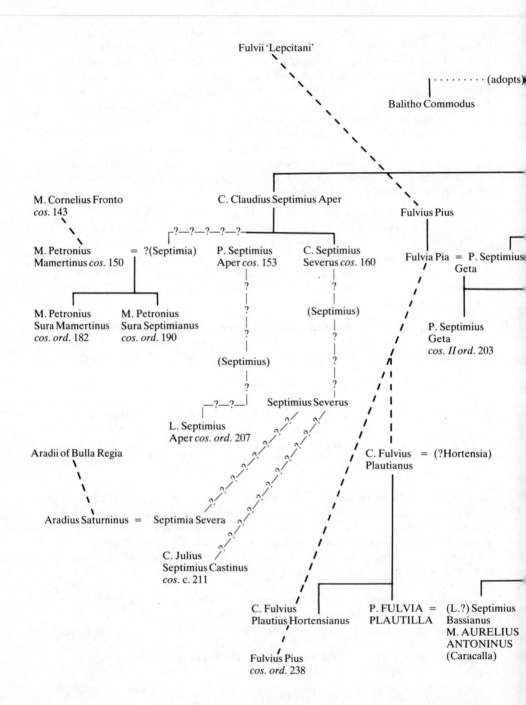

Fulvii 'Lepcitani'

· · · · · · · · (adopts)

Balitho Commodus

M. Cornelius Fronto
cos. 143

C. Claudius Septimius Aper

Fulvius Pius

M. Petronius
Mamertinus *cos.* 150

= ?(Septimia)

?—?—?—?—?

P. Septimius
Aper *cos.* 153

C. Septimius
Severus *cos.* 160

Fulvia Pia = P. Septimius
Geta

M. Petronius
Sura Mamertinus
cos. ord. 182

M. Petronius
Sura Septimianus
cos. ord. 190

?

?

?

(Septimius)

?

?

P. Septimius
Geta
cos. II ord. 203

(Septimius)

?

?

?

—?—?—

L. Septimius
Aper *cos. ord.* 207

Septimius Severus

Aradii of Bulla Regia

C. Fulvius = (?Hortensia)
Plautianus

Aradius Saturninus = Septimia Severa

C. Julius
Septimius Castinus
cos. c. 211

C. Fulvius
Plautius Hortensianus

P. FULVIA =
PLAUTILLA

(L.?) Septimius
Bassianus
M. AURELIUS
ANTONINUS
(Caracalla)

Fulvius Pius
cos. ord. 238

SEPTIMIUS SEVERUS

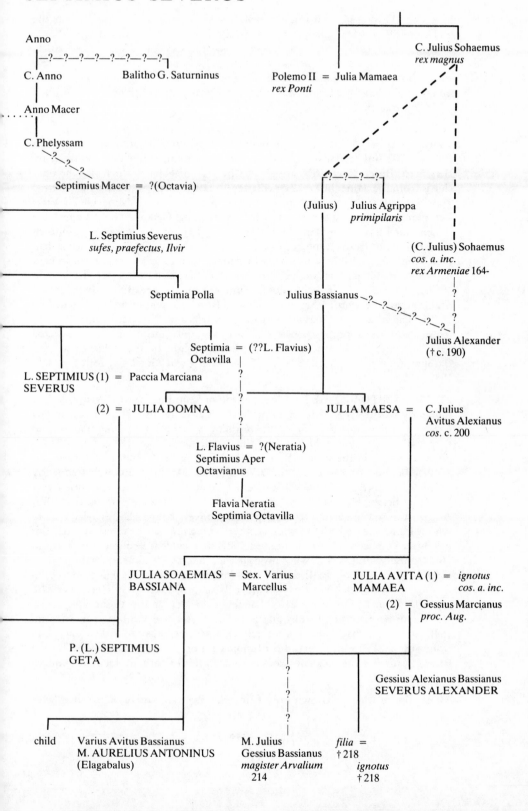

Severus' fellow-pupil Vitorius Marcellus, with whom he is associated in the preface to *Silvae* 4, dedicated to Marcellus. Cf. also on 'Polla' under no. 10 above. In Birley 1971, 302 n. 1 it was suggestd that the story in Victor, *Caes.* 20.28, Eutropius 8.8 and *HA Geta* 2.4, that Septimius himself was *advocatus fisci* and equestrian military tribune before entering the senate might derive from a misunderstanding of Marius Maximus (who dilated at length on this man), i.e. that Septimius' father held these posts.

21. P. Septimius Geta *cos. II ord.* 203. Brother of Septimius. His career is fully known from *IRT* 541, set up in his honour at Lepcis by one of the *curiae* between 198 and 202 (his second consulship is not registered), originally published by Bersanetti. Birley 1969, 262f. argues that he was the elder brother, but the only clue is from the name: he was named after his father, Septimius after the paternal grandfather (but it must be conceded that practice varied: Mme G. Di Vita-Evrard informs me that she hopes to demonstrate that Geta was the younger). He is mentioned several times in *HA Sev* (also *Get.* 2.1): in 8.10 he met Septimius en route to the east from Rome in 193 and was told to remain in the province he had been assigned, probably still Moesia Inferior, which he is assumed to have held from at least 192; he was later governor of Dacia, attested in 195 (*CIL* III 905); in 196 he seems to have met Septimius at Viminacium, *HA Sev.* 3; shortly before his death, in 204, he warned Septimius about Plautianus, whom he had hated, Dio 76.2.4. The contacts he may have made and details of his career before 193 are registered in the appropriate places of this biography and need not be repeated here. No wife or children are known, but he might be the father of no. 24. Barbieri no. 469; Corbier 1982, 723; Thomasson 1975, 73f.; 1984, 28f., 138, 155; 1985, 135.

22. P. (L) SEPTIMIUS GETA. Younger son of Septimius. Born 7 March 189, as shown by Barnes 1968, 522ff. and murdered on 26 December 211, the date in *HA Geta* 3.1 being spurious. The true birthday is supplied by the tradition of Perpetua's martyrdom which fell on the 'natale Getae Caesaris' and Dio 77.2.5 gives his age at death, see also Barnes 1971, 253ff. Made Caesar in 198, when his brother became Augustus, *cos.* in 205, *cos. II* in 208, but, although frequently called Augustus especially in Africa from 198, not in fact promoted until a year before his death. The date has been assumed to be late in 209, from *IG* II 2, 1077, Athens, the sole evidence (quoted p. 186, above), but G. Di Vita-Evrard, to whom I am indebted for showing me her typescript, can demonstrate that this belongs a year later, cf. her summary, 1987. The evidence collected in Mastino 161, naturally limited following his *damnatio*, shows only four inscriptions with *tr.pot.* II, three with *tr.pot.* III, none with *I* (or no number) or *IV*. His grant would then belong to c. October or November 210, *tr.pot.* II from 10 December 210, *tr.pot. III* from 10 December 211. (The few coins that appear to show *tr.pot. IV* (*IIII*) may be discounted.) His *praenomen* fluctuates, see the listing in Mastino 153ff. It may be that it was deliberately changed, perhaps more than once, e.g. from original P. to L., to avoid confusion with no. 21, and back to P. after the latter's death; but the incidence does not match this hypothesis. He is not known to have married.

23. Septimius Macer. Known only from *HA Sev.* 1.2, where he is called 'avus paternus'. This must be wrong as *IRT* 412 gives the grandfather as L. Septimius Severus (no. 26). The latter should have been listed; perhaps omitted in error or in transmission, likewise 'proavus' before Macer. He should be the great-grand-father. 'Macer' is found at Lepcis (and Oea), borne by non-Romans, cf. under no. 3 above, suggesting that it could be a latinisation of a Punic or Libyan name. The *gentilicium* 'Septimius' (not specifically attested in his case) could have been chosen because of the presence of Septimius Flaccus, evidently legate of III Augusta, at Lepcis, in the Flavian period, thus Birley 1969, 255f. But that person is only so called in Ptolemy 1.8.4 and it is often assumed that 'Septimius' is a mistake for 'Suellius': Suellius Flaccus was active as legate, in the Syrtica, in 87 and could be Ptolemy's man, cf. e.g. Thomasson 1984, 395, with further references. An unknown senatorial Septimius could have been at Lepcis as legate or even proconsul, cf. *AE* 1973. 543 for one who was legate in Cilicia in AD 75. Alternatively, it is conceivable that the name was selected because to a Punic ear or eye it evoked *špṭm*, the plural of *špṭ* = Latin *sufes*. See further Birley 1988.

24. Septimius Severus. Named only by Herodian 4.6.3 as a cousin of Caracalla killed after Geta's death (*cognomen* only). If a first cousin he should be a son of no. 21, which is perfectly possible. He might be a grandson of no. 25. Barbieri no. 470 suggests he could be the same as no. 15, also killed at this time (*HA Carac.* 3.6–7, where the MSS have 'Afer'); if so he had at least two *cognomina*, cf. no. 17. Herodian could well have guessed the name, however, so this person remains slightly wraith-like. Corbier 1982, 725; Torelli 398.

25. C. Septimius Severus *cos.* 160, has emerged since 1963, when G. Di Vita-Evrard published the inscription from the arch of M. Aurelius at Lepcis giving his name as proconsul in 174, with Septimius as his legate (*AE* 1967. 536 repeats the text); she showed that he can be identified with '-mius Severus', proconsul and patron of Thubursicu Numidarum on *ILAlg* I 1283, giving his full career, with minor gaps. The *tabula Banasitana* (*AE* 1971. 534) supplies his filiation, 'C.f.', and tribe, 'Quirina'. That at last demonstrated that the Septimii were granted citizenship in the Flavian (or just possibly Claudio-Neronian) period, Birley 1976, and disposed of the identification with a homonymous patron of Praeneste, in the 'Pupinia' (*CIL* XIV 3004): that tribe is confined to Italy, and by inference the Septimii would have been Italian settlers. Praeneste is close to the *ager Hernicus*, where Statius' friend had property, as well as at Veii and Cures, as pointed out in *PIR*[1] S 345, and pressed by Barnes 1967, 89. The filiation makes no. 16 a likely parent, and at any rate rules out no. 26, hence this man and no. 15 cannot be 'patrui' as in *HA Sev.* 1.2, but quite probably 'fratres patrueles' of Septimius' father. This person will also be the 'adfinis' who secured Septimius the *latus clavus* in the early 160s, but 'bis iam consulari' there must be an error, perhaps from textual corruption, Birley 1970, 63f. For his career, Thomasson 1975, 75f. and Alföldy 1977, 174f., 188 n. 203, 227, 257; Eck 178f.; Schumacher 83f., 238; Corbier 1982, 723. After preliminary stages (no military tribunate), a road curator, legate of XVI Flavia in Syria, legate of Lycia-Pamphylia, consul, legate of one of the German provinces, almost certainly Inferior, proconsul of Africa; also *XVvir s.f.* and *sodalis Hadrianalis*. Last recorded July 177, in *consilium* of Marcus and Commodus (*AE* 1971. 534).

26. L. Septimius Severus. Grandfather of Septimius, *sufes, praefectus* when Roman citizenship was granted to Lepcis, i.e. when it became a *colonia* under Trajan, and first *duumvir* of the *colonia: IRT* 412, much discussed, notably in an article by Guey 1951, cf. also Birley 1969, 253ff., 1970, 63, 75ff. and now Di Vita-Evrard 1984. His identity with Statius' friend, the rich Roman knight from Lepcis called Septimius Severus, brought to Italy as a child, commemorated in *Silvae* 4.5 and 4. *praef.*, from at latest AD 95, is disputed, but is perfectly plausible. (The argument of Pflaum 1968, 57ff. that Statius' friend could not be the *iudex selectus* of *IRT* 412 is misconceived: he could have been *iudex* at an early stage, rather than after being *duumvir*, as Pflaum assumes.) To the arguments brought forward elsewhere I would add simply the observation that the names of his children Polla and Geta evoke the circle of Statius, cf. above under nos. 10 and 20. Assumed to be the son of a Septimius Macer, no. 23 above; mother unknown, perhaps a different one from that of his assumed brother, no. 16. The Italian property may well have been divided, but the Veii part went to Septimius and perhaps his brother, *HA Sev.* 4.5, brilliantly emended by Hammond, 142ff., backed by *CIL* XI 3816, a lead pipe found on the Via Cassia near Veii with the name 'P. Septimi Geta', either Septimius' brother or father (overlooked by Saller 176 n. 156, who expresses scepticism). Also recorded in *IRT* 413. Cf. also Torelli 379ff., and on Statius' poem Vessey. See further Birley 1988.

27. L. SEPTIMIUS SEVERUS. His year of birth, 146 in *HA Sev.* 1.3, works out as 145 from Dio 76.17.4, giving his age at death sixty-five years, nine months, twenty-five days, and birthday as 11 April (9 April in *HA*, perhaps a corrupt text). Guey 1956 produced strong arguments (astronomical) for 145 being correct. Further discussion in Birley 1970, 65f.; Barnes 1976, 19f., 40; Rubin 33ff.: Septimius may have falsified the year. His titulature as emperor is briefly discussed by Murphy, 102f.

C. FULVII

They seem to be an immigrant family, calling themselves 'Fulvii Lepcitani' in 3/2 BC, *IRT* 320, 328, as interpreted by Romanelli. But the names of nos. 29, 32–3 show they intermarried with enfranchised natives, as would be expected, viz. the Plautii, a powerful family in second century Lepcis: Torelli, 385ff., plausibly suggesting (404) Ti. Plautius Silvanus Aelianus, son of the proconsul Lamia, as patron and source of the name, and Iddibal son of Balsillec, etc., the last dated non-citizen notable (*IRT* 300, AD 72), as an ancestor, citing *IRT* 734 (Torelli 402). Intermarriage with Marcii (perhaps descended from Annobal Ruso who paid for the temple of Ceres in AD 36, *IRT* 269: Torelli 402) is suggested in Birley 1969, 256ff. (citing *IRT* 705). On the Plautii see now esp. Di Vita-Evrard 1982.

28. Fulvia Pia. Mother of Septimius, known only from *IRT* 415–6 (after AD 198) and *HA Sev.* 1.2. Birley 1969, 256; 1970, 64 f.

29. PU(BLIA) FULVIA PLAUTILLA. Daughter of no. 32, sister of 33, betrothed to 18 in 200, married in 202, divorced in 205, killed 212. Augusta 202–05. No children known, cf. under 18. *PIR*² F 564.

30. Fulvius Pius. Maternal grandfather of Septimius, known only from *HA Sev.* 1.2.

31. Fulvius Pius *cos. ord.* 238. Presumed descendant of Septimius' grandfather, no. 30. *PIR*[2] F 553; Barbieri no. 1054; Dietz 165f. Perhaps 'Gaius', if identical with the C. Fulvius Pius of *AE* 1930.67.

32. C. Fulvius Plautianus. Kinsman of Septimius (Herodian 3.10.6), hence one of the Lepcis Fulvii, and perhaps the son of a Plautia, cf. above under C. Probably the 'Fluvius' in a fragment of Dio, 73.15.4, convicted by Pertinax as proconsul of Africa, for serious offences, probably in 188 or 189, but given some important post or distinction by Pertinax as emperor 'as a favour to Severus'. His career before he became Guard Prefect is difficult to establish because of his *damnatio* in 205, but Grosso 14ff. shows that *CIL* XIV S 4380 ought to be Plautianus as prefect of the *vigiles* in 195, not later than summer; and 17ff. that he was already Guard Prefect, not yet *c.v.*, on 1 January 197 (from *AE* 1935. 156). He was not necessarily given command of the *vigiles* by Pertinax, as Grosso argues, and may be the man whose names are erased on *IRT* 572, as the editors suggest *ad loc.*, honoured by his sister Fulvia Nepotilla, her husband, also a Fulvius and their sons. If so, he was *praefectus vehiculorum* and *procurator XX hereditatium*, cf. *CP* no. 238. It remains uncertain. He was *comes* of Septimius 'on all his expeditions': Corbier 1974 discusses this question in detail. The theory of Hasebroek, 109, 131ff., that there were two 'rifts' between Septimius and Plautianus before his overthrow was disputed by Judeich, rejected by Grosso. On the statues row, cf. p. 154 above. *PIR*[2] F 554; Barbieri no. 255; Schumacher 36 (he was *pontifex* as well as augur, yet another sign of his exceptional influence). Evidence for his being an oil-producer: Manacorda; Di Vita-Evrard 1985.

33. C. Fulvius Plautius Hortensianus. Son of no. 32. Surely 'Plautius' as in Dio 77.1.2, in spite of *PIR*[2] F 555. For his presumed mother see no. 54. *CIL* XIV 4392 shows he was in the 'Quirina'. Exiled with his sister and put to death with her.

D. THE EMESENE DYNASTY

34. Gessius Alexianus Bassianus = M. AURELIUS SEVERUS ALEXANDER. Son of no. 37 by her second husband, no. 36. Only twelve in 221 according to Herodian 5.7.4, hence not the *magister Arvalium* of 214 (no. 35), who may be an elder brother. His sister and brother-in-law were murdered by Macrinus, as was his father, in 218 (Dio 78.31.4, 33.2–34.1[2], fragmentary). Bowersock 1975, 231ff. argues that Herodian 5.3.3, 7.3 is correct in calling him Alexianus, but Dio 78.30.3, 79.17.2, 18.3 wrong, giving him Bassianus, before his change of name to Alexander in 221. Surely both are right. The family favoured double *cognomina*, cf. nos. 37, 41, 45. *PIR*[2] A 1610; Barbieri no. 966 + Agg.; Kettenhofen.

35. M. Julius Gessius Bassianus. *Magister* of the Arval Brethren in 214, but did not attend their ceremonies, probably because he was in the east. Unless Herodian is completely mistaken about no. 34's age (not impossible), the suggestion in *PIR*[2] J 342 that the *magister* is the future emperor seems implausible. An elder brother is more likely. Barbieri no. 296.

36. Gessius Marcianus. From Arca Caesarea in Syria, second husband of no. 37, father of no. 34 and of a daughter, murdered with her husband in 218; his own death followed soon after (cf. above under 34). He was a procurator, no details known (Dio 78.30.3). Mentioned by implication in *Digest* 1.9.12. *PIR*[2] G 171; Bowersock 1982, 665 takes him to have been adlected to the senate, but see Raepsaet-Charlier 12 and n.74.

37. JULIA Avita MAMAEA. Mother of no. 34, and Augusta from 222, killed with him in 235. Her first *cognomen* comes from her father (no. 45), the second is 'dynastic' at Emesa (see under no. 40). First married to a consular and allowed to retain her rank when married to her second husband, the equestrian Gessius Marcianus (see under 36). *PIR*[2] J 649; Kettenhofen, esp. 43ff.

38. JULIA DOMNA. Could be the lady of this name who eventually inherited from her great-uncle, 'patruus', a *primipilaris* named Julius Agrippa (see no. 43). Daughter of no. 46, date of birth unknown, married to Septimius at latest in 187. Her name was claimed to be a Latin translation—'dom(i)na'—of Syrian 'Martha' by Domaszewski, but see Kettenhofen 76f.; Shahid 41, who shows its relation to Arab names (meaning 'black'). On the supposed horoscope, Kettenhofen, 77f.; Syme, 87ff.; Rubin, 178ff. (with the convincing argument that the story, ascribed to Marius Maximus in *HA Sev. Alex.* 5.4, also used in *Sev.* 3.6, *Get.* 3.1, was spread as propaganda). On the allegations of adultery and conspiracy, of incest with Antoninus and supposed marriage with him (and the stepson idea), see especially Rubin 173ff. In general, Kettenhofen; Raepsaet-Charlier no. 436 (both with full bibliography).

39. JULIA MAESA. Sister of no. 38, wife of no. 45, mother of nos. 37 and 41. Augusta from 218 until her death. *PIR*[2] J 678; Kettenhofen, esp. 23ff., 33ff., who shows that her role was greatly inflated by Herodian, and that Dio must be preferred. Further references in Raepsaet-Charlier no. 445. On her name, Shahid 41: 'most probably the feminine *nomen agentis* of Arabic *masa*, a verb which signifies walking with a swinging gait.'

40. Julia Mamaea. Wife of Polemo II of Pontus (no. 60), as revealed by a bronze coin published by Seyrig; see also Sullivan, 926 n.85; Chad 68. She is taken to be daughter of Samsigeramus II, dynast of Emesa AD 14–47, and sister of the last ruler, the *rex magnus* C. Julius Sohaemus (no. 47). On the name, related to the Arab *Mama*, Shahid 42. The emergence of this woman helps to support the descent of nos. 38–9 from the old royal house of Emesa.

41. JULIA SOAEMIAS Bassiana. Elder daughter of no. 39, sister of no. 37, wife of Sex. Varius Marcellus (no. 51) and mother of no. 50 and at least one other child (*ILS* 478, the sarcophagus of her husband was dedicated by her 'cum filis'). Kettenhofen, 23ff. admirably corrects the often imaginary version of her role from 218 onwards, based on Herodian's romanticised account. Note especially his welcome exposition of the true role of Gannys Eutychianus (often confused with another man, Valerius Comazon), Soaemias' lover, who had been brought up in Maesa's household (Dio 80.6.1—but this does not say he was the boy's *tropheus*, as Kettenhofen 30). She was Augusta from 218 and murdered with her son in 222. *PIR*[2] J 704; Raepsaet-Charlier no. 460 (with further references). For the name 'Soaemias', related to the 'Sohaemus'—*Suhaym* name of the Arab dynasts of Emesa, Shahid 41f. (like 'Domna' it is linked to the colour black). 'Bassiana' is taken from her father the high-priest.

42. (Julius). Presumed father of 46 and brother of 43.

43. Julius Agrippa. This man, a *primipilaris*, left a will which was the subject of litigation some time after his death, his property eventually going to his grand-niece Julia Domna (*Digest* 32.38.4, from Book XIX of the *Digesta* of Cervidius Scaevola, repeated by him in his third book of *Responsa*, *Dig.* 32.93 *pr.*, although there with stock names). Identity of the grand-niece with the empress is doubted in *PIR*² J 662, and elsewhere and not discussed by Kettenhofen or Raepsaet-Charlier no. 436, but is perfectly possible. 'Agrippa' is of course a favoured name in the region, cf. esp. Rey-Coquais for a powerful Julius Agrippa at Apamea, and it is not inconceivable that a member of Julia's family entered the centurionate, cf. Dobson, 15ff. His nos. 73, 75, 76, 94, 95 come from Heliopolis, and the man could have started 'ex equite Romano'.

44. Julius Alexander. A man of Emesa, hunted down and killed on Commodus' orders c.190, allegedly for provoking his jealousy by his prowess at lion-hunting, Dio 72.14; for conspiracy according to *HA* 8.3. Letta argues that the lion-hunt was a royal activity and that Julius Alexander deliberately infringed on the imperial prerogative and had serious designs on the throne. At all events, he ought to be linked to the dynastic family, cf. *IGLS* V 2213–4, two Alexanders buried at Emesa in the second century AD, and Alexander, brother of the dynast Iamblichus, killed after Actium (Dio 51.2.2).

45. C. Julius Avitus Alexianus *cos.* c. 200. This man's identity and career has finally been pieced together properly, combining the inscriptions from Salonae (*AE* 1921. 64 = 1963. 42) and Augusta Vindelicorum (*AE* 1962. 229) with the mentions of him, as Avitus, husband of Maesa (no. 39) in Dio. An equestrian officer, after the *tres militiae* a procurator, *ad annonam Ostiis*, whence he was adlected to the senate by Septimius, made legate of the legion IV (Flavia, almost certainly), then legate of Raetia, where he dedicated an altar to Elagabalus, the Emesene god (*AE* 1962.229) and consul. Thereafter he was long out of service, probably through hostility from Plautianus, but reappears as *comes* of the emperors in Britain, i.e. 208–211, twice prefect of the *alimenta* in Italy under Caracalla, legate of Dalmatia and proconsul of Asia, *comes* of Caracalla, dying on a mission to Cyprus shortly before Caracalla's murder. See Halfmann for the above reconstruction; there may be slight room for doubt over the date of his Asian proconsulship, cf. Barnes 1986. For his last name, cf. C. Julius Alexio of Emesa, father of C. Julius Sampsigeramus who built himself a monumental tomb there in AD 78 or 79, clearly from the royal house, *PIR*² J 541; Chad 92. A useful summary in Thomasson 1985, 122f.

46. Julius Bassianus. Named only in *Epit. de Caes.* 21.1, 23.2, presumably deriving from Marius Maximus. His second name, deriving from the Syrian *basus*, a priestly title (Domaszewski 209ff.), was borne by nos. 18 and 41, his grand-children and by nos. 34 and 50 his great-grandchildren (hence 35 surely belongs in this family too).

47. C. Julius Sohaemus. King of Emesa from AD 53, shortly afterwards made king of distant Sophene as well, called 'rex magnus' as king of more than one kingdom, also 'philocaesar', 'philorhomaeus', given 'ornamenta consularia', was *dummvir quinquennalis* and patron of the *colonia* at Heliopolis, *ILS* 8958, the inscription from his statue at that city. Son of Samsigeramus II, brother of Aziz, Iotape and—as now appears—of Julia Mamaea (no. 40). Assisted Rome against the Jewish rebels in 66, was among the first to support Vespasian in 69, brought troops to the siege of Jerusalem in 70 and against Commagene in 73. Thereafter disappears from the record. *PIR*² J 582 and Seyrig. His kingdom is assumed by most to have been absorbed in Syria on his death, but there is no explicit evidence. The high-priesthood of the god Elagabalus is generally thought to have been retained by members of his family. On the name 'Sohaemus' see above, under 41. Other bearers of the name, *PIR*¹ S 541ff.

48. (C. Julius) Sohaemus, consul before 164, Alföldy 1977, 195, made king of Armenia in 164, expelled once but restored; length of his reign unknown, Dio 71.3.1¹. Iamblichus, the Emesene novelist, explicitly claims Sohaemus as a fellow-countryman (Photius, *Bibl.* 94), which the name would in any case suggest, cf. no. 47, says that he had been consul before becoming king of Armenia, and also labels him 'the Achaemenid and Arsacid', dismissed by Bowersock 1982, 665 as 'ignorant glosses'. But the explanation must be descent from a Median Iotape: the name occurs in the Emesene dynasty as that of a daughter of Samsigeramus II, *PIR*² I 45 (all based on Josephus, *Ant.* 18. 135), presumably derived by descent from the Median princess once betrothed to Alexander Helios, thus Macurdy 42, cited approvingly by Chad 66, who later, however, 119n.6 rejects the 'Arsacid' label as gratuitous (he also adheres to the old-fashioned dating of this Sohaemus, 118ff.; see Chaumont 147ff.)

49. Varius Avitus Bassianus = M. AURELIUS ANTONINUS = 'Elagabalus'. Probably born in 203, priest of Elagabalus at Emesa in 218, son of nos. 41 and 50. On his names, see the comment under 34; in spite of doubts by Bowersock 1975, there is no reason to reject Dio, who calls him 'Avitus', the first of two *cognomina* borne by his mother's father (no. 45); his cousin was the given other one, Alexianus, and they both took 'Bassianus', the name of the priestly great-grand-father (no. 46). Kettenhofen, especially 23ff., is indispensable on this person, not least on the circumstances of his elevation. Otherwise, Barbieri no. 963 + Agg.

50. Sex. Varius Marcellus. His career, frequently discussed, e.g. by Pflaum in *CP* no. 237, Birley 1981, 296ff. (following the line in 1971, 304ff.), has now been reinterpreted by Halfmann on the lines of his treatment of no. 45. He shows that the puzzling appointment 'vice praefectorum praetorio et urbis functus' can best be explained as a short-term post following the murder of Geta, rather than earlier; further that Marcellus was probably excluded, like no. 45, from holding appointment during Plautianus' main period of power. The second post, procurator in Britain, can be assigned to the expedition, 208–11, followed by the powerful charge as *a rationibus*, the vice-prefecture, and adlection to senatorial rank within the first year or so after Septimius' death; then prefecture of the military treasury (important in 212) and governorship of Numidia, where he probably died, without having been consul. His home was Apamea.

E. OTHERS

51. Aradius Saturninus. See above under no. 11, and, on the Aradii of Bulla

Regia, Corbier 1982, 689ff., 713. Their first consular seems to be Q. Aradius Rufinus Optatus Aelianus, 'Severan'; the exact date is doubtful and much discussed, cf. e.g. Birley 1981, 175f.; but new information keeps appearing, see also the brilliant conjectures of Champlin 1981. This man should belong to the Bulla Regia family, but his wife Septimia Severa may not be from Lepcis and the couple may be later, as the lettering of their sarcophagus from Italian Interpromium, *EE* VIII 132 is said to look. The Aradii went on a long time, their latest representative being City Prefect in 376. This man might have been polyonymous, and must remain doubtful.

52. M. Cornelius Fronto *cos.* 143. The famous orator. Kinsman of the Petronii Mamertini, as pointed out by Champlin 1980, 10, 145 n. 22, picking up Fronto, *Ad amicos* 1.10.2. See nos. 56–8 below.

53. (Hortensia). Conjectured wife of no. 32, based on the name of his son, no. 33. Hortensii are not found at Lepcis.

54. (Neratia). Conjectured wife of no. 17, from the name borne by his daughter, no. 9. Presumably from the famous Saepinum family.

55. (Octavia). Conjectured wife of no. 23 (or perhaps of 26), to explain 'Octavilla' and 'Octavianus' in the names of nos. 8, 9 and 17.

56. Paccia Marciana, first wife of Septimius, whom she married in 175. She died at latest in 187, evidently childless: the alleged daughters mentioned in *HA Sev.* 8.1, provided with dowries and husbands in 193, could only have been hers, not Julia's; but they are fictional, Hasebroek 49. Her marriage is mentioned in *HA Sev.* 3.2 (she is called 'Marciam'): Septimius is there said to have omitted mention of her from his autobiography but to have set up statues to her as emperor; cf. *IRT* 410–11, Lepcis, *CIL* VIII 19494, Cirta. Her two names derive from first century proconsuls, Marcius Barea and Paccius Africanus, Birley 1969, 256, showing that her family was of Punic origin. Raepsaet-Charlier no. 590 (with further references).

57, 58, 59. M. Petronius Mamertinus *cos.* 150, was a kinsman of the orator Fronto, *Ad amicos* 1.10.2, as pointed out by Champlin 1980, 10, which supports the argument in Birley 1969, 259f. for the African origin of these Petronii. The *cos.* 150 was probably nephew rather than son of the Guard Prefect of this name under Pius. His own sons, Sura Mamertinus *cos.ord.* 182 and Sura Septimianus *cos. ord.* 190, may have been the product of his marriage with a Septimia, the natural explanation for the *cognomen* 'Septimianus'. A sister of nos. 15 and 25, or perhaps a daughter of one of them, would be suitable, although other Septimii could be found (not the procurator L. Septi—Petro—, who served in Egypt under the future Guard Prefect or his possible kinsman M. Petronius Honoratus; *CP* no. 146 *bis*). The *cos.* 182 was son-in-law of M. Aurelius, married to Cornificia. He and his brother were killed by Commodus in 190 or 191, *HA Comm.* 7.5.

60. Polemo II of Pontus. Husband of no. 40, as shown by Seyrig, yet another royal name lurking in the background of Julia Domna's family. Also king of Cilician Olba, descended via his mother Antonia Tryphaena, wife of the Thracian king Cotys, from Antony and Cleopatra: *RE* 21.2 (1952), 1285ff. (W. Hoffmann); Sullivan 908ff.

BIBLIOGRAPHY

Alföldy, G. 1967 — *Die Legionslegaten der römischen Rheinarmeen* (*Epigraphische Studien* 3, Bonn 1967)

Alföldy, G. 1968 — 'Septimius Severus und der Senat', *Bonner Jahrbücher* 168 (1968), 112–60

Alföldy, G. 1977 — *Konsulat und Senatorenstand unter den Antoninen* (Bonn 1977)

Barbieri, G. — *L'Albo senatorio da Settimio Severo a Carino* (Rome 1952)

Barnes, T. D. 1967 — 'The family and career of Septimius Severus', *Historia* 16 (1967) 87–107

Barnes, T. D. 1968 — 'Pre-Dacian *acta martyrum*', *Journal of Theological Studies* n.s. 19 (1968) 509–31

Barnes, T. D. 1971 — *Tertullian: a literary and historical study* (Oxford 1971)

Barnes, T. D. 1976 — *The Sources of the Historia Augusta* (Collection Latomus 155 Brussels 1976)

Barnes, T. D. 1986 — 'Proconsuls of Asia under Caracalla', *Phoenix* 40 (1986) 202–5

Bersanetti, G. M. — 'P. Settimio Geta, fratello di Settimio Severo', *Epigraphica* 4 (1942) 105–26

Birley, A. R. 1969 — 'The coups d'état of the year 193', *Bonner Jahrbücher* 169 (1969) 247–80

Birley, A. R. 1970 — 'Some notes on *HA Severus* 1–4', *HAC 1968–9* (Bonn 1970) 59–77

Birley, A. R. 1971 — *Septimius Severus the African Emperor* (London 1971)

Birley, A. R. 1976 — 'C. Septimius C.f. Qui. Severus: a note', *HAC 1972–4* (Bonn 1976) 63–4

Birley, A. R. 1981 — *The Fasti of Roman Britain* (Oxford 1981)

Birley, A. R. 1988 — 'Names at Lepcis Magna', *Libyan Studies* 19 (1988)

Bowersock, G. W. 1975 — 'Herodian and Elagabalus', *Yale Classical Studies* 24 (1975) 229–36

Bowersock, G. W. 1982 — 'Roman senators from the near east: Syria, Judaea, Arabia, Mesopotamia', *Epigrafia e ordine senatorio* (*Tituli* 5, Rome 1982) 651–88

Chad, C. — *Les dynastes d'Émèse* (Beirut 1972)

Champlin, E. 1980 — *Fronto and Antonine Rome* (Cambridge, Mass and London, 1980)

Champlin, E. 1981 — 'Serenus Sammonicus', *Harvard Stud. in Class. Phil.* 85 (1981) 189–212

Chastagnol, A. — '*Latus clavus* et *adlectio* dans l'Histoire Auguste', *HAC 1975–6* (Bonn 1978), 107–31

Chaumont, M.-L. — 'L'Arménie entre Rome et l'Iran I. De l'avènement d'Auguste à l'avènement de Dioclétien', *ANRW* 2.9.1 (1976) 71–194

Corbier, M. 1974   'Plautien, *comes* de Septime-Sévère', *Mélanges P. Boyancé* (Rome, 1974) 213–18

Corbier, M. 1982   'Les familles clarissimes d'Afrique proconsulaire (Ier-IIIe siècle)', *Epigrafia e ordine senatorio* (*Tituli* 5, Rome 1982) 685–754

Dietz, K.   *Senatus contra principem. Untersuchungen zur senatorischen Opposition gegen Kaiser Maximinus Thrax* (Munich 1980)

Di Vita-Evrard, G. 1963   'Un nouveau proconsul d'Afrique, parent de Septime Sévère', *Mélanges d'arch. et d'hist. école franç. de Rome* 75 (1963) 389–414

Di Vita-Evrard, G. 1981   'Le proconsul polyonyme IRT 517', *Mélanges d'arch. et d'hist. école franç. de Rome* 93 (1981) 183–226

Di Vita-Evrard, G. 1982   'Note sur "trois" sénateurs de Lepcis Magna. Le clarissimat des Plautii', *Epigrafia e ordine senatorio* (*Tituli* 4, Rome 1982) 453–65

Di Vita-Evrard, G. 1984   ' "Municipium Flavium Lepcis Magna" ', *Bull. du comité des travaux hist.* n.s. 17 B (1984) 197–210

Di Vita-Evrard, G. 1985   'Note sur quelques timbres d'amphores de Tripolitaine', *ibid.* 19 B (1985) 147–59

Di Vita-Evrard, G. 1987   'De la date du procés d'Hérode Atticus à l'ére d'Hadrien et à l'association au pouvoir de Géta', *Praktika tou 8 diethnous synedrious ellenikes kai latinikes epigraphikes 1982* II (Athens 1987)

Dobson, B.   *Die Primpilares* (Bonn 1978)

Domaszewski, A. V.   'Die politische Bedeutung der Religion von Emesa', *Abhandlungen zur römischen Religion* (Leipzig & Berlin 1909) 197–216

Duncan-Jones, R. P.   *The Economy of the Roman Empire. Quantitative Studies* (Cambridge 1974)

Eck, W.   *Die Statthalter der germanischen Provinzen vom 1.-3 Jahrhundert* (*Epigraphische Studien* 14, Bonn 1985)

Elmayer, A. F.   'The reinterpretation of Latino-Punic inscriptions from Roman Tripolitania', *Libyan Studies* 15 (1984) 93–105

Grosso, F.   'Richerche su Plauziano e gli avvenimenti del suo tempo', *Rendiconti. Accademia dei Lincei*[8] 23 (1968) 7–58

Guey, J. 1948   '28 janvier 98—28 janvier 198, ou le siècle des Antonins', *Revue des études anciennes* 50 (1948) 60–70

Guey, J. 1951   'L'inscription du grand-père de Septime-Sévère à Leptis Magna', *Mémoires . . societé nationale . . antiq. de France* 82 (1951) 161–226

Guey, J. 1956   'La date de naissance de l'empereur Septime-Sévère d'après son horoscope', *Bull. . . . soc. nationale . . antiq. de France* 1956, 33–5

Halfmann, H.   'Zwei syrische Verwandte des severischen Kaiserhauses', *Chiron* 12 (1982) 217–35

Hammond M.   'Septimius Severus, Roman bureaucrat', *Harvard Studies Class. Philology* 51 (1940) 137–73

Hasebroek, J. *Untersuchungen zur Geschichte des Kaisers Septimius Severus* (Heidelberg 1921)

Jenkins, G. *Sylloge Nummorum Graecorum. North Africa Syrtica Mauretania* (Copenhagen 1969)

Judeich, W. 'Plautianus und Severus', *Festschrift Alexander Cartellieri* (Weimar 1927) 63–71

Kajanto, I. *The Latin Cognomina* (Helsinki 1965)

Kettenhofen, E. *Die syrischen Augustae in der historischen Uberlieferung* (Bonn 1979)

Letta, C. 'Dal leone di Giulio Alessandro ai leoni di Caracalla. La dinastia di Emesa verso la porpora imperiale', *Studi E. Bresciani* (Pisa 1985) 289–302

Macurdy, G. 'Iotape', *Journal Roman Studies* 26 (1936) 40–2

Manacorda, D. 'Testimonianze sulla produzione e il consumo dell'olio nel III secolo', *Dialoghi di Archeologia* 9–10 (1977) 542–601

Mastino, A. *Le titolature di Carcalla e Geta attraverso le iscrizioni (indici)* (Bologna 1981)

Murphy, G. J. *The Reign of the Emperor L. Septimius Severus from the Evidence of the Inscriptions* (1947)

Pflaum, H. G. 1968 'Les juges des cinq décuries originaires d'Afrique', *Antiquités africaines* 2 (1968) 153–95

Raepsaet-Charlier, M.-T. *Prosopographie des femmes de l'ordre sénatoriale (Ier-IIe siècles)* (Louvain 1987)

Rey-Coquais, J. P. 'Inscriptions grecques d'Apamée', *Annales archéol. Syrie* 23 (1973) 39–84

Rössler, O. 'Libyen von der Cyrenaica bis zur Mauretania Tingitana', *Die Sprachen im Römischen Reich*, eds. G. Neumann, J. Untermann (Bonn 1980) 267–84

Romanelli, P. 'Fulvii Lepcitani', *Archaeologia Classica* 10 (1958) 258–61

Rubin, Z. *Civil-War Propaganda and Historiography* (Collection Latomus 173, Brussels 1980)

Saller, R. P. *Personal Patronage under the Early Empire* (Cambridge 1982)

Schumacher, L. *Prosopographische Untersuchungen zur Besetzung der vier hohen römischen Priesterkollegien im Zeitalter der Antonine und der Severer (96–235 n. Chr.)* (Diss. Mainz 1973)

Seyrig, H. 'Monnaies hellénistiques. XVI. Polémon II et Julia Mamaea', *Revue numismatique*, 6e sér., 11 (1969) 45–7

Shahid, I. *Rome and the Arabs* (Washington D.C. 1984)

Soproni, S. 'Die Caesarwürde Caracallas und die syrische Kohorte von Szentendre', *Alba Regia* 18 (1980) 39–51

Sullivan, R. D. 'The dynasty of Emesa', *ANRW* 2.8 (1977) 198–219; 'The dynasty of Judaea in the first century', ibid. 296–354; 'Papyri reflecting the eastern dynastic network', ibid. 908–38

Syme, R. 'Astrology in the Historia Augusta', *Historia Augusta*

	Papers (Oxford 1983) 80–97 (reprinted from *HAC 1972–4* (Bonn 1976) 291–309
Thomasson, B. E. 1975	*Senatus Populusque Romanus* (Gothenburg 1975)
Thomasson, B. E. 1984	*Laterculi Praesidum* (Gothenburg 1984)
Thomasson, B. E. 1985	'Zur Laufbahn einiger Statthalter des Prinzipats', *Opuscula Romana* 15 (1985) 109–41
Torelli, M.	'Per una storia della classe dirigente di Leptis Magna', *Rendiconti . . Accademia dei Lincei*[8] 28 (1973) 377–410
Vessey, D. W. T. C.	'*Non solitis fidibus*: some aspects of Statius, *Silvae* 4.5', *Antiquité Classique* 39 (1970) 507–18

References and Notes

For Bibliography to Chapters 1–3, see pp. 258–61

1. The Emporia(pages 1–7)

1 App. 2 nos. 27; 20; 28—consuls of 145: Birley1987, 89.
2 grandfather: App. 2 no. 26—self-adoption: Dio 76. 9.4; cf. pp. 117, 122 above. Geta: App. 2 no. 20—Aper, C. Septimius Severus: nos. 15; 25—Polla: no. 10—'another son ... Octavilla': nos. 21; 8—Maximus: *HA Geta* 2.1 (cf. App. 1.A4).
3 Phoenicians: Harden provides a useful introduction—language: Röllig 285f.—Carthage: Warmington—Cyrene: Herodotus 4. 151ff.—Carthage's response: Di Vita 1969—*Lpqy* and the other names: Rössler 272—'little island': called *Lyd*[...], *IPT* 32, and commentary, p.84—'Neapolis': *IRT* p. 75.—Herodotus 4. 175 (Hill of the Graces); 198 (Cinyps region).
4 Cinyps, Dorieus: Herodotus 5.42—Carthage: Whittaker 1974; 1978.
5 Tripolitania, geography and climate: Haynes 13ff. gives a concise introduction—indigenous peoples: Bates remains fundamental; cf. also Desanges. On both topics I have benefited from consulting the as yet unpublished Ph.D. thesis by D. J. Mattingly (1984).
6 Punic wars: Harris 182ff.; 200ff. provides an acute analysis of their causes—Massinissa in the Syrtica: Livy 29. 33. 9 (205 BC)—'one talent': Livy 34. 62. 2—'commissioners': 34. 61–2; Badian 1958, 125ff.; Walsh 1965, 156ff.—'160s': Polybius 31. 21—'relative independence ... Alexandria': Di Vita 1968a; 1982, 528f.
7 third Punic war: Harris 234ff.—formation of province, C. Gracchus: Romanelli 1959, 43ff.; Lassère 35ff.—Jugurtha: Sallust, *BJ* 77.1–4—*fossa regia*: Badian 1958, 138f. ('Rome's first recorded attempt to mark out an artificial frontier'); Di Vita-Evrard 1986, 33f. and figs. 1–11.
8 'free states': Di Vita 1982, 518ff.—coinage: Jenkins—'abomination': *II Kings* 23.13.—Sallust, *BJ* 78. 4–5—'inscription': *IPT* 31; Di Vita 1968b—*sufetes: RE* 4A (1931) 643ff.—Melquart and Shadrapa: Gese 198ff.—Ba'al Hammon, Tanit: Di Vita 1982, 562ff.
9 Herennius: Cicero, *II Verr.* 1.14; 5. 155f.; Rebuffat 1986—Cyrenaica: Badian 1968, 22; 29f.—Arsinoe: Moretti—'new city centre': Di Vita 1968b, 202 n. 1, 203; 1982, 553ff.
10 Juba: Caesar, *Bell. civ.*2.38; *Bell. Afr.* 97.—Cato: Aumont.—'fine': *Bell. Afr.* 97; Plutarch, *Caes.* 55; Di Vita 1982, 521f.; Mattingly 1988.
11 Romanelli 1959, 111ff.; Lassère 145ff.; 166ff.; 199ff.

2 Lepcis Magna: from Free State to Colonia (pages 8–22)

1 'free cities': Di Vita 1982, 522ff.—'Italians settled': Lassère 1977, 145ff. (he

excludes Tripolitania)—Virgil, *Ecl.*1.64; Deman 1969—Herennius; chapter 1, n.9 above—Perperna: *IRT* 335 (dedicated statue to Drusus Caesar)—Fulvii: *IRT* 320; 328; Romanelli 1958; App. 2.C.

2 'triumphs': Thomasson 1984, 371—Balbus: Pliny, *NH* 5.36–7; other sources on this man in *PIR*² C 1331. Garamantes: Daniels 1970—trade: Di Vita 1982, 588ff. (convincingly reasserting its importance).

3 'first dated inscription': *IRT* 319 + *IPT* 21—'presumably . . . of Melqart now rebuilt': I follow Di Vita 1968b.

4 Annobal: *IRT* 321 + *IPT* 24; *IRT* 322–3—Fulvii: *IRT* 320; 328—Piso: *IRT* 520; Di Vita 1982, 555f. Syme 1986, 369f. favours a date of 4–3BC. It was Piso who offered Strabo (2.130) the famous simile comparing North Africa to a leopard's skin—'spotted with inhabited places surrounded by waterless desert'.

5 Quirinius: Florus 2.31; generally assumed to have been proconsul of Cyrenaica, e.g. Thomasson 1984, 361; Syme 1986, 320 suggests he could have governed Africa, either in 3 BC or AD 2—Lentulus (*cos.* 3 BC): Thomasson 1984, 373—Cossus (*cos.* AD 1): *IRT* 301; Thomasson 373.

6 'cult of Augustus': Di Vita 1982, 558f.—Chalcidicum: *IRT* 324—Caecina: not yet published; Di Vita-Evrard 1982, 467f.—Asprenas: *AE* 1952. 232; 1905. 177; Thomasson 1984, 373.

7 Lamia: *IRT* 930; properly explained by Di Vita-Evrard 1979, 73ff. in the light of the Gallicus inscriptions, p. 16 above, n.16 below. *IPT* 76.

8 Tacfarinas: Tacitus, *Ann.* 2.52; 3.20–1; 73–4; 4.23–6 (3.9 refers to IX Hispana on its way through Italy)—Dolabella: *AE* 1961. 107f. Romanelli 1959, 227ff. discusses the war.

9 'statues': *IPT* 22—Marsus: *IRT* 308—Blandus: 330–1; also on 269; 540.

10 'legion': Syme 1984, 1358 shows that Dio 60.20.7 rather than Tacitus, *Hist.* 4.48.1 has the details right—Ptolemy, Mauretania: *RE* 23 (1959) 1780ff.; 14(1930) 2372f.; Daniels 1987, 239.

11 Claudius and citizenship: Sherwin-White 1973, 237ff.—Ti. Claudii at Lepcis: Torelli 1974, 377f.—Iddibal: *IRT* 273—Marcii: Birley 1969, 257f.; Torelli 1974, 402; already in Guey 1951b, 315—Cornutus: *PIR*² A 609—Lucan: A 611—Seneca at Alexandria; *Cons. Helv.* 19.4–7; *PIR*² A 617.

12 Patrons: Barea (*IRT* 273); Crassus Frugi (319); Caninius (521); Blandus and Lupercus (330–1); Lamia: for his son Silvanus Aelianus, Syme 1988, 168f.; postulated as a patron by Torelli 1974, 404.

13 Silvanus: *IRT* 338 + *IPT* 26; *IRT* 615; *AE* 1968. 549 (amphitheatre); Thomasson 1984, 376.—statues: *IPT* 22; App. 2 nos. 1–6. Contrast the lowly patrons of e.g. Thugga, Harmand 274.

14 amphitheatre: *AE* 1968. 549; Di Vita-Evrard 1965—Orfitus, Ithymbal: *IRT* 341—harbour: Di Vita 1974 (on the old harbour); Bartoccini 1958.

15 'Punic inscription': *IPT* 18—Clodius Macer; *PIR*² C 1170—Festus: Tacitus, *Hist.* 2.98; 4. 49–50; Thomasson 1984, 393; Vitellius and Vespasian proconsuls of Africa: id. 376f.—Statilius Capella: Suetonius, *D. Vesp.* 3.1—Festus' campaign: Daniels 1970; Di Vita 1982, 530ff.; Romanelli 1959, 285ff.

16 Nero's confiscations: assumed from Pliny, *NH* 18.35—Vespasian's financial problems and remedies: Suetonius, *D. Vesp.* 16.1–3—Gallicus: Di Vita-Evrard 1979 publishes and discusses the inscriptions which show him at work

in the Gebel; other evidence summarised, Thomasson 1984, 377; on his career, Syme 1988, 504; 514ff.—Paetina: *CIL* V 6990. Plautius: n.12 above—*municipium*: this much debated question (the prime evidence being *IRT* 342; 346; 347) should now be regarded as settled, see Di Vita-Evrard 1984—privileges of Latin communities: Sherwin-White 1973, 112; 360ff. (Spain under Vespasian)—*mahazim*; *IIIIv[ir aed.]pot.*: *IRT* 305 + *IPT* 30 (confirming that *[aed.]* is correct).

17 Iddibal: *IRT* 300—Sestius: *IRT* 347; 318 + *IPT* 27—cf. *IPT* 86 (Gebel Msellata) and, apparently late second or early third century, a bilingual in the western Gefara, chapter 3, n.14 below.

18 Pliny, *NH* 5.34ff.—Zliten: Di Vita 1982, 530—Septimius Flaccus, Julius Maternus: Ptolemy 1.8.4; Birley 1969, 255f.—Domitian: Di Vita 1982, 532—Colosseum: Dio 66. 25; Martial, *De spectaculis*, etc.

19 Suellius: Thomasson 1984, 395; Romanelli 1959, 204 favours identification with Septimius Flaccus; against, Birley 1969, 255f. But the matter must naturally remain open—'Macer' and ancestors: App. 2 nos. 1–6; 23 —'olive plantations': explicit evidence is not to hand until the Tripolitanian amphorae begin to be stamped with producers' initials, in the Severan period: Manacorda 1977; 1983; Di Vita-Evrard 1985; Mattingly 1988. They include L.APRI and L.S.A. CV = L. Septimius Aper *cos. ord.* 207 (App. 2 no. 14), as well as the emperor and his sons (AVGG; AVGGG) and Plautianus (CFPCV; CFPPPCV).

20 'estates': Statius, *Silvae* 4.5. 53–6; Veii is confirmed by a lead pipe found near the Via Cassia, five miles from Veii, seventeen from Rome, hearing the name 'P. Septimi Geta': *CIL* XI 3816. The place was evidently called 'Baccanae', *CIL* XI p. 557 n.3. In the *Acta Sanctorum* (VI 227ff., 21 September), *Acta* of Alexander, he is said to have been tried near a villa of the emperor Antoninus (Caracalla) at 'vicus Baccatensis' or 'Baccanae', close to find-spot of the lead pipe. *CIL* IX 4868, the epitaph of L. Septimius Primigenius, from Montopoli (territory of Forum Novum), not far from Cures, might be evidence for a freedman of the family ('dis manibus' is written out in full; hence it could be early).—'child': Statius, *Silvae* 4.5.36–40—'educated': *Silvae* 4 pr. (to Vitorius Marcellus: 'tuum quidem et condiscipulum'; cf. chapter 3 n.1 below); cf. 4.5.41–3 ('hinc parvus inter pignora curiae ... crescis'). Pliny as Quintilian's pupil: *Ep.* 2.1.9; 6.6.3—'narrow stripe': *Silvae* 4.5.42.—'barrister': 4.5. 49–52—'verses': 4.5.57–60—Statius on Gallicus: *Silvae* 1.4, cf. 1 pr.; Syme 1988, 514ff.—'tribute': *Silvae* 1.4 83–6.

21 'provincial Romans': Syme 1958, esp. 585ff.; 1988, 473 (Montanus); 472 (Pactumeius); 10; 12f.; etc. (Domitian's promotion of Greek senators)—Silius Italicus: Martial 4.14; 7.63; Pliny, *Ep.* 3.7. Silius lists the three cities of Tripolitania as providing troops for Hannibal's army, *Punica* 3. 256–7—Statius' road poem: *Silvae* 4.3 ('certe non Libycae sonant catervae/nec dux advena peierante bello/Campanos quatit inquietus agros', lines 4–6)—'Punica fides': e.g. Sallust, *BJ* 108.3—Hercules: *Silvae* 4.6. 75–85—On the poem to Septimius Severus, see esp. Vessey 1970.

22 4.5.29–30; 33–4; 37–44; 45–6—'accent': cf. chapter 3 n.28 below.—Rufina: Martial 11.53.—Martial had several friends called Severus: for the poet, 11.57 (identification favoured by Vessey 1970, 508 n.9)—Alba: *Silvae* 4.5. 21–8. The

festival took place in March 90: Hardie 1983, 63—'country retreat': *Silvae* 4.53–6. These lines encourage Vessey 1970, 512ff. to label Septimius Severus an Epicurean. Plausible enough.

23 Nerva, Trajan: Syme 1958, esp. 1–44; 88f. (death or withdrawal of poets)— *iudex selectus*: as revealed by *IRT* 412. This of course assumes the identity of Septimius' grandfather and the friend of Statius; argued by Birley 1970, 75ff.; see also App. 2 no. 26; and chapter 3 n.1 below—'iron control': Suetonius, *Domitian* 8.2 (contrasting what followed)—trial of Priscus: Pliny, *Ep.* 2. 11; Syme 1958, 70f.

24 Pliny, *Ep.* 2.11.

25 Pliny, *Ep.* 2.11; Juvenal 1. 49–59; cf. 8.119–20—*colonia*: *IRT* 412; 353; 284; Guey 1951a, esp. 202; *IRT* p. 81—*Curiae*: Kotula 1968, 83ff.; Torelli 1971— Arch: *IRT* 353 (AD 110) also 523 (another proconsul, presumably earlier). The Arch marks the *terminus ante quem*: the award of colonial status could have been several years earlier. *IRT* 543 refers to the restoration of the 'Ulpian basilica and forum' in late antiquity. Presumably built at this time; but not located.

3 Life in Roman Tripolitania (pages 23–36; for bibliography, pp. 258–61)

1 Severus: App. 2 no. 26—Polla, Geta: nos. 10; 20.—Marcellus and son: Statius, *Silvae* 4 *pr.*; 4.4 (the son Geta: line 72. For his grandfather Hosidius Geta: Birley 1981, 222); Syme 1984, 1133; 1160; 1269; 1306. Marcellus may have become proconsul of Africa (c. 120): id. 1305; 1306; 1313—Polla: Statius, *Silvae* 2.2 and 7; Nisbet 1978, convincingly identifying Lucan's widow Argentaria Polla with Polla the wife of Pollius Felix.

2 Servilius Candidus: *IRT* 357–9; 275. Rogate: *KAI* no. 178—Candidus ben Candidus (*Q'ndd' bn Q'ndd' bn Hn' bn 'bdmlqrt*): *IPT* 18.—C. Cl. Septimius Aper: *IRT* 316; Birley 1976; App. 2 no. 16.—Aper, C. Septimius Severus: App. 2 nos. 15; 25.

3 App. 2, nos. 15; 25.

4 Suetonius: Syme 1984, 1337ff.; Birley, *JRS* 1984, 245f.; 249f.—Mamertinus: cf. App. 2, nos. 57–9—C. Septimius Severus: App. 2 no. 25.

5 Fronto: Champlin 1980, *passim*; App. 2 no. 52.—Tuticius Proculus: *HA Marcus* 2.3; Birley 1968, 39ff.—Apollinaris: *PIR*[1] S 707; Champlin 1980, 18; 36; 48; 50; 54—Urbicus: Birley 1981, 112ff.; 1987, 275 n.9; Vidman 1977— Julianus: Corbier 1982, 719f.

6 'already senators': Corbier 1982, 721f.; 727f.; 729; Di Vita-Evrard 1982, 453ff.—Apuleius: Hijmans 1987, 412ff. discusses the chronology of his life and writing again—'extracts': the *Florida*; quotation from 8.

7 'Madauros . . . equestrian rank': *Apol.* 24.1; 7–9; Lassère 252ff. Apuleius' father was presumably *praefectus* acting on behalf of an emperor who was (honorary) *IIvir* ('loco principis IIviralem'); cf. *RE* 22 (1954) 1318ff. for parallels.— Carthage: *Florida* 18. 15, 36; 20.10—Athens: 18.15; 20.4—Samos: *Florida* 15— Hierapolis: *De Mundo* 17—Pontianus: *Apol.* 72.3.

8 Orfitus: *Florida* 17.4—On the *Metamorphoses*: Walsh 1968; Millar 1981.

9 *Apol.* 72.1–6. The date emerges from the proconsuls Avitus and Maximus, n.12 below.

10 'language was Punic', etc.: *Apol.* 98.8—'fluent Punic': *Epit. de Caes.* 20.8

(quoted p. 35 above)—'made himself at home ... four million sesterces':
Apol. 73.1–7.

11 *Apol.* 68.2–72.1.

12 'a year or so ... toga of manhood': *Apol.* 7–9—'study oratory': 73.1—Avitus:
24.13; *IRT* 533–5; Guey 1951b—'recommended': *Apol.* 94.3—Pertinax: *HA
Pert.* 1.5; cf. *Epit. de Caes.* 18.4; pp. 63f above.

13 'largesse': *Apol.* 87.10—Rufinus: 74.3–78.4, etc.—letter: quoted in full 83.1;
discussed 78.5ff.—'returned .. two months': 87.6.

14 marriage: 87.10–99.7—'late husband's property': 9.3.3–6—'fifteen slaves': 44.
5ff.'—'town house': 72.6—'a hundred miles': 44.4–6. It is worth asking
whether the nonagenarian Q. Apuleus Maxssimus (*sic*), 'qui et Rideus
vocabatur Iuzale f. Iurathe n.', whose sons were Pudens, Severus and
Maximus, his wife Thanubra, commemorated by a Latin and Neo-Punic
tombstone at El-Amrun, might be a tenant on the estate of the Sicinii: he
could have taken Apuleius' name on enfranchisement—and named one son
after Sicinius Pudens. El-Amrun lies in the Gefara, a long way from Oea.
Dated to late second or early third century by Brogan 1968, 54f.; Millar 1968,
132; Röllig 1980, 292; but cf. Mattingly 1987, 81—'modest property': *Apol.*
101.4–5—Lamia: *IRT* 930; its true significance elucidated by Di Vita-Evrard
1979, 73ff.; 87ff. (on size of Lepcis' territory; further, Mattingly 1988)—
Carthage: Gascou 1982, 136ff.—Cirta: Garnsey 1978, 226.

15 *Apol.* 93.6–94.6.

16 'homeward ... his uncle': *Apol.* 28.8; 96.4–98.4—Aemilianus: *Apol.* 2.9–12;
Vidman 1977—Pudens: 98.5–8; 99.3–5.

17 'change of proconsul': Thomasson 1984, 382 summarises the evidence;
Maximus is referred to in *Apol.* 1.1–7 and repeatedly throughout, cf. n.23
below—Granii: *Apol.* 1.5—'scepticism': 1.7—Pudens, Aemilianus: 2.1–3—
Tannonius: 4.2.

18 'names ... matched': Guey 1954—'agrarian economy': Pavis d'Escurac
1974—'multitude': *Apol.* 28.3.

19 'poems': *Apol.* 6ff.—'magic' 25–65 (fish: 29ff.; slave boy: 42ff.; cloth: 53ff.;
nocturnal rites: 57ff.; image: 61ff.

20 Quintianus, Crassus: *Apol.* 57–9—Mercury: 61–3.

21 letter: 78. 5ff.—'sixty': 89.1–7. Did the prosecution-deliberately-confuse the
consuls of 116 (*Aeliano et Vetere*) with those of 96 (*Valente et Vetere*)? If so, that
would make Pudentilla just over forty when she married Apuleius—Rufinus:
74.3–76.6—'astrologers': 97.4.

22 Zaratha: *Apol.* 23.6; 24.10—'austerity ... boorish': 10.6—'long passage':
16.10–13—'a good joke ... been hung': 56.3–6—'lucifugus': 16.13, cf.
Minucius Felix, *Octavius* 8.4; 10.1ff.; the parallel was noted by Griset 1957;
Barnes 1971, 271f. notes that Griset misdates Minucius and regards the notion
of an allusion to Christianity as implausible—Thyestes: *Apol.* 16.7 (not
mentioned by Barnes), cf. Fronto, ap. Minuc. Fel. *Octavius* 8.3–9.6 (cf.
30.2–31.2), interpreted by Champlin 1980, 64ff.

23 Maximus: *Apol.* 11.5; 25.3; 35.7; 38.1; 41.4; 48.5; 81.2; 91.3. Cf. *PIR*[2] C 933;
Alföldy 1977, 143—'trump card': *Apol.* 94.6–95.7—'at Carthage': *Florida*
16.1, 25ff.; Augustine, *Ep.* 138.19.—Granii: *Apol.* 1.5; *IRT* 532, 642, 708–9;
Guey 1954, 115ff.—Pudens: *IRT* 295 (cf. pp. 142f. above)—'nurse of

pleaders': Juvenal 7.148—'plead his own case': 2.1–2 (pp. 45f. above).

24 'judges ... prowess': *HA Sev.* 1.4—'Punic': *Epit. de Caes.* 20.8—'eager for more': Dio 76.16.1—'speech': *HA Sev.* 1.5—Geta: App. 2 no. 21—Agricola: Birley 1981, 127ff.

25 'ferment ... war': Birley 1987, 116ff.; 121ff.—'to study': *HA Sev.* 1.5.

26 Circus: Di Vita-Evrard 1965; Humphrey 1985, 25ff.—'superstitious': cf. *HA Geta* 2.6 ('gnarus geniturae illius, cuius, ut plerique Afrorum, peritissimus fuit')—Apuleius, *Apol.* 97.4—'phallic symbols': Vergara Caffarelli 1966, 111—Sarapis: *HA Sev.* 17.3–4; *IRT* 309–12.

27 Statius, *Silvae* 4.5.45–6—*Epitome de Caes.* 20.8—Maximus: App. 1.A.4.

28 'voice .. accent': *HA Sev.* 18.9—Apuleius, *Apol.* 24.1; *Florida* 9.7—'aitches': Augustine, *Confess.* 1.18—'L': Isidore, *Orig.* 1.31.8; Pompeius Maurus, *Gramm. Lat.* (ed. Keil) 286—'lengthening': Consentius, *Gramm. Lat.* 392—'whistling': Jerome, *Ep.* 103.5. As Röllig 1980, 295ff. points out, the three sibilants, for which Latin has only 'S', are represented in the late Latino-Punic inscriptions by S, sigma and a third sign $ (e.g. *IRT* 889; 892). The accent is discussed by Monceaux 1899, 185ff.—Octavilla: *HA Sev.* 15.7; pp. 131f. above.

29 Malalas 12, p. 291—colour portrait: pl. 16; Neugebauer 1936; and see McCann 1968, *passim*, on the portrayal of Septimius.

4 The Broad Stripe (pages 37–46; for Bibliography, see pp. 261–3)

1 'dying emperor': *HA Pius* 12.4ff., Birley 1987, 114—war, id. 121ff.—kinsmen: App. 2, nos. 15, 25.

2 Verus: Birley 1987, 123ff.—Priscus: Birley 1981, 123ff.—Agricola, Eck 65ff.—'transfers, promotions': Birley 1987, 122ff.

3 Marcianus: *PIR*² J 340; Alföldy 1977, 182; Adventus, Agricola, Priscus, Laelianus, Julius Verus: Birley 1981, 129ff., 127ff., 123ff., 273ff., 118ff. Cassius, Pompeianus: Bowersock, 664, 665—Claudius Fronto: Halfmann 636—Martius Verus: *PIR*² M 348—Vindex: Birley 1982, 535—Maximianus: *CP* no. 181 bis.

4 'dynasty': Birley 1987, 232ff.

5 *HA Sev.* 1.5; App. 2 no. 25. Cf. p. 18, above.

6 'tribune': App. 2 no. 25—'I Minervia': *ILS* 1097–8.

7 'tribunate': *HA Sev.* 2.2, Birley 1970, 69—Geta: App. 2 no. 21—Pertinax: p. 65 and n.5—'Hadrian's Wall': Breeze-Dobson 125ff.

8 Birley 1981, 8ff.

9 Geta: App. 2 no. 21—'vigintivirate: Birley 1981, 4ff.

10 *laticlavii*: Talbert, 11ff., 513; Chastagnol 112ff. believes that S. only became senatorial as quaestor, pressing *HA Sev.* 3.1 too hard in my view.—Anullinus, Cilo: *PIR*² C 1322, F27—Albinus: Birley 1981, 146ff.—Niger: Dio 74.6.1 (much of the *vita* in the *HA* is bogus)—Didius: Alföldy 1982, 354; Corbier 720.

11 'autobiography', Dio: App. 1, A.1–2—astrology: Cramer 208ff.; Rubin 27ff.

12 *HA Sev.* 1.6 (cf. Augustine, *Confessions* 6.3.3 on reading habits), 7–10; Dio 74.3.1,3.

13 Dio 76.16.1; Herodian 2.9.2; *HA Sev.* 19.7–10 (including at least some invention, as well as the error about his size)—grandfather: p. 20 above—Hadrian: *HA Had.* 3.1; 1.3, 2.1; 2–5 with *ILS* 308 (a record equalled later only

by the younger L. Minicius Natalis, *ILS* 1061; cf. Birley 1981, 8ff.)—Pliny, *Ep.* 9.23. 2–3—Fronto, *Ad M. Caes.* 1.10.5, discussed by Champlin 7f.

14 'literary salon': Champlin 29ff.—Sextus: Philostratus, *v. soph.* 2.1.9–Galen: *On Prognosis* 2.24; 5.17ff. (ed. V. Nutton, Berlin 1979), Bowersock 1969, 62ff.—'dwarf': A. Gellius, *Noctes Atticae* 19.13; cf. Birley 1987, 65ff., 93ff.

15 Verus in the east, Birley 1987, 129f.—Fronto and family: Champlin 27f. On the grandson, cf. p. 140 below—Fronto, *De feriis Als.* 3; *De bello Parth, Ad Verum Imp.* 2.6; *HA Verus* 7.10, 4.6ff., 6.1–5; Fronto, *Ad amicos* 1.12.

16 Antoninus: *Ad amicos* 2.6–8; Optatus: 1.9; Mamertinus: 1.10 and App. 2 no. 57.

17 Pliny, *Ep.* 5.8.8, cf. 1.18.3; Victor, *De Caes.* 20. 28. The *HA Sev.* 1.5 does indeed say S. went to Rome 'studiorum causa'. At this stage in his life he needed to study oratory—'plead a case': *HA Sev.* 2.1–2, pp. 45f. above.

18 Birley 1987, 140ff., 249ff.

19 Birley 1987, 147ff.—'Italian land': Pliny, *Ep.* 6.19.4; *HA Marcus* 11.8, Talbert 142 (a reflection of the growing numbers of non-Italian senators).—'Veii': *HA Sev.* 4.5, emended, p. 220 above.

20 Geta: *IRT* 541, App. 2 no. 21.—Apuleius at Carthage in the 160s: p. 33 above.

21 *HA Sev.* 2.1–2, Birley 1970, 68; Alföldy 1977, 209 n.18.

2ʾ Birley 1981, 12ff.; Talbert 16ff., 131ff. ('six hundred')—'sixty million': any estimate is largely guesswork, cf. eg. Charles-Picard 45ff.

5 Into The Emperor's Service (pages 47–56; for Bibliography see pp. 261–3)

1 'lots': Talbert 348ff.—quaestors: Birley 1981, 12ff.; Talbert 13ff., 348ff.—'13 April': Dio 60.17.3 (cf. 60. 11.6), and cf. Talbert 497f.—consuls: Alföldy 1977, 185; *PIR*² E 95, cf. 94, 96–7; G 98; II 189.

2 Birley 1987, 155ff.

3 Birley 1987, 160; 247f.; cf. App. 2 nos. 57–9—Pertinax: p. 65 above.

4 'gladiators': *HA Marcus* 21.8. 'games': Talbert 59—'offensive': Birley 1987, 163ff.

5 invaders: Birley 1987, 164f., 250f.—offensive renewed: id. 171ff., 251f. Geta: App. 2 no. 21; curators: Eck 1979, 190ff., but 238 puzzlingly dating the post 'c. 190' (its order in Geta's *cursus*, *IRT* 541, is unambiguous, between aedileship and praetorship).

6 double quaestorship: Birley 1981, 282 n.1 (to which add *ILS* 1002, 8842), eight other cases—Baetica, Anullinus: Alföldy 1969, 122f.; 1985.

7 '13 April': Dio 60.17.3—father's death : *HA Sev.* 2.3–4—Moors: Alföldy 1985, 100ff.—Victorinus: Alföldy 1969, 38ff.—Julianus: *CP* no. 180.

8 Sardinia: *HA Sev.* 2.4—'Punic influence': an inscription at Bitia in Punic from the reign of an emperor 'M. Aurelius Antoninus', i.e. some time between 161 and 222, Mastino 1985, 71, cf. 70 n.237 (public works carried out under *sufetes*). See generally, on African-Sardinian relations in the Roman period, Mastino 1985, 27ff.

9 Talbert 16ff.—Pertinax: pp. 66f. above.

10 *HA Sev.* 2.5, confirmed, with the identity of the proconsul, by *AE* 1967. 536 of 174—legates: Di Vita-Evrard 1985, 155ff.: the proconsul of Africa had once had three *legati*, but with the removal of the legion and its commander from

his control by Caligula (pp. 51–61 above), he was left with two only—Oea
arch: *IRT* 232;—Apuleius, *Florida* 17.
11 The arch: Di Vita-Evrard 1963—Thubursicu: *ILAlg.* I 1283, corrected by Di
Vita-Evrard—Agueneb: *CIL* VIII 21567, a dedication by a centurion of III
Augusta after a successful expedition, Alföldy 1985, 103. Cf. p. 147 above.
12 *HA Sev.* 2.6
13 *HA Sev.* 2.8, cf. Dio 76.11.1.
14 App 2 no. 56
15 *HA Sev.* 3.1, Birley 1970, 70f. 'suspect story': *HA Sev.* 8.1, their supposed
marriage in 193, an invention: Hasebroek 49
16 Talbert 185ff., etc.—Pliny, *Ep.* 1.23.
17 Birley 1987, 184ff.—'detachments': *AE* 1920. 45.
18 Birley 1987, 188, 253f.
19 Pertinax: p. 67 above—Geta: *IRT* 541—Victorinus: Alföldy 1969, 38ff.—
kinsman: App 2 no. 25.
20 *HA Sev.* 3.—Commodus: Birley 1987, 197.
21 Talbert 185ff., etc.—'supervised': *HA Marcus* 24.2, cf. 12.3–4.
22 *AE* 1971. 534, Banasa.
23 games: Talbert 59f.—gladiators: *Hesperia* 24 (1955) 320ff., Birley 1987,
200f.—Spain: *HA Sev.* 3.4, Alföldy 1969, 88f.
24 *HA Sev.* 4.4; *Had.* 12.3. Marcus' death: Birley 1987, 209f.
25 Ammianus 31.5.14.

6 A Caesar Born to the Purple (pages 57–62; for Bibliography see pp. 261–3)

1 'nobilissimus': *ILS* 397, cf. Herodian 1.5.5–6. On Commodus the massive
study by Grosso remains essential.
2 Dio 71.33.42 believed the poisoning story.
3 'five sisters': Birley 1987, 247f.—Pompeianus: *PIR*[2] C 973—Praesens: B
165—Pollio: *ILS* 1112—Victorinus: Alföldy 1969, 38ff—Marcus' hope:
Grosso 95ff., perhaps valuing Herodian 1.4–5 too highly.
4 'IV Scythica': *HA Sev.* 4.4 and p. 68 above—*HA Comm.* 3.1 refers to
dismissals of Marcus' senior advisers, 4.8 to the appointment of criminals or
criminally recommended as provincial governors.
5 *Meditations* 1.17.19—teachers: *HA Comm.* 1.6—Sanctus: *CP* no. 178 bis—
'twenty-sixth year': Birley 1987, 92ff.
6 Dio 72.1.1; *HA Comm.* 1.7ff.—Maximus: App.1.A.4; *PIR*[2] M 308 (tribune in
the legions XXII Pr. and III Italica).
7 Herodian 1.7.5.
8 Faustina I: *HA Pius* 3.7—Verus: *HA Verus* 2.9–10, 4.4ff., 8.8ff., etc.—
'illegitimate': *HA Marcus* 19.1–11.
9 Grosso 99ff.—Saoterus: id. 113ff.—'brothers-in-law': Birley 1987, 247f.
10 Alföldy 1988, warns against uncritical acceptance of this view, derived
principally from the romanticised and distorted version of Herodian.
11 pp. 48 above (brothers-in-law); 74, 77 (British army).
12 Herodian 1.8.3–8; *HA Comm.* 4.1–5; Dio 72.4.4–5. Cf. Grosso 145ff.—
Paternus' *nomen* emerges from AE 1971. 534 (Banasa).
13 Grosso 153ff.—*HA Comm.* 4.1.7–10; 3.2; Dio 72.5.1–2; *HA Did. Jul.* 1.9–2.2;
Dio 73.11.2. It is not known where Salvius' command was.

14 Grosso 158f.—Dio 72.6.1–7.2, cf. *HA Comm.* 4.9—dismissals, pp. 67, 73 above.

7 The Great Marshal (pages 63–67; for Bibliography see pp. 261–3)

1 See further chapter 8.

2 There is now an extensive literature on Pertinax. His origin and career are dealt with in *HA Pert.* 1.1–4 4, the basic accuracy of which is largely confirmed by the Bonn inscription, *AE* 1963. 52, giving his career up to the promotion from the German fleet to the Dacian procuratorship. His career from c. 158–79 is admirably handled by Alföldy, *Situla* 14/15 (1974) 199–215, reprinted as Alföldy 1987, 326–42, with addenda 342–8 giving comprehensive bibliography. Cf. also *PIR²* H 73; *CP* no. 179—Horace: *PIR²* H 198—Apollinaris: Champlin 18, 36, 48, 50f., 54. Avitus: *PIR²* H 40. This is the proconsul whom Apuleius knew, p. 33 above. Champlin 36 comments: 'The tight network of literary society may be ... observed, for Pertinax was a pupil of Sulpicius Apollinaris and a client of Lollianus Avitus, both friends of Fronto.' On the Lolliani, Alföldy 1982, 325ff. This man's younger son, Lollianus Gentianus, was to be a prominent ally of Septimius. His wife, Plautia Servilia, was surely a daughter of Verus' sister Ceionia Plautia and her husband Q. Servilius Pudens of Hippo Regius (Corbier 721): *CIL* XV 7514, generally read as 'Servilla', likewise in the names of her own daughter, *ILS* 1155—Turbo: *CP* no. 94—'failed to acquire': thus, interpreting *HA Pert.* 1.5–6, E. Birley in *PIR²* H 73, confirmed by *AE* 1963. 52—his unit was VII Gallorum: Roxan 246f.

3 Dio 73.3.1—Pompeianus: *PIR²* C 973—Cornelianus: *HA Marcus*: 8.6, *PIR²* A 1341—'made to walk': *HA Pert.* 1.6 (not naming him).

4. Parthian war: Birley 1987, 121ff.—Verus, Priscus, Agricola: Birley 1981, 120, 126, 127ff.—*ab epistulis*: E. Birley 1953, 142f.; 1963, 21f.

5 'mainly administrative': E. Birley 1953, 143ff.—VI Victrix: *AE* 1963. 52—Agricola: Breeze & Dobson 128ff.—'Coria': i.e. Corbridge on Tyne, for which new evidence seems to confirm that this name, discussed by Rivet & Smith 322ff., cf. 320, is the right form. *RIB* 1120, 1122, 1125, 1130–32, 1137, 1159–63, 1175, 1190 all show men of VI Victrix at this place—'Tungrians': this seems the only unit he could have commanded in the second *militia*, a military cohort anomalously commanded by a prefect, which is required by *AE* 1963. 52. It was at Housesteads in the third century, location uncertain between c. 158 and 198, perhaps already at Housesteads. Summary of evidence in Breeze & Dobson 251f.; Holder 122f.—Geta: *IRT* 541; App. 2 no. 21—men from II Aug. at Corbridge: *RIB* 1127, 1136, 1155–8.

6 Pompeianus: *PIR²* C 973—altar: *ILS* 407—Avitus: *CP* no. 188+add.

7 'retire': E. Birley 1953, 145—'fourth *militia*': E. Birley 1966, 55ff.—*alimenta*: *CP* no. 179—fleet: *HA Pert.* 2.2–3; *AE* 1963. 52—Dacia: ibid.; Alföldy 1987, 328f.

8 *HA Pert.* 2.4–2.11; Alföldy 1987, 329ff., who draws attention throughout his study to the close association, in the period c. 158–79, between the careers of Pertinax and Valerius Maximianus, the other military phenomenon of these wars.—'clearing the invaders': Birley 1987, 168f.—'Miracle': id. 171–4—consulship: Alföldy 1977, 189—Euripides, *Supp.* 119, quoted by Dio

71.22.1—'praised': *HA Pert.* 2.10—Cassius: Birley 1987, 184ff.—governorships: Alföldy 1987, 335ff. He was still in Dacia on 1 April 179, as shown by *RMD* 123.

9 Retirement: not explicitly stated in *HA Pert.* 3.1–2, but implied by 3.3 ('ordered at once to withdraw from Rome to his father's villa in Liguria').

8 Julia Domna (pages 68–80; for Bibliography see p. 263)
1 legions: *RE* 12 (1925) 1525f.; 1560f.; 1765f. (E. Ritterling; 1560 on prestige of IV Scythica)—'uncle': App. 2 no. 25—'Massilia': *HA Sev.* 3.6, emended by Thomsen, who locates 'Massyas' in the modern Masyaf. But this is too far south, too close to Raphaneae. 'Massias' or 'Marsyas', *vel sim.* is common in Syria, *RE* 14 (1930) 1985f., 2165f. For the western tributary of the Euphrates: Pliny, *NH* 5.86.
2 'Antioch': *HA Sev.* 9.4, cf. Herodian 2.10.2—Olympics: Downey 230ff.—Verus: Fronto, *Princ. Hist.* 17; *HA Verus* 4.6, 6.1, etc.—population: Downey 582f.
3 Edessa: Drijvers 863ff.—'form of Aramaic', i.e. Syriac. Millar 1987, 144, 159ff. is instructive.
4 Palmyra: Matthews provides a stimulating introduction; Drijvers 846ff.; Teixidor; Millar 1987, 155ff.—Emesa: Chad's monograph is the only one on the subject, worth consulting if antiquated and over-speculative in places; Millar 1983, esp. 58f.; 1987, esp. 157ff.—Samsigeramus I: *RE* 1A.2 (1920) 2227—Iamblichus I: Cicero, *Ad fam.* 15.1; Josephus, *AJ* 14.129; *BJ* 1.188; Strabo 16. 753; Dio 50.13.7—Iamblichus II: *PIR²* I 7—Samsigeramus II: *PIR²* J 541—Iotape: I 47—Aziz: A 1693—In general, Sullivan 198ff.
5 Mamaea and Polemo: App. 2, nos. 40, 60.
6 'absorbed into Syria': Chad 103ff. argues that Emesa remained independent until the reign of Pius—Agrippa II's kingdom: Sullivan 329–45—names: *IGLS* 2212, 2217, 2385; 2362, 2366, 2216; 2339; 2565, etc.—Sohaemus: App. 2 no. 48—Iamblichus the novelist: Millar 1987, 150.
7 Chad 24ff. evokes the setting—Millar 1983, on the Phoenician cities.
8 Millar 1983, on the Phoenician cities; 1987, 157f. on the god; Herodian 5.3.2–7; *AE* 1962. 229, set up at Augusta Vindelicorum by no. 45 in App. 2—The novelist: Heliodorus, *Aethiopica* 10.41.4, perhaps the Arab sophist of that name, Millar 1987, 149 n.16.
9 Coins: Wroth 237ff.—Bassianus: App. 2 no. 46. Herodian 5.3.2–7—names: App. 2 nos. 38–9—horoscope: *HA Sev. Alex.* 5.4; *Sev.* 3.6; *Get.* 3.1, discussed App. 2 no. 38.
10 Sohaemus: App. 2 no. 48—Agrippa: no. 43—Emesenes in army: e.g. *CIL* III 7500 (V Macedonica), III 3301, 3334–10316 (II Adiutrix), VIII 2568,36 (III Aug.) and the *cohortes Emesenorum*, and note the *primipilares* from the region cited in App. 2 no. 43—'plebeian': Dio 78,24.1.
11 Oracle: Dio 78.8.6 (*Iliad* 2.478f.)
12 *HA Pert.* 3.1–3; Grosso 145, 162f.—Juncus, Rufus: *HA Comm.* 4.10, with the observations of Bowersock 1982, 662 (and 666 on their origins).
13 Dexter: *PIR²* D144—Cilo: F27—Athens: *HA Sev.* 3.7, Birley 1970, 72—Pontianus: p. 26 above—Hadrianus and others: Philostratus, *v. soph.* 2.1, 10, 11, 12, 24.

14 'four emperors': Birley 1987, 23, 126, 194—Apollonius: Philostratus, *v. soph.* 2.19.

15 Grosso 164ff.; Birley 1981, 140ff. (Marcellus); 260f. (Priscus), on Dio 72.8.2–6, 9.2a—'legates dismissed': *HA Comm.* 6.2.

16 'hostility . . . Danube': *HA Comm.* 5.1–6.2—Herodian 1.9.2–5 has a romantic yarn about a Cynic philosopher denouncing Perennis at the Games, probably complete fiction, Hohl 16f.—'army of Danube': this army had indeed won the final round in the civil wars of 69; subsequently it had grown in size.

17 Herodian 1.9.7; Dio 72.9.2–3; *HA Comm.* 6.2—Cleander: Dio 72.9.3.

18 Marcellus: Dio 72.8.6—Cleander: *CP* no. 180 bis + *mantissa add.* (p. 1007f.); Alföldy 1988.—Victorinus: Dio 72.11.1–4—Pertinax: *HA Pert.* 3.5–6, 8–9; Dio 72.9.2, 73.4.1; Birley 1981, 145—Lugdunensis: *HA Sev.* 3.8.

19 Urban Cohort: *RE* Supp. 10 (1962) 1129f.—Maternus: only in Herodian, regarded as a fictional creation by Hohl 17ff.; Alföldy 1971, esp. 373f. is more judicious—The war gets a passing mention in *HA Comm.* 16.2, further in *Niger* 3.3–5, regarded as bogus by Alföldy 1971, 369f., more favourably by Barnes, 51.

20 *HA Sev.* 3.9. App. 2 nos. 56, 38–9, 45–6. Trade; cf. e.g. Jones.

21 Dio 74.3.1, 2.3; *HA Sev.* 3.5.

22 languages: useful indications in Millar 1983; 1987—Bassianus: App. 2 no. 18; *HA Sev.* 3.9; Dio 77.6.1.

23 Gentianus, Avitus: Alföldy 1982, 325f.—Cilo: *PIR²* F 27—Niger: n.19 above—Pertinax may well have passed through Lugdunum on his way back from Britain to Rome in 187, while S. was there.

24 Sicily: *HA Sev.* 4.2; Birley 1970, 73—Geta: *IRT* 541, App. 2 no. 21.

25 Pertinax: *HA Pert.* 3.5–10; Comm. 6.10–12; 8.4; Dio 72.9.2; 73.4.1; Birley 1981, 145; Alföldy 1988.

26 Aebutianus: *HA Comm.* 6.11.12; Grosso 239ff.—Antoninus: n. 28 below—Pertinax: *HA Pert.* 3.10–11.

27 Horse: Dio 73.4.1–2 (it reappeared later, p. 87 above)—Burrus: *HA Comm.* 6.11–12; Alföldy 1988—Cleander: *CP* no. 180 bis (p. 1007f. on *AE* 1961. 280); Alföldy 1988.

28 Africa: *HA Pert.* 4.2, cf. Did. 2.3; Dio 73.15.4 (he convicted Plautianus of serious offences, App. 2 no. 32).—Asia: Tertullian, *Scap.* 5.1—Attalus; *HA Comm.* 7.1; Alföldy 1988—Thomasson 1984, 232; 384 summarises evidence for the two proconsuls.

29 consuls: Dio 72.12.4; *HA Sev.* 4.4; Birley 1970, 74—Septimianus: App. 2 no. 59—Cleander: Alföldy 1988, passim, showing the unreliability of Herodian's version, 1.9.2–5. Dio 72.13 must be preferred.

30 Dio 72.13; Alföldy 1988.

31 Julianus, Dionysius: *CP* nos. 180–1—Regillus; *HA Comm.* 7.4.

32 Date: Alföldy 1988. Sicily: *HA Sev.* 4.3; Birley 1970, 73.

33 'sole Prefect': *CIL* XIV 4378—Motilenus: *HA Comm.* 9.2—Rufinus, 'without employment': *HA Sev.* 4.4.

9 The Conspirators (pages 81–88; for Bibliography see pp. 264–6)

1 Grosso 1964, 321; *HA Comm.* 11. 2–3; 7.4; Dio 72.14.1.

2 Dio 72.14.1–3; *HA Comm.* 8.3—Julius Alexander: App. 2 no. 44 (where the

theory that the lion-killing was part of a serious bid for power is discussed).

3 'purge': *HA Comm.* 7.5–8; Grosso 1964, 357ff.—'plague': Dio 72.14.3–4; Millar 1964, 131 (Grosso 250ff. prefers Herodian's implied date, AD 188–9).

4 Coins: *BMC* IV, pp. clxvi, clxxvii, clxxxi–ii; Grosso 1964, 331ff. (on the cults).—debasement: Walker 51, 126f. provides important data and draws instructive conclusions. The imminent financial ruin (cf. p. 91 above on the almost empty treasury) could only be averted by drastic means. Pertinax and others were no doubt strongly influenced by these considerations.

5 Laetus: *AE* 1949.38 revealed the *origo*; Birley 1969, 252f.; Jarrett 154—Eclectus: *PIR²* E 3—Marcia: M 261.

6 Victor: Eusebius, *HE* 5.22.1 (tenth year of Commodus), in office ten years, 5.28.7; African according to the *Liber Pontificalis* 1. 137f. (Duchesne)—'planned a visit': *HA Comm.* 9.1—'two thirds': Josephus, *BJ* 2.383, 386, a much discussed passage, e.g. Rickman 231ff.

7 Pudens: *AE* 1949. 38; Birley 1969, 252f. He seems out of place in Halfmann's list of *comites*, 1986, 250 no. 64, cf. 98. 'in comitatu' means something different—Pannonia: *HA Sev.* 4.4; Birley 1969, 261—On the province, and specialisation, Birley 1981a, 29ff.

8 *HA Sev.* 4.5; p. 220 above.

9 Birley 1969, 252ff.—Marii: App. 1.A.4.

10 legionary legates: Birley 1981a, 18ff.—patronage: E. Birley 1953, 141ff.—army of Pannonia: see e.g. the summary table (based on calculations by P. A. Holder, to whom I am indebted) in Birley 1981b, 40f., showing the numbers of units, auxiliary and legionary, in each province c. AD 150—Castinus: App. 2 no. 19.

11 *HA Pert.* 4.3–4; Birley 1969, 250ff.

12 Egypt: Thomasson 1984, 353—Sabinus: Birley 1969, 268f.—Vologaeses III: *RE* Supp. 9 (1962) 1851—Niger: Dio 74.6.1; *HA Pesc. Nig.* 1.5. Dio says that Niger and Albinus had performed well in a Dacian war (72.8.1). Piso argues that he was consular governor of III Daciae, 369 and n.35. In that case he was much senior to Albinus and Septimius. He cites *CIL* III 1066, on which he reads part of a deleted *cognomen* as GE. Barnes 1978, 51 accepts the story about Niger owing to his job to the athlete Narcissus in *HA Nig.* 1.5, cf. *Comm.* 17.2. *Sev.* 14.1 Aemilianus: Dio 74.6.1f. (noting his kinship with Albinus, often neglected); Herodian 3.2.3 (Niger's predecessor in Syria, where he is attested apparently in 184–5 or 185–6; Thomasson 1984, 314, who doubts the date on *IGR* III 1262; but he could easily be the predecessor of Julius Saturninus, id. 313f., in which case Herodian, as often, is imprecise: Aemilianus would then not be Niger's *immediate* predecessor as Herodian says)—Anullinus: Thomasson 1984, 385; 1985, 113; cf. p. 49 above.

13 Dio 72.15. 1ff.; *HA Comm.* 8.5–9; 11.8–12.9; Grosso 1964, 360ff.; 365ff.; 369ff.; Nesselhauf 1966.

14 Maximus: *PIR²* M 308. He was legate of I Italica under Geta. Note the freedman (surely his) L. Marius Doryphorus, of this period, scribe of the aediles and tribunes (*ILS* 1899), an obvious source of information—fire: Dio 72. 24. 1–3; Galen 2.216K; 13. 362K; Herodian 1.14.1–6; Grosso 1964, 361ff.

15 Herodian 1.15.1–6; Dio 72.20.1; 72.18.1–4—'plebeian games': Birley 1969, 248 n.5. Kolb 25–37 argues that Herodian is not an independent witness but

has distorted and garbled Dio. Alas, Kolb is probably right, but without Dio's original text certainty is beyond our reach.

16 Dio 72.19.1–21.2; Herodian 1.15.1; Dio 73.4.3–4 (horse and club); 72.22.1–6 (murder); *HA Comm.* 16.3 (Vectilian House). Kolb 38–47 argues convincingly that Herodian has made up the extra details in his version, raiding Dio's story of Domitian's murder (67.15.3–4).

17 Herodian 1.16–17; Birley 1969, 249f. Contrast *HA Pert.* 4.4.

18 Marcia: *HA Comm.* 8.6—'urgent insistence': Dio 72.22.3; Birley 1969, 248ff.

19 'dark': Hohl 4.—'sent word': Dio 73.1.1; *HA Pert.* 4.5 (omitting the first stage)—'in secret . . . troops' fears': Dio 73.1.2—'thrust . . . power': HA Pert. 4.6–7—'donative: . . threat': Dio 73.1.2–3. Walker acutely interprets the 'disturbing features' as a veiled reference to the imminent financial catastrophe, 127ff. 'mediocre . . . smooth': *HA Pert.* 12.1—'response . . . rest followed': *Pert.* 4.7, cf. Dio 73.1.2. 'not yet midnight': this is clear from *Pert.* 4.8, giving the *dies imperii* as 31 December ('pr. kal. Ian'.), presumably overlooked by Herz 35 and others. The Kalends began at midnight: Plutarch, *Quaest. Rom.* 84. Hohl has shown that Herodian 2.1.1–2.10 is grossly inaccurate and is better discounted for these transactions.

10 the Year 193 (page 89–107; for Bibliography see pp. 264–6)

1 'mist': *HA Comm.* 16.2—dark . . . fate of Commodus . . . Pompeianus': *HA Pert.* 4.9–10. Dio 73.1.4 also says that it was still dark—'not seen at Rome': Dio 73.3.2. In what survives of his work, Dio says not that Pompeianus was at Rome before dawn on 1 January or that Pertinax offered him the throne; but that he had been absent on his Tarracina estate with the excuse of bad health and failing sight; under Pertinax both improved; then they worsened and he withdrew again (back at Tarracina under Didius: *HA Did. Jul.* 8.3). Kolb 47–54 disbelieves the story of the offer in the Temple of Concord; but seems to me to miss the point; see my review, *JRS* 64 (1974) 267. He also rejects the Herodian version, 2.3.3–4, that it was Glabrio who was offered the throne. This is taken seriously by Champlin, who argues hard that Glabrio's mother was from the Antonine dynasty, 288ff.; this is doubtful, but Champlin's general thesis (referred to in later parts of this chapter) that the pull of the Antonine dynasty was important, deserves serious attention. Glabrio (*cos. II* 186) is mentioned by Dio 73.3.3, being given a seat in the senate next to Pompeianus and Pertinax. Herodian has invented the rest, as Hohl 12, followed by Kolb argues.

2 'curia . . . speeches in his honour': *HA Pert.* 4.11–5.1; Dio 73.1.4–2.1—health: *HA Pert.* 12.1; Dio 73.1.5—Marius Maximus quoted a lengthy letter of Pertinax attesting his 'horror imperii': *HA Pert.* 15.8—'savage litany': *HA Comm.* 18–19 contains a full text; Nesselhauf 1966—Larensis and Cilo: ibid. 20.1–2—Larensis: *CP* no. 194; he is the host in Athenaeus' *Deipnosophistae*—Cilo; *PIR*² F 27,

3 'outcry': *HA Comm.* 20.2–5, cf. Dio 73.2.1–3—'thanks' . . an opportunity': *HA Pert.* 5.1–3; Birley 1969, 250f.; Hohl 7f.

4 Dio 73.5.1; *HA Pert.* 5.4–6.2, cf. 6.9.

5 *HA Pert.* 6.3–5—Maternus: Alföldy 1969, 87f.; Champlin 297ff.

6 'concessions': *HA Pert.* 6.6—'7 January': Herz 124f.—'proposals': *HA Pert.* 6.7–8; Dio 73.5.2–3; *HA Pert.* 7.3–9.10; Dio 73.5.4–5. The precedent was Marcus' auction in 169; *HA Marcus* 17.4–5—'old man's pleasure', reading 'senem' as in the MSS of *HA Pert.* 7.9 (emended to 'Severum' by editors, but Pertinax was no paragon and the *HA vita* is quite hostile in places).

7 'coinage': Walker 51 ('the denarius returns to a purity it had not known for fifty years'); 127ff.—Herodian 2. 5–7.—'regulate the senate': *HA Pert.* 6.10— Maximus: PIR^2 M 308 (he had omitted the praetorship by adlection; Dio 73.12.2).

8 'trick': Dio 73.2.5–6—AD 69: Tacitus, *Hist.* 1.12ff.—Icelus: Suetonius, *Galba* 22.—Rufus: Alföldy 1969, 42f.—Egypt: *Loeb Select Papyri* no. 222; on the chronology, Martin—Titiana: PIR^2 F 444—younger Pertinax: H 74. Titiana is also 'Augusta' on the Alexandrian coins; otherwise only on a milestone in Gaul. Likewise with the son (also on three Arabian milestones)—Birley 1969, 269f. 'children': Herodian. 2.3–4 (Asellius Aemilianus was a victim, p. 102 above).

9 'dream': Herodian 3.9.5–6, fuller than Dio 73.3.3; Bloch; Rubin 23f.—'21 April': *HA Pert.* 12.8; Birley 1969, 251—Sulpicianus; Birley 1969, 266— Plautianus: Dio 73.15.4, cf. Herodian 3.10.6; App. 2 no. 32.

10 Dio 73.6.1–3.

11 Dio 73.8.1–5—Alexianus: App. 2 no. 45.

12 Falco: *HA Pert.* 10. 1–7 (not mentioning Ostia); Dio 73.8.1–5. Falco was married to a grand-niece of Avidius Cassius: PIR^2 C, p. 166 (stemma). Champlin 300ff. offers interesting suggestions on possible links between Falco and the house of Antonines—Walker 128f. stresses Dio's tribute to Pertinax's *oikonomia beltiste*, 73.5.2. He had hoped to cancel 'ea ... quae Commodus exigerat' (*HA Pert.* 6–7) and was attacked, for reneging on the promise, by Lollianus Gentianus, his old patron's son—On his meanness: *HA Pert.* 9. 4ff.

13 *HA Pert.* 10. 1–7; Birley 1969, 252 n.12; Champlin.

14 *HA Pert.* 10.8–11.13; Dio 73.9.1–10. Herodian is inadequate, Hohl 17ff.

15 Birley 1969, 273. It was later asserted that Albinus was the guiding spirit, p. 118 above. Presumably propaganda from 195–7, superficially plausible because Albinus came from Hadrumetum, home of Didius Julianus' mother (p. 41, above).

16 Hohl 19ff. is the best study—Repentinus: Corbier 730 (he turns out to be African, from Simitthu). Kolb 54–70 seeks to prove the dependence of *HA Didius Julianus* on Dio; Barnes 1978, 43ff. summarises the factual content of *HA Did. Jul.* (high).

17 Dio 73. 11. 2ff. (very hostile to Didius); *HA Did. Jul.* 2.6–7 (restrained); Herodian 2.6.8–14 adds a good deal of detail. All subject to a complex analysis by Kolb 54ff.

18 Hohl 23ff.—Didius' career: *HA Did. Jul.* 1.1–2.3 combines with *ILS* 412 to make the stages quite clear. On the origin and family, Corbier 720; Alföldy 1982, 354—'betrothal': this may be bogus (*HA Pert.* 14.4–5; Did. Jul. 2.3), since only one daughter, Didia Clara, wife of Cornelius Repentinus (p. 95 above) is otherwise known—'Add "Severus"': *HA Did. Jul.* 7.1–2.

19 'no fears': *HA Did. Jul.* 5.1—Hadrumetum: Birley 1981a, 147, against Barnes

1970, 51ff.—'29 March': Dio 73.13.2–5. He sent an assassin against Niger: *HA Did. Jul.* 5.1—Chronology: Martin 92ff. (earliest attestation in Egypt of Niger as emperor is 30 May.

20 donative: *HA Did. Jul.* 3.2.

21 Domaszewski argued that S. was Laetus' candidate all along, a theory that is implausible—'683 miles': Hasebroek 18; thirty-four days march at normal rates—'south-western borders': *Epit. de Caes.* 19.2 in fact has 'Savaria' as the place of his proclamation, regarded as plausible by Šašel-Kos 364f. (Victor, *De Caes.* 19.4, Zonaras 12.7 and *HA Did. Jul.* 5.2 put him in 'Syria', usually taken as confusion between S. and Niger, but perhaps misled by 'Savaria' in a source)—Plautianus, Octavilla, Alexianus: App. 2 nos. 32, 8, 45.—Cilo: *PIR*² F 27—Pudens: Thomasson 1984, 115; Birley 1981a, 155ff.—Geta: App 2 no. 21—other provinces: Birley 1969, 265ff.—*dies imperii:* Herz 36, 178f., supplied by the *Feriale Duranum*—*repugnans: HA Sev.* 5.1—'avenger': ibid. 5.5, cf. Herodian 2.10.1–9, etc.—'children': Herodian 3.2.4.

22 Albinus' origin: Birley 1981, 147; his kinship with Niger's supporter Aemilianus (Dio 74.6.2) gave S. reason to be nervous of his response—'emissaries': Dio 73.15.1–2 shows they went before S. reached Rome, indeed suggests that it was before he left Pannonia. Cf. Herodian 2.15.1–5; *HA Sev.* 6.9–10; *Nig.* 4.7; *Alb.* 3.2–6. *Alb.* 10.3 seems to be clear and straightforward. Rubin 138ff. subjects it and *Nig.* 4.7 to an exhaustive analysis, concluding that they derive from Marius Maximus, who endorsed S.'s claims happily slandered Niger, but was favourable to Albinus (151f.). I am not sure that I can grasp his argument—*HA Sev.* 6.10 names an emissary: Heraclitus.

23 Niger: Martin 92ff.—Rufus: Alföldy 1969, 42f.—Quadratianus: Thomasson 1984, 401f.; perhaps from African Mastar, Alföldy 1968, 418—'Thrace': Dio 73.15.2; Herodian 2.14.6; *HA Sev.* 8.12, no doubt commanded by Marius Maximus (*PIR*² M 308), although conceivably Fabius Cilo was already with the armies (F 27).

24 Vitulus: *CP* no. 224. He was later a resident of Bulla Regia, but his tribe 'Pupinia' shows that he is Italian; probably from Tergeste, which is in this tribe, Kubitschek 271, and living at home—Valerianus: Speidel 1985 seems to me to have improved on all the numerous interpretations of *AE* 1966. 495—Laetus: *PIR*² J 373 + L 69.

25 'coins': *BMC* V 11f.; 14ff.—'public enemy ... amnesty': Dio 73.16.1; *HA Sev.* 5.5, etc.—Catullinus, Candidus: *HA Did. Jul.* 5.6–7, cf. Alföldy 1968, 152f.—Felix: *HA Did. Jul.* 5.8, etc.; *CP* no. 225.

26 'borders of Italy': Herodian 2.11.3—Ravenna, Crispinus: *HA Did. Jul.* 6.3–4; Dio 73.17.1—'elephants' etc.: ibid. 5.9; Dio 73.16.1–3—Laetus, Marcia: *HA Did. Jul.* 6.2; Dio 73.16.5—Candidus: Dio 73.17.1—Felix: *CP* no. 225. 'panic ... programme': *HA Sev.* 5.6–9; *Did. Jul.* 6.3; 6.5–8.2; Dio 73.17.1–3—Macrinus, Juvenalis: *CP* no. 179 bis; *PIR*² F 300—*HA Did. Jul.* 7.9–11 reports that Didius resorted to magic, including the hypnotising of a young boy (the practice of which Apuleius had been accused at Sabratha twenty-five years before, p. 31 above); Dio 73.16.5 soups this up and alleges human sacrifice, reproducing propaganda, Rubin 56f. argues—Plautius Quintillus: Birley 1987, 182, husband of Fadilla, also the nephew of L. Verus. Barnes 1978, 52, otherwise generally sceptical (e.g. of Albinus' Hadrumetine origin) surpris-

ingly suggests that *HA Clod. Alb.* 10.7, which, in a bogus letter, calls Albinus son-in-law of 'Plautillus', may be evidence for this man. Such a father-in-law for Albinus would be remarkable indeed.

27 *HA Did. Jul.* 8.2–8; *Sev.* 5.9–10; Dio 73.17.3–5. The date is supplied by 73.17. 5—Interamna: *HA Sev.* 6.2 (note that Fabius Cilo was curator of this town: *PIR²* F 27. Conceivably for a short period that spring?)—Herodian 2.11. 1ff. gives a breathless description of S.'s march; Dio 73.15.3 has the vivid detail— 'messengers ... children': *HA Sev.* 6.7–8.10—Aemilianus: Herodian 3.2.3; Birley 1969, 270.

28 Interamna: *HA Sev.* 6.1–4. Hasebroek 38 has an elaborate theory on the money present: it may represent the equivalent of 25,000 denarii, nominally worth 1,000 aurei; but denarii of very different fineness were now in circulation: Walker 51—Juvenalis: *HA Sev.* 6.5; *PIR²* F 300—Macrinus: *CP* no. 179 bis.

29 Juvenalis: *HA Sev.* 6.5; *PIR²* F 300—Macrinus: *CP* no. 179 bis.

30 This famous scene has been much discussed. *HA Sev.* 6.11 is very brief; Dio 74.1.1–2; Herodian 2.13.1–12 provide details—'secret instructions': Cn. Marcius Rustius Rufinus (*CP* no. 234 + add.) was probably one of the co-operative officers, probably then a tribune of the Guard, ultimately prefect of the *vigiles* and perhaps Guard Prefect—'increases', etc.: E. Birley 1969, 64f.

31 'panic': Herodian 2.12.1–2—Dio 74.1.3–5—Tertullian, *Apol.* 35.4—*Sev.* 7.1–3. Cf. Herodian 2.14.1–2, emphasising the bloodless nature of the capture of Rome—Hasebroek 40 proposed 9 June as the day of entry, Herz 222 is cautious. It could have been a few days earlier.

32 'following day': Herodian 2.14.3–4; *HA Sev.* 7.4; 5.8—decree: ibid. 7.5; Dio 74.2.1–2—disturbance: *HA Sev.* 7.5–7; Dio 46.46.7; Watson 113, 198 suggests that some of the men had been reading Appian, *BC* 3.94 on the donative of 43 BC. Why not?—'special issue': *BMC* V lxxxiif., xcvii, 21ff., 118.

33 Dio 74.4.1–5.5; cf. *HA Pert.* 15.1–5; *Sev.* 7.8–9.

34 'claimed': Herodian 2.3; Birley 1969, 273—'refused': *HA Sev.* 8.6.—Cilo: *PIR²* F 27—Maximus: *PIR²* M 308.

35 'mint': *BMC* V 20ff., 117ff. Walker 59 calculates the fineness of the silver as below the restored level of Pertinax's coinage but better than that of Commodus. It did not last—*saeculum*: *BMC* V 2; 20; 119; 38; 134ff.—Venus; ibid. 27f. Julia of course became Augusta, perhaps from 1 June: *PIR²* J 663; Kettenhofen 78f.

36 'consulship': explicit only in *HA Alb.* 6.8 (garbled)—'little time': *HA Sev.* 8.1–2 on his alleged daughters and their husbands is rejected by Hasebroek 54, rightly. 7.9; 8.3, that he paid off his friends' debts and executed Julianus' friends, may be authentic. But 8.4–5 (especially on the 'res frumentaria') looks suspect. '27 June': *CJ* 3.28.1—Dexter: *PIR²* D 144— Bassus is named in *HA Sev.* 8.8 and is perhaps the friend enriched by S., mentioned with Anullinus, Cilo and Lateranus in *Epit. de Caes.* 20.6.

37 Felix: *CP* no. 228—Claudianus: Alföldy 1968, 139; Fitz 1983—Gallus: Alföldy 1968, 139—Alexianus: App. 2 no. 45—Plautianus: App. 2 no. 32.

38 'new legions': E. Birley 1969, 67f.—'in the east': *HA Sev.* 8.6—'children': Herodian 3.2.5; *HA Sev.* 8.12.—Africa: ibid. 8.7—Sabinus: see p. 84 above.

39 'great departments': he may have already chosen Aelius Antipater as *ab epistulis Graecis* (*PIR²* A 137)—Galen: 14. 64–6K;217K.

11 The War against Niger (pages 108–120; for Bibliography see pp. 264–6)

1 Saxa Rubra: *HA Sev.* 8.10—Vitulus: *CP* no. 224.
2 Perinthus, Byzantium: Dio 74.6.3; *HA Sev.* 8.12–13; Herodian 3.1.5–2.1—Cilo: *PIR²* F 27—coins: *BMC* V 73f.—Alexander: Dio 74.6.2a—'public enemies': *HA Sev.* 8.13—Aemilianus: Birley 1969, 270f. See Rubin 60ff.; 103ff.; 215ff.; Alföldy 1976.
3 Carnuntum: Dio 74.8.1–2; Rubin 68.
4 Candidus: the career is given by *ILS* 1140; Alföldy 1968, 139; 1969, 43ff.
5 Geta: *HA Sev.* 8.10; Thomasson 1984, 155f.; 138. Auspex: there is a famous problem about the elder and younger Auspex (*ILS* 8841 and other evidence). For this interpretation, Birley 1981a, 151ff., esp. 154 n.22—Maximus: *PIR²* M 208.
6 Byzantium: Dio 74.6.3; cf. Herodian 3.2.1—Aemilianus: Herodian 3.2.2ff.; Dio 74.6.1—Perinthus: Dio 74.6.3; Halfmann 1986, 219—children: *HA Sev.* 8.14–15.
7 Cyzicus: *HA Sev.* 8.16 (confused, cf. n.13 below); Dio 76.6.4; Herodian 3.2.1–9. Cilo was curator of Nicomedia (*PIR²* F 27), perhaps briefly at this very time—rivalry: Robert—Niger at Nicaea: Dio 74.6.6; Herodian 73.2.10.
8 'detailed account': Dio 74.6. 4–6—Rome: *CIL* XVI 134 has '*imp. III*'; cf. *BMC* V lxxxvii, etc.—Egypt: Martin 93ff.
9 Cilo: *PIR²* F 27—Candidus: *ILS* 1140; Alföldy 1969, 43ff.—Xenophon: *CP* no. 222—'no executions': *HA Sev.* 9.3 (9.6 refers to the aftermath of Issus).
10 '*imp II, III*': Rubin 202f.—*pater patriae*: *BMC* V lxxxviiff., xcviiff.—*saeculum frugiferum*: ibid. lxxxixf.; Birley 1981a, 147.
11 Anullinus: p. 49 above; Alföldy 1969, 122f. Dio 74.7.1–8 names him as commander at Issus.
12 Prusias: Halfmann 1986, 216; 219—Niger: Herodian 3.2.10–3.3.2—Arabia: Šašel 1982 568—VI Ferrata became 'constans': *RE* 12 (1925) 1593—Laodicea, Tyre: Herodian 3.3.3–5; Ziegler—Emesa: the coins are very dubious; Rubin 202ff., Walker 60.
13 'passes': Herodian 3.3.1–2; 3.3.6–8—Issus: Dio 74.7.1–8; Herodian 3.4.1–5. Rubin 66ff.; 101ff.; 104ff.; 117ff.; 224f.—Valerianus: the man named by Dio is surely the L. Valerius Valerianus of the much discussed *AE* 1966.495. Speidel 1985 seems to have produced the best interpretation of this inscription so far. *HA Sev.* 9.1 repeats the error in Victor, *De Caes.* 20.8; Eutropius 8.18.4, that Niger was killed at Cyzicus. Presumably an error in the 'Kaisergeschichte'—Date of Issus: Herz 36f. 421 favours 31 March; Rubin 202 'spring'; Walker 70 n.6 argues for the second half of 194.
14 Niger: *RE* 19 (1937) 1086ff.; Alföldy 1968, 149—Parthia: *RE* Supp. 9 (1962) 1851—coins: *BMC* V cvii ff. (too inclined to believe *HA Nig.*). See further Rubin 92ff.
15 21 May: Herz 92; 210; 501; cf. 440 n.8—coinage: Walker 59; 60ff.; 129f.
16 '*imp. IV*': n.14 above—Clemens: Dio 74.9.1–4—Athenagoras: *Digest* 22.1.6; Halfmann 1982, 633 for persons of this name in Caria (not citing the *Digest*).

17 Rufus: Alföldy 1968, 153; Birley 1969, 276f.—Fuscus: *PIR*² M 137—'rewards and punishments': Dio 74.8.4–5; see now esp. Ziegler—Syria divided: only in Dio 55.23.2 (list of legions in his own day by province), not in surviving excerpts of book 74; perhaps vaguely alluded to by Herodian 3.5.1. Fuscus is shown as legate of Phoenice in 194 by *AE* 1930. 141.

18 'Niger's troops . . . Nisibis': Dio 75.1. 1ff. Herodian is ignorant of this war— glory: Dio 75.1.1; cf. 75.3.2—Osrhoene: Wagner, publishing new inscriptions showing Pacatianus, previously known as governor from his career inscrip- tion (*ILS* 1353; *CP* no. 229 + add.; *PIR*² J 444), governor in 195 and Abgar still having a (reduced) kingdom round Edessa—Abgar at Rome: mentioned by Dio 79.1.2, a comparison with something completely different—Aramaic, etc.: p. 69 above.

19 '*mater castrorum*': Herz 37; Kettenhofen 80f.—Faustina: Birley 1987, 178; 191; 254; Dio 72.10.5. 'titles': *HA Sev.* 9.9–11; *BMC* V 33, 35 (no. 86)—other salutations: Rubin 205ff.—triumph, arch: *HA* 9.10–11 (cf. p. 155 above)— 'desert conditions': Dio 75.2.1–3; Rubin 68ff. sees propaganda behind this story, unnecessarily in my view—Lucan 9.607ff—Nisibis: Dio 75.2.3.

20 'five generals': Dio 75.2.3; 3.2—Candidus: *ILS* 1140—Lateranus: *PIR*¹ S 469 (cf. 463–5; 468; 471–2)—Laetus: *PIR*² L 69—Gentianus: Alföldy 1982, 324–6; Thomasson 1985, 120ff.—Anullinus: Alföldy 1969, 122f.—Probus: the name is very common (Kajanto 253 knows 200 cases, including nine senators) 'one sentence': *HA* 9.10 ('deinde circa Arabiam plura gessit', etc.).—'Syriac source': *RE* Supp. 9 (1962) 1851.

21 'son of M. Aurelius': *BMC* V p. 136 (with *Imp. V*)—'rainstorm': Rubin 66ff.—'northern weather-miracle': id. 72ff. on Dio 74.3.1—Marcan miracles: Birley 1987, 171ff.—Aurelian column: id. 267—Goths: Speidel 1977, 712f.

22 Nisibis: Dio 75.3.2—Valerianus: Speidel 1985.

23 Albinus: Herodian 3.5.1–8; *HA Alb.* 7.2–8.3—murder of Pertinax: Birley 1969, 266 on Eutropius 8.18.4; Victor, *De Caes.* 20.9; *HA Alb.* 1.1; 14. 2 and 6.

24 Herodian 3.5.3—Dio 75.4.1—'dedications': e.g. *CIL* VIII 9317—3 Sep- tember: *AE* 1941. 166—Candidus: *JRS* 64 (1974) 173f.

25 Dio 74.14.2.

26 Dio 74.10.1–14.6. He does not mention Maximus (*PIR*² M 308), perhaps deliberately: one suspects there was no love lost between historian and biographer. Tertullian, *Scap.* 3.4 tells how 'in illo exitu Byzantino' (which must mean its fall to Maximus' army) one Caecilius Capella shouted out: 'Christiani gaudete'.

27 '*imp. VIII*': *BMC* V 111ff.; 145ff.—Aezani: *IGR* IV 566 = *ILS* 8805. The date of Antoninus being made Caesar, much discussed, is now established by the Ulcisia Castra inscription published by Soproni; thus Halfmann 1986, 220.

28 'journey back': *HA Sev.* 10.1–3; Herodian 3.6.1–10 (most of this a speech by S., 1–7, placed before the fall of Byzantium; but Herodian is hopelessly ignorant and careless)—'Dio's reference'; 75.4.2–7; Alföldy 1968, 118 n.4; Rubin 79f. prefers a later date. I do not believe this is necessary.

29 Dio 75.4.6–7; Rubin 80ff. offers this acute interpretation.

12 The War against Albinus (pages 121–128; for Bibliography see pp. 264–6)

1 Herodian 3.6.8 places the declaration of Albinus as a *hostis*, by the army,

before the fall of Byzantium—'racing': id. 3.6.10—'unsuccessful attempt': chapter 11 n.23 above—Herodian 3.5.8 has Albinus beginning preparations 'as against a declared enemy' immediately after the failed murder attempt; but 3.7.1 puts his crossing to Gaul only after hearing of S.'s 'rapid approach'—Dio 75.4.1—S.'s claim: HA Alb. 10.3; cf. Nig. 4.7. Rubin 138ff. makes very heavy weather of this—'Augustus': PIR² C 1186.

2 Cilo: PIR² F 27—Alexianus: App. 2 no. 45—Plautianus: ibid. no. 32—Candidus (PIR² C 823): ILS 1140; Alföldy 1968, 139—Claudianus (PIR² C 834): ILS 1146; Alföldy 1968, 139—Dexter: PIR² D 144—Anullinus: PIR² C 1322.

3 Perinthus: Halfmann 1986, 217; RE 2A (1923) 1962—Barbarus: Birley 1969, 277; Thomasson 1984, 169—Auspex: Dio 76.9.4; Birley 1981a, 151ff., esp. 154 n.22.

4 HA Sev. 10.3; cf. chapter 11 n.27—Geta: App 2 no. 21—Claudianus: PIR² C 834—Maximus: PIR² M 308—'conspiracy': ILS 3029, Poetovio.

5 Candidus: ILS 1140—Rufus: Alföldy 1969, 42f. I am unconvinced by Christol's suggested redating—Philippianus: ILS 1152; Alföldy 1968, 142—Lupus: Dio 75.62; Birley 1981a, 149ff.—Gallus: AE 1957.123; Alföldy 1968, 139—Pacatianus: ch. 11 n.18 above—Alpine passes: cf. also ILS 1368 (CP no. 226)—Vitulus: CP no. 224.

6 Numerianus: Dio 75.5.1. Pekáry 476f. places this in Galatia, unjustifiably. The story illustrates the point that recruiting for the legions was in full swing. Rubin 77f. has a forced interpretation of Numerianus (as a brigand).

7 Cilo: PIR² F 27—coins: BMV V 50ff.; 150ff.—issues: Pekáry 456f.

8 Albinus: BMC V civff.; Walker 59f.; 130 finds that Albinus' silver coinage was of superior fineness to that struck by S. from late 194 onwards.

9 Nerva: ILS 418—Code: CJ 9.1.1 (195; the speech of 13 June 195 will have been read out in S.'s absence, Digest 27.8.1).

10 Cilo: PIR² F 27—roads: Hasebroek 95—augurs: HA Sev. 10.7; cf. Alb. 9.1–4; Rubin 181ff.; Alföldy 1988, revising his study of 1960.

11 Dio 75.6.1, misunderstood by all modern scholars until the truth was demonstrated by Graham—British army: Birley 1981b, 40 offers a summary (for which I am indebted to P. A. Holder)—Sarmatians: Dio 71.16—Marcellus: id. 72.8.2–6; Birley 1981a, 140ff.; cf. Dio 75.5.4—VII Gemina; modest auxilia: Le Roux—Urban Cohort: RE Supp. 10 (1962) 1129f.

12 S.'s forces: for the auxilia, Birley 1981b, 40; legions, 41—'worsted': 75.6.2.

13 Tinurtium: HA Sev. 11.1–19 February: ibid. 11.7. Rubin 210 implausibly argues that Tinurtium and Lugdunum were a single battle. The distance is too great. It may be noted that a suggested redating of Lugdunum from 197 to 196, attributed to C. L. Clay and favoured by Barnes, Gnomon 47 (1975) 373, without giving evidence, seems too implausible to require discussion here—on the battle: Dio 75.6.1–8; Herodian 3.7.2–6; HA Sev. 11.2—Laetus: PIR² L 69.

14 'pursued': Herodian 3.7.6–7; Dio 75.7.1–8; HA Sev. 11.6–9—Rubin 210 (but cf. n.13 above for reservations about Tinurtium).

15 Candidus: ILS 1140—Rufus: HA Sev. 12.1; Alföldy 1968, 119ff.; 1970, 1ff.—VII Gemina: RE 12 (1925) 1642—'olive oil': Remesal 104f.—terra sigillata: E. Birley in Stanfield xli—Gentianus: Thomasson 1985, 120ff.; more plausible than Christol.

16 Xenophon: *CP* no. 222—other procurators: nos. 228; 239; 240—Albinus' allies: Alföldy 1968, 120.

17 Maximus: *PIR²* M 308—Pudens, Lupus: Birley 1981a, 155ff., 149ff.—'Lupus faced': Dio 75.5.4; Birley 1972; cf. p. 171 above.

18 envoys: *ILS* 1143—Gallus: *AE* 1957. 123; Alföldy 1968, 139—Laetus: *PIR²* L 69.

19 'correspondence': Herodian 3.8.6—'laurel branches': id. 3.8.3–4—'first speech': Dio 75.7.4–8.3; cf. Herodian 3.8.6—Commodus: *HA Sev.* 11.4,8, etc.—'openly praised': Dio 75.8.1–3; *HA Sev.* 12.7—executions: Dio 75.8.4; *HA Sev.* 12.9–13.9; Alföldy 1970 for a detailed analysis.

20 Dio 75.8.5—Solon: id. 74.2.2; *HA Sev.* 13.4; Alföldy 1969, 145; 1970, 4; 8; 10. Narcissus, who strangled Commodus, was also killed: *HA Sev.* 14.1.

21 '*res privata*': Nesselhauf 1964—Felix: *CP* no. 225—'sixty or more': Birley 1981b, 40—coinage: Walker 59ff.; 129ff.—pay: Watson 188; Develin—marriage: Campbell (on Herodian 3.8.4–5, the only explicit source for S.'s grants to the army at this time).

22 Grosso 1968, 14ff.

23 Antoninus: Mastino 29f.; Šašel 1983—'lavish games': Herodian 3.8.9—'departed': *HA Sev.* 14.11; Halfmann 1986, 217.

13 Parthia and Egypt (pages 129–145; for Bibliography see pp. 266–8)

1 'Aegeae': Hasebroek 111—'new legions': *RE* 12 (1925) 1435f.; 1476ff.; 1539f.—Anullinus, Cilo, Geta et al.: Alföldy 1968, esp. 156ff.

2 Julia and sons: *CIL* VI 225, 227, 738, 31322, etc., cited by Hasebroeek 111—Nisibis: Dio 75.9.1–3—Laetus: *PIR²* L 69—Euphrates: *HA Sev.* 16.1—king of Armenia: Herodian 3.9.2—*imp. x*: *BMC* V 59ff.—Rubin 1975, 231ff.; 1980, 210f. argues that *imp. x* was for the capture of Ctesiphon; an unnecessary hypothesis, even if there are difficulties over *imp. xi* and other matters of chronology, n.4 below.

3 Dio 75.9.1, though brief, is the fullest version; *HA Sev.* 16.1 (end of summer)—Verus, Cassius: Birley 1987, 129; 140ff.—'king's brother': Dio 75.9.3.—Ctesiphon: Dio 75.9.3–4; *HA Sev.* 16.2; Herodian 3.9.9–11 (peculiar: the campaign, in his version, was originally aimed at Hatra and the army got to Ctesiphon by mistake, swept downstream; but captured it anyway, 'more by good luck than by good judgement', ibid. 12).

4 28 January: Herz 37; 135, from the *Feriale Duranum*, following the interpretation of Guey 1948. Rubin 1975, 231ff.; 1980, 210f. doubts that Ctesiphon was taken so late because of apparent evidence that Antoninus was Augustus before the end of 197; not borne out by Mastino 87ff.; cf. also Šašel 1983 on 'imp. destinatus'. It is perfectly feasible to attach *imp ix* to Tinurtium and Lugdunum, *imp. x* to the opening phases of the war, *imp. xi* to the sack of Ctesiphon. Coins which show 'Parthicus Maximus' with *imp. x* need not present a problem—*HA Sev.* 16. 2–4 associates Ctesiphon with the elevation of S.'s sons—'plunder': Dio 75.9.4–5—Hatra: Drijvers 803ff.—Barsemius: named only in Herodian 3.1.3; 3.9.1 (as aiding Niger, hence to be punished).

5 Dio 75.10.1–3 (Virgil, *Aeneid* 11. 371–3)—Laetus: *PIR²* L 69—Plautianus: *HA Sev.* 15.4—Candidus: *ILS* 1140 = *RIT* 130—astrologers: *HA Sev.* 15.5.

6. Octavilla: App. 2 no. 8, cf. 17.

7 Mesopotamia: Kennedy 1979 on Subatianus Aquila (*AE* 1979. 625)—'bulwark': Dio 75.3.2.3—Osrhoene: Wagner—Senecio: Birley 1981, 157ff.—garrison: Speidel and Reynolds; Kennedy, *Antichthon*.

8 Hatra: the second siege is reported only by Dio 75.11.1–13.1. It has generated an extensive modern literature: Drijvers 803ff. on the city; Rubin 1975 on the propaganda aspects, particularly on the depiction of Hatra on the Arch in the Roman Forum; Speidel 1986 on the 'European' soldiers, with the reply by Kennedy 1986; Campbell.

9 Thus Rubin 1975, 424—*coh. IX Maurorum*: *AE* 1958. 239f.

10 'another excerptor': Dio ed. Boissevain III 150 (not in Loeb version)—Ulpian: he himself gives his origin in *Digest* 50.15.1 *pr.*—Papinian: *HA Carac.* 8.2 asserts the relationship 'per secundam uxorem'. See esp. Syme 1984, 1393ff. on their careers and the fiction surrounding them—Zeus Belos: Dio 78.8.6 (no date; the quotation is Euripides, *Phoenissae* 20)—family: App. 2 nos. 41; 50; 45; 36; 37.

11 Frontiers: survey in Kennedy 1987, 283–6. Of the now extensive literature I cite Bowersock 1983, 110ff.; Kennedy 1980; 1982, 69ff.; Speidel 1987 (on Dumata and Wadi Sirhan); Invernizzi; Kennedy and Northedge. On Palmyra: Mann.

12 Claudius the brigand: Dio 75.2.4—'privileges': *HA Sev.* 17.1, cf. 14.6—'banned conversion': endlessly discussed, but almost certainly spurious, thus, concisely, Barnes 1968, 40f.—'Jewish triumph': *HA Sev.* 16.7, accepted by Rubin 1980, 211f. (and associated with *imp. xi*), but highly doubtful, Hasebroek 70ff. and see id. 117; 120ff. for a convenient survey of Roman-Jewish affairs in this period.

13 Athens: *HA Sev.* 3.7; p. 73 above—Egypt: Thomasson 1984, 352f., nos. 70–9 (but no. 76, Dionysius, never got to the province, p. 78 above)—'fascination': *HA Sev.* 17.3–4; Dio 75. 13. 1–2—divination edict: Rea on *P. Yale Inv.* 299, issued before S.'s arrival, hence important for the date, but as Rea points out, the month, in the last line, is too fragmentary for certainty. Still, other evidence indicates that Hannestad's early date for S.'s arrival will not do, Halfmann 220f.

14 Pelusium: Dio 75. 13. 1—Hadrian: Dio 69.11.1; *HA Had.* 14. 4—'curse': Dio 43.3. 3ff.—Lucan 8. 608ff. Other references to L. Septimius: *RE* 2A (1923) 1561f.—M. Aurelius and Pompey: through his great-grandfather Rupilius Libo, *PIR*² L 166.

15 Niger, Cybele, baths: Malalas 293; gymnasium, *Chron. Pasch.* 493 (also a 'Pantheon'); Hasebroek 118; 123—council: *HA Sev.* 17.2; Bowman—Coeranus: Dio 76.5.5, but not until 212; *PIR*² A161.

16 Plautianus: Dio 75. 14.2–5—Antipater: Philostratus *v. soph.* 2.24–5; *CP* no. 230; Bowersock 1969, esp. 55f.

17 *libelli, apokrimata*: *P. Columbia* 123; some new readings in Merentitis—Apollinaris: Thomasson 1984, 353f.—delegations: *P. Oxy.* 3019.

18 Sarapis: *HA Sev.* 17.3–4. I am indebted to Fowden 20ff—Lepcis: *IRT* 309–12—'portrayed': McCann 55f.; 79f.; 110f.—'painted portrait': Neugebauer.

19 Memphis; *Oracle of the Potter*, etc.: Fowden 21f., Apuleius, *Met.* 2.28;

Tertullian, *Adv. Valent.* 15.1 ('Mercurius ille Trismegistus, magister omnium physicorum').

20 pyramids, Sphinx, Labyrinth, Memnon: *HA Sev.* 17.4—'repaired': *IGR* I 1113—'statue sang'; Bowersock 1984 (showing that S. did not silence it by repair-work). Plague: Dio 75. 13. 1—Nile journey: I follow Hannestad, but cf. n.13 above on chronology—frontier: Daniels 223ff.

21 taboo: Hannestead—Syria: Halfmann 220f.—*toga virilis: HA Sev.* 16.8 (misplaced)—Commodus: Birley 1987, 188f.; 197.

22 consuls: Alföldy 1968, 158f.

23 Antioch: *HA Carac.* 1.7; Downey 242f.

24 Dio 76. 15. 3–6.

25 Julia: Dio 75.6–7; Philostratus, *v. Apoll.* 1.3; Bowersock 1969, 101ff. Dio 72.23.1–3 on the genesis of his historical work is much discussed (App. 1.A.2) but no exact date is imposed—Nicaea: Robert, esp. 30ff.—Byzantium: id. 28 n.134, on *HA Carac.* 1.7.

26 Dio's career: App. 1.A.2—Hannibal: Dio 18. 65. 7 (Tsetzes, *Chil.* 1. 798ff.; Zonaras 9.21).

27 Sicinius: I follow Guey 1952, 40ff.—Pudens: *IRT* 295—Pizos: *IGR* I 766.

28 Halfmann 218; 221 on the journey—Gallus: Alföldy 1968, 135—Faustus: id. 134—*limes Transalutanus*: Bogdan-Cătăniciu 461; 466 (rejects Severan date). Claudianus: Alföldy 1968, 138; with Fitz—Cilo: Alföldy 1968, 141f.

29 Dio 76. 1. 1–5; Chastagnol.

14 Return to Africa (pages 146–154; for Bibliography see pp. 268–70)

1 In spite of doubts by Romanelli 1959, 413ff.; Kotula 1985, there can be no doubt that there was a visit to Africa, further, that it took place in 202–03: Halfmann 1986, 88; 132f.; 218; 222f. (cf. n.8 below)—Hadrian's visit: id. 192; 203—Dio on 'cos.II' in the case of those who had had 'ornamenta consularia' and then a consulship (Octavian was an example; Plautianus the first to be called 'cos. II'): 46.46.3–4.

2 Carthage, *ius Italicum, pertica*: Gascou 1982, 215ff.—Thugga and other cities: id. 209ff.—Marii: App. 1.A.4—Gargilii: Corbier 1982, 736f.—The ius *Italicum* is registered in *Digest* 50.15.8.11.

3 Lambaesis: *CIL* VIII 2702; 18250 (*ratio castrensis*); Halfmann 1986, 88; 219; 222—Gallus: Thomasson 1984, 403; Alföldy 1968, 139 (on his origo)— province de iure: Subatianus Proculus, in office 208–10 is the first dated legate of 'Numidia' rather than 'of the legion III Aug.'); *ILS* 9488; Thomasson loc. cit.—Cirta: the description is based on that by Pflaum 1959, 96; cf. also Champlin 1980, 5ff.—Faustus: Thomasson 1984, 402f. lists the enormous number of inscriptions which attest his activity—Dimmidi: Charles-Picard 1949—Agueneb: *CIL* VIII 21567; cf. p. 51 above. A valuable *tour d'horizon* is provided by Daniels 1987, 253ff.

4 III Gallica: Charles-Picard 1949, 47ff.—'task . . . formidable': Daniels 1987, 253ff.—Moors: Alföldy 1985—Pudens: *PIR*² o 51—Auzia: Gascou 1982, 207ff.—Victory monument: Daniels 1987, 255; Romanelli 406ff.—Haius, Sallustius: Thomasson 1984, 412f.

5 P. 51 above.

6 Baths: *IRT* 396—Barton 1977 provides a helpful conspectus of the dedications—197: *IRT* 387; 418 (note also 291, to Julia Domna as 'deae Iunoni orbis
terrae', dedicated by one of the Lepcis Fulvii)—'double L': Mastino 1981, 33f.
(doubting official inspiration)—Geta: *IRT* 437. No doubt there were others
to S. himself, Antoninus, Julia. Geta's has survived, by paradox, because it was
removed after his *damnatio* and re-used for building.—Tyre: Rey-Coquais.

7 Cerealis: *IRT* 388; 440—Punicus: 392; 403; 422; 434—Galba: 395; 407; 424—
Celer: 432.

8 AD 202: *IRT* 393; 423; 441—*ius Italicum: Digest* 50.15.8.11—*curiae: IRT* 416;
420—Arch: V. M. Strocka 1972 dates this, and the imperial visit, to the years
205–09. But he depends on the notion that the coins of 206–07 prove an
African visit then, emanating from *BMC* V p. clix. See Halfmann 1986, 132f.;
222f. (There might, for all that, have been a *second* visit: cf. p. 000 n.10
below)—Lamia: *IRT* 930; p. 12 above.

9 'free oil': *HA Sev.* 18.3—'stamped': Di Vita-Evrard 1985; Mattingly 1988—
Dioga: *PIR*² M 231.

10 'only direct mention': Philostratus, *v. soph.* 2.20.2. Kotula 1985 attempts
unsuccessfully to explain this away. However, Procopius, *De aedif.* 4.4.5,
referring to S. building a 'palace' (*basileion*, probably the new Basilica) at
Lepcis, cited by Hasebroek 133 (followed by Halfmann 1986, 126; 222) as
further direct evidence, is irrelevant, as Kotula 165 n.55 points out: *enthende
hormōmenos* means that S.'s *origo* was Lepcis, nothing more—On the buildings: Guey 1950, 73ff.; Haynes 71ff.; meanwhile the forthcoming publication
of the late J. B. Ward-Perkins' work on the Severan building complex is
eagerly awaited—'completed in 216': *IRT* 427–8—Plautianus: *IRT* 530.

11 'great temple': it is not in fact certain to which divinity this was dedicated.
Hasebroek 149f. proposed that Dio 76.16.3 meant Lepcis, a suggestion
dismissed by Di Vita 1982, 552 n.85 (but he does not refer to the possibility of the
new Forum temple being the one in question. There are substantial areas as yet
unexplored—note that the 'Ulpian basilica with its forum' restored in late
antiquity, *IRT* 543, is unlocated). The new Forum complex certainly honours
Hercules (Melqart) and Dionysus/Bacchus (Shadrapa) with its relief decoration—
Dio as proconsul: App. 1.A.2—'displayed at Rome': p. 159 above.

12 Vezereos: *ILAfr.* 26; *ILTun.* 5; 58—Tisavar: *CIL* VIII 11048—Tillibari:
Trousset 1974, 117f. (restoration in 197)—Si Aioun: *ILAfr.* 9; *ILS* 9117;
Trousset 1974, 120—Cydamus: *IRT* 909—Auru: Brogan and Reynolds 1960,
51—Thenadassa: *IRT* 868—Bir Tarsin: *IRT* 887—Gheriat-el-Garbia: *Supp.
to Libya Antiqua* 2 (1966) 107ff. Note also Gasr Zerzi: Brogan and Reynolds
1960, 43f.—Gholaia: *AE* 1976. 698; 700; *IRT* 913–5; Rebuffat 1985 (with
bibliography of his very numerous other publications).

13 On the olive cultivation in the pre-desert, the work of the G. D. B. Jones and
G. W. W. Barker UNESCO mission has fundamentally changed our
understanding. See Mattingly 1985; 1987; 1988 for convenient and lucid
exposition. Further results are awaited—'Julius Masthalul': *IRT* 886b (Bir ed
Dreder in the W. Sofeggin) registers the stone (not read and thought then to
be 'in the Libyan language'); see now Elmayer 1984—Ghirza: Brogan and
Smith 1984.

14 Victor, *De Caes.* 20.9 (= *HA Sev.* 18.3).

15 Quintianus: *IRT* 918—'11 April': *IRT* 292; Guey 1950, 55ff. 'urbem suam' in the case of emperors ought to mean Rome; thus e.g. Halfmann 1986, 222. At Lepcis it might be otherwise.

16 Geta's birthday: Barnes 1971, 263ff.; 71ff. (on Perpetua's martyrdom); 163 (with the acute observation that the procurator Hilarianus is the same as the P. Aelius Hilarianus who earlier, in Spanish Asturica, dedicated an altar 'to the gods and goddesses in the pantheon to whom it is right and lawful to pray', *AE* 1968. 228; a pious persecutor). On the *Passio Perpetuae*, see now Robert 1982; further, Barnes' *addenda* (321–39) in the 1985 reprint of his work— 'Hittite storm-god' (i.e. Dolichenus): Speidel 1978, 76f. has an evocative description and explanation of the deity's success among the military— Tertullian, *Scap.* 4.5 (Proculus: a servant of Antoninus' *educator* Euodus); Barnes 1971, 70—'not .. change of policy': Barnes 1971, 143–63.

17 Dio 75.16.2–5; *HA Sev.* 14.7. The fact that the governor of Sardinia is the only named official to have misjudged what happened may not be coincidence. That province would get wind of rumours, from Rome or Lepcis, sooner than most and Constans presumably acted at once, before the rumour had been suppressed—'10 June 203': *AE* 1968. 8.

15 The Years in Italy (pages 155–169; for Bibliography see p. 270)

1 *ovatio: HA Sev.* 14.7 (misplaced)—Arch: I rely on Brilliant, although not convinced by his interpretation of the reliefs, on which Rubin 1975.

2 *ILS* 425.

3 Alföldy 1968, 134; 141f.; 159.

4 See above all the monograph by Pighi.

5 'kinsman': App. 2 no. 25.

6 role of *XVviri*: Syme 1958, 65f.—prophecy: *Or. Sib.* 8.139ff.; Syme 1958, 773.

7 Pighi 140ff.; 144ff.; 146ff.; 222ff.—Troy Game: 167; 173—Piso: *PIR*² C 295— Augustan Messallae: Pighi 236—the consuls of 196 and 214: Barbieri nos. 570–1.

8 Augustan *XVviri*: Syme 1939, 382—in 204: Pighi 232ff.; Schumacher 157ff.— Africans: Aiacius Modestus (Corbier 743); Cocceius Vibianus (id. 741); Salvius Tuscus (id. 720); Gargilius Antiquus (id. 737); Julius Pompeius Rusonianus (*cognomen* only in *IRT* 396, 750; the case in Philostratus, *v. soph.* 2.25.2 is dubious); Venidius Rufus (Birley 1969, 277); Fulvius Fuscus (Corbier 722). Cassius Pius Marcellinus (*RE* Supp. 9 (1962) 19) and Fabius Magnus (in 'Quirina' tribe) are possibly from Africa too. Mucianus: Alföldy 1982, 344.

9 Pighi 116f.; 241ff.—Soaemias and Marcellus: App. 2 nos. 41; 50.

10 Herodian 3.9–10; Zosimus 2.4.3; 7.2 registers these games.

11 App. 2 nos 21, 22—'deathbed': Dio 76.2.4.

12 Dio 76. 2.1–3.

13 Dio 76.2.5; cf. Herodian 3.10.8.

14 Dio 76. 3.1–6.3—Macrinus: 78.11.2; *CP* no. 257.

15 Herodian 3.11.1–12.12, demolished by Hohl—city: *CIL* VI 32365. Dio 75.14.6–15.2a.

16 Herodian 3.11.2–3.

17 Benario provides a convenient survey—'Septizodium' proves to be the correct form of the name; even if it has, strictly, no connection with 'septem', this would not stop people so interpreting it. Guey 1946 is still worth consulting on the matter—horoscope: Dio 76.11.1; Rubin 1980, 33ff.

18 Laetus: *PIR*² M 54. Papinian: *HA Carac.* 8.2; *CP* no. 220. Ulpian: *Digest* 50.15. 1 *pr.* Syme 1984, 1393ff. is essential reading on the three jurists.

19 Dio 76.16.4—Gorgus: *Digest* 48. 5.2.6—Victor, *De Caes.* 20. 23. 'principle': *Digest* 1.3.31—'pronouncement': *Int.* 2.17.8.

20 Dio 76.7.3–9.2.

21 Dio 76.17.1–3—Sammonicus: Macrobius, *Sat.* 3.17.4; see further the intriguing discussion by Champlin.

22 *Frag. Vat.* 294.2; *Digest* 24.1.32.2.

23 Dio 76.9.2–4.

24 Tertullian, *Apol.* 30.4.

25 App. 1.A.1—Saturninus: *CP* no. 231—Ulpian: *Digest* 1.6.3.

26 Dio 75.15.7; 77.18.3; Philostratus, *v. soph.* 2.30; *v. Apoll.* 1.3; Bowersock 1969, 101ff.

27 Victor, *De Caes.* 21.3 = *HA Sev.* 18.8—Herodian 4.9.3, etc.; Rubin 1980, 173ff. offers a plausible interpretation for Victor's further charge, treason.

28 Dio 76.7. 1–3.

29 Dio 76. 10. 1–7; cf. 6.2; 74.2. 4–6; MacMullen 255ff.

30 'not long to live': Dio 76. 11. 1–2.

16 Expeditio Felicissima Brittannica (pages 170–187; for Bibliography see pp. 271–2)

1 'angry'; Dio 76.10.6—'idleness': 76.11.1—Herodian 3.14.1–2.

2 Senecio: Birley 1981, 157ff—Bainbridge: id. 155—'next year': reading '[Sen]ecio[ne et Aemiliano cos.]' in the last line of *RIB* 722, as suggested in *Northern History* 20 (1984) 240, pursuing a suggestion of Alföldy 1969, 4 n.1. The polyonymous first consul of 206, generally 'Albinus', is 'Senecio' e.g. in *CIL* VIII 6985. After 197 the former name might have been better avoided in Britain, the latter was shared by the governor. See further Alföldy 1969 on the Bainbridge stones—Birdoswald: *RIB* 1909—Habitancum: *RIB* 1234—Cilurnum: *RIB* 1462—Adventus: *CP* no. 247 + add.; Birley 1981, 160, 298f.; Rankov. His career is outlined by Dio 78.14.1–3; 79.8.2.

3 Lupus: *RIB* 757 (Verterae, name not preserved); 637 (Verbeia); 730 (Lavatrae); 1163 (Coria). Dio 75.5.4; Birley 1972; 1981, 149ff.

4 changes to two Walls: Breeze and Dobson, esp. 128f.—Geta, Pertinax: p. 65 above—Lupus, Pudens, Senecio: Birley 1981, 149ff.; 155ff.; 157ff.

5 Dio 76.10.6—Condercum: *RIB* 1337—Coria: 1138; Birley 1981, 265f. Herodian: Birley 1972, 186ff., comparing 6.1.2; 6.7.2; see further on this author App. 1A.3.

6 'governor defeated': Dio 72.8.1–2; Birley 1981, 135ff.—Vindolanda: *Britannia* 8 (1977) 432; other sites, n.2 above—Arbeia: Dore and Gillam 61ff. On the name: Kennedy 1986; he suggests a fourth-century date for the Tigris bargemen (also at Lancaster: Shotter), but early third is quite possible—Barathes: *RIB* 1065; 1071.

7 Agricola: Dio 39. 50. 4; 66. 20—Tertullian, *Apol.* 16, etc.—grandfather: pp.

18ff. above—Bolanus: Statius, *Silvae* 5.2.140ff.—Dio 75.1.1; 76. 13.1—'outermost island' Aristides, *or* 26.82.—Tertullian, *Adv. Iudaeos* 7.4.

8 Asper: *CIL* XIV 2508; Birley 1981, 433f.—Polus: id. 261ff.—Haterianus: Di Vita-Evrard 1982—Antius Crescens: Birley 1981, 137ff.—Alexianus, Marcellus: App. 2 nos. 45, 50—Papinian: *CP* no. 220—Faustinus, younger Ulpius Marcellus: Birley 1981, 161ff., 164ff.

9 Castor, Euodus: Dio 76.14.1–2, 5; 77.1.1—*classis: CIL* VI 1643; *CP* no. 259; 'granaries': *RIB* 1143.

10 'two inscriptions': 429–30—Castinus: App. 2 no. 19—coins in 208: *BMC* V 262; in 207: 265ff.; 348f.—Victor, I Adiutrix: *CIL* III 11082—Africa: cf. Robertson 137—On the British references on the coinage, see esp. the salutary discussion by Robertson.

11 Maximus: *PIR*² M 308—Martialis: M 608—Perpetuus: M 31.; Thomasson 1984, 129; 1985—Aquila: Thomasson 1984, 339; 354—Proculus: id. 403.—Senecio: Birley 1981, 158—Aiacius: p. 253 n.8 above—Victor: Alföldy 1968, 141—Castinus: App. 2 no. 19.

12 consuls: Alföldy 1968, 159—Aper: App. 2 no. 14—'Commodus': revealed by *RMD* 73, where the other consul is correctly identified—'daughters': Pflaum 36f.; 37f.

13 coins: *BMC* V 208ff.; 349ff.—'gout': Dio 76.13.4; Herodian 3.14.3, 5; *HA Sev.* 23.3.

14 Eboracum: Victor, *De Caes.* 20.27.

15 Dio 76. 12. 1–4; Herodian 3.14.5–8.

16 'bridge': Robertson corrects widespread error on this whole matter—208: *BMC* V 351, no. 857—209: 353 (frequently misdated)—Herodian 3.14.5; Dio 76.13.1–4.

17 Herodian 3.14.9–10—Alban: argued by Morris.

18 Aenus: Kaygusz 66f.

19 Dio 76. 13. 4; Herodian 3.15.1—Britannicus: Dietz 382f. points out that neither *ILS* 431 nor *AE* 1965. 338 of AD 209 can be used to date the title to this year: the former should read 'f[ort. fel.]' not 'B[ritann.]', the latter was doctored after Geta's murder. For the evidence for 'Britannicus': Mastino 51f. and n.186—camps: *JRS* 59 (1969) 114ff.; 63 (1973) 230ff.

20 camps: see previous note—'extremity': Dio 76.13.3—'money': 76.11.2: Herodian 3.14.2.

21 Carpow: identified as belonging to this expedition by R. E. Birley 1962; 1963. Further work reported by Leach and Wilkes; cf. also *JRS* 55 (1965) 208f.; 56 (1966) 199; 57 (1967) 175; 58 (1968) 177f.; 59 (1969) 202, 63 (1973) 231; 67 (1977) 144; *Britannia* 9 (1978) 277f. For 'VI Vic. B. pf.', ibid. 52 (1962) 197; 53 (1963) 164 (which also reports an example from Eboracum); and *ILAlg* I 539.1 from Zattara in Numidia may register the title on a veteran's tombstone—II Augusta: Wright, assigning the fragmentary inscription decorated with its emblem to 212; hard to prove or disprove—'horehound': *JRS* 53 (1963) 166.

22 *HA Sev.* 18.2; Victor, *De Caes.* 20. 18; Eutropius 8.19; *Epit. de Caes.* 20.4; Jerome, *Chron.* p. 212 (Helm); Orosius 7.17.7 (a little extra detail—ditch and turrets)—207: a quarrying inscription, *RIB* 1009.

23 Dio 76. 14.1–7; cf. Rubin 174f.

24 Dio 76. 11. 1–2; *HA Sev.* 22.1–7—Aballava: *RIB* 2042—Bellona: *RIB* 890.

25 Carvetii: *JRS* 55 (1965) 224; Higham and Jones, esp. 9ff.—Syrian Goddess: *RIB* 1791—Vindolanda: 1700—Phoenician deities: 1124; 1129.

26 Eboracum: *CJ* 3.32.1; 8.25.2; 2.11.9; 3.28.4; 6.35.2; 8.13.4; 2.11.10; 6.53.4; 8.40.3 (208); 7.62.1; 8.18.1; 7.8.3 (209); 3.32.1; 8.53.1; 6.4.1; 8.44.3; 8.37.2; 3.1.2 (210). The issue of 28 April 211 (6.37.3) which bears his name may have been delayed—Ephesus: *Die Inschriften von Ephesos* (Bonn 1979–84) no. 881. Sarapis: *RIB* 658; Birley 1981, 263ff.

27 Dio 76.16.5.

28 revolt: Dio 16.15.1–2 (*Iliad* 6.57–9); Herodian 3.15.1—proto-Picts: Chadwick in Dillon and Chadwick 73f. on the view from the 'great Iron Age hill fort of Castle Law above Abernethy . . . surely the heart of Pictavia'—Geta: *IG* II/III 1077, redated by Di Vita-Evrard 1987, cf. App. 2 no. 22.

29 Dio 76.15.2; 17.4; Herodian 3.15.2; Victor, *De Caes.* 20. 29. *HA Sev.* 20–1 was exposed as crass fiction by Straub.

17 Aftermath and Assessment (pp. 188–200; for Bibliography see pp. 272–3)

1 'purple stone': Dio 76.15.4 (also quoting S.'s words); Herodian says alabaster, 3.15.7. Probably Derbyshire Blue John, often various shades of purple. *HA Sev.* 24.2 says 'a little gold urn'; trying to be different). 'preparations': . . . at Eboracum': Herodian 3.15.4–5; Dio 77.1.1 (with names). One of the officers bribed could be Tineius Longus, prefect of cavalry at Condercum, designated quaestor (*RIB* 1329; Birley 1981b, 165)—'resemblance': Dio 77.1.3.

2 withdrawals, etc.: Dio 77.1.1 and Herodian 3.15.6 make this clear enough. Wright believes the fragmentary inscription from Carpow cannot be earlier than 212. Not certain: but a slight delay may be allowed—'concerted attempt': cf. chapter 16 n. 22 above—younger Marcellus: not believed in by everyone, argued by Birley 1981b, 168ff.—Herodian 3.15.6–4.4.2; Dio 77.1–6 describe the return. Herodian produces the story that there was a serious plan to divide the empire; implausible, Alföldy 1988.—Geta's character: Dio 77.1.3; elaborated by Herodian 3.3.2–3 (and the *HA*).

3 Dio 77.2.1 says Antoninus wanted to murder Geta at the Saturnalia but failed to carry it out. The date seems to have been established by Barnes 51f. Dio 77.2.2–6 describes the murder; also Herodian 4.4.3; *HA Carac.* 2.4. The aftermath is given by Dio 77.3.1–5.2; Herodian 4.4.4–6.5: *HA Carac.* 2.4–4.10 (same re-used in *Geta* 6.1–8). To be used with caution, see Dietz; Alföldy 1988—Inscriptions: Mastino 175f.

4 'Caracalla': the correct form is established by a leaden curse tablet from Aquae Sulis, Wild—Dio on Caracalla: 78.3.3; 9.3, etc. Herodian 4.7.4–7. 'Dio's hatred' etc.: see Books 77, 78. 1–9—'soldierly conduct': 77.13.1–2. Detailed annotation on events after 211 lies beyond the scope of this work.

5 Dio 77. 9.4–5—Marcellus: App. 2 no. 50. Rome as the common fatherland has been much written about.

6 My views on the division of Britain are set out in Birley 1981b, 166ff. (Julius Marcus as last governor of undivided Britain)—Gordianus: id. 181ff.

7 *ILS* 1159—army pay: Develin; Watson 188 (with varying calculations).

8 Dio 78.4.1–23.6. Herodian 4.12.1ff. is better disregarded and the *HA Macrinus* and *Diadumenianus* are mostly fiction—Haius: *PIR²* H 8.

9 See above all the fundamental study by Kettenhofen.

10 On the reign of Alexander, in addition to Kettenhofen; Syme 146ff.
11 See esp. Alföldy 1968.
12 E. Birley; Smith; Graham offer estimates on military matters.
13 Birley 1974 summarises the evidence for Septimius as '*propagator imperii*'.
14 Galen 14. 217K; Tertullian, *De pallio* 1.1; 2.7; Herodian 3.7.7–8; Victor, *De Caes.* 20.6, 10.
15 Dio 76.16.1–4; Millar 139; Dio 78.10.1–2; Millar 180.
16 Dio 75.7.4; *HA Sev.* 15.5; Dio 76.7.3. Perhaps I may be permitted to refer to my papers dealing with aspects of the third century: Birley 1976; 1981a.

Bibliographies

Chapters 1–3

Alföldy, G. 1977   *Konsulat und Senatorenstand under den Antoninen* (Bonn 1977)

Aumont, J. 1968   'Caton en Libye (Lucain, Pharsale IX 294–949)', *Rev. et. anc.* 70 (1968) 304–20

Badian, E. 1958   *Foreign Clientelae* (Oxford 1958)

Badian, E. 1968   *Roman Imperialism in the Late Republic* (2nd ed., Oxford 1968)

Barnes, T. D. 1971   *Tertullian. A literary and historical study* (Oxford 1971)

Bartoccini, R. 1958   *Il porto romano di Leptis Magna* (Rome 1958)

Bates, O. 1914   *The Eastern Libyans* (London 1914)

Birley, A. R. 1968   'Some teachers of Marcus Aurelius', *Historia-Augusta-Colloquium 1966–7* (Bonn 1968) 39–42

Birley, A. R. 1969   'The *coups d'état* of the year 193', *Bonner Jahrbücher* 169 (1969) 243–80

Birley, A. R. 1970   'Some notes on *HA Severus* 1–4', *Historia-Augusta-Colloquium 1968–9* (Bonn 1970) 59–77

Birley, A. R. 1981   *The Fasti of Roman Britain* (Oxford 1981)

Birley, A. R. 1987   *Marcus Aurelius. A biography* (London 1987)

Brogan, O. 1968   'Henschir el-Ausaf by Tigi (Tripolitania) and some related tombs in the Tunisian Gefara', *Libya Antiqua* 2 (1965) 47–56

Champlin, E. 1980   *Fronto and Antonine Rome* (Cambridge, Mass. 1980)

Corbier, M. 1982   'Les familles clarissimes d'Afrique proconsulaire', *Epigrafia et ordine senatorio* II (*Tituli* 5, Rome 1982) 685–754

Daniels, C. M. 1970   *The Garamantes of Southern Libya* (Harrow 1970)

Daniels, C. M. 1987   'Africa', *The Roman World*, ed. J. S. Wacher (London 1987), I 223–65

Deman, A. 1962   'Virgile et la colonisation romaine en Afrique du Nord', *Hommages Grenier* (Collection Latomus 68, Brussels 1962) 514–62

Desanges, J. 1980   *Pline l'Ancien. Histoire naturelle, livre V, 1–46, lère partie (L'Afrique du Nord)* (Paris 1980)

Di Vita, A. 1968a   'Influences grecques et tradition orientale dans l'art punique de Tripolitaine', *Mélanges . . école française de Rome* 80 (1968) 7–83

Di Vita, A. 1986b   'Shadrapa et Milk'ashtart dèi patri di Leptis ed i templi del lato nord-ovest del Foro vecchio leptitano', *Orientalia* 37 (1968) 201–11

Di Vita, A. 1969 · 'Le date di fondazione di Leptis e di Sabratha sulla base dell'indagine archeologica e l'eparchia cartaginese d'Africa', *Hommages M. Renard* III (Collection Latomus 103, Brussels 1969) 196–202

Di Vita, A. 1974 · 'Un passo dello *Stadiasmos tes megales thalasses* ed il porto ellenistico di Leptis Magna', *Mélanges P. Boyancé* (Rome 1974) 229–49

Di Vita, A. 1982 · 'Gli *Emporia* di Tripolitania dall'età di Massinissa a Diocleziano: un profilo storico-istituzionale', *ANRW* 2.10.2 (1982) 515–95

Di Vita-Evrard, G. 1965 · 'Les dédicaces de l'amphithéatre et du cirque de Lepcis', *Libya Antiqua* 2 (1965) 29–37

Di Vita-Evrard, G. 1979 · 'Quatre inscriptions du Djebel Tarhuna: le territoire de Lepcis Magna', *Quaderni di arch. della Libia* 10 (1979) 67–98

Di Vita-Evrard, G. 1982 · 'Note sur "trois" sénateurs de Lepcis Magna. Le clarissimat des Plautii', *Epigrafia e ordine senatorio* I (*Tituli* 4, Rome 1982) 453–65; 'Contribution de la Tripolitaine à la prosopographie de deux sénateurs, proconsuls d'Afrique', ibid. 467–70

Di Vita-Evrard, G. 1984 · ' "Municipium Flavium Lepcis Magna" ', *Bulletin . . comité des travaux historiques*, n.s. 17B (1984) 197–210

Di Vita-Evrard, G. 1985 · 'Notes sur quelques timbres d'amphores de Tripolitaine', ibid. 18B (1985) 147–59

Di Vita-Evrard, G. 1986 · 'La *Fossa Regia* et les diocèses d'Afrique proconsulaire', *L'Africa Romana* 3, ed. A. Mastino (Sassari 1986) 31–58

Garnsey, P. D. A. 1978 · 'Rome's African empire under the principate', *Imperialism in the Ancient World*, eds. Garnsey and C. R. Whittaker (Cambridge 1970, and 1978) 223–54

Gascou, J. 1982 · 'La politique municipale de Rome en Afrique du Nord', *ANRW* 2.10.2 (1982) 136–320

Gese, H., Höfner, M., Rudolph, K. 1970 · *Die Religionen Altsyriens, Altarabiens und der Mandäer* (Stuttgart 1970)

Griset, E. 1957 · 'Un cristiano di Sabrata', *Rivista di studi classici* 5 (1957) 35–9

Guey, J. 1951a · 'L'inscription du grand-père de Septime-Sévère à Leptis Magna', *Mémoires soc. nat. ant. de France* 82 (1951) 161–226

Guey, J. 1951b · 'Au théâtre de Leptis Magna. Le proconsulat de Lollianus Avitus et la date de l'Apologie d'Apulée', *Rev. ét. lat.* 29 (1951) 307–17

Guey, J. 1954 · 'L'Apologie d'Apulée et les inscriptions de Tripolitaine', ibid. 32 (1954) 115–119

Harden, D. B. 1962 · *The Phoenicians* (London 1962)

Hardie, A. 1983 · *Statius and the Silvae* (Liverpool 1983)

Harmand, L. 1957 · *Le Patronat sur les collectivités publiques des origines au Bas-Empire* (Paris 1957)

Harris, W. V. 1979   *War and Imperialism in Republican Rome* (Oxford 1979)

Haynes, D. E. L. 1959   *The Antiquities of Tripolitania* (Tripoli 1959)

Hijmans, B. L. 1987   'Apuleius, philosophus Platonicus', *ANRW* 2.36.1 (1987) 395–475

Humphrey, J. H. 1986   *Roman Circuses. Arenas for Chariot Racing* (London 1986)

Jenkins, G. K. 1969   *North Africa, Syrtica, Mauretania* (Sylloge Nummorum Graecorum, Copenhagen 1969)

Kotula, T. 1968   *Les curies municipales en Afrique romaine* (Wroclaw 1968)

Lassère, J. M. 1977   *Ubique populus* (Paris 1977)

McCann, A. M. 1968   *The Portraits of Septimius Severus* (Rome 1968)

Manacorda, D. 1977   'Testimonianze della produzione e il consumo dell'olio tripolitano nel III secolo', *Dial. di Archeologia* 9–10 (1976–7) 542–601

Manacorda, D. 1983   'Prosopografia e anfore tripolitane: nuove osservazioni', *Prodduccion y comercio del aceite en la Antiguedad*, ed. J. M. Blázquez Martínez and J. Remesal Rodríguez (Madrid 1983) 483–500

Mattingly, D. J. 1984   *Tripolitania. A comparative study of a Roman frontier province* (unpublished Ph.D. thesis, Manchester 1984)

Mattingly, D. J. 1987   'Libyans and the 'limes': culture and society in Roman Tripolitania', *Antiquités africaines* 23 (1987) 71–94

Mattingly, D. J. 1988   'The olive boom. Oil surpluses, wealth and power in Roman Tripolitania', *Libyan Studies* 19 (1988)

Millar, F. 1968   'Local cultures in the Roman empire: Libyan, Punic and Latin in Roman Africa', *JRS* 58 (1968) 126–34

Millar, F. 1981   'The world of the Golden Ass', *JRS* 71 (1981) 63–75

Monceaux, P. 1899   *Les Africains. Étude sur la littérature latine d'Afrique* (Paris 1899)

Moretti, L. 1976   'Un decreto di Arsinoe in Cirenaica', *Rivista di Filologia* 104 (1976) 385–98

Neugebauer, K. A. 1936   'Die Familie des Septimius Severus', *Die Antike* 12 (1936) 155–72

Nisbet, R. G. M. 1978   '*Felicitas* at Surrentum (Statius, *Silvae* II 2)', *JRS* 68 (1978) 1–11

Pavis d'Escurac, H.   'Pour une étude sociale de l'Apologie d'Apulée', *Antiquités africaines* 8 (1974) 89–101

Rebuffat, R. 1986   'Un banquier à Lepcis Magna', *L'Africa Romana* 3, ed. A. Mastino (Sassari 1986) 179–87

Röllig, W. 1980   'Das Punische im Römischen Reich', *Die Sprachen im Römischen Reich der Kaiserzeit*, eds. G. Neumann, J. Untermann (Bonn 1980) 285–99

Rössler, O. 1980   'Libyen von der Cyrenaica bis zur Mauretania Tingitana', ibid. 267–84

Romanelli, P. 1958   'Fulvii Lepcitani', *Archeologia Classica* 10 (1958) 258–61

Romanelli, P. 1959   *Storia delle province romane dell' Africa* (Rome 1959)

Sherwin-White, A.   *Roman Citizenship* (2nd ed. Oxford 1973)
N. 1973

Syme, R. 1958   *Tacitus* (Oxford 1958)

Syme, R. 1984   *Roman Papers* III (Oxford 1984)

Syme, R. 1986   *The Augustan Aristocracy* (Oxford 1986)

Syme, R. 1988   *Roman Papers* IV–V (Oxford 1988)

Thomasson, B. E.   *Laterculi Praesidum* I (Gothenburg 1984)
1984

Torelli, M. 1971   'Le "curie" di Leptis Magna', *Quaderni . . archeologia della Libia* 6 (1971) 105–11

Torelli, M. 1974   'Per una storia della classe dirigente di Leptis Magna', *Rendiconti . . Accad. Lincei*, ser. 8 28 (1974) 377–410

Vergara Caffarelli,   *The Buried City. Excavations at Leptis Magna* (London
E. and Caputo, G.   1966)
1966

Vessey, D. W. T. C.   '*Non solitis fidibus*: some aspects of Statius, *Silvae* 4.5',
1970   *L'antiquité classique* 39 (1970) 507–18

Vidman, L. 1977   'Die Stadtpräfektur des Q. Lollius Urbicus und Apuleius, *Apologia* 2–3', *Arheološki Vestnik* 27 (1977) 373–84

Walsh, P. G. 1965   'Massinissa', *JRS* 55 (1965) 149–60

Walsh, P. G. 1968   'Lucius Madaurensis', *Phoenix* 22 (1968) 143–57

Warmington, B.   *Carthage* (London 1964)
1964

Whittaker, C. R.   'The western Phoenicians: colonisation and assimilation',
1974   *Proc. Cambridge Philol. Soc.* n.s. 20 (1974) 58–79

Whittaker, C. R.   'Carthaginian imperialism in the fifth and fourth cen-
1978   turies', *Imperialism in the Ancient World*, eds. P. D. A. Garnsey and C. R. Whittaker (Cambridge 1978) 59–90

Chapters 4–7

Alföldy, G. 1969   *Fasti Hispanienses. Senatorische Reichsbeamte und Offiziere in den spanischen Provinzen des römischen Reiches von Augustus bis Diokletian* (Wiesbaden 1969)

Alföldy, G. 1977   *Konsulat und Senatorenstand unter den Antoninen* (Bonn 1977)

Alföldy, G. 1982   'Senatoren aus Norditalien. Regiones IX, X und XI', *Epigrafia e ordine senatorio* II (*Tituli* 5, Rome 1982) 309–68

Alföldy, G. 1985   'Bellum Mauricum', *Chiron* 15 (1985) 87–105 (reprinted in Alföldy 1987, 463–81)

Alföldy, G. 1987   'P. Helvius Pertinax und M. Valerius Maximianus', *Situla* 14/15 (1974) 199–215, reprinted with addenda in the same scholar's *Römische Heeresgeschichte. Beiträge 1962–1985* (Amsterdam 1987) 326–48

Alföldy, G. 1988   'Cleanders Sturz und die antike Überlieferung', *Geschichte, Geschichtsbetrachtung und Geschichtsschreibung in der Krise des Römischen Reiches* (Heidelberg 1988).

Birley, A. R. 1970   'Some notes on *HA Severus* 1–4', *Historia-Augusta-Colloquium 1968–9* (Bonn 1970) 59–77

Birley, A. R. 1981   *The Fasti of Roman Britain* (Oxford 1981)

Birley, A. R. 1982   'Senators from Britain?', *Epigrafia e ordine: senatorio* II (*Tituli* 5, Rome 1982) 531–8

Birley, A. R. 1987   *Marcus Aurelius. A Biography* (London 1987)

Birley, E. 1953   *Roman Britain and the Roman Army* (Kendal 1953)

Birley, E. 1963   'Promotions and transfers in the Roman army. 2. The centurionate', *Carnuntum Jahrbuch* 1963–4, 21–33

Birley, E. 1966   '*Alae* and *cohortes milliariae*', *Corolla E. Swoboda* (Graz 1966) 54–67

Bowersock, G. W. 1969   *Greek Sophists in the Roman Empire* (Oxford 1969)

Bowersock, G. W. 1982   'Roman Senators from the near east', *Epigrafia e ordine senatorio* II (*Tituli* 5, Rome 1982), 651–88

Breeze, D. J. and Dobson B. 1987   *Hadrian's Wall* (3rd ed., London 1987)

Champlin, E. 1980   *Fronto and Antonine Rome* (Cambridge, Mass., 1980)

Charles-Picard, G. 1959   *La civilisation de l'Afrique romaine* (Paris 1959)

Chastagnol, A. 1978   '*Latus clavus* et *adlectio* dans l'Histoire Auguste', *Historia-Augusta-Colloquium 1975–6* (Bonn 1978) 107–31

Corbier, M. 1982   'Les familles clarissimes d'Afrique proconsulaire', *Epigrafia e ordine senatorio* II (*Tituli* 5, Rome 1982) 685–754

Cramer, F. H. 1954   *Astrology in Roman Law and Politics* (Philadelphia 1954)

Di Vita-Evrard, G. 1963   'Un "nouveau" proconsul d'Afrique, parent de Septime-Sévère: Caius Septimius Severus', *MEFRA* 75 (1963) 389–44

Di Vita-Evrard, G. 1985   'L. Volusius Bassus Cerealis, légat du proconsul d'Afrique T. Claudius Aurelius Aristobulus, et la création de la province de Tripolitaine', in Mastino (below) 149–77

Eck, W. 1979   *Die staatliche Organisation Italiens in der hohen Kaiserzeit* (Munich 1979)

Eck, W. 1985   *Die Stalthalter der germanischen Provinzen* (Cologne 1985)

Grosso, F. 1964   *La lotta politica al tempo di Commodo* (Turin 1964)

Halfmann, H. 1982   'Die Senatoren aus den Kleinasiatischen Provinzen des römischen Reiches vom 1. bis 3. Jahrhundert', *Epigrafia e ordine senatorio* II (*Tituli* 5, Rome 1982) 603–50

Hasebroek, J. 1921   *Untersuchungen zur Geschichte des Kaisers Septimius Severus* (Heidelberg 1921)

Holder, P. A. 1980   *The Roman Army in Britain* (London 1980)

Mastino A. (ed.) 1985   *L'Africa Romana* II (Cagliari 1985), including the editor's own contribution, 'Le relazioni tra Africa e Sardegna in età romana: inventario preliminare', 27–91

Rivet, A. L. F. & Smith, C. C. 1979   *The Place-Names of Roman Britain* (London 1979)

Roxan, M. M. 1972   'Epigraphic notes', *Epigraphische Studien* 9 (1972) 246–50

Rubin, Z. 1980   *Civil-War Propaganda and Historiography* (Collection Latomus 173, Brussels 1980)

Talbert, R. J. A. 1984   *The Senate of Imperial Rome* (Princeton 1984)

Chapter 8

Alföldy, G. 1971   '*Bellum desertorum*', *Bonner Jahrbücher* 171 (1971) 367–76, reprinted with addenda in Alföldy 1988

Alföldy, G. 1982   'Senatoren aus Norditalien. Regiones IX, X und XI', *Epigrafia e ordine senatorio* II (*Tituli* 5, Rome 1982) 309–68

Alföldy, G. 1988   'Cleanders Sturz und die antike Überlieferung', *Geschichte Geschichtsbetrachtung und Geschichtsschreibung in der Krise des Römischen Reiches* (Heidelberg 1988)

Barnes, T. D.   *The Sources of the Historia Augusta* (Collection Latomus 155, Brussels 1978)

Birley, A. R. 1970   'Some notes on *HA Severus* 1–4', *Historia-Augusta-Colloquium 1968–9* (Bonn 1970) 59–77

Birley, A. R. 1981   *The Fasti of Roman Britain* (Oxford 1981)

Birley, A. R. 1987   *Marcus Aurelius. A biography* (London 1987)

Bowersock, G. W. 1982   'Roman senators from the Near East: Syria, Judaea, Arabia, Mesopotamia', *Epigrafia e ordine senatorio* II (*Tituli* 5, Rome 1982) 651–68

Chad, C. 1972   *Les dynastes d'Emèse* (Beirut 1972)

Downey, G. 1961   *A History of Antioch in Syria* (Princeton 1961)

Drijvers, H. J. W. 1977   'Hatra, Palmyra und Edessa', *ANRW* 2.8 (1977) 799–906

Grosso, F. 1964   *La lotta politica al tempo di Commodo* (Turin 1964)

Hohl, E. 1954   *Kaiser Commodus and Herodian* (Sitzungsber. Berlin 1954)

Jones, C. P. 1978   'A Syrian in Lyon, *AJP* 99 (1978) 336–53

Matthews, J. F. 1984   'The tax law of Palmyra', *JRS* 74 (1984) 157–80

Millar, F. 1983   'The Phoenician cities: a case-study of Hellenisation', *Proc. Cambridge Phil. Soc.* n.s. 29 (1983) 55–71

Millar, F. 1987   'Empire, community and culture in the Roman Near East: Greeks, Syrians, Jews and Arabs', *J. Jewish Studies* 38 (1987) 143–64

Sullivan, R. D. 1977   'The dynasty of Judaea in the first century', *ANRW* 2.8 (1977) 296–354; 'The dynasty of Emesa', ibid. 198–219

Teixidor, J. 1985   *Un port romain du désert: Palmyre* (Paris 1985)

Thomasson, B. E. 1984   *Laterculi Praesidum* (Gothenburg 1984)

Thomsen, P. 1945   'Massilia in Syrien, Ein Beitrag zur Historia Augusta und zur Ortskunde Syriens', *Zeitschr. d. deutschen Palästina-Vereins* 67 (1945) 75–81

Wroth, W. 1899   *Catalogue of the Greek Coins of Galatia, Cappadocia, and Syria* (London 1899)

Chapters 9–12

Alföldy, G. 1968   'Septimius Severus und der Senat', *Bonner Jahrbücher* 168 (1968) 112–60

Alföldy, G. 1969   *Fasti Hispanienses. Senatorische Reichsbeamte und Offiziere in den spanischen Provinzen des römischen Reiches von Augustus bis Diokletian* (Wiesbaden 1969)

Alföldy, G. 1970   'Eine Proskriptionsliste in der Historia Augusta', *Historia-Augusta-Colloquium 1968–69* (Bonn 1970) 1–12; repr. in Alföldy 1988

Alföldy, G. 1976   'Das neue saeculum des Pescennius Niger', ibid 1972–4 (Bonn 1976) 1–10; repr. in Alföldy 1988

Alföldy, G. 1982   'Senatoren aus Norditalien. Regiones IX, X, und XI', *Epigrafia e ordine senatorio* II (*Tituli* 5, Rome 1982) 309–68

Alföldy, G. 1988   *Geschichte, Geschichtsbetrachtung und Geschichtsschreibung in der Krise des Römischen Reiches* (Heidelberg 1988)

Barnes, T. D. 1970   'A senator from Hadrumetum and three others', *Historia-Augusta-Colloquium 1968–9* (Bonn 1970) 45–58

Barnes, T. D. 1978   *The Sources of the Historia Augusta* (Collection Latomus 155, Brussels 1978)

Birley, A. R. 1969   'The *coups d'état* of the year 193', *Bonner Jahrbücher* 169 (1969) 247–80

Birley, A. R. 1972   'Virius Lupus', *Archaeologia Aeliana*, 4th ser. 50 (1972) 179–89

Birley, A. R. 1981a   *The Fasti of Roman Britain* (Oxford 1981)

Birley, A. R. 1981b   'The economic effects of Roman frontier policy', *The Roman West in the Third Century*, eds. A. King, M. Henig (BAR Int. Ser. 109, Oxford 1981) 39–53

Birley, A. R. 1987   *Marcus Aurelius. A biography* (London 1987)

Birley, E. 1953   *Roman Britain and the Roman Army* (Kendal 1953)

Birley, E. 1969   'Septimius Severus and the Roman army', *Epigraphische Studien* 8 (1969) 63–82

Bloch, H. 1943   'A dream of Septimius Severus', *Classical World* 37 (1943–4) 31–2

Campbell, J. B. 1978   'The marriage of soldiers under the empire', *JRS* 68 (1978) 153–66

Champlin, E. 1979   'Notes on the heirs of Commodus', *AJP* 100 (1979) 288–306

Christol, M. 1981   'La carrière de Q. Hedius Rufus Lollianus Gentianus', *Rev. études anciennes* 83 (1981) 75–84

Corbier, M. 1982   'Les familles clarissimes d'Afrique proconsulaire (Ier–IIIe siècle', *Epigrafia e ordine senatorio* II (*Tituli* 5, Rome 1982) 685–754

Develin, R. 1971   'Pay rises under Severus and Caracalla and the question of the *annona militaris*', *Latomus* 30 (1971) 687–95

Domaszewski, A. v. 1898   'Der Staatsstreich des Septimius Severus', *Rheinisches Museum* 53 (1898) 638–9

Fitz, J. 1983   'A la carrière équestre de Ti. Claudius Clandianus', *Alba Regia* 20 (1983) 275–6

Graham, A. J. 1978 'The numbers at Lugdunum', *Historia* 27 (1978) 625–30

Grosso, F. 1964 *La lotta politica al tempo di Commodo* (Turin 1964)

Grosso, F. 1968 'Ricerche su Plauziano e gli avvenimenti del suo tempo', *Rendiconti Acc. Lincei*, 8th ser. 23 (1968) 7–58

Halfmann, H. 1982 'Die Senatoren aus den Kleinasiatischen Provinzen des römischen Reiches vom 1. bis 3. Jahrhundert', *Epigrafia e ordine senatorio* II (*Tituli* 5, Rome 1982) 603–50

Halfmann, H. 1986 *Itinera Principum. Geschichte und Typologie der Kaiserreisen im Römischen Reich* (Stuttgart 1986)

Hasebroek, J. 1921 *Untersuchungen zur Geschichte des Kaisers Septimius Severus* (Heidelberg 1921)

Herz, P. 1975 *Untersuchungen zum Festkalender der römischen Kaiserzeit nach datierten Weih- und Ehreninschriften* (Diss. Mainz 1975)

Hohl, E. 1956 *Kaiser Pertinax und die Thronbesteigung seines Nachfolgers im Lichte der Herodiankritik* (Sitz. Berlin 1956)

Jarrett, M. G. 1972 'An album of the equestrians from North Africa in the emperor's service', *Epigraphische Studien* 9 (1972) 146–232

Kajanto, I. 1965 *The Latin Cognomina* (Helsinki 1965)

Kettenhofen, E. 1979 *Die syrischen Augustae in der historischen Überlieferung* (Bonn 1979)

Kolb, F. 1972 *Literarische Beziehungen zwischen Cassius Dio, Herodian und der Historia Augusta* (Bonn 1972)

Kubitschek, J. W. 1889 *Imperium Romanum tributim discriptum* (Vienna 1889)

Le Roux, P. 1982 *L'Armée romaine et l'organisation des provinces ibériques d'Auguste à l'invasion de 409* (Paris 1982)

Martin, A. 1982 'Les évènements des années 193–194 dans le papyrus, les ostraca et les inscriptions d'Egypte', *Anagennesis. Papyrologike Ephemeris* 2 (1982) 83–97

Mastino, A. 1981 *Le titolature di Caracalla e Geta attraverso le iscrizioni (indici)* (Bologna 1981)

Millar, F. 1964 *A Study of Cassius Dio* (Oxford 1964)

Nesselhauf, H. 1964 'Patrimonium und res privata des römischen Kaisers', *Historia-Augusta-Colloquium 1963* (Bonn 1964) 73–93

Nesselhauf, H. 1966 'Die Vita Commodi und die Acta Urbis', ibid. 1964–5 (Bonn 1966) 127–38

Piso, I. 1982 'La place de la Dacie dans les carrières sénatoriales', *Epigrafia e ordine senatorio* I (Rome 1982) 369–95

Pekáry, T. 1959 'Studien zur römischen Währungs- und Finanzgeschichte von 161–235 n. Chr.', *Historia* 8 (1959) 443–89

Remesal Rodríguez, J. 1986 *La Annona Militaris y la exportacion de aceite betico a Germania* (Madrid 1986)

Rickman, G. 1980 *The Corn Supply of Ancient Rome* (Oxford 1980)

Robert, L. 1977 'La titulature de Nicée et de Nicomédie: la gloire et la haine', *Harvard Stud. in Class. Philol.* 81 (1977) 1–39

Rubin, Z. 1980 *Civil-War Propaganda and Historiography* (Collection Latomus 173, Brussels 1980)

Šašel, J. 1982   'Senatori ed appartenenti all'ordine senatorio provenienti dalle province romane di Dacia, Tracia, Mesia, Dalmazia e Pannonia', *Epigrafia e ordine senatorio* II (Tituli 5, Rome 1982) 553–81

Šašel, J. 1983   'Dolichenus-Heiligtum in Praetorium Latobicorum. Caracalla, Caesar, imperator destinatus', *Zeitschr. f. Papyrol. u. Epigr.* 50 (1983) 203–8

Šašel-Kos, M. 1986   *A Historical Outline of the Region between Aquileia, the Adriatic, and Sirmium in Cassius Dio and Herodian* (Ljubljana 1986)

Soproni, S. 1986   'Die Cäsarwürde Caracallas und die syrische Kohorte von Szentendre', *Alba Regia* 18 (1980) 39–51

Speidel, M. P. 1977   'The Roman army in Arabia', *ANRW* 2.8 (1977) 687–730

Speidel, M. P. 1985   'Valerius Valerianus in charge of Septimius Severus' Mesopotamian campaign', *CP* 80 (1985) 321–6

Stanfield, J. A. & Simpson, G.   *Central Gaulish Potters* (Oxford 1958)

Thomasson, B. E. 1984   *Laterculi Praesidum* (Gothenburg 1984)

Thomasson, B. E. 1985   'Zur Laufbahn einiger Statthalter des Prinzipats', *Opuscula Romana* 15 (1985) 109–41

Wagner, J. 1983   'Provincia Osrhoenae: new archaeological finds illustrating the military organisation under the Severan dynasty', *Armies and Frontiers in Roman and Byzantine Anatolia*, ed. S. Mitchell (BAR S156, Oxford 1983) 103–30

Walker, D. R. 1978   *The Metrology of the Roman Silver Coinage. III. From Pertinax to Uranius Antoninus* (BAR S40, Oxford 1978)

Watson, G. R. 1969   *The Roman Soldier* (London 1969)

Ziegler, R. 1978   'Antiochia, Laodicea und Sidon in der Politik der Severer', *Chiron* 8 (1978) 493–514

Chapter 13

Alföldy, G. 1968   'Septimius Severus und der Senat', *Bonner Jahrbücher* 168 (1968) 112–60

Barnes, T. D. 1968   'Legislation against the Christians', *JRS* 58 (1968) 32–50

Birley, A. R. 1981   *The Fasti of Roman Britain* (Oxford 1981)

Birley, A. R. 1987   *Marcus Aurelius. A biography* (London 1987)

Bogdan-Cătăniciu, I. 1986   'Repères chronologiques pour le limes sud-est de la Dacie', *Studien zu den Militärgrenzen Roms* III (Stuttgart 1986) 461–8

Bowersock, G. W. 1969   *Greek Sophists in the Roman Empire* (Oxford 1969)

Bowersock, G. W. 1983   *Roman Arabia* (Cambridge, Mass., 1983)

Bowersock, G. W. 1984   'The miracle of Memnon', *Bull. American Soc. Papyrologists* 21 (1984) 21–32

Bowman, A. K.
1971

The Town Councils of Roman Egypt (New York 1971)

Campbell, D. B.
1986

'What happened at Hatra?', *The Defence of the Roman and Byzantine East*, eds. P. Freeman and D. L. Kennedy (BAR Int. 297, Oxford 1986) 51–8

Chastagnol, A. 1984

'Les jubilés décennaux et vicennaux des empereurs sous les Antonins et les Sévères', *Revue numismatique*, 6e série, 26 (1984) 104–24

Daniels, C. M. 1987

'Africa', *The Roman World*, ed. J. S. Wacher (London 1987), I 223–65

Downey, G. 1971

A History of Antioch in Syria (Princeton 1971)

Drijvers, H. J. W.

'Hatra, Palmyra und Edessa', *ANRW* 2.8 (1977) 799–906

Fitz, J. 1983

'Notes. 20. A la carrière équestre de Ti. Claudius Claudianus', *Alba Regia* 20 (1983) 275–6

Fowden, G. 1985

The Egyptian Hermes (London 1985)

Guey, J. 1948

'28 janvier 98–28 janvier 198, ou le siècle des Antonins', *Revue ét. anciennes* 50 (1958) 60–70

Guey, J. 1952

'Lepcitana Septimiana VI. 2', *Revue africaine* 96 (1952) 25–63

Halfmann, H. 1986

Itinera Principum. Geschichte und Typologie der Kaiserreisen im Römischen Reich (Stuttgart 1986)

Hannestad, K. 1944

'*Sollemne sacrum praefecti Aegypti* and its historical background', *Classica et Medievalia* 6 (1944) 41–59; 'Septimius Severus in Egypt. A contribution to the chronology of the years 198–202', ibid. 194–222

Hasebroek, J. 1921

Untersuchungen zur Geschichte des Kaisers Septimius Severus (Heidelberg 1921)

Herz, P. 1975

Untersuchungen zum Festkalender der römischen Kaiserzeit nach datierten Weih- und Ehreninschriften (Diss. Mainz 1975)

Invernizzi, A. 1986

'Kifrin and the Euphrates lines', *The Defence of the Roman and Byzantine East*, eds. P. Freeman and D. L. Kennedy (BAR Int. 297, Oxford 1986) 357–81

Kennedy, D. L.
1979

'Ti. Claudius Subatianus Aquila, "first prefect of Mesopotamia"', *Zeitschr. f. Papyrol. u. Epigr.* 36 (1979) 255–86

Kennedy, D. L.
1980

'The frontier policy of Septimius Severus: new evidence from Arabia', *Roman Frontier Studies 1979*, eds. W. S. Hanson and L. J. F. Keppie (BAR S71, Oxford 1980) 879–88

Kennedy, D. L.
1986

' "European" soldiers and the Severan siege of Hatra', *The Defence of the Roman and Byzantine East*, eds. P. Freeman and D. L. Kennedy (BAR Int. 297, Oxford 1986) 397–409

Kennedy, D. L.
1987

'The East', *The Roman World*, ed. J. S. Wacher (London 1987) I 266–300

Kennedy, D. L.,
Antichthon

'The garrisoning of Mesopotamia in the late Antonine and early Severan period', *Antichthon* (forthcoming)

Kennedy, D. L. and Northedge, A. — 'Ana in the classical sources' (forthcoming)

McCann, A. M. 1968 — *The Portraits of Septimius Severus* (Rome 1969)

Mann, J. C. 1985 — 'The "Palmyrene" Diplomas', *Roman Military Diplomas 1978–84* (London 1985) 217–19

Mastino, A. 1981 — *Le titolature di Caracalla e Geta attraverso le iscrizioni (indici)* (Bologna 1981)

Merentitis, J. 1978 — 'Die neugefundenen Reskripte des Septimius Severus', *Platon* 30 (1978) 31–43

Neugebauer, K. A. 1936 — 'Die Familie des Septimius Severus', *Die Antike* 12 (1936) 155–72

Rea, J. R. 1977 — 'A new version of P. Yale Inv. 299', *Zeitschr. f. Papyrol. u. Epigr.* 27 (1977) 151–6

Robert, L. 1977 — 'La titulature de Nicée et de Nicomédie: la gloire et la haine', *Harv. Studies in Class. Phil.* 81 (1977) 1–39

Rubin, Z. 1975 — 'Dio, Herodian, and Severus' second Parthian war', *Chiron* 5 (1975) 419–41

Rubin, Z. 1980 — *Civil-War Propaganda and Historiography* (Collection Latomus 173, Brussels 1980)

Šašel, J. 1983 — 'Dolichenus-Heiligtum in Praetorium Latobicorum. Caracalla, Caesar, Imperator destinatus', *Zeitschr. f. Papyrol. u. Epigr.* 50 (1983) 203–8

Speidel, M. P. 1986 — ' "Europeans"—Syrian elite troops at Dura-Europos and Hatra', *Roman Army Studies* I (Amsterdam 1986) 301–10

Speidel, M. P. 1987 — 'The Roman road to Dumata (Jawf in Saudi Arabia) and the frontier strategy of *praetensione colligare*', *Historia* 26 (1987) 213–21

Speidel, M. P and Reynolds, J. M. 1985 — 'A veteran of legio I Parthica from Carian Aphrodisias', *Epigraphica Anatolica* 5 (1985) 31–5

Syme, R. 1984 — *Roman Papers* III (Oxford 1984)

Thomasson, B. E. 1984 — *Laterculi Praesidum* I (Gothenburg 1984)

Wagner, J. 1983 — 'Provincia Osrhoenae: new archaeological finds illustrating the military organisation under the Severan dynasty', *Armies and Frontiers in Byzantine Anatolia*, ed. S. Mitchell (BAR S156, Oxford 1983) 103–30

Chapter 14

Alföldy, G. 1968 — 'Septimius Severus und der Senat'. *Bonner Jahrbücher* 168 (1968) 112–60

Alföldy, G. 1985 — 'Bellum Mauricum', *Chiron* 15 (1985) 87–105

Barnes, T. D. 1971 — *Tertullian. A Literary and Historical Study* (Oxford 1971)

Barton, I. M. 1977 — 'The inscriptions of Septimius Severus and his family at Lepcis Magna', *Mélanges L. Senghor* (Dakar 1977) 3–12

Brogan, O. and — 'Seven new inscriptions from Tripolitania', *Papers British*

Reynolds, J. M. 1960 — *School at Rome* 28 (1960) 1–5

Brogan, O. and Smith, D. J. 1986 — *Ghirza. A Libyan Settlement in the Roman Period* (Tripoli 1984)

Champlin, E. 1980 — *Fronto and Antonine Rome* (Cambridge, Mass., 1980)

Charles-Picard, G. 1949 — *Castellum Dimmidi* (Algiers 1949)

Corbier, M. 1982 — 'Les familles clarissimes de l'Afrique romaine', *Epigrafia e ordine senatorio* II (*Tituli* 5, Rome 1982) 685–754

Daniels, C. M. 1987 — 'Africa', *The Roman World*, ed. J. S. Wacher (London 1987), I 223–65

Di Vita, A. 1982 — 'Gli *Emporia* di Tripolitania dall'età di Massinissa a Diocleziano: un profilo storico-instituzionale', *ANRW* 2.10.2 (1982) 515–95

Di Vita-Evrard, G. 1985 — 'Notes sur quelques timbres d'amphores de Tripolitaine', *Bulletin du comité des travaux historiques* 19B (1985) 147–59

Elmayer, A. F. 1984 — 'Latino-Punic inscriptions', *Libyan Studies* 15 (1984) 93–105

Gascou, J. 1982 — 'La politique municipale de Rome en Afrique du Nord', *ANRW* 2.10.2 (1982) 136–320

Guey, J. 1950 — 'Lepcitana Septimiana VI.1', *Revue africaine* 94 (1950) 51–84

Halfmann, H. 1986 — *Itinera Principum. Geschichte und Typologie der Kaiserreisen im Römischen Reich* (Stuttgart 1986)

Hasebroek, J. 1921 — *Untersuchungen zur Geschichte des Kaisers Septimius Severus* (Heidelberg 1921)

Haynes, D. E. L. 1959 — *The Antiquities of Tripolitania* (Tripoli 1959)

Kotula, T. 1985 — 'Septime-Sévère, a -t -il visité l'Afrique en tant qu'empereur?', *Eos* 73 (1985) 151–65

Mastino, A. 1981 — *Le titolature di Caracalla e Geta attraverso le iscrizioni (indici)* (Bologna 1981)

Mattingly, D. J. 1985 — 'Olive oil production in Roman Tripolitania', *Town and Country in Roman Tripolitania*, eds. D. J. Buck and D. J. Mattingly (BAR Int. 274, Oxford 1985) 27–46

Mattingly, D. J. 1987 — 'Libyans and the 'limes': culture and society in Roman Tripolitania', *Antiquités africaines* 23 (1987) 71–94

Mattingly, D. J. 1988 — 'The olive boom. Oil surpluses, wealth and power in Roman Tripolitania', *Libyan Studies* 19 (1988)

Pflaum, H. G. 1959 — 'Remarques sur l'onomastique de Cirta', *Limes Studien* (Basel 1959) 96–133

Rebuffat, R. 1985 — 'Les centurions de Gholaia', *L'Africa Romana* 2, ed. A. Mastino (Sassari 1985) 225–38

Rey-Coquais, J.-P. 1986 — 'Une double dédicace de Lepcis Magna à Tyr', *L'Africa Romana* 4, ed. A. Mastino (Sassari 1987) 597–602

Robert, L. 1982 — 'Une vision de Perpetue martyre à Carthage en 203', *Comptes-Rendues Acad. des Inscriptions* 1982, 228–76

Romanelli, P. 1959 — *Storia delle province romane dell' Africa* (Rome 1959)

Speidel, M. P. 1978   *The Religion of Iuppiter Dolichenus in the Roman Army* (Leiden 1978)

Strocka, V. M. 1972   'Beobachtungen an den Attikareliefs des severischen Quadrifrons von Lepcis magna', *Antiquités africaines* 6 (1972) 147–72

Thomasson, B. E. 1984   *Laterculi Praesidum* I (Gothenburg 1984)

Trousset, P. 1974   *Recherches sur le 'limes Tripolitanus' du chott el-Djerid à la frontière tuniso-libyenne* (Paris 1974)

Chapter 15

Alföldy, G. 1968   'Septimius Severus und der Senat', *Bonner Jahrbücher* 168 (1968) 112–60

Alföldy, G. 1982   'Senatoren aus Norditalien. Regiones IX, X und XI', *Epigrafia e ordine senatorio* II (*Tituli* 5, Rome 1982) 309–68

Barbieri, G. 1952   *L'Albo senatorio da Settimio Severo a Carino* (Rome 1952

Benario, H. W. 1958   'Rome of the Severi', *Latomus* 17 (1958) 712–22

Birley, A. R. 1969   'The *coups d'état* of the year 193', *Bonner Jahrbücher* 169 (1969) 243–80

Bowersock, G. W. 1969   *Greek Sophists in the Roman Empire* (Oxford 1969)

Brilliant, R. 1967   *The Arch of Septimius Severus in the Roman Forum* (Rome 1967)

Champlin, E. 1981   'Serenus Sammonicus', *Harvard Stud. in Class. Philol.* 85 (1981) 189–212

Corbier, M. 1982   'Les familles clarissimes d'Afrique proconsulaire', *Epigrafia e ordine senatorio* II (Tituli 5, Rome 1982) 685–754

Guey, J. 1946   'Note sur le Septizonium du Palatin', *Mélanges soc. toulousaine d'études classiques* I (1946) 147–66

Hohl, E. 1956   *Herodian und der Sturz Plautians* (Sitz. Berlin 1956)

MacMullen, R. 1966   *Enemies of the Roman Order* (Cambridge, Mass., 1966)

Pighi, G. B. 1941   *De ludis saecularibus populi Romani Quiritium* (Rome 1941)

Rubin, Z. 1975   'Dio, Herodian, and Severus' second Parthian war', *Chiron* 5 (1985) 419–41

Rubin, Z. 1980   *Civil-War Propaganda and Historiography* (Collection Latomus 173, Brussels 1980)

Schumacher, L. 1973   *Prosopographische Untersuchungen zur Besetzung der vier hohen römischen Priesterkollegien im Zeitalter der Antoninen und der Severer (96–235 n. Chr.)* (Diss. Mainz 1973)

Syme, R. 1939   *The Roman Revolution* (Oxford 1939)

Syme, R. 1958   *Tacitus* (Oxford 1958)

Syme, R. 1984   *Roman Papers* III (Oxford 1984)

Chapter 16

Alföldy, G. 1968   'Septimius Severus und der Senat', *Bonner Jahrbücher* 168 (1968) 112–60

Alföldy, G. 1969   'Ein *praefectus* der *cohors VI Nerviorum* in Britannia', *Hommages M. Renard* II (Collection Latomus 102, Brussels 1969) 3–6 (reprinted with addenda in Alföldy, *Römische Heeresgeschichte*, Amsterdam 1987, 223–7)

Birley, A. R. 1972   'Virius Lupus', *Archaeologia Aeliana*, 4th ser. 50 (1972) 179–89

Birley, A. R. 1981   *The Fasti of Roman Britain* (Oxford 1981)

Birley, R. E. 1962   'Excavation of the Roman fortress at Carpow, 1961–2', *Proc. Society of Ant. of Scotland* 96 (1962–3) 184–207

Birley, R. E. 1963   'The Roman legionary fortress at Carpow', *Scottish Historical Review* 42 (1963) 126–134

Breeze, D. J. and Dobson, B. 1987   *Hadrian's Wall* (3rd ed. Harmondsworth 1987)

Dietz, K. 1983   'Caracalla, Fabius Cilo und die Urbaniciani. Unerkannt gebliebene Suffektkonsuln des J. 212 n.Chr.', *Chiron* 13 (1983) 381–404

Di Vita-Evrard, G. 1982   'Note sur "trois" senateurs de Lepcis Magna. Le clarissimat des Plautii', *Epigrafia e ordine senatorio* I (Tituli 4, Rome 1982) 453–65

Di Vita-Evrard, G. 1987   'De la date du procès d'Hérode Atticus à l'ére d'Hadrien et à l'association au pouvoir de Géta', *Praktika tou 8 diethnous synedriou ellenikes kai latinikes epigraphikes 1982* II (Athens 1987)

Dillon, M. and Chadwick, N. K. 1967   *The Celtic Realms* (London 1967)

Dore, J. N. and Gillam, J. P. 1979   *The Roman Fort at South Shields* (Newcastle upon Tyne 1979)

Higham, N. J. and Jones, G. D. B. 1985   *The Carvetii* (Gloucester 1985)

Kaygusz, I. 1986   'Neue Inschriften aus Ainos (Enez)', *Epigraphica Anatolica* 8 (1986) 65–70

Kennedy, D. L. 1986   'The place-name Arbeia', *Britannia* 17 (1986) 332–3

Leach, J. D. and Wilkes, J. J. 1978   'The Roman military base at Carpow, Perthshire, Scotland: summary of recent investigations (1964–70, 1975)', *Limes. Akten d. XI Int. Limeskongresses* (Budapest 1978) 47–62

Mastino, A. 1981   *Le titolature di Caracalla e Geta attraverso le iscrizioni (indici)* (Bologna, 1981)

Morris, J. 1968   'The date of St Alban', *Hertfordshire Archaeology* 1 (1968) 1–8

Pflaum, H. G. 1961   'Les gendres de Marc-Aurèle', *J. des Savants* 1961, 28–41

Rankov, N. B. 1987   'M. Oclatinius Adventus in Britain', *Britannia* 18 (1987) 243–9

Robertson, A. S.   'The bridges on the Severan coins of AD 208 and 209', *Roman Frontier Studies 1979*, eds. W. S. Hanson and L. J. F. Keppie (BAR S71, Oxford 1980) 131–9

Rubin, Z. 1980   *Civil-War Propaganda and Historiography* (Collection Latomus 173, Brussels 1980)

Shotter, D. C. A.   '*Numeri Barcariorum*: a note on *RIB* 601', *Britannia* 4 (1973) 206–9

Straub, J. 1964   'Die *ultima verba* des Septimius Severus', *Historia-Augusta-Colloquium 1963* (Bonn 1964) 171–2

Thomasson, B. E. 1984   *Laterculi Praesidum* I (Gothenburg 1984)

Thomasson, B. E. 1985   'Zur Laufbahn einiger Statthalter des Prinzipats', *Opuscula Romana* 15 (1985) 109–41

Wright, R. P. 1974   'Carpow and Caracalla', *Britannia* 5 (1974) 289–92

Chapter 17

Alföldy, G. 1968   'Septimius Severus und der Senat', *Bonner Jahrbücher* 168 (1968) 112–60

Alföldy, G. 1988   *Geschichte, Geschichtsbetrachtung und Geschichtsschreibung in der Krise des Römischen Reiches* (Heidelberg 1988)

Barnes, T. D. 1968   'Pre-Decian *acta martyrum*', *Journ. Theol. Stud.* n.s. 19 (1968) 509–31

Birley, A. R. 1974   'Septimius Severus, *propagator imperii*', *Actes du IXe congres International d'Etudes sur les frontieres romaines* (Bucharest 1974) 297–9

Birley, A. R. 1976   'The third century crisis in the Roman empire', *Bulletin John Rylands Library Manchester* 58 (1976) 253–81

Birley, A. R. 1981a   'The economic effects of Roman frontier policy', *The Roman West in the Third Century*, eds. A. King and M. Henig (BAR Int. 109, Oxford 1981) 39–53

Birley, A. R. 1981b   *The Fasti of Roman Britain* (Oxford 1981)

Birley, E. 1969   'Septimius Severus and the Roman army', *Epigr. Stud.* 8 (1969) 63–82

Develin, R. 1971   'The army pay rises under Severus and Caracalla and the question of the *annona militaris*', *Latomus* 30 (1971) 687–95

Dietz, K. 1983   'Caracalla, Fabius Cilo und die Urbaniciani. Unerkannt gebliebene Suffektkonsuln des J. 212 n.Chr.', *Chiron* 13 (1983) 381–404

Graham, A. J. 1973   'Septimius Severus and his generals, AD 193–7', *War and Society. Essays in memory of J. Western*, ed. M. R. D. Foot (London 1973) 255–75; 336–45

Kettenhofen, E. 1979   *Die syrischen Augustae in der historischen Überlieferung* (Bonn 1979)

Mastino, A. 1981   *Le titolature di Caracalla e Geta* (Bologna 1981)

Millar, F. 1964   *A Study of Cassius Dio* (Oxford 1964)

Smith, R. E. 1972 'The army reforms of Septimius Severus', *Historia* 21 (1972) 481–500

Syme, R. 1971 *Emperors and Biography* (Oxford 1971)

Watson, G. R. 1969 *The Roman Soldier* (London 1969)

Wild, J. P. 1986 'Bath and the identification of the *caracalla*', *Britannia* 17 (1986) 352–3

Wright, R. P. 1974 'Carpow and Caracalla', *Britannia* 5 (1974) 289–92

INDEX